CHILDREN
OF THE
TROUBLES

CHILDREN
OF THE
TROUBLES

The Untold Story of the Children Killed in the
Northern Ireland Conflict

JOE DUFFY &
FREYA McCLEMENTS

HACHETTE
BOOKS
IRELAND

First published in 2019 by Hachette Books Ireland
An Hachette UK Company

1

A CIP catalogue record for this title is available from the British Library.

ISBN: 978 1 47369 735 5

Typeset in Dante by Anú Design, Tara
Book text design by Anú Design, Tara
Cover design by Anú Design, Tara
Printed and bound in Italy by L.E.G.O. SpA

Hachette Books Ireland policy is to use papers that are natural, renewable and recyclable products and made from wood grown in sustainable forests. The logging and manufacturing processes are expected to conform to the environmental regulations of the country of origin.

Hachette Books Ireland
8 Castlecourt Centre
Castleknock
Dublin 15
Ireland

A division of Hachette UK, Carmelite House, 50 Victoria Embankment, London EC4Y 0DZ, England
www.hachettebooksireland.ie

Contents

Foreword by Mary McAleese   page xvi

Introduction   page xix

Timelines and Children's Biographies

Essays

For the children

'Darkness cannot drive out darkness; only light can do that.
Hate cannot drive out hate; only love can do that.'

Martin Luther King Jnr,
1929–1968

Places where children died in the Northern Ireland conflict

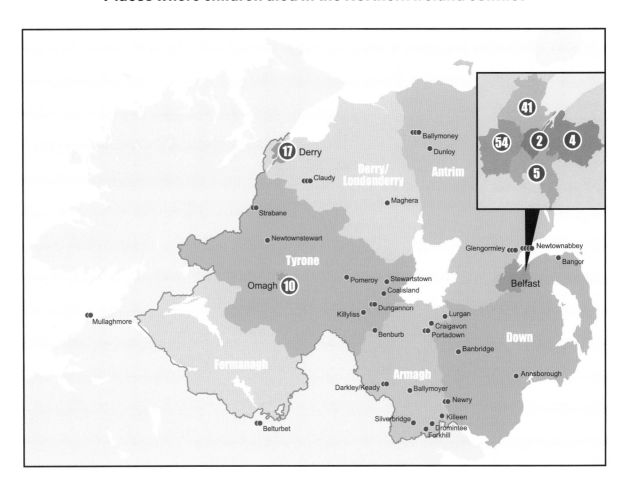

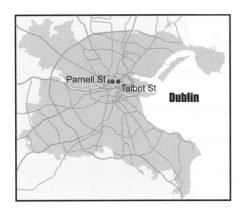

Names, ages, places of residence and dates of death of the children who died as a result of the Troubles

Patrick Rooney (9), Divis Flats, West Belfast. Died: 15/08/1969

Gerald McAuley (15), Lower Springfield Road, Belfast. Died: 15/08/1969

Jim Dorrian (3), Short Strand, East Belfast. Died: 12/01/1970

Francis McGuigan (23 months), Ballymurphy, West Belfast. Died: 07/04/1970

Ann Gilligan (2), Falls Road, West Belfast. Died: 09/05/1970

Bernadette McCool (9), Creggan, Derry. Died: 27/06/1970

Carole McCool (3), Creggan, Derry. Died: 27/06/1970

Denise Dickson (5), New Lodge, North Belfast. Died: 08/02/1971

Damien Harkin (8), Bogside, Derry. Died: 24/07/1971

Desmond Healey (14), Lenadoon, West Belfast. Died: 09/08/1971

Leo McGuigan (16), Cliftonville, North Belfast. Died: 09/08/1971

Alphonsus Cunningham (13), Lower Falls, West Belfast. Died: 11/08/1971

James O'Hagan (16), Waterside, Derry. Died: 19/08/1971

Angela Gallagher (18 months), Falls Road, West Belfast. Died: 03/09/1971

Annette McGavigan (14), Bogside, Derry. Died: 06/09/1971

Gary Gormley (3), Foyle Road, Derry. Died: 09/09/1971

Maria McGurk (14), New Lodge, North Belfast. Died: 04/12/1971

Jimmy Cromie (13), New Lodge, North Belfast. Died: 04/12/1971

Tracey Munn (2), Oldpark, North Belfast. Died: 11/12/1971

Colin Nicholl (17 months), Oldpark, North Belfast. Died: 11/12/1971

Martin McShane (16), Coalisland, Co Tyrone. Died: 14/12/1971

James McCallum (16), Turf Lodge, West Belfast. Died: 18/12/1971

Michael Sloan (15), Ballymurphy, West Belfast. Died: 11/01/1972

David McAuley (15), Ardoyne, North Belfast. Died: 19/02/1972

Gerard Doherty (16), Creggan, Derry. Died: 25/02/1972

Michael Patrick Connors (14), Coalisland, Co Tyrone. Died: 01/03/1972

Tony Lewis (16), Clonard, West Belfast. Died: 09/03/1972

Sean O'Riordan (13), Clonard, West Belfast. Died: 23/03/1972

Patrick Campbell (16), Ballymurphy, West Belfast. Died: 25/03/1972

Francis Rowntree (11), Lower Falls, West Belfast. Died: 22/04/1972

Rosaleen Gavin (8), Oldpark, North Belfast. Died: 29/04/1972

Michael Magee (15), Springfield Road, West Belfast. Died: 13/05/1972

Martha Campbell (13), Ballymurphy, West Belfast. Died: 14/05/1972

Harold Morris (15), Shankill, West Belfast. Died: 18/05/1972

Manus Deery (15), Bogside, Derry. Died: 19/05/1972

Joan Scott (12), Oldpark, North Belfast. Died: 30/05/1972

Joseph Campbell (16), Ardoyne, North Belfast. Died: 11/06/1972

John Dougal (16), Ballymurphy, West Belfast. Died: 09/07/1972

Margaret Gargan (13), Ballymurphy, West Belfast. Died: 09/07/1972

David McCafferty (15), Ballymurphy, West Belfast. Died: 09/07/1972

Gerard Gibson (16), Turf Lodge, West Belfast. Died: 11/07/1972

David McClenaghan (14), Oldpark, North Belfast. Died: 12/07/1972

Alan Jack (5 months), Ballymagorry, Co Tyrone. Died: 19/07/1972

William Crothers (15), Newtownards Road, East Belfast. Died: 21/07/1972

Stephen Parker (14), Cavehill Road, North Belfast. Died: 21/07/1972

Daniel Hegarty (15), Creggan, Derry. Died: 31/07/1972

Kathryn Eakin (8), Claudy, Co Derry. Died: 31/07/1972

William Temple (16), Donemana, Co Tyrone. Died: 31/07/1972

Patrick Joseph Connolly (15), Claudy, Co Derry. Died: 08/08/1972

James Boyle (16), Glen Road, West Belfast. Died: 27/09/1972

Alex Moorehead (16), Newtownstewart, Co Tyrone. Died: 07/10/1972

Jim Doherty (6), Turf Lodge, West Belfast. Died: 15/10/1972

William Warnock (15), Newtownards Rd, East Belfast. Died: 17/10/1972

Tony Diamond (12), Creggan, Derry. Died: 23/10/1972

Michael Turner (16), Cavehill, North Belfast. Died: 29/10/1972

Claire Hughes (4), Sailortown, North Belfast. Died: 31/10/1972

Paula Strong (6), Sailortown, North Belfast. Died: 31/10/1972

Rory Gormley (14), Lisburn Road, South Belfast. Died: 27/11/1972

Bernard Fox (16), Ardoyne, North Belfast. Died: 04/12/1972

James Reynolds (16), Shore Road, Newtownabbey. Died: 15/12/1972

Geraldine O'Reilly (15), Belturbet, Co. Cavan. Died: 28/12/1972

Patrick Stanley (16), Clara, Co Offaly. Died: 28/12/1972

Peter Watterson (14), Falls Road, West Belfast. Died: 29/01/1973

Philip Rafferty (14), Andersonstown, West Belfast. Died: 30/01/1973

Gordon Gallagher (9), Creggan, Derry. Died: 25/02/1973

Kevin Heatley (12), Newry, Co Armagh. Died: 28/02/1973

Alan Welsh (16), Beersbridge, East Belfast. Died: 12/03/1973

Bernard McErlean (16), Grosvenor Road, West Belfast. Died: 20/03/1973

Patrick McCabe (16), Ardoyne, North Belfast. Died: 27/03/1973

Martin Corr (12), Grosvenor Road, West Belfast. Died: 30/03/1973

Tony McDowell (12), Ardoyne, North Belfast. Died: 19/04/1973

Eileen Mackin (14), Ballymurphy, West Belfast. Died: 17/05/1973

Paul Crummey (4), FInaghy Road, West Belfast. Died: 26/05/1973

David Walker (16), Belvoir, South Belfast. Died: 21/06/1973

Henry Cunningham (16), Carndonagh, Co Donegal. Died: 09/08/1973

Patrick Quinn (16), Dungannon, County Tyrone. Died: 16/08/1973

Anthony McGrady (16), Donegall Road, West Belfast. Died: 25/08/1973

Bernard Teggart (15), Ballymurphy, West Belfast. Died: 13/11/1973

Kathleen Feeney (14), Brandywell, Derry. Died: 14/11/1973

Lee Haughton (5), Manchester. Died: 04/02/1974

Robert Haughton (2), Manchester. Died: 04/02/1974

Thomas Donaghy (16), Rathcoole, Newtownabbey. Died: 11/02/1974

Michael McCreesh (15), Dromintee, Co Armagh. Died: 10/03/1974

Baby Doherty (Unborn), Sheriff Street, Dublin. Died: 17/05/1974

Jacqueline O'Brien (16 months), Lower Gardiner Street, Dublin. Died: 17/05/1974

Anne Marie O'Brien (4½ months), Lower Gardiner Street, Dublin. Died: 17/05/1974

Michelle Osborne (12), Ligoniel, North Belfast. Died: 09/06/1974

Michael Browne (16), Bangor, Co Down. Died: 12/07/1974

Joseph McGuinness (13), New Lodge, North Belfast. Died: 15/08/1974

Patrick McGreevy (15), New Lodge, North Belfast. Died: 19/09/1974

Michael Hughes (16), Newry, Co Armagh. Died: 18/10/1974

Michael Meenan (16), Shantallow, Derry. Died: 30/10/1974

John McDaid (16), Strand Road, Derry. Died: 07/12/1974

Patrick Toner (7), Forkhill, Co Armagh. Died: 19/01/1975

Eddie Wilson (16), Cavehill, North Belfast. Died: 26/01/1975

Robert Allsopp (15), New Lodge, North Belfast. Died: 23/03/1975

Baby Bowen (Unborn), Killyliss, Co Tyrone. Died: 21/04/1975

Michelle O'Connor (3), Ormeau Road, South Belfast. Died: 13/06/1975

John Rolston (16), White City, North Belfast. Died: 28/06/1975

Charles Irvine (16), Divis Flats, West Belfast. Died: 13/07/1975

Patrick Crawford (15), Glen Road, West Belfast. Died: 10/08/1975

Siobhan McCabe 4, Lower Falls, West Belfast. Died: 10/08/1975

James Templeton (15), Ormeau Road, South Belfast. Died: 29/08/1975

Stephen Geddis (10), Divis Flats, West Belfast. Died: 30/08/1975

Eileen Kelly (6), Beechmount, West Belfast. Died: 30/10/1975

Kevin McCauley (13), Andersonstown, West Belfast. Died: 06/11/1975

Michael Donnelly (14), Silverbridge, Co Armagh. Died: 19/12/1975

Thomas Rafferty (14), Portadown, Co Armagh. Died: 07/02/1976

Robert McLernon (16), Stewartstown, Co Tyrone. Died: 07/02/1976

Anthony Doherty (15), Turf Lodge, West Belfast. Died: 14/02/1976

James McCaughey (13), Dungannon, Co Tyrone. Died: 17/03/1976

Patrick Barnard (13), Dungannon, Co Tyrone. Died: 18/03/1976

Joanne Maguire (8), Andersonstown, West Belfast. Died: 10/08/1976

Andrew Maguire (6 weeks), Andersonstown, West Belfast. Died: 10/08/1976

John Maguire (2), Andersonstown, West Belfast. Died: 11/08/1976

Majella O'Hare (12), Ballymoyer, Co Armagh. Died: 14/08/1976

Brigeen Dempsey (10 months), New Lodge, North Belfast. Died: 27/08/1976

Brian Stewart (13), Turf Lodge, West Belfast. Died: 10/10/1976

Anne Magee (16), Cliftonville Road, North Belfast. Died: 11/10/1976

Carol McMenamy (14), New Lodge, North Belfast. Died: 06/11/1976

Philomena Greene (16), Lurgan, Co Armagh. Died: 28/11/1976

Geraldine McKeown (14), Ardoyne, North Belfast. Died: 08/12/1976

Graeme Dougan (15 months), Glengormley, Co Antrim. Died: 01/01/1977

Kevin McMenamin (7), Ballymurphy, West Belfast. Died: 10/04/1977

Paul McWilliams (16), Springhill Avenue, West Belfast. Died: 09/08/1977

Michael Neill (16), Unity Flats, North Belfast. Died: 24/10/1977

Marcia Gregg (15), Ligoniel, North Belfast. Died: 16/11/1977

Lesley Gordon (11), Maghera, Co Derry. Died: 08/02/1978

Michael Scott (10), Oldpark, North Belfast. Died: 12/02/1978

John Boyle (16), Dunloy, Co Antrim. Died: 11/07/1978

Graham Lewis (13), Woodvale, North Belfast. Died: 14/10/1978

James Keenan (16), Darkley, Co Armagh. Died: 24/02/1979

Martin McGuigan (16), Darkley, Co Armagh. Died: 24/02/1979

Nicholas Knatchbull (14), Mersham, Kent. Died: 27/08/1979

Paul Maxwell (15), Enniskillen, Co Fermanagh. Died: 27/08/1979

Doreen McGuinness (16), Grosvenor Road, West Belfast. Died: 01/01/1980

Hugh Maguire (9), Ballymurphy, West Belfast. Died: 10/02/1980

Paul Moan (15), Glen Road, West Belfast. Died: 31/03/1980

Michael McCartan (16), Lower Ormeau, South Belfast. Died: 23/07/1980

Paul Whitters (15), Bishop Street, Derry. Died: 25/04/1981

Desmond Guiney (14), Rathcoole, Newtownabbey. Died: 08/05/1981

Julie Livingstone (14), Lenadoon, West Belfast. Died: 13/05/1981

Carol Ann Kelly (12), Twinbrook, West Belfast. Died: 22/05/1981

John Dempsey (16), Turf Lodge, West Belfast. Died: 08/07/1981

Danny Barrett (15), Ardoyne, North Belfast. Died: 09/07/1981

Alan McCrum (11), Loughbrickland, County Down. Died: 15/03/1982

Stephen McConomy (11), Bogside, Derry. Died: 19/04/1982

Patrick Smith (16), Lower Ormeau, South Belfast. Died: 02/06/1982

Stephen Bennett (14), Divis Flats, West Belfast. Died: 16/09/1982

Kevin Valliday (11), Divis Flats, West Belfast. Died: 17/09/1982

David Devine (16), Strabane, Co Tyrone. Died: 23/02/1985

David Hanna (6), Hillsborough, Co Down. Died: 23/07/1988

Emma Donnelly (13), Benburb, Co Tyrone. Died: 23/11/1988

Seamus Duffy (15), Oldpark, North Belfast. Died: 09/08/1989

Nivruti Islania (6 months), Wildenrath, West Germany. Died: 26/10/1989

Charles Love (16), Strabane, Co Tyrone. Died: 28/01/1990

Katrina Rennie (16), Craigavon, Co Armagh. Died: 28/03/1991

Colin Lundy (16), Glengormley, County Antrim. Died: 09/11/1991

James Kennedy (15), The Markets, South Belfast. Died: 05/02/1992

Patrick Harmon (15), New Lodge, North Belfast. Died: 25/03/1992

Danielle Carter (15), Basildon, Essex. Died: 10/04/1992

Johnathan Ball (3), Warrington, Cheshire. Died: 20/03/1993

Tim Parry (12), Warrington, Cheshire. Died: 25/03/1993

Michelle Baird (7), Forthriver, North Belfast. Died: 23/10/1993

Leanne Murray (13), Shankill, West Belfast. Died: 23/10/1993

Brian Duffy (15), Ligoniel, North Belfast. Died: 05/12/1993

Barbara McAlorum (9), Skegoneill, North Belfast. Died: 15/03/1996

Darren Murray (12), Portadown, Co Armagh. Died: 10/10/1996

James Morgan (16), Annsborough, Co Down. Died: 24/07/1997

Richard Quinn (10), Ballymoney, Co Antrim. Died: 12/07/1998

Mark Quinn (9), Ballymoney, Co Antrim. Died: 12/07/1998

Jason Quinn (8), Ballymoney, Co Antrim. Died: 12/07/1998

James Barker (12), Buncrana, Co Donegal. Died: 15/08/1998

Fernando Blasco Baselga (12), Madrid, Spain. Died: 15/08/1998

Breda Devine (20 months), Donemana, Co Tyrone. Died: 15/08/1998

Oran Doherty (8), Buncrana, Co Donegal. Died: 15/08/1998

Shaun McLaughlin (12), Buncrana, Co Donegal. Died: 15/08/1998

Maura Monaghan (20 months), Augher, Co Tyrone. Died: 15/08/1998

Monaghan Twins Unborn, Augher, Co Tyrone. Died: 15/08/1998

Alan Radford (16), Omagh, Co Tyrone. Died: 15/08/1998

Lorraine Wilson (15), Omagh, Co Tyrone. Died: 15/08/1998

Thomas McDonald (16), White City, North Belfast. Died: 04/09/2001

Glen Branagh (16), Tiger's Bay, North Belfast. Died: 11/11/2001

Thomas Devlin (15), Fortwilliam, North Belfast. Died: 10/08/2005

Michael McIlveen (15), Ballymena, County Antrim. Died: 08/05/2006

Foreword

by Mary McAleese

One of the proudest days of my life was on 11 November, 1997 when I was inaugurated as the 8th President of Ireland and, as I said in Dublin Castle that day, the first President from Ulster.

In my inauguration speech, with the theme 'building bridges', I spoke about my own life experience. Born in Ardoyne in Belfast, I came of age in a deeply militarised and violent society.

My family ran a pub in Belfast, and, like everyone featured within these pages, we were never far from the violence of the Troubles. My brother John was badly beaten for no other reason than his religion. Our family home, with nine children, was often attacked for the same reason – indeed our parish had the highest incidence per capita of sectarian deaths.

Our family pub, the Long Bar on Belfast's Leeson Street, was the target of a car bomb in October, 1972. As the terrorists ran away from the car, they inadvertently left the handbrake off. The car rolled forward as pedestrians, including my sister's good friend Olive Campbell – at 23 only a couple of years older than I was – tried to protect her baby daughter. Olive was killed when the car exploded – she died in my father's arms. Newspapers the following day showed her daughter being comforted by strangers.

My father was traumatised by this atrocity for the rest of his life. On my own wedding day a few years later, two of my dearest friends and neighbours, Myles and Tony O'Reilly, were murdered. It made for a sombre honeymoon and a dedication of our lives to the vision and values of Daniel O'Connell, whose home we made a pilgrimage to during those strange honeymoon days.

I was thinking of these horrors and the catalogue of other tragedies during the Troubles when I wrote my inaugural address as the first President of Ireland from Ulster. That day I said:

> We know only too well the cruelty and capriciousness of violent conflict. Our own history has been hard on lives, young and old. Too hard on those who died and those left behind with only shattered dreams and poignant memories.
>
> We hope and pray – indeed we insist – that we have seen the last of violence. We demand the right to solve our problems by dialogue and the noble pursuit of consensus. We hope to see that consensus pursued without the language of hatred and contempt and we wish all those engaged in that endeavour well.
>
> The greatest salute to all those dead and the living who they loved would be the achievement of peace. No side has a monopoly of pain, each has suffered intensely.

Little did I know that before I had even served one year as President, I would be sitting in a hospital in Omagh trying to comfort a bereft group of Spanish students after a beautiful Saturday afternoon trip turned into unimaginable horror when another car bomb exploded, killing 29 people and two unborn twins. Two Spanish members of their trip were killed as well as three of their friends from their host families in Buncrana.

I felt my energy evaporate in Omagh: those deaths almost made me lose hope. It was an awful moment of disbelief. A feeling of 'How can we ever again gather the fragments of the peace process?' But we did and were compelled to do so because of all those fragmented and shattered lives.

It is these children's lives that are so vividly remembered, reclaimed and rededicated in this important book. In a lesson to all of us, this book is not about recrimination, or blame. Instead, it is a powerful reminder of the catastrophic, enduring effects of violent and premature death. In the words of one of the bereaved parents in this book, bullets never stop travelling.

I truly believe that this powerful book, in its humanity, and its by turns joyous and tragic recollections, is another stepping stone on our road to recovery. It reminds us of the futility of violence, no matter what its source. Joe Duffy and Freya McClements recount the stories of both the lives of those young people, and their tragic and unnecessary deaths.

I am struck by how many deaths of children they uncovered which had not been previously publicly recorded. The revised figure of 186 children aged 16 or under who died violently in the Troubles is truly shocking.

One of the many funerals I attended as President of Ireland for the victims of the Omagh bombing was for twelve-year-old Shaun McLaughlin. I subsequently discovered that he had visited me at the Áras only eight weeks previously.

For my family and me, school visits were joyous, often raucous occasions, as young people ran and played in the house and around the grounds, often with my own three young children. Shaun wrote a poem, 'The Bridge', which he gave to me on that visit. Shaun's words, his story and the shortened lives of all those in this book, will not only stop you in your tracks, it will check all who consider resorting to violence, regardless of the circumstances.

'Scatter the seeds of peace across our land/so we can travel hand in hand/ across the bridge of hope.'

Mary McAleese, June 2019

Introduction

'When you lose a child, you just can't forget it. You have those last
moments forever. A lot of people have said to me, "Why on earth would
you want to bring all that back?". I've said, we don't bring it back.
It's with us all the time.'

Wendy Parry's 12-year-son Tim had gone into town to buy a Mother's Day card
and a pair of Everton football shorts. The next time Wendy saw her son, he was
in a hospital bed. Fatally injured in the IRA bombing of Warrington in 1993, his
family had no choice but to switch off his life support machine.

Tim is one of 186 children – aged 16 and under – who died as a result of the
Troubles in Northern Ireland.

The first, Patrick Rooney, was killed 50 years ago in 1969; the last, Michael
McIlveen, died in 2006, more than three decades later.

'He's not special to everyone but he's so special to me and my family,' says
Maggie Crawford of her 15-year-old brother Patrick.

Her words could stand for the families of each of the 186 children who are
remembered in this book. While their loss is always with their parents and
siblings, their wider family circle, their friends and their communities, all too
often their names have been publicly forgotten.

In the midst of a conflict which cost the lives of more than 3,700 people, it is
perhaps inevitable; with *Children of the Troubles*, this is something which we have
sought to remedy.

Children of the Troubles grew from *Children of the Rising*, Joe Duffy's
investigation into the lives of the 40 children who died during the Easter Rising
in 1916. Yet even as he wrote, Joe found himself continually reminded of the

parallels between the children killed in Easter week and the children who died in the bloodiest conflict of 20th century Ireland, the North's Troubles.

Children died in their homes, or at play, or at work. They died in their prams, or on their way to the shop, or while fighting. They died because of childish curiosity, or unexpected circumstance, or simply because violence had come to the streets where they lived. The majority – approximately 42.5% – were killed by republicans. Loyalists were responsible for 27% of child deaths, and the security forces for 26%.

This final percentage, comprised of children killed by either the British army or by the RUC, is significantly higher than the figure, based on *Lost Lives*, that the security forces were responsible for 10% of deaths among those of all ages killed during the Troubles.

There have been convictions – for murder or manslaughter – in fewer than 15% of child deaths, all amongst either loyalist or republican paramilitaries or their associates. There have been convictions for lesser offences in connection with a handful more.

It seems incredible that there is no single, official list of Troubles' fatalities. The closest is *Lost Lives*, by David McKittrick, Seamus Kelters et al., which has made the single greatest contribution to our knowledge of the Troubles and our understanding of its consequences. It was the starting point for our research, and a work to which we referred constantly during the writing of this book; it is frequently cited in our pages, and we are forever indebted to its scholarship.

In the course of our research, we have uncovered the stories of nine additional children who we believe should be acknowledged as victims of the Troubles.

Aside from age – 16 or under – our only criteria have been that in each case we believe the child's death was as a result of the Troubles. In many cases, this was clear-cut; in others, less so.

For example, while only road accident deaths which were known to have taken place during disturbances were included in *Lost Lives*, we believe that deaths such as those of Jim Dorrian, Damien Harkin and others were nevertheless a result of the Troubles and should be included.

Moreover, while many factors – not least the passage of time – make it virtually impossible to prove definitively whether, for example, 23-month-old Francis McGuigan did indeed die as a result of inhaling CS gas, we adjudged that the circumstances of his death and his sister's testimony was sufficient to merit his inclusion.

Similarly, the parents of Thomas Devlin revealed that at the time of their son's murder they had been asked not to claim it was sectarian; they told us that they are in no doubt that Thomas was killed because of his religion, and that he should be regarded as a victim of the Troubles.

In other instances, we have been forced to make a decision as to how far the line of cause and effect extends. For this reason, we have chosen not to include two-year-old James Coleman, one of the many refugees who fled west Belfast at the start of the Troubles and who died, along with his parents, of carbon monoxide poisoning in their caravan in Co. Kildare.

We also have not included five-year-old John Morrow, who was electrocuted by a loose cable while playing in burnt-out houses in Farringdon Gardens in north Belfast in 1971, nor 12-year-old Cathy McGartland who – though a member of the Cailíní – died in 1974 in an accidental fall which was unrelated to her membership, nor the young brother and sister Brian and Elaine Boylan, who were killed in an accident involving a lorry which had been diverted as a result of a series of IRA hijackings in Dublin in 1974.

We acknowledge, too, that this is a work in progress, and would invite any readers who are aware of any other children who they believe should be included to contact us at childrenofthetroubles@gmail.com

We have included four unborn children – baby Doherty and baby Bowen, both of whom have been officially recognised as Troubles' victims – and the Monaghan twins, who died along with their sister, mother and grandmother in the 1998 Omagh bombing.

We would like to acknowledge here the other unborn children who died, either as a result of their mother's death or because of a miscarriage brought on by a Troubles-related incident or trauma. Their loss is no less significant, and their families' sorrow no less great.

The majority of the book is comprised of biographies of each child. These are arranged chronologically, with a timeline at the beginning of each year which sets the time in its political and social context. These pieces are interspersed with essays which examine particular aspects of childhood during the Troubles and its impact both on families and wider society.

Where possible, we made contact with family members. *Children of the Troubles* is based on more than 100 original interviews, the majority with relatives of the children remembered in these pages; for some, it was their first ever interview. Time after time, we were overwhelmed by your dignity, and by your kindness and generosity towards us, and we are deeply grateful to you for placing your trust in us.

Across Northern Ireland, you welcomed us into your homes. You showed us your treasured photographs, your keepsakes – the wooden rattle, the pair of plimsolls, the 50-year-old schoolbag. We felt privileged that you would share your precious memories with us; they will stay with us.

Frequently, we cried; often, at unexpected moments – driving home from an interview, while writing, or while simply staring at the computer screen. We felt loss, and anger at 186 wasted lives.

In *Children of the Troubles*, we tell their stories: the story of 'Wee Pat' Toner, who loved his pet cows and wanted to be a vet; the story of James Keenan and Martin McGuigan, who were on their way to see their first showband; the story of Denise Dickson, who never got her first taste of peanut butter.

The story of Tim Parry, who loved Everton FC and loved girls – so much so, that his parents are sure he would have given them plenty of grandchildren. After he was killed, his parents set up a peace centre in Warrington. 'We wanted to make sure Tim was not forgotten,' said his mother Wendy. "We didn't want him to be like other children in Northern Ireland, where they were basically a number on a list of young people killed. We wanted to make sure that Tim did count."

In *Children of the Troubles*, we acknowledge the lives of the 186 children who were killed during the conflict. We remember that they lived and were loved, and celebrate them: their characters, their passions, their hopes and dreams. They do count.

13-year-old Philip Rafferty wanted to become an architect and had promised his mother he would build her a house. He was killed in 1973 by a loyalist gang who took him from the street in west Belfast, tortured him and then shot him in the head.

His mother, Maureen, was one of the first people who spoke to us. 'Nobody knows my Philip's name,' she told us. 'I want the world to know my Philip's name.'

Throughout the research and writing of *Children of the Troubles*, her words have been our inspiration and our guide. We hope we have done all the children justice.

Joe Duffy & Freya McClements, July 2019

Derry, 1969.
Opposite: Civil rights march, Derrry.

1969

- People's Democracy civil rights march from Belfast to Derry is attacked by loyalists at Burntollet Bridge

- Moderate unionist prime minister Terence O'Neill is forced from office, replaced by James Chichester-Clark

- Bernadette Devlin becomes youngest woman to be elected to Westminster

- Rioting sparked by an Apprentice Boys march in Derry develops into the three-day 'Battle of the Bogside'

- The British army arrives in Northern Ireland; it is deployed first in Derry on 14 August, and in Belfast the following day

- Nine-year-old Patrick Rooney becomes the first child victim of the Troubles

Leabharlanna Poiblí Chathair Baile Átha Cliath

- Catholic residents are burnt out of their homes as loyalists attack the Lower Falls area of Belfast. Seven others are killed in the rioting, and Bombay Street is burned to the ground. Almost 2,000 people become refugees

- Taoiseach Jack Lynch moves troops and field hospitals to the border and calls for UN intervention

- In December the Northern-based Provisional IRA splits from the Official IRA, headquartered in Dublin; the Provisionals' leadership commences an 'armed struggle' in an effort to achieve a united Ireland

- Popular toys include Corgi and Matchbox cars, and Sindy, Barbie and Action Man dolls.

Name: *Patrick Rooney*

Age: *9*

From: *Divis Flats, West Belfast*

Date of Death: *15/08/1969*

As night fell on 14 August 1969, it seemed to Neely and Alice Rooney as if all of Belfast was on fire. Unable to leave their ground-floor flat, they watched as tracer bullets fired by the RUC sent flashes of light through the sky. Fearful for their six children's safety, they gathered them together in one room.

Nine-year-old Patrick was the eldest; he was 'a thoughtful child', Alice remembers, who loved Hallowe'en. 'His father used to cut the turnips out for him, and skeletons' faces, and hung them up around the walls for him."

'You looked up to him because he was the oldest,' says his sister Sharon. 'He made us say our prayers at night. We weren't allowed to go to bed unless we'd knelt down and said our prayers.'

An altar boy, Patrick had been serving at eight o'clock mass all week. 'He always loved horror movies on the TV, so I'd have kept him up that wee bit late,' says Alice. 'The others were all in bed and when he was going up the stairs that night he said, "Don't be waking me in the morning, I'm not on until one because it's the feast of Our Lady." That was the last thing he said.'

Alice and Neely contemplated their escape. Could they make it to Neely's sister's house? Alice reached into the wardrobe to get a coat for Patrick's brother, Felix. Suddenly she felt a burning sensation; a bullet had grazed her cheek.

'Then Patrick slid down the wall,' says Alice. I thought he'd fainted but when I lifted him up there was blood coming from the back of his head.'

She laid her son on the bed. 'That's why people keep saying he was shot on the bed but he wasn't, he slid down the wall. Neely said, "Get down and pray."' Patrick was the first child to die as a result of the Troubles.

His teacher came to see Alice and told her that Patrick had wanted to be a priest. 'He was very smart,' says his younger brother Con. 'He did well at school – he was a brainbox. They made a programme about Patrick later, and people were saying he could have been anything.'

Patrick had been shot with a machine gun mounted on an RUC armoured car; that same year, the Scarman Tribunal concluded it could not be justified.[1]

A year after their son's death, Patrick's parents named their new baby Patrick in his memory.

Neely campaigned for the rest of his life to have the policeman who killed his son brought to justice. 'They can't say to me he was in the wrong place at the wrong time,' he told *The Irish Times*. He was in his home when he was shot dead.'[2]

✳ ✳ ✳ ✳ ✳

Name: *Gerald McAuley*

Age: *15*

From: *Lower Springfield Road, Belfast*

Date of Death: *15/08/1969*

Gerald McAuley loved the outdoors. From the age of ten he and his friends would walk out to Dundrod, County Antrim, to watch the motorcycle racing.

'They used to take bread and butter with them for their lunch,' says Gerald's mother Ellen. 'He'd say, "I'm away to Dundrod," and that'd be him all day.'

Gerald loved fishing and birds, and going walking with his father on Black Mountain, high above west Belfast; at school he played Gaelic football and hurling, and won medals for his sporting achievements.

He could also be a daredevil – Ellen remembers being on a bus and suddenly seeing her son 'flying past me on the back of this trailer'. 'He said, "I was only going to the Markets to see could I get a job."'

Gerald had just started working in a clothing factory three weeks before he was killed, and had planned to join the Irish merchant navy that September.

In June, Gerald and his friends had been playing handball when the ball went up onto a factory roof. Tall for his age, Gerald climbed up after it and fell right through the roof, just missing the machines and hitting the concrete instead. 'He should have been dead that June,' says Ellen, 'but instead he died in August.'

Gerald was shot and killed by a loyalist gunman as he helped local people who had been burnt out of their homes in and around Bombay Street amid the violence that had erupted in Belfast; he was attempting to bring them to what he hoped was the safety of Clonard Monastery. Fr P.J. Egan, the superior of the monastery, heard the shots ring out and saw Gerald lying on the street outside. He gave him absolution and anointed him. 'Apparently Gerald knew he was a priest, and he died in his arms,' says Ellen.

'I took all my children when they were born over to Clonard to get them blessed. I had him consecrated to the Blessed Virgin and she took him on her day, 15th August, and he had a priest with him too, so there's a lot to be thankful for.'

A member of the Fianna, Gerald was the first republican to die in the Troubles. Today, a plaque marks the spot where he died; his picture looks down from a gable wall in the rebuilt Bombay Street over a memorial to the local civilians and IRA volunteers who would subsequently lose their lives. Behind it, the corrugated sheeting and wire mesh of a so-called peace wall remain.

Now 88, Ellen finds it a comfort that her son is remembered. 'His friends called him Geraldo,' she says. 'I didn't know that until after he died, but Gerry Adams was speaking at a commemoration one day and kept referring to him as Geraldo. That was nice.'

✳ ✳ ✳ ✳ ✳

The British army starts to use rubber bullets. Opposite: British army patrol, Belfast, 1970.

1970

- The first civilians are killed by the IRA and the British army. The year also marks the first female fatalities, as well as the first Garda to die as a result of the Troubles

- British army starts to use rubber bullets in riot situations

- The nationalist SDLP is formed, as is the cross-community Alliance Party

- Ian Paisley is elected MP for North Antrim

- Dana, an 18-year-old Derry schoolgirl, wins the Eurovision Song Contest; in December Santa arrives for some lucky children by British army helicopter.

Name: *Jim Dorrian*

Age: *3*

From: *Short Strand, East Belfast*

Date of Death: *12/01/1970*

Jim Dorrian was in a rush to get out to play. The three-year-old was on his way up the street; as he left the house he had taken a sausage from his uncle's plate.

Jim was 'my sister's wee boy', explains Jimmy McLarnon. 'He was called after me.'

The little boy was the first child to be killed by a British army vehicle. 'The soldier said he had seen kids on the right-hand side of the street and cut the corner,' says Jimmy.

'When he realised he'd hit Jim, he cried like a child.'

Jim's father, Robert Dorrian, joined the IRA in 1971 and was killed in 1972 in an accidental explosion.[3]

⁂ ⁂ ⁂ ⁂ ⁂

Name: *Francis McGuigan*

Age: *23 months*

From: *Ballymurphy, West Belfast*

Date of Death: *07/04/1970*

To this day, Margaret McGuigan can picture her younger brother Francis perfectly. 'He was the most gorgeous little boy, with the darkest curly hair and dark, chocolate eyes. He was so pleasant, always smiling, and he looked like a wee cherub because he had such rosy cheeks.'

Ten years old and the eldest in her family, Margaret often looked after her little brother. She and her sister Louise, who was nine, used to push Francis up and down the street in his pram. 'Everybody used to stop us because he was just so pleasant and would gurgle away at people.

'Francis had a little pull-along toy, a little red horse, that he used to play with all the time. He used to pull it along and it made a clicking noise and he loved it; he would play with it for ages. He also loved it if you threw him up in the air and caught him, you would have heard the chuckles out of him.'

He called his sister 'Mar-Mar' – 'because he couldn't say Margaret' – and he would 'put out his wee chubby arms to get lifted up'.

The day before he died, there had been serious rioting in Ballymurphy, in west Belfast. 'The army suddenly came in,' says Margaret, 'and I remember the bin lids going and the whistles blowing and the doors being kicked in.'

She and her siblings sheltered in the back bedroom of their house, Francis in his cot, while their parents watched from the landing window. 'I remember them screaming, "They're shooting tear gas into the houses," and I remember hearing the window smash and then the gas. I can still get that sensation where my eyes were streaming and burning and you're coughing. Francis got so ill. I can remember him just vomiting, and Mummy saying he had diarrhoea and phoning for an ambulance.'

The baby never came home. 'My dad carried the little white coffin from the house to the church and it was the first time I had ever seen a man cry.'

The army denied that the gas had caused Francis' death and said the assistant state pathologist 'was of the opinion that death was not caused by the gas'.[4] Local community associations and politicians disputed this, and there was a call in parliament for an inquiry into his death.[5]

An inquest jury decided that Francis's death had been due to natural causes; the coroner, Dr Herbert Lowe, 'ruled out any allegation that the military or police were in any way responsible'.[6]

Four years later Francis' parents received a letter from the regiment that had been in Ballymurphy that day, offering their 'sincere condolences'.

Margaret is in no doubt that the gas caused her brother's death. 'Francis had a bad chest but otherwise he was perfectly healthy,' she said. 'All I remember is a little boy who was very much loved and brought so much joy to us, who was there one minute and was gone the next.'

✳ ✳ ✳ ✳ ✳

Name: *Ann Gilligan*

Age: *2*

From: *Falls Road, West Belfast*

Date of Death: *09/05/1970*

Ann Gilligan was playing cowboys and Indians. She and the other children – her siblings and the two 12-year-old boys who were babysitting them – would have been laughing and giggling as they ran around the house.

When the Gilligan children ran upstairs, the boys followed. 'On pushing open a bedroom door,' the inquest heard, 'a pair of trousers fell to the floor and a loaded revolver fell out of the pocket.'

The boys began playing with the gun. One of them pointed it at Ann, and pulled the trigger. 'It went off. The girl fell to the floor.'[7]

The coroner described Ann's death as 'another of these terribly tragic cases arising out of the present circumstances in Northern Ireland'.[8]

Hours after his daughter's death, Ann's father John was charged with possessing a thousand rounds of ammunition. He was released on bail to allow him to attend Ann's funeral, and the *Evening Herald* reported that 'women relatives burst into tears and sobbed bitterly' when he was remanded in custody days after her burial.

In a statement at the inquest into her death, John said the loaded gun had been in his house for a month, and he had known it was in his trouser pocket. 'He accepted responsibility,' the statement said.[9]

In death notices in *The Irish News*, Ann was described as 'dearly beloved little daughter … very deeply regretted by her sorrowing Mummy and Daddy'.[10]

✷ ✷ ✷ ✷ ✷

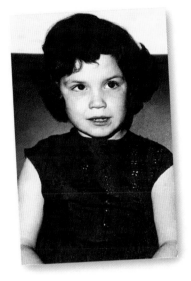

Name: *Bernadette McCool*

Age: *9*

From: *Creggan, Derry*

Date of Death: *27/06/1970*

When Bernadette McCool's older brother John looks at photographs of his sister, he is struck by how pretty she was. 'I'd say she would have been a stunner,' he says. 'One of the memories I have of Bernadette is that she had lovely hair, and she loved brushing her hair out.'

Her younger sister Sinead still has the bows Bernadette was wearing in her hair the day before she died. 'She had two lovely green tartan bows, and she pulled them out of her hair that night before going to bed. She'd set them on top of the television, and they're still exactly the way they were when they came out of her hair.'

Bernadette liked school – she was in Mrs Casey's class at Nazareth House Primary School, in Bishop Street in Derry – and was popular with her friends and with the neighbours.

She loved singing. 'I often remember my mother saying she would have been sitting at the foot of the stairs singing,' remembers Sinead. 'One of the songs was "Nobody's Child". She would have sat singing that at the foot of the stairs.'

Bernadette and her youngest sister Carole died, along with their father Tommy and two other men, Thomas Carlin and Joseph Coyle, after an explosion engulfed the McCool home in Dunree Gardens in flames.

The three had been members of the IRA during the 1956–62 Border Campaign; Tommy and his former comrades found themselves among the most senior republicans in Derry when the Troubles erupted.

That night they had been attempting to make a bomb in the kitchen when there was an accident; a stack of crates had been knocked over. John was in the sitting room. 'I just heard, "boom".' He rushed out. 'I heard screams and I saw the flash coming out, it was like a fireball.'

Rescuers were unable to reach Bernadette and Carole, who were asleep upstairs. Four-year-old Sinead – who had refused to go to bed that night –

survived because she was asleep on the sofa. 'I remember my mother grabbing Sinead and us all running out to the street. The smoke was just billowing out of the house," says John. 'Neighbours had to pull me away because I was trying to get in to reach them. They had to sit on me to hold me down.'

The inquest into their deaths heard that firemen had found 'what appeared to be the remnants of a wooden crate containing bases of two pint milk bottles and five large mineral bottles'. A colleague had discovered a tin containing sodium chlorate and a white cloth gauze in the kitchen, and in the backyard 'a brown paper bag containing one and three quarter pounds of sodium and a plastic funnel.'[11]

He and Sinead are thankful that many of their family photographs survived the fire; they had been stored safely in a tin box. 'When I look at them now, I often wonder,' says John. 'She was good-looking. She would have gone places.'

✳ ✳ ✳ ✳ ✳

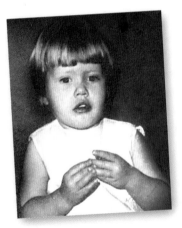

Name: *Carole McCool*

Age: *3*

From: *Creggan, Derry*

Date of Death: *27/06/1970*

Carole was the youngest in a family of five – 15-year-old John, 13-year-old Kieran, and then the girls: Bernadette (9), Sinead (4), and three-year-old Carole. 'When the girls came on the scene,' says John, 'suddenly they were the ones getting all the attention.'

Their Granny McCool's house, on Moore Street, was a focal point for the family. When a photographer appeared on the street, he was brought inside to take a picture of the girls. 'It's the only one of the three of us together,' says Sinead.

A big attraction at their granny's was Peggy the horse. Their great-uncle was a horse dealer, and Peggy pulled a cart and lived in stables at the back of the house. 'It was just any child's dream,' remembers John. 'Carole loved Peggy the horse, just like any wain would.'

Only a year older than Carole, Sinead still keeps 'a wee kimono belonging to Carole and a poncho that was crocheted for the two of us. It was a green poncho, and we used to fight over it.'

Sinead recalls her mother, Josie, saying that Carole had been a strong-willed child. 'I'd say she would have been the type of girl if she had her mind fixed on something she would have went for the top.'

Carole could also have a temper. 'I remember my father teasing her, for a laugh, just to get her going,' adds John.

'I think it was the day of the accident,' says Sinead, 'and my father had to go somewhere and Carole sunk her teeth into my mother because she wanted to go too.'

Carole and her nine-year-old sister Bernadette were asleep upstairs when an explosion in the kitchen of their home sent a fireball through the house. One eyewitness said the house was 'gutted within three minutes of the start of the fire'.[12] Their mother Josie and their three siblings – who were in the living room – were able to escape, but rescuers were unable to reach Carole and Bernadette. They died of smoke inhalation.

Among the few items that were salvaged from the house was a Pinocchio puppet that Bernadette had given Carole. 'Bernadette was a very motherly sort, and my mother remembered her going on a bus run with the school and bringing back that puppet for Carole,' says Sinead. 'I miss them terribly. I miss having sisters.'

✳ ✳ ✳ ✳ ✳

1971

- The level of violence continues to escalate. Gun battles between the IRA and British army are now commonplace in parts of Belfast

- Gunner Robert Curtis becomes the first British soldier to be killed

- James Chichester-Clark resigns as Northern Ireland PM and is replaced by Brian Faulkner

- Internment – the arrest and imprisonment of suspects without trial – is introduced in August; it is used almost exclusively against the Catholic population

- Violence in the 48 hours after the introduction of internment leaves 17 people dead, 11 of them civilians shot by the British army's Parachute Regiment in west Belfast in what would become known as the 'Ballymurphy Massacre'

- The loyalist Ulster Defence Association (UDA) is formed and organises paramilitary shows of strength

- Ian Paisley sets up the Democratic Unionist Party in a direct challenge to Faulkner's Ulster Unionist Party

- An unusual attempt at peacebuilding sees comedian Peter Sellers bring love, flowers and an Indian guru to Unity Flats in Belfast, while Mother Teresa and four nuns move into a house in Ballymurphy

- The Space Hopper is the year's must-have toy.

Name: *Denise Dickson*

Age: *5*

From: *New Lodge, North Belfast*

Date of Death: *08/02/1971*

Denise Dickson was only five, but she knew who she was and what she wanted. Within days of starting school at Star of the Sea Primary School the previous September, she had asked her mother for a new schoolbag – one that she could put on her back and keep her hands free 'so she could run if she had to'.

When she saw the other girls in her class with peanut butter sandwiches, she wanted to know what they tasted like. 'I promised I would go to the new Marks & Spencer in the city centre to get her some,' her mother, May, recalls.

She still keeps her daughter's school books, with their mature handwriting – all marked ten out of ten – and laughs when she remembers how Denise had promised to help her with decimalisation, which was introduced the following week. 'She was a wee angel. She loved school, she obeyed the teachers, and she was always helping.'

Denise ran messages for her neighbours to the local corner shops and loved skipping on the street outside her house – and waving in the window to her mother as she did so.

Her favourite toys were the doll and pram Santa had brought her the previous Christmas and she loved singing, with her toy record player and plastic records – another Christmas present – 'constantly on the go'. Her favourite programme was Ulster Television's *Romper Room*, and she proudly told her brother, sister and parents that one day she would be on TV.

That Monday afternoon she had grabbed her skipping rope and headed to the shops with her brother Gerard. He remembers hearing the roar of an engine as a convoy of British army jeeps and Ferret armoured cars came around the corner.

A Ferret hit her; it did not stop. 'It was put down as a traffic accident,' says Gerard. 'There was no investigation. The police never called to the hospital or the house, then or since.'

Denise never got to taste peanut butter. But she knew she was a good girl. The day she was killed, she wrote in her copybook, 'Today is Monday. I am a good girl. I talk to God.'

Name: *Damien Harkin*

Age: *8*

From: *Bogside, Derry*

Date of Death: *24/07/1971*

Damien Harkin has many namesakes. His best friend Paul's baby brother was named Mark Damien in his memory; over the years Damien's mother Lily has heard of lots of other Damiens who were called after her son. 'It was nice of people to do that,' she says. 'In a way, it's him being carried on.'

Lily remembers her son's blond hair and 'beautiful smile'. A 'happy boy' who was 'always full of go', he was always out on the street playing, especially with the toy guitar he had received the Christmas before. 'I remember the man down the street laughing over the way Damien was standing playing his guitar, shaking it up and down,' says Lily.

'He never wanted to sit about. He would run over to his granny's and climb over the back gate and say, "Do you want any messages, Granny?", on a Saturday morning.' He was 'reliable and smart', Lily adds. 'I could have sent him anywhere.'

That Saturday, eight-year-old Damien had been to the minors' matinee at the cinema with his friends and was walking home. An eyewitness recalled how the 'ground vibrated'[13] as a British army convoy made its way along Westland Street in Derry's Bogside. A 'three-tonner' transport lorry mounted the pavement and hit Damien.

The Harkins lived only a few minutes' walk away. Lily was hoovering when her daughter came running in. 'She said a wee boy at the door said our Damien was lying dead out there. I went down to see. People kept saying, "No, it's not him, it's not him." He was covered by a blanket, and somebody lifted the bottom of the blanket. I hadn't to see any more.'

Lily identified her son from his shoes – the same shoes he had worn for his First Holy Communion only a few months earlier.

She remembers how a photograph of Damien and his classmates from Long

Tower Primary School making their Communion appeared in the *Derry Journal*, 'all looking so happy'; only a few months later, his friends and schoolmates led his funeral cortege.

'You wonder what he would have done in life and how he would have got on,' says Lily. 'Would he have been married, had children, things like that. I always remember the bishop in the cathedral, when he was buried, said he was taken before the evils of the world touched him. It's a nice thing to remember.'

✳ ✳ ✳ ✳ ✳

Name: *Desmond Healey*

Age: *14*

From: *Lenadoon, West Belfast*

Date of Death: *09/08/1971*

Dessie was the taller of the Healey twins, and the more adventurous – even though he was the younger, by an hour. 'A bit wild', is how his brother Ted describes him. 'We used to go up to a place where there were banks of red muck and there was a dam there and we used to go swimming.'

The twins also swam in the 'half-moon lake' near their home, though Dessie spent a lot of time with friends in Leeson Street on the Lower Falls, where the family used to live.

Internment had been introduced that morning. In Lenadoon, Ted was among the rioters; he had no idea his twin was also there. 'We heard the shots, and everybody dispersed. I went up to the house and said to my mummy someone had been shot dead down there.'

Believing Dessie was staying with friends in Leeson Street, the family did not realise for several days that he was dead. 'It was a real shock for me personally. I think a bit of myself died with him,' says Ted. 'I remember the funeral, it was bad. When they were throwing in the earth someone brought me away and I thought, *I want to put it in his grave.* But I never got to do it.'

Dessie had been shot by the British army's elite Parachute Regiment, though the circumstances remain disputed. The army maintained he had been throwing a petrol bomb; eyewitnesses told Ted his brother was throwing a HP sauce bottle that had been taken from a hijacked lorry.

After Dessie's death, his mother went to the Official IRA (OIRA) headquarters. 'He was supposed to have been in the Fianna,' says Ted, 'and she wanted to know why they didn't give him an IRA funeral. She would have liked it to be known that he was in the IRA or the Fianna and that he was shot.'

Ted is unsure if his brother was a member. 'I've never met anybody who said they were in it with him, so maybe it was just talk. There's a plaque up in Lenadoon, from his friends and neighbours. It was nice that they remembered him.'

✳ ✳ ✳ ✳ ✳

Name: *Leo McGuigan*

Age: *16*

From: *Oldpark, North Belfast*

Date of Death: *09/08/1971*

Leo McGuigan was to go for a trial at Sunderland Football Club that September. 'He was so excited about that trial,' says his brother Kieran. 'His only interest was football.'

The 16-year-old was a student at St Malachy's College, where the future Republic of Ireland manager Martin O'Neill was also a pupil. 'Martin would play football after school,' says Kieran, 'and he would always pick Leo as his first choice.'

Leo's father had been a professional footballer with Belfast Celtic, but he was keen that his son's talent should speak for itself. 'Our father used to go to Leo's matches and people beside him would say, "Who's that young fella there, he's a great player," says Kieran. 'He never let on who he was.

'A well-known football scout stood beside him one day and said, "That's a great wee player," and again he never let on. At the end of the match the scout asked if he knew where he could find Leo, and he said, "Well, he's my son."

'The scout laughed and said, "Why didn't you say?", but he said he always liked people to find out about Leo for themselves.'

Leo was shot by a British soldier during rioting in Ardoyne which followed the introduction of internment that morning, 9 August 1971. The journalist Kevin Myers witnessed his death. 'His shot ricocheted off a wall, and fragments of one bullet hit the three boys he couldn't even see; one lost the fingers of one hand, another lost the back of his head but survived, the third was Leo McGuigan. I crouched beside him, but he was dead to my fingers, and no blood came from the tiny hole in his young cheek.'[14]

Kieran remembers his brother as 'a great character – a good, kind-hearted soul who was never in trouble'.

Leo had been going out with a Protestant girl when he was killed; she and her parents came to his funeral.

Among those who expressed their condolences in *The Irish News* were the members of St Gabriel's Youth Club and football team; Martin O'Neill wrote to Leo's parents after his death, a gesture they always appreciated.

'He was so talented,' says Kieran. 'He had a great football career ahead of him when he died.'

✳ ✳ ✳ ✳ ✳

Damien Harkin's funeral,
4 July 1971.

Name: *Alphonsus Cunningham*

Age: *13*

From: *Lower Falls, West Belfast*

Date of Death: *11/08/1971*

Thirteen-year-old Alphonsus Cunningham was the third child to die following the introduction of internment on 9 August 1971.

In the Lower Falls, where Alphonsus lived, it must have seemed as if the Troubles had become a war. People in working-class nationalist areas 'woke up to the sound of splintering wood and glass as their front doors were kicked in. Whole families were assaulted and clubbed as arrested men were dragged, half dressed, into the street, some with sacks over their heads and their mouths stuffed with cotton wool. Outside, the district was swamped with soldiers … within minutes of the first arrests, the area was in uproar.'[15]

'Operation Demetrius', an attempt by the unionist prime minister Brian Faulkner to curb the rising violence, instead sent Northern Ireland spiralling into near-civil war. The policy of arrest and imprisonment without trial was used overwhelmingly against Catholic civilians – few IRA members were arrested – and its main achievement was to further alienate the nationalist population. It sparked rioting and gun battles between the IRA and the British army, with up to 2,500 people forced out of their homes in the unrest that followed.

Newspaper front pages showed teenage rioters confronting the army with petrol bombs, rows of burning houses, and families with young children huddled with suitcases waiting to be taken to safety over the border.

In Belfast alone, 20 people died[16] in the four days following its introduction; among them, 11 civilians – including a priest – shot dead by the British army's Parachute Regiment in what became known as the Ballymurphy Massacre.

There had been rioting at the junction of the Springfield and Falls roads; according to *Lost Lives*, youths had been attempting to hijack a car and set it on fire to create a barricade.

The driver accelerated away, hitting Alphonsus; he died in hospital the following day.

'Although he is indirectly a victim of the Troubles,' the *Belfast Telegraph* reported, 'his name is not being included in the riot death list.'[17]

Name: *James O'Hagan*

Age: *16*

From: *Waterside, Derry*

Date of Death: *19/08/1971*

James O'Hagan's father, Thomas, thought his son was out delivering civil rights pamphlets. 'A young fellow came to the door and told me there had been an accident and that my son had been slightly injured. He asked me to go with him to the house of a friend. When I got there, I found my son dying.'[18]

The 16-year-old – who was known as Jim – had been shot and mortally wounded; three other boys brought the dying teenager to a nearby house to seek help.

It is believed he was shot accidentally in a disused stable on land off the Limavady Road, which was owned by the sister of the local unionist MP. Found in the stable were 'a length of fuse wire, a Smith and Wesson revolver, some ammunition, a quantity of gelignite and one spent cartridge case. There was blood on the floor.'[19]

Two teenagers, aged 16 and 17, were later jailed in connection with the discovery of firearms and explosives in the stable.

Jim O'Hagan is listed as a Volunteer on the Republican Roll of Honour; it also states that he was 'shot accidentally'.[20]

Former IRA member Shane Paul O'Doherty later wrote in his memoir that he and Jim had become friends when they were in the IRA's Waterside section together.[21]

The eldest of six – three boys and three girls – Jim had just left St Brecan's High School.; O'Doherty remembers him as 'quiet, and very innocent'.

His 'distraught' father wept as he spoke of Jim's death. 'He may have been a member of the IRA, I do not know, but I wish to God I knew who killed him.'[22]

✳ ✳ ✳ ✳ ✳

Name: *Angela Gallagher*

Age: *18 months*

From: *Falls Road, West Belfast*

Date of Death: *03/09/1971*

Angela Gallagher was the best child in Ireland. 'I said to someone once that she was the best child in Ireland for sleeping,' recalls her mother Irene. 'She remembered that, and if you asked her, "What are you?", she would say, "The best child in Ireland."'

'She always had a bow in her hair and she'd try to take it out, and we'd tell her to keep it in because it was a nice bow. From then on, she'd pat it and say, "Nice bow."'

'When we went out on a Sunday she would lift the stones off the graves and we'd tell her just to take one special stone, and every time after that she'd give you a stone and say, "Special stone."'

Though she was only 18 months old, Angela was already 'a real livewire, a real wee character'.

'I met a man the other day who said his last memory of her was of her waving at him and shouting, "Hiya." She would go down the street shouting "Hiya" at everyone.

'The night before she died, she was quiet, so I knew she was up to something. She'd bitten a piece out of the corner of a packet of jelly. I still have that jelly.'

That day, her father Peter had come home for lunch. 'Angela had finished all hers and she took a bit from her daddy's plate and he pretended to be angry and he chased her round the house. That was his last memory of her.'

Angela and her older sister Paula had just left their grandmother's house, just off Belfast's Falls Road, to buy sweets. Angela had insisted on bringing her pram and was pushing it in front of her when 'I heard a bang. Angela fell down and I could not pick her up.'[23]

The toddler had been struck by a bullet fired by the IRA, which ricocheted off the wall; a second bullet had passed through Paula's skirt.

When her father Peter died, Angela was reinterred along with him. 'We always said whichever one of us went first, we'd have her buried with us,' says Irene.

At the ceremony, the mourners were presented with bags of sweets. 'They represent the sweets that Angela never got.'

※ ※ ※ ※ ※

Name: *Annette McGavigan*

Age: *14*

From: *Bogside, Derry*

Date of Death: *06/09/1971*

Among the murals which decorate the gable ends in Derry's Bogside, there is a portrait of a girl in a green school uniform: Annette McGavigan.

'She was a bubbly girl, very good-natured,' remembers her brother Martin. 'She was always with my mother – she would have been like a mother figure in the home.'

She was a kind, caring child. 'She would never have said a bad word about anybody,' says her sister May, who believes Annette would have gone on to become a nurse.

Annette was also creative. 'She used to write poems,' says Martin. 'She always had pieces of paper with poems on them, and she loved art and drawing.'

She and her friends had been let out of school early because of rioting in the area. Still wearing her green St Cecilia's College uniform, Annette had gone to see what was happening. 'The girls went down to see the talent,' according to Martin.

Shot as she knelt to pick up a rubber bullet from the street for her collection, the 14-year-old was the hundredth civilian to die in the Troubles.

Twelve-year-old May heard on the street that a girl had been shot, and ran home and told her mother. '"God help her poor mother and father, whoever they are." That's what my mammy said,' recalls May. 'I'll never forget those words as long as I live.'

The *Derry Journal* reported that her funeral was one of the largest ever seen in the city. 'Counting those in the cortege and the silent thousands lining the route, the attendance must have been in the vicinity of 10,000.'[24]

After their sister's death, the McGavigan children grew used to seeing their mother up on the landing when they came home from school. 'She would have all the clippings from the newspapers about Annette and her clothes all spread out, and my mother would have been crying,' says Martin. 'My father would have spent hours standing at the railings in front of the mural of Annette, that's the way he dealt with it.'

Annette had planted a tree in the back garden of the family home; 'Annette's tree' was never allowed to be cut down.

The British army claimed they had shot a gunman; Martin and May have tried for decades to have Annette's name officially cleared. 'How could they say they shot a gunman when it was a young girl with a school uniform on?'

✳ ✳ ✳ ✳ ✳

Name: *Gary Gormley*

Age: *3*

From: *Foyle Road, Derry*

Date of Death: *09/09/1971*

Gary Gormley was killed just yards from his front door. One of a family of six children from Carrigans Lane in Derry, the three-year-old had been out in the street playing when a British army 'Pig' armoured personnel carrier came along Foyle Road at 'powerful speed'.

Gary was knocked down. Eyewitnesses said the 'Pig' failed to stop but that two soldiers jumped down from a second vehicle. 'After looking at the child it, too, made off quickly.'[25]

In a statement read out at the inquest, the driver – a gunner in the Royal Artillery – said he saw a child 'dash out into the road into the path of my vehicle.

I braked and accelerated to the left away from the child.' Another soldier said the driver fainted after the impact.[26]

A local eyewitness said that he heard a soldier shout, 'My God, we've killed him.'[27]

That evening 14-year-old Eamonn MacDermott was with his father, Dr Domhnall MacDermott, who was making a house call in the area. 'Somebody came and said a child had been knocked down. We could already see a crowd gathering, and it was obvious the boy was dead. I can still remember the atmosphere. It was volatile, people were extremely angry and distraught because a child had been killed.

'My father had to then go and tell his parents, and I remember him being angry because it was the second time in a few days he'd had to go and tell a mother and father their child had been killed by the British army.'

There were calls for an investigation. SDLP MP Ivan Cooper said, 'I have often seen army drivers breaking every traffic regulation in the book – and they seem immune from prosecution for these breaches.'[28]

Gary's death was followed by rioting. Petrol bombs were thrown at the army and barricades erected in the Brandywell area of Derry. A crowd of around a hundred women and girls marched from the Bogside to an army post in the city centre chanting, 'Hey, hey British army, how many children have you killed today?'[29]

✳ ✳ ✳ ✳ ✳

Name: *Maria McGurk*

Age: *14*

From: *New Lodge, North Belfast*

Date of Death: *04/12/1971*

Fourteen-year-old Maria McGurk died alongside her mother, Philomena, and her uncle, John Colton, when her father's pub – which was also the family's home – was blown up by the UVF. Fifteen people died.

McGurk's – on the corner of North Queen Street and Great Georges Street – was a family bar; Patrick and Philomena McGurk 'ran a tight ship, and were renowned for their intolerance of bigotry and prejudice.

'Mr and Mrs McGurk therefore sought to create an environment that was not only fitting for a well-run pub, but also one appropriate for the raising of their children. They even had a swear box on the counter.'[30]

Maria and her mother had just returned from the nearby St Patrick's Church. 'The bombers watched Mrs McGurk and her daughter going through the door,' says Gary Roberts, whose 13-year-old cousin James Cromie was also killed. 'They'd just come back from confession and she'd stopped off at the shop on the way back to buy them all lollipops. She was on the stairway going up to the house above.'

Maria's brother John was upstairs when the bomb went off. 'In the white heat of pure terror, I realised that I was trapped under slabs of concrete and tons of rubble – walls which used to be my happy family home. I was utterly alone, trapped in the abyss, roaring for help; and smelling gas as I feverishly recited my childhood prayers over and over again.'[31]

Police and army intelligence initially claimed the bomb had been 'an IRA plan that went wrong'.[32] This was denied by the IRA; a member of the UVF was later convicted of the bombing. The families of the victims continue to campaign, alleging security force collusion and cover-up in regard to the atrocity. In 2011 the Police Ombudsman found that 'investigative bias' by the RUC 'precluded an effective investigation'.[33]

As John McGurk had lain there, trapped in the rubble, he believed he heard his sister's voice. 'It sounded like the low wail of a ghost, calling directly to me. Was it my sister Maria? I roared her name over and over again. But there was no response, no recognition … just a dwindling, weaker call, until I could hear nothing more above the noise of others literally pleading for their lives.'[34]

✳ ✳ ✳ ✳ ✳

Name: *Jimmy Cromie*

Age: *13*

From: *New Lodge, North Belfast*

Date of Death: *04/12/1971*

From Jimmy Cromie's front door to McGurk's Bar is exactly 147 steps. After his death, Gary Roberts counted them.

'Up until that day, I can't remember a time when Jimmy wasn't in my life,' he says. The pair were cousins, but were more like brothers; Jimmy, 11 months older, was the more adventurous of the two, had a great imagination.

'This Sunday night we'd nothing to do, so we went up onto the Crumlin Road – my parents would have went mad – and Jimmy told me this whole story about how the scales on top of the court building tilt one way for innocent, and the other way for guilty. I remember looking up at it and thinking, *that's marvellous*, and for years afterwards looking to see if the scales moved.

'He also told me this fantastic story about the Poor Clares [convent] and the wall around it, and how inside there were elephants and tigers; he described it almost like a zoo. He said he got to see them because his mummy gave money to the Poor Clares, and one day I might be able to see all this as well. Of course, I believed every word he said.'

Jimmy was mad about football – he was an Everton supporter – and loved playing all kinds of sport, playing Gaelic football and hurling for his school teams.

Nicknamed Bunter, he was a hero in the playground, known for standing up for other boys in school. 'He had guts,' says Gary, 'but he also had a sense of justice and a sense of righteousness.'

Jimmy lived with his grandparents and was friends with the McGurk boys, who lived above their father's bar.

That evening Jimmy couldn't wait to get up to McGurk's, where he and his friends were planning a game of Subbuteo.

'When the explosion went up,' recalls Gary, 'my great-granny – Jimmy's granny - ran out and she was one of the first ones there. The whole bar had just collapsed in on top of itself, and she screamed and screamed and screamed.'

Fifteen people had been killed, including Jimmy and 14-year-old Maria McGurk. Jimmy would have turned 14 two weeks later. 'I think to myself what sort of life would Jimmy have had ahead of him,' says Gary. 'He passed his eleven-plus, I didn't. He was at the grammar school. He was going to make it.

'In my mind's eye I can still see him running down that street, full of devilment, kicking anything that was on the ground, so excited to get to McGurk's.'

✳ ✳ ✳ ✳ ✳

Name: *Tracey Munn*

Age: *2*

From: *Oldpark, North Belfast*

Date of Death: *11/12/1971*

Two-year-old Tracey Munn and her 17-month-old friend Colin were enjoying a day out with Tracey's mother Helen. Sitting together in Colin's pram, the two babies would been babbling away to each other, playing games or looking out at the people and places they passed on the way to the Shankill Road.

Tracey lived next door to Colin's granny; Colin's mum was away, so Colin and his dad Jackie were at Jackie's mother's house. Helen and Tracey were going shopping, and Helen offered to take Colin with them. 'I didn't really want her to because I knew my mother would miss him,' says Colin's father Jackie, 'but I said alright. Colin's pram was outside, so she put them in the pram and away she went.

'When my mum came up from the shop, she ate the head off me. "I wanted to mind him today," she said.'

When Helen reached the Shankill the street was busy with Christmas shoppers. She took the babies to a café and was pushing the pram past the Balmoral Furniture Company showrooms when the bomb exploded. There had been no warning.

'The whole front of the building fell onto the pavement and the three floors collapsed on top of one another,' *The Irish Times* wrote. 'Dust and smoke rose in the air and people were running hysterical and screaming in all directions … local people had already begun to dig at the smoking ruins with their bare hands.'[35]

A wall collapsed on the babies' pram, killing them both; two men also died. Helen was seriously injured.

A 15-year-old eyewitness, James Wilson, told the inquest that he had seen two men plant a box in the shop doorway just before the explosion.[36] The IRA was believed to have carried out the attack in retaliation for the loyalist bombing of McGurk's Bar the week before.

Many young local Protestants would later cite the bombing of the furniture shop as the turning point which persuaded them to join loyalist organisations such as the UDA.

As the babies' funerals made their way through north Belfast, crowds lined the route. The two corteges came together on the Cliftonville Road and about a thousand mourners, some in tears, followed the tiny coffins to Carnmoney Cemetery.

✳ ✳ ✳ ✳ ✳

Name: *Colin Nicholl*

Age: *17 months*

From: *Oldpark, North Belfast*

Date of Death: *11 / 12 / 1971*

Summer, 1971. Neil Diamond's song 'Sweet Caroline' was on the radio, but the Nicholls had their own version. 'I used to hold him and I would sing, "Sweet Colin mine", says his father Jackie.

That summer Colin's parents had taken him on holiday to the seaside resort of Portrush. 'We had the greatest week,' remembers Jackie. 'We were staying in a boarding house and there were other kids there and they just lapped him up. They loved playing with him, and of course he loved it.'

The Nicholls had adopted Colin the year before. Initially, Jackie had been uncertain, but as soon as he saw the baby, 'everything in my life changed. I couldn't let him go, and then they said we had to wait a week to adopt him and it nearly broke my heart waiting.

'He was fantastic, a beautiful child. He probably would have grown up saying, "Thank God I'd a different dad to you for looks."'

Colin had just begun talking – 'mostly "Mum", none of the "Dad"', says Jackie – and was his Granny Nicholl's pride and joy. 'My mum loved minding him, it was like a new lease of life for her.'

With Colin's mother Ann away – her nephew had been knocked down and killed in England – his granny had been looking forward to babysitting that Saturday. Instead, her neighbour Helen Munn offered to take the children for a walk.

Colin and Tracey were killed when the IRA bomb exploded outside the Balmoral Furniture Company on Belfast's Shankill Road. In England, Ann saw Colin being carried out of the wreckage wrapped in a blanket; she had no idea it was her son.

The Nicholls went on to adopt two more boys; every time Jackie hears 'Sweet Caroline', he thinks of Colin. 'You think of wee things, like whenever I was working and I came home his wee head would have lifted, even though I know it was probably my own imagination telling me he knows I'm home.

'He'd have been almost 50 now. There's a void – he should have been here to look after us.'

Jackie still keeps Colin's favourite toy – a wooden rattle given to him by his neighbour. 'Margaret next door gave it to him and it was with him all the time. You can see his wee teeth marks on it. I have it by my bedside, and it's going to go into my coffin.'

✳ ✳ ✳ ✳ ✳

Name: *Martin McShane*

Age: *16*

From: *Coalisland, Co Tyrone*

Date of Death: *14/12/1971*

Martin McShane loved getting up early. He would rise between five and six in the morning and set off with his Uncle Paddy Joe to Roughan Lough – near his home in Coalisland, County Tyrone – where they would fish for pike, perch, rainbow trout and eel.

His catch was sold locally, or eaten at home – especially when he arrived back with a rabbit he and his pet dog, Cheeky, had snared.

'All the money he earned he handed to his mother like a trophy,' remembers his brother Pearse.

The eldest of seven – five boys and two girls – Martin was well used to hard work. At primary school in Edendork, after school the siblings would head straight to their Granny Donaghy's farm a mile away for their dinner. 'She fed us every day,' says Pearse. 'It was great food – veg, chicken, potatoes. We all ate together and you couldn't be fussy. You had to grab it, or you'd starve.'

Martin had been helping out on the farm from a young age and had learnt to drive the tractor by the time he was eleven. Evenings were spent at home getting the lead weights and tackle ready for the next morning's fishing.

The four eldest McShane boys – Martin, Seamus, Pearse and Anthony – were inseparable. In the family home in Meenagh Park, they shared a bedroom. 'We even all got chickenpox together,' says Pearse.

That December evening the brothers had been to the youth club at the nearby GAA ground, and afterwards began playing 'Jailbreak' – a game similar to hide and seek – outside. Martin ran home to get his coat, and as he returned he was shot dead by Royal Marine commandos who were concealed near the GAA ground, armed with sub-machine guns; the teenager was hit seven or eight times.

An independent committee of inquiry, set up in the Coalisland area after Martin was shot, found that the 16-year-old had been unarmed and called on the prime minister to hold a public inquiry into the killing.[37]

Today, Pearse is the only surviving McShane brother. He recounts how the youngest, Daniel, was only ten months old when Martin was killed; the brothers never got over their loss.

Martin, Daniel and Anthony are buried together.

✳ ✳ ✳ ✳ ✳

Name: *James McCallum*

Age: *16*

From: *Turf Lodge, West Belfast*

Date of Death: *18 / 12 / 1971*

James McCallum had only been working in the Star Bar for a few weeks. Jim – as he was known – had been glad to leave school the previous summer and had immediately begun working as a barman.

When he got the job in the Star – also known as Murtagh's – on the Springfield Road in west Belfast, his mother Theresa was concerned; Murtagh's had already been attacked by loyalists. His brother Sean remembers Jim reassuring her. 'Don't worry, it'll be alright,' he told her.

Jim was one of ten children. The eight boys all shared a bedroom, with the four youngest in a single double bed.

Sean remembers his brother as a 'generous, happy-go-lucky' boy who loved football and boxing. He followed Glentoran – even though its supporters would have been predominantly Protestant – and boxed for St John Bosco's Boxing Club.

The family couldn't afford holidays but, according to Sean, their one treat was 'torturing our father every Sunday to take us on a trip in his Ford Corsair'.

Jim and his friends used to go to the local youth club to play table tennis, and always went to the disco on a Wednesday night. 'Jimmy had just the most beautiful brown eyes,' remembers his friend Patricia Roberts. 'He was the first of our group to turn 16, and he was a lovely guy, very good-looking. He and my friend Kate were an item, and he was the love of her life – she was just devastated when he died.'

That evening Jim was washing bottles in the stockroom when a bomb – which had been left against an outside wall – exploded without warning. 'The force of the blast blew him the length of the room, down stairs and into a cellar.'[38] Five others were injured. The UVF were believed to be behind the attack.[39]

Sean remembers coming home from his paper round when 'we saw the commotion on our road. We thought it was a party. Then we saw the police, and we were told Jim had been killed.'

It was exactly a week until Christmas. 'We got extra presents for Christmas,' says Sean, 'but it was never the same again.'

✳ ✳ ✳ ✳ ✳

Paul Maxwell and his parents
on the beach at Mullaghmore.

1

Childhood of the Troubles

'Anyone raised during this time will remember
the empty roads and streets as there was essentially
a self-imposed curfew.'

Mullaghmore is a memory. Year-round, the tiny fishing village on the Sligo coast lives on in the mind's eye of its visitors as a seaside idyll, a land of golden sands, sparkling blue water, and long, hot summer days.

It has always been popular with Northerners, attracted not just by the beauty of the harbour or the proximity of the beach, but by its safety. A few weeks at Mullaghmore, over the border in the Republic, was a welcome escape from the Troubles which would sustain families after they returned home to the grey reality of the killings in the North.

The Maxwell family went every year; days were spent swimming in the sea and hanging around with the other teenagers holidaying in the village. The eldest, 17-year-old Donna, had met a boy and her younger brother Paul, 15, delighted in following them around the headland; he and Lisa, 12, would get up to all sorts of mischief together.

Paul had also found a job, as a boat boy for Lord Mountbatten, who was also on holiday with his family. The Mountbattens – part of the British royal family – stayed in Classiebawn Castle, a nineteenth-century construction with round turret which sits atop the headland overlooking Mullaghmore like a vision from a fairy tale.

Lord Mountbatten (third from left) with family members, including Nicholas Knatchbull, on *Shadow V* at Mullaghmore, Co Sligo, c. 1975.

Paul had become friends with Lord Mountbatten's grandsons, the 14-year-old twins Nicholas and Timothy Knatchbull; Timothy recalls being out on their grandfather's boat and Paul asking him the time. '11.39 and 30 seconds,' he replied jokily.[1]

The bomb exploded. Paul and Nicholas were both killed, as were Lord Mountbatten and the twins' grandmother, Lady Doreen Brabourne.

It is a bright summer's day in July 2017. Paul's sisters, Donna and Lisa, sit in the bar of the hotel in Mullaghmore. The hotel is right beside the slipway; on this beautiful day the concrete is bleached almost white, and the water lapping at its edges is a dazzling blue.

Lisa points out the window. 'That's where they brought the bodies,' she says. 'They laid them out on the slipway.'

Both sisters were watching. 'Daddy had gone out on the boat to look for Paul and I was on the pier,' says Donna. 'I remember him yelling over at me, "Paul's dead."'

Donna and Lisa bring their own children to Mullaghmore every summer; they have shown them the cottage where they used to stay and told them stories of their Uncle Paul.

'This is where Paul was,' says Lisa. 'He loved it here. I feel closer to him. I don't want this place to be overshadowed by this traumatic event.'

The long summer holidays are one of the constants of childhood. In Northern Ireland, school finished at the end of June and started again on 1 September; in between was fun, freedom and opportunity. For families who could afford them, holidays were almost always in Ireland; Butlins – in Mosney, County Meath – was a popular destination, as were coastal resorts.

James Morgan had just returned from a week in Killarney when he was killed; that he had made the most of his time away has been a comfort to his parents in the years since. Others never got their holiday – like Tony McDowell, due to go to Lourdes; another experience missed in a life cut short. Majella O'Hare returned from the Isle of Man – for ever afterwards, her sister Marie Grew thought, if only she'd stayed.

Colin Nicholl's first holiday was to Portrush, County Antrim. He and his parents spent a week in a boarding house by the seaside; a treasured family

Colin Nicholl's body is carried from the bomb site.

Colin's rattle.

photograph shows a blond, chubby baby sitting on the sand, spade in hand, with a large sandcastle in front of him. Colin was killed the following December, one of two young children who died in the bombing of the Balmoral Furniture Company showroom on Belfast's Shankill Road.

His father Jackie still keeps a wooden rattle marked with his son's teeth marks. It is a privilege to be allowed to hold the treasured toy. To run finger and thumb over it, to feel their indentations, is to be connected to the child that made them. Time falls away; for that moment, Colin is present.

Of the children killed as a result of the Troubles, it is mementoes like these which hold the greatest power. Stephen McConomy's toy army truck; the big old coins belonging to Daniel Hegarty which he called his 'lucky money' for playing pitch and toss; the tiny pair of gloves still hidden in Denise Dickson's schoolbag.

Teresa Campbell still treasures her sister Martha's Timex watch; after Jimmy Cromie was killed, his cousin Gary Roberts was given the brown shoes he had bought for Christmas, and the black Chelsea boots he had been wearing the night he was killed. 'I wore those boots and those shoes with a passion,' says Gary. 'That was the last bit I had of him.'

Such mementos are all the more precious because they are so rare. Family after family explains that, particularly during the early part of the Troubles, 'we didn't have much'.

Patrick Gibson and his three sisters Margaret, Pauline and Kathleen chat excitedly, their eyes shining as they recall their childhood in Turf Lodge in west Belfast. Their eldest brother, Gerard, was shot and killed in 1972. Like many others, they look back with nostalgia on the sense of community, on the large families and the neighbours who helped each other out.

'It was all street games, and everybody was out playing, boys and girls played together, rally-o and red rover, calling people over, swinging on the lamp, it was a good street,' remembers Patrick.

'The girls would have played skips, two-ball hopscotch, rounders,' adds Pauline. 'We had good wee neighbours, and we had respect – we knew what would happen if we didn't do what we were told.'

'We really hadn't got much, we were hungry plenty of times,' says Patrick.

Ballymurphy estate, west Belfast.

'Many's a time we had to sleep on the bedroom floor, not even in beds,' says Pauline.

'Blankets up at the windows,' remembers Patrick.

'If somebody in the street made a pot of stew it might have been up and down a few houses in the street, or a pot of soup,' says Pauline.

'Always shared,' adds Kathleen.

'Our door would have been left wide to the world,' says Pauline. 'We had a brilliant childhood.'

'It seems like we played outdoors all the time,' says John Dempsey's sister, Martina Toner. 'We had a game in our street called "TASKS". John and his mates would make jumps like hurdles from old doors, they would jump from trellis to trellis and climb through hedges. We played hide and seek, kick the can, rally-o, rounders and flashlight. While the girls played two ball and skips, the boys played football and skateboarded. I remember the best time to play skips or rounders was when the street was barricaded to keep the Brits out.'

Inevitably, the contours of childhood adapted to the circumstances around them. Richard Moore, who was blinded when he was hit by a rubber bullet at the age of ten, remembers watching adults build barricades at the top of his street in the Creggan area of Derry. 'I used to stand with my friends in our street and count bombs going off in the city centre. There was one day when we heard ten explode. Of course it was frightening, but also, to children, exciting.'[2]

At night-time he would be afraid – 'For a child it was frightening listening to the bin lids clanging and angry voices, but worse when there were explosions and gunfire.' Yet life continued as normal. 'We still played football in the street, and sometimes I sat on top of the Malin Street barricades with my friends. Now and then our street gang would have its meeting in the vigilante hut … we'd sit in it and chat and tell jokes. It was like camping for the day.'

They also played 'IRA and British soldiers'. 'Nobody wanted to be the army; we all wanted to be the IRA. In the end we had to agree to take turns. One group would pretend to be an army foot patrol making its way down the street, while the others hid in the gardens waiting to ambush them; we'd pretend to open fire on them.

'Once we used my brother Liam's car as an IRA getaway vehicle. We pretended to drive to another part of the estate, got out, ran round to the back of our house and "opened fire". We used to wear masks or balaclavas or tie handkerchiefs over our noses like the rioters did. We'd collect rubber bullets and spent tear gas canisters so that those of us playing soldiers could throw them at the others.'[3]

The friends of Bernard Fox remembered how they had invented a new game: 'snatch squad'; in March 1973, the *Belfast Telegraph* carried a picture of two boys aiming sticks at a British army Saracen as if they were guns.

Under the headline, 'The Games Children Play', the newspaper warned: 'It's all just a game – a game the Army has constantly warned against, for obvious reasons. The danger of playing with toy guns is clearly illustrated by these children during a recent bomb alert.'[4]

Paddy McCauley remembers how he and his brother Kevin had a 'really true-to-life Tommy gun'. 'My mother said, "You can't bring that outside, you'll get shot."'[5]

Yet in other respects the streets of the 1970s were regarded as safer than those of today. Damien Harkin was killed as he walked home from the cinema; he had walked from his home in Derry's Bogside to call for a friend in Creggan, then to the city centre to go to the matinee and then back home.

Damien was a reliable, sensible child, his mother Lily explains, who was always running messages for his granny and other neighbours. 'It was safe enough for them to go that far themselves because there wasn't a lot of traffic other than the army then,' she says. 'Imagine letting your wain out now at eight to go to the pictures themselves, but that's the way it was then. People just tried to get on with living a normal life.'

For children, the Troubles were part of that normality. In Derry, Eamonn McCann wrote how, by 1970, the Bogside 'was raising a sudden generation of kamikaze children whose sport it was to hurtle down Rossville Street, stones in hand, to take on the British army. The Saturday riot became a regular thing. It was known as "the matinee".'

The rioters would gather at the bottom of William Street in the early afternoon and throw stones towards the police barracks. 'Eventually the armoured personnel carriers would trundle out. The rioters would withdraw … the army would first use rubber bullets, then gas. Then they would send in the snatch squad.'

Few were caught – the rioters were too nimble on their feet, writes McCann. Instead, 'the snatch squad would withdraw, the rioters would regroup and battle would continue. There were few variations from Saturday to Saturday.'[5]

'I loved to riot,' admitted a friend of Glen Branagh's. 'I lived to riot, we all did. We didn't know anything else. We started when we were eight or ten years old.'[6]

Ten-year-old Colette O'Connor lived on William Street; the bottom of the street had become known as 'Aggro Corner' because of all the riots. 'It was very scary sometimes and you just wanted to hide under your bed. I used to lie in our back bedroom with the radio on full blast to try to drown out the noise outside from all the missiles and glass being broken, the constant roaring and the smashing of petrol bombs.'[7]

Her sister Christine Robson, who was a year younger, remembers that the rioting had become 'commonplace'. 'It's a terrible thing to say, but I think we almost got used to it … we just amused ourselves with toys and TV and accepted we weren't allowed out.'[8]

Fifteen-year-old Eileen Fox remembers going with her sister and friends to watch the riots. 'It was great craic to us. We would pull ourselves up on the windowsills of the old houses on William Street and from there we could watch everything. We would chat about which fellas were out today and who was throwing stones. I fancied Charlie, my husband, back then.'[9]

Fourteen-year-old Annette McGavigan was watching the riots when she was shot and killed by the British army in September 1971.

In the former family home in Drumcliff Avenue in Derry's Bogside, her brother Martin opens a large plastic bag; he has brought it down specially from his sister May's attic.

We unpack its contents carefully: it is his sister Annette's exercise books, and her 'teddy bear' – a stuffed dragon, hand-made out of felt. In another bag is her clothes – her plimsolls, and the green school skirt she was wearing when she was shot.

Annette had backed some of the books with leftover wallpaper, and her name, age and address are written neatly on the front cover. Martin has never noticed until now that they are mostly empty; they only contain a few days' work. Annette was killed on 6 September – the start of the new school year.

There is also a note to 'Bobby', apologising for standing him up. 'I am really very sorry I didn't turn up last night, but a boy I used to go with called – and my father kept me in because of it. Are you really going away for a week? If you are bring me back something (ha).' It is signed, 'See you soon, all my love, Annette.'

Martin looks out the window to the back wall; he remembers his sister sitting on the wall and laughing. For a moment, Annette's ghost perches there, looking on.

Just as childhood went on during the Troubles, so too did teenage life. Like teenagers everywhere, those in Northern Ireland hung around on street corners, chatting to their friends; they went to the shop, or for chips; they gathered at the youth club or went to local discos; they listened to records in friends' bedrooms; they found girlfriends and boyfriends, often unbeknownst to their parents.

'He'd started showering himself away into nothing,' says Seamus Duffy's mother Kathleen. Seamus was killed in 1989, aged 15, after being shot by a plastic bullet. 'After he died I knew all about the girls he was with, for there was enough came to the door looking for his memorial card.'

Sometimes the only photograph of a child might have been from their First Communion, or a Confirmation; in the 1970s, most Catholic children would have been brought to Mass regularly. Attendance was high; latecomers might have to stand in the porch, and as new estates were constructed, so too were new churches. In 1976 chapels opened in both Galliagh and Carnhill in Derry; the two are less than a mile apart.

'In 1972, being Catholics, it was okay,' says Michael Turner's brother Peter. 'Michael was in Heaven so we didn't have to worry. I was nearly jealous – if you

Michael Turner in his Communion suit.

asked what time Michael had to go to bed at, well there was no bedtime in Heaven, and all the priests came and all the bishops and all the mass cards. You believed it. It was a big comfort.'

Youth clubs, run by the church or by community workers, were set up to keep teenagers off the streets. Geraldine – Dina – McKeown's friend and neighbour Angela Willett recalls Dina's last summer as 'long and hot and filled with hanging out with the Mountainview kids', sitting on the wall of the petrol station or wandering aimlessly, generally wasting time but which provided an opportunity to "eye up the talent"'.

There were 'long walks to the Water Works, stopping off in Tommy Maguire's for a drink on the way and chips from Fusco's on the return, if funds allowed'. The Saturday night disco in Toby's Hall was 'not to be missed'; in the midst of the Troubles the walk home meant watching out for 'suspicious traffic or people'.

'Anyone raised during this time will remember the empty roads and streets as there was essentially a self-imposed curfew,' says Angela. 'If going into and returning from Ardoyne, it was done in stages, undertaking an initial "juke" then hugging fences and peeking around corners until you entered the relative safety [of] near home.'

Inevitably, parents worried. Peter Watterson's mother went to his school principal for advice because she was concerned about her son being out at night, says his brother Johnny. 'She didn't know what to do with Peter, because he was 14 and out in the evenings around the Falls Road and she knew it was dangerous, but she also knew she couldn't lock up a kid who's 14 years old when his friends are literally standing right outside your shop door.

He [the principal] said, "You have to let kids do what kids do," but I know that when Peter was killed she definitely suffered guilt. Our [newsagent's] shop was on the corner and the chipper across the road was open until ten, so you could guarantee there would always be loads of kids on both sides of the road, just out talking.'

Julie Livingstone loved being out with her best friend Nuala. Her interest was music and discos – either the 'Olly bop' at St Oliver Plunkett's School, or at the Horn Drive Youth Club.

Julie and Nuala 'just wanted to enjoy themselves,' remembers her sister Elizabeth. 'They were into the smoking – even when she was injured, she said, "Get those cigarettes out of my pocket, I don't want my mummy to see the cigarettes."'

Kathleen Feeney was the same. Due to go to the youth club the night she was killed, she had a single cigarette in her coat pocket. She treasured her signed photograph of Derry's Eurovision Song Contest winner, Dana, though her favourite song was Michael Jackson's 'Ben'.

Julie's favourite song had been Stevie Wonder's 'Lately'; she and her friends had even formed their own group, The Sweet Roses. 'I think they thought they were The Nolan Sisters,' says her sister Elizabeth.

Majella O'Hare also loved music and singing; her older sister Marie is adamant that, had she lived, she would have become a singer in a showband like her older brother Michael.

Showbands were popular, particularly in rural areas. The evening he was killed, Henry Cunningham and his brothers were to go to the Lilac Ballroom in Carndonagh, County Donegal; Martin McGuigan and his friend Jim Keenan were blown up as they walked to Keady to catch a bus to the Nuremore Hotel in Carrickmacross to see The Memories. They were hoping the band would do some covers from the new Status Quo album, or Thin Lizzy.

For Martin, Jim and their friends, their shared love of music was part of the glue that held their group together; other children found friendship and a sense of identity in the many marching bands which exist in Northern Ireland on both sides of the community.

Thomas McDonald was a member of the loyalist Whitewell Defenders Flute Band, and was buried in his band uniform; a flute band in north Belfast is named after Fianna member Robert Allsopp.

A promising violinist, Philip Rafferty had just started playing in the James Connolly Youth Band; he was abducted as he walked to band practice. Thomas Devlin played the tenor horn, but his real love was heavy metal. He was a Goth, and would congregate in the 'neutral' Belfast city centre with other Goths, punks and skaters where he made friends with other young people from all backgrounds. His parents now award a bursary in his memory to teenagers studying music or the arts.

Dina McKeown was also mad about music. She and her best friend Kate McCurdy spent most of their time in Dina's room listening to records. 'She loved Abba and The Eagles,' says Kate. 'She used to get the tennis racket and pretend she was playing the guitar while I sang into the hairbrush.'

One day, Dina and Kate brought Dina's portable Dansette record player outside; they were playing Abba's 'Dancing Queen' when it began to rain. 'She ran up to the house and got a bit of cardboard and an umbrella. She set the record player on top of the cardboard and put the umbrella over it. Then me and her stood dancing with it raining like we were two eejits. Every time I hear "Dancing Queen" I think of her.'[10]

At weekends, the friends would stay in each other's houses; they would stand outside clubs listening to the music because they were too young to go in. Dina was 14 when she was killed.

Angela Willett also remembers Dina's 'red Dansette and a few records which were played in the shed at the back of the garden. I can never hear "Blue Moon" without thinking of her; it's an old record, as were the others she possessed, because her money was for important things like clothes and makeup – probably no different to any other 14-year-old, then or now.'

Clothes were important. Michael Turner 'loved the style', says his brother Peter. He points out a photograph of Michael dressed in a paisley shirt. 'He had a cravat as well.'

James Morgan was 'a snappy dresser', remember his parents, Justin and Philomena. He would wear 'a nice white shirt, always spick and span, and loved the jeans. He always kept himself well.'

In Benburb, County Tyrone – where Emma Donnelly lived – one of the big events of the year was Benburb Sunday, at the local priory.

'The Saturday before Benburb Sunday she went looking for something to wear [with her aunt], and it was gorgeous,' remembers her mother Bernie. 'She bought herself a wee wool skirt and a wee jumper with three-quarter-length sleeves and she went to Benburb Sunday and she looked a million dollars.'

Like many teenagers, Michael McCartan loved the Bay City Rollers. He had all the gear; 'I used to say, "Michael, you're not going out in those trousers,"' says his mother Molly Lyttle.

'He'd say, "Well, if you buy me a good pair of Wranglers." It took me weeks and weeks to get them for him. He also had those big heavy shoes they used to wear – he only had them on him a couple of times – and he thought he was great walking up and down the street in them.'

Michael was wearing his Wranglers when he was shot; they had to be cut off him. Molly has none of her son's clothes. 'You had to be careful, there wasn't a lot of money around and you had to pass things down. Things like old jumpers, he used to say, "Ah Mummy, that there went out with the flood, and you expect me to wear it?"'

If clothes and music were among the constants for teenagers, so too was sport. For Johnny Watterson and his brother Peter, their hero was George Best. 'In our bedroom one side of the walls was Celtic posters and Manchester United was the other, but George Best was the most inspirational, untouchable, gold standard of sport. There really was no other.'

They played football on the street 'all the time'; from the Rockville Street off the Falls Road, their local team would play against a team from the nearby Whiterock. They played on the GAA ground at McCrory Park 'until the army took over and it became Fort Pegasus'.

A team pic with Jimmy Cromie, back row, third from right.

Most boys had their team. For Jimmy Cromie, it was Everton, and for his cousin Gary Roberts it was Celtic, though 'I still have a bit of a liking for Everton because of Jimmy,' he admits.

Jimmy loved sport – he played soccer, Gaelic football and hurling; he and Gary would go to a pitch in Ballysillan in north Belfast to play their matches for their school teams. 'We played on their rugby pitches – there was no Gaelic pitch – and I remember coming out and there was a crowd waiting for us,' says Gary. 'We had to run the gauntlet of the crowd, getting beat up, to get home. The following week we went up and played hurling and there was nobody waiting for us that week because we had our hurley sticks with us.'

Sport, like much in Northern Ireland, was a marker of identity. Just as Gaelic games were played almost exclusively by members of the Catholic community, so too was support for a particular soccer team like Celtic or Rangers regarded as a marker of religious affiliation, though this was not always the case.

According to a 'loyalist source' cited in *The Guardian*, Glen Branagh – a member of the loyalist paramilitary organisation the Ulster Young Militants – had chosen to be buried in a Celtic shirt. 'He was just a wee lad who supported Celtic and thought sport should remain separate from everything else,' the source said.[11]

He was not the only one obsessed with sport; Jim Rowntree remembers how his brother Frank walked through riots in order to get to football practice. Yet for John Dougal's brother, also called Jim, it was a part of childhood which the Troubles took away. 'Young lads at our age would have been into football. We weren't, because the Troubles consumed everything. I've never followed football teams – I still don't, because that stage in life where a boy gets interested in things like that had gone.'

Yet sport could still provide moments of glory. James Kennedy's brother David still remembers how James scored two goals in the Schools Cup final. It was unheard of for St Augustine's to even make it to the final, and suddenly they were 2-0 ahead against Boys' Model. For a brief moment, James was a hero – until their opponents equalised.

David still keeps the video of his brother's performance. 'He played for Rosario FC, and Gaelic for St Malachy's. He was a good footballer – he had to be to play for Rosario. Would he have been good enough to play professionally? Who knows?'

James was 15 when he was killed, the same age as Billy Crothers. He had been spotted by Bob Bishop, the football scout who first discovered George Best,

Billy's hero; Billy was due at Bob's soccer school the evening he was killed.

'He was a good footballer and would have done very well here,' Bob told the *Belfast Telegraph*. 'His whole life seemed to revolve around football.'[12]

Alan Welsh was awaiting a trial at Spurs; Leo McGuigan, too, was due to have a trial at Sunderland FC the month after he was killed. He had been spotted by the future Ireland manager, Martin O'Neill, from a young age. 'Martin would play football after school,' says Leo's brother Kieran, 'and he would always pick Leo as his first choice.'

Emma Donnelly, her mother is convinced, would have played camogie for her county; her cousin won two All-Ireland Gaelic football titles with Tyrone.

The year she was killed Emma had won player of the year at her club; the year after, it was awarded to her posthumously. She is one of many children killed in the Troubles who have sporting awards dedicated to their memory. A snooker trophy named after John Boyle is awarded in Dunloy, County Antrim every year; in Basildon, Essex, a hockey tournament is held in Danielle Carter's memory.

Members of the Celtic football team attended Oran Doherty's funeral, and travelled to Omagh for a fundraiser held by the local supporters' club.

Oran had asked for a Celtic tracksuit the previous Christmas. 'I remember him going up to the pub with his daddy to see the match,' says his mother Bernie. 'It was Celtic playing Rangers, and he was so happy because they won. His brothers all like Celtic, I don't know if it's because of Oran or not, but they always want Celtic to win.'

Oran played underage football in Buncrana, and had won 'a few wee plaques', as Bernie puts it. 'I don't know if he'd have been a great footballer or not. He was only eight. We didn't really get the chance to know.'

Danielle Carter's father Danny makes that same point. 'She was only 15 years old. She didn't have much of a life.'

Of the 186 children aged 16 and under who died as a result of the Troubles, more than 50 of them – or 28 per cent - were 16. The vast majority had left school as soon as they were old enough, and were either working or about to start work. One, Pat McCabe, was already engaged – he had proposed to his girlfriend on her sixteenth birthday – and was working as a mechanic.

A significant number, such as 16-year-old Anne Magee, also had part-time jobs – in her case, in the local shop; others, like seven-year-old Pat Toner, worked on the family farm, or – like 16-year-old John McDaid – helped out with his father's bakery business.

This could be prompted by family circumstances. As the eldest son, Michael Hughes knew his mother needed a wage to help raise his younger siblings after his father was killed; he had just found a job in the Nylon factory in Newry when he was shot.

Others had no love of school, or were simply keen to get out in the world and start earning. Michael Neill had just completed his first week at work when he was killed; he was employed in a shop which supplied hessian bags and coal sacks. 'He was ecstatic when he got that job,' says his sister, Patricia Friel. 'He was all, "I'm a big boy now, I'm a working man. I'm the man of the house."'

For some children, their work put them in harm's way. Anne Magee was shot in the shop where she worked; so too was Katrina Rennie, who had been employed in the mobile shop in Craigavon because the owner 'felt that if there was any trouble in the area, nobody would harm young women.'[13]

Jimmy McCallum was washing bottles in the pub where he worked when a bomb exploded without warning; he was blown the length of the room. Anthony McGrady was working as an apprentice in a garage on Belfast's Cliftonville Road when loyalists attacked, killing Anto and his two employers.

Younger children died with their parents – among them Desmond Guiney, who was helping his father Eric on his milkman's round when they became caught up in rioting following the death of Bobby Sands on hunger strike.

When a series of bombs exploded in Claudy, County Derry, in July 1972, William Temple was there because he had volunteered to help deliver milk that morning. Joe Connolly had gone into Claudy to see about a job he was to start in Desmond's clothing factory; eight-year-old Kathryn Eakin was washing windows outside her family's shop.

Each was only starting out in life. When David Temple thinks of his brother, he emphasises William's good education and friendly personality. 'He would have had a brilliant life,' he says.

Paul Maxwell's sisters feel the same. Paul had been an entrepreneur from a young age; he was also 'incredibly sociable' and got on well with people. 'I wonder what he would have been like as a man,' says Donna. 'I think he would have been a good man.'

Square from a memorial quilt commemorating William Temple.

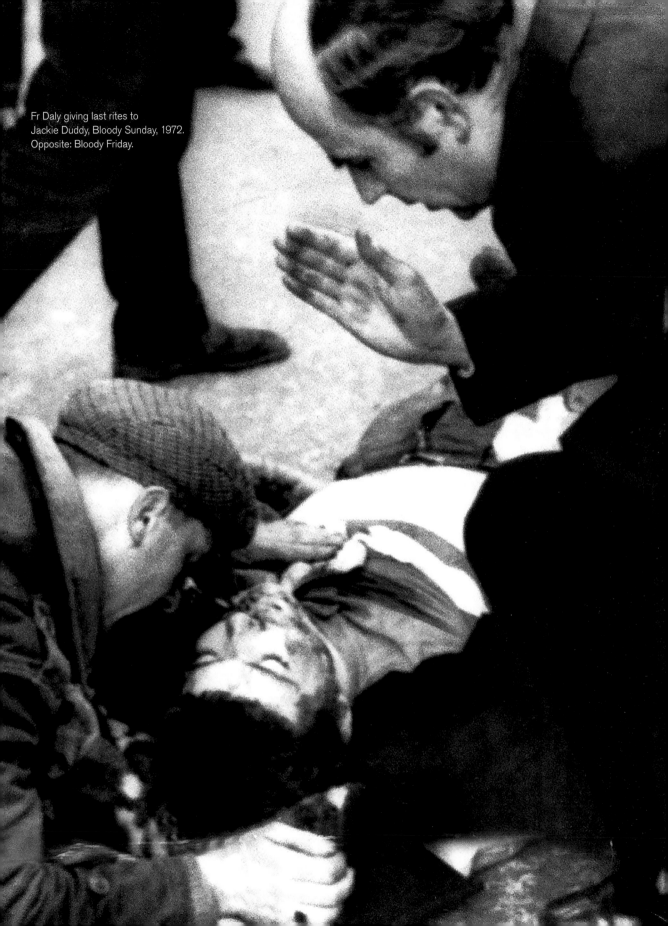

Fr Daly giving last rites to
Jackie Duddy, Bloody Sunday, 1972.
Opposite: Bloody Friday.

1972

- The worst year of the Troubles, with almost 500 lives lost

- On 30 January the British army shoots dead 13 unarmed anti-internment marchers in Derry; a fourteenth victim dies later. The day becomes known as 'Bloody Sunday'

- In response, the British embassy in Dublin is burned by rioters

- Seven die in an official IRA bomb at Aldershot army barracks

- British prime minister Edward Heath suspends Stormont and imposes Direct Rule from Westminster

- Francis Rowntree becomes the first child to be killed by a rubber bullet

- On 21 July, 'Bloody Friday', the IRA explodes 22 bombs across Belfast, killing nine and seriously injuring 130 people

- Belfast widow and mother of ten Jean McConville is kidnapped and killed by the IRA, in one of the most controversial Troubles' atrocities to date

- Northern Ireland resident Mary Peters wins gold in the pentathlon at the Munich Olympics; boxer Charlie Nash, whose brother William was one of the victims of Bloody Sunday, represents Ireland at the same games.

Name: *Michael Sloan*

Age: *15*

From: *Ballymurphy, West Belfast*

Date of Death: *11/01/1972*

Michael Sloan was found dead in a house in New Barnsley Park in Ballymurphy.

From nearby Westview Pass, the 15-year-old – who was a member of the Fianna – was said by the police to have had a loaded revolver in his pocket when his body was found by security forces after a tip-off from neighbours; and there was another gun in the room.

Michael 'had been shot through the head' and 'was lying in a pool of blood in a downstairs room'.[40]

'It was being said by people in the district that the youth's death was accidental and that it may have happened during a weapon instruction lesson.'[41]

The Irish News quoted IRA sources as describing his death as 'accidental'.[42]

Michael was described in death notices as a staff officer in the second battalion of Na Fianna Éireann. A student at St Thomas's Secondary School, his main interest is said to have been playing soccer; he is listed on the Republican Roll of Honour as a student and Fianna member who was 'shot accidentally'.[43]

About 200 teenage boys and girls, many of them wearing black berets, walked in formation behind Michael's coffin as it was brought to Corpus Christi Church in Ballymurphy for requiem mass, and then to Belfast's Milltown Cemetery, watched by British army troops who were stationed along the route.[44]

His niece, Caoimhe Ní Shluáin, became the Republic of Ireland's youngest mayor when she was elected mayor of Navan in 2012.[45] She said her uncle had 'provided inspiration to her throughout her life'.[46]

✳ ✳ ✳ ✳ ✳

Name: *David McAuley*

Age: *15*

From: *Ardoyne, North Belfast*

Date of Death: *19/02/1972*

Fifteen-year-old David McAuley was shot and fatally wounded in his own kitchen.

Michael Donnelly, who grew up beside him in Fairfield Street, has vivid memories of his friend. 'As kids we did all the normal things together, played football, went camping.

'I have no recollection of Davy ever being at school. He was full of mischief. He would get up early and do all the wee things on his own.

'I remember one morning he got up about six o'clock and stole a horse from the Travellers in Flax Street. He tied the horse to his ma's front door and they couldn't get it opened.'[47]

The youngest of seven, David had a milk round and worked in the Saunders Social Club. He was a student at St Gabriel's Boys Secondary School though, according to his sister Rita, 'David didn't have a favourite subject in school, he wasn't really interested; rioting would have been his interest. He would have started a riot in an empty house. I suppose that was a reflection of the era he grew up in.'[48]

'If there was a riot, Davy was at the front,' says Michael. 'He was a great rioter.'[49]

When his friends went to join the Fianna, they found David was already in it. At the time of his death he held the rank of Officer Commanding (OC). 'It came really as no surprise to us when we heard that he had been shot,' says Michael, 'or that he had been close to guns because he was always around IRA Volunteers.'[50]

That Saturday afternoon David had been in the kitchen when his mother heard a shot. 'He came out and said to my mummy in the living room, "I'm shot,"' says Rita. 'She didn't believe him because there was no blood. She said he was really, really white but he was still walking around the house.'[51]

According to 'Jackie', an 'eyewitness and comrade', 'weapons required for an operation' had been brought into the house. An IRA inquiry was held afterwards and found that a gun which had a bullet jammed in the breech had accidentally discharged, hitting David in the side.[52]

David was taken to hospital in Dundalk, where he died early the following morning. At his funeral, soldiers charged mourners after a volley of shots was fired over his Tricolour-draped coffin.

'A large crowd,' the *Irish Independent* reported, 'cheered when five girls and one man in dark berets and dark glasses fired shots over the coffin. Immediately the troops, who had been waiting nearby, rushed forward, scattering the mourners and up to 50 members of Fianna Éireann who had formed up behind the coffin.'[53]

Among the guard of honour was 16-year-old Bernard Fox, who would be shot and killed ten months later.

✳ ✳ ✳ ✳ ✳

Name: *Gerard Doherty*

Age: *16*

From: *Creggan, Derry*

Date of Death: *25/02/1972*

Gerard – Gerry – Doherty joined the Official Fianna at 14. By the time he was 16, he had become a member of the Official IRA.

As a member of the James Connolly Republican Club, he was 'endlessly cheerful and pleasant in accepting the tasks given to him', and the IRA had been 'happy to accept him into their ranks' as soon as he was old enough.[54]

He was found, seriously injured, in an empty building in Central Drive, in Derry's Creggan estate. A nurse, Jean Donohoe, told the inquest into his death that she had gone in and 'saw a boy lying on the bottom floor of the building. The boy did not say anything but started roaring.'[55]

The teenager had been shot in the chest; at his funeral, an unnamed individual who delivered an oration at his graveside said his death had been an accident, and nobody else had been involved.[56]

Gerard's coffin was draped in a Tricolour and flanked by an Official IRA colour party. A volley of shots was fired over his grave.

Following an Official IRA commemoration in 1975, his parents issued a statement. 'Like many boys of his age, he was caught up in the mood of the time. His present-day outlook would have been different. To describe him as a revolutionary socialist is far from the truth, as his family knows it.

'To reopen our sense of loss on the tragedy of our son's death merely to make an occasion for propaganda for political views is no service to his sorrowing family nor to our son. May he rest in peace.'[57]

✴ ✴ ✴ ✴ ✴

Name: *Michael Patrick Connors*

Age: *14*

From: *Coalisland, Co Tyrone*

Date of Death: *01/03/1972*

Michael Patrick Connors – known as Paddy – was a member of a Traveller family originally from the Gorey area of County Wexford, but which had been living in Coalisland.

He and other friends from the Travelling community, including 19-year-old John Maughan, had gone to Belfast to collect scrap and rags, often sleeping in the van at night.[58]

The army opened fire on the van after it sped off when police approached it in the city centre; it was found two miles away outside the Royal Victoria Hospital, riddled with bullets, and the bodies of Paddy and John inside.

'It is thought the driver raced through the city in a rush against time to get medical aid for his companions,' *The Irish News* wrote.[59]

He abandoned the van on the footpath outside the hospital's outpatient department and ran off. "Hospital staff carried the bodies inside but the boys were already dead'.[60]

At the inquest into their deaths, a statement was read out on behalf of a man who had been in the van, who said they had been to the pub for a pint and then left. 'We drove around, blowing the horn at the girls,' he said.[61]

Paddy's funeral took place in Coalisland. 'Despite a bitterly cold snow shower at the funeral time hundreds of the Coalisland people joined in the funeral cortege … black flags were carried on both sides of the hearse.'[62]

The family's grief was compounded when Paddy's three-year-old niece died accidentally at home the day after his death. They had a joint funeral, the two coffins lying beside each other at the altar, and were buried together in Coleraine, County Derry.

Paddy's uncle, John Delaney, said his nephew's killing was 'a foul and despicable deed'. 'This child's only crime was that he was young and a member of the travelling people and was in the wrong place at the wrong time.'[63]

✳ ✳ ✳ ✳ ✳

Name: *Tony Lewis*

Age: *16*

From: *Clonard, West Belfast*

Date of Death: *09/03/1972*

Tony Lewis grew up in Belfast's Bombay Street. As a 14-year-old, he witnessed the street being burnt to the ground by loyalists in August 1969.

He 'played an active role in the defence of the Clonard area', according to the Greater Clonard Ex-Prisoners Association;[64] the teenager joined the Fianna that same year and was 'very active, defending his area once again with great courage in 1971 during the internment riots'.[65]

By the time he was 16, Tony had left school, and was working as an apprentice butcher. He also played football and hurling, winning medals for his club, Cumann an Phiarsaigh.[66]

He died along with three other members of the IRA's Second Belfast Battalion when a bomb exploded prematurely. The 16-year-old was the youngest of the four fatalities; the eldest was 20.

According to *The Irish Times*, Tony and his comrades had been attempting to make a bomb in Clonard Street in west Belfast when it accidentally went off; the army said the blast had been caused by 30 lb of gelignite at the rear of the house.[67]

The explosion destroyed three houses, and civilians and members of the security forces worked side by side to try and rescue survivors from the rubble. Priests from nearby Clonard Monastery tended to the injured and anointed the dead.

His name is remembered on a memorial in Clonard Street.

✳ ✳ ✳ ✳ ✳

Name: *Sean O'Riordan*

Age: *13*

From: *Clonard, West Belfast*

Date of Death: *23 / 03 / 1972*

Sean O'Riordan dreamt that when he left school he would go to South America.

'He had brains to throw away,' says his mother Flo. 'He did all my messages, and the old people loved him because he used to carry their groceries. He was just everything that anybody could have wanted in a son.'[68]

Sean was an 'all-round athlete', says his mother. 'He had medals for swimming, he had a hurley, he played football – he had been footballer of the year that year.'[69]

He excelled at Irish, and when he was 12 won a scholarship to the Donegal Gaeltacht.[70]

He was also a member of Na Fianna Éireann; at 13, he was one of the youngest members of any such organisation to die during the Troubles.

Sean's father Jack said his son had been playing near his home when he was shot by British soldiers; rioting had been going on at the time but at his inquest the coroner said there was no firm evidence he had been involved.[71]

Sean was small for his age; his mother points out that he was shot under a streetlight. 'They saw he was only a child.'[72]

His coffin was draped with a Tricolour and flanked by a Fianna guard of honour; about 50 members of the Fianna and a similar number of his schoolmates followed the cortege through west Belfast's streets.[73]

The death notice inserted in *The Irish News* by his family read: 'You died for your country, my hero-love; in the first grey dusk of spring on your lips was a prayer to God above: that your death will have helped to bring freedom and peace to the land you love.'[74]

In the hospital, Flo had got down on her knees and prayed her son would survive. She prayed until the doctor lifted her up. 'He just said to me, "What a waste, what a waste."'[75]

✳ ✳ ✳ ✳ ✳

Name: *Patrick Campbell*

Age: *16*

From: *Ballymurphy, West Belfast*

Date of Death: *25/03/1972*

Patrick Campbell's nickname was 'Peachy'. He had left St Thomas's Secondary School in 1970, and according to the republican pamphlet had found work as a "bread-server".[76]

He had joined the Fianna in 1970; this 'came as no surprise to family or friends', *Belfast Graves* wrote, as Patrick's grandmother and her child had been killed by the Black and Tans and his second cousin had been interned on the prison ship the *Al Rawdah*.[77]

In August 1971 Patrick was arrested but not interned; from then on, his home was regularly raided by the British army and he was often arrested.[78] The following year, he became a member of the IRA's 2nd Belfast Battalion.

It is believed Patrick was shot and killed accidentally by another IRA member at the top of Springhill Avenue in west Belfast early on a Saturday morning. According to Ciaran de Baroid, the accident happened during 'an IRA stand-by'.[79]

Death notices in the *Irish News* said Patrick had been "shot by enemy forces",[80] but according to *Lost Lives* both the police and the British army said they were not involved in the shooting.[81]

A former member of the Fianna recounted how 'an attack was planned, and as Patrick climbed over a low wall or fence a gun was discharged and he died.'

Patrick was taken to a nearby house. 'He was shot several times in the head. Outside, police found 24 spent cartridges lying in a pool of blood.'[82]

✳ ✳ ✳ ✳ ✳

Name: *Francis Rowntree*

Age: *11*

From: *Lower Falls, West Belfast*

Date of Death: *22/04/1972*

Francis Rowntree 'loved running and loved moving about. He was sports mad,' says his brother Jim.

As long as 11-year-old Frank was playing sport, he was happy. He played soccer for Donegal Celtic FC, GAA for Patrick Sarsfields, and he loved to run. 'The only thing I never saw him play was hurling,' adds Jim.

From Lower Clonard Street, off Belfast's Falls Road, Jim says Frank was aware of the trouble going on around them, but this took second place to his beloved sport. 'One day in particular there was terrible rioting and my mother was out looking for him. She found him standing at the corner of the Springfield Road with his bag over his shoulder, waiting to get picked up to go to training.'

Jim remembers his brother as 'a good kid' who was 'usually about the street' playing football or handball.

He hated smoking, and used to empty all the ashtrays in the house as soon as he came in. 'I was a smoker,' says Jim, 'and he always smelt the smoke off me and it turned him something shocking. He hated it with a passion.'

Frank was the first person to be killed by a rubber bullet during the Troubles. He had been playing with other boys in Divis Flats, and went to look at an army vehicle which had stopped nearby. 'It was childish curiosity,' says Jim.

He remembers his grandmother telling him Frank had been shot. 'I said, "Was he hit in the arm or the leg because he'll go mad because of his sport," but she said, "No, he was hit in the head."'

The British army had claimed that Frank had been shot because he was involved in rioting and throwing stones; at a fresh inquest into his death in 2017, the coroner said he was confident Francis had not been involved in rioting. Frank's death was not justified, and the soldier involved had used 'excessive force', he said.[83]

After her son's death, Frank's mother Theresa became a prominent campaigner against the use of rubber – and later plastic – bullets. 'She felt very strongly about it until the day she died,' says Jim.

Before her death, Jim was able to show his mother a report from the Historical Enquiries Team. 'I got her the page and showed her that according to them Frank was completely innocent, he was involved in no trouble. It lifted her.'

✳ ✳ ✳ ✳ ✳

Name: *Rosaleen Gavin*

Age: *8*

From: *Oldpark, North Belfast*

Date of Death: *29/04/1972*

As Francis Gavin got into his car that Saturday afternoon, his eight-year-old daughter Rosaleen pleaded with her father to take her with him. He promised he would – the following day.

That evening – unknown to his family – Francis was arrested for driving under the influence of alcohol and held in a police cell.

As midnight approached, Rosaleen – who was one of five children – was at home in Ardilea Street. Her mother Mary handed her daughter 12p and sent her out to buy a packet of cigarettes from the nearby shop, The Candy Store.

When Rosaleen arrived the shop was closed, but she knew to knock on the owner's hall door – beside the shop – for the cigarettes. She gave Ann Saunders the money, took the packet, and began to run home. 'I still had the 12p in my hand when I heard four quick shots,' Ann told the *Belfast News Letter*. 'I rushed out and the child was dead.'[84]

The IRA initially denied responsibility, claiming Rosaleen had been 'brutally murdered by Orange extremists';[85] it subsequently emerged that she had been hit by an IRA sniper who had been aiming at soldiers.[86]

At the inquest into her death the deputy coroner described it as 'a tragic case symptomatic of our times'.[87]

In the police station, Francis Gavin was suddenly released. 'A policeman unlocked the door and came in … he threw my car keys to me and stuck a packet of cigarettes into my hand and told me to go straight home.'

The following day, Francis wept as he described how he had arrived home to be told, 'Your baby is dead.'

'The last I saw of her was when I left the house at a quarter to two and she asked me to take her out in the car. I promised to take her out today instead.'[88]

✳ ✳ ✳ ✳ ✳

Name: *Michael Magee*

Age: *15*

From: *Springfield Road, West Belfast*

Date of Death: *13/05/1972*

The youngest of five, Michael Magee hated being cooped up in the house. 'He loved the outside, loved the country,' remembers his sister Alice McCusker. 'He loved going up the Black Mountain, up to the Hatchet Field with his friends and would pick wild flowers and collect them for my mummy.'

Michael's mother had taken him and his older brother to England when the Troubles broke out, but the boys hated it so much that the family returned, moving into a house on the Springfield Road.

Michael enjoyed making Airfix models of aeroplanes, which hung in the bedroom alongside posters of Pelé and George Best. He supported Celtic, and Alice still has a Celtic flag that belonged to her brother.

He also loved *Doctor Who* and The Monkees – 'especially the TV show', says Alice – and was 'a great wee lad for running messages for everyone'.

Michael had left school the previous Christmas, and Alice believes he had started working in the *Belfast Telegraph* as an errand boy.

A member of Na Fianna Éireann, he was shot accidentally amid the confusion that followed a gun and bomb attack by loyalists on Kelly's Bar on the Whiterock Road.

To this day, Alice is unsure exactly what happened. 'In the republican plot it says shot by accident. We were told Michael had a gun and was running across the road, or that he had a loaf and was crossing the road, and then somebody else said he was on lookout. We don't know.'

At his funeral a volley of shots was fired over his coffin; nearly 100 Fianna members marched behind the funeral cortege.[89]

Each year Alice carries his black-framed photograph in the republican Easter commemoration. 'I'm proud to do so, as his sister,' she says. 'I'm proud of him as a brother.'

✳ ✳ ✳ ✳ ✳

PIRA Easter Commemoration, April 1972.

Name: *Martha Campbell*

Age: *13*

From: *Ballymurphy, West Belfast*

Date of Death: *14/05/1972*

'I'm not going to school tomorrow,' were the last words Martha Campbell said to her mother Betty. 'I can still see her coming through the kitchen door saying that,' says Betty. 'I said to her, "You're definitely going to school tomorrow," and she just started to laugh.'

That was typical of Martha. 'She was full of life,' says Betty. If Betty was home late, Martha would wait for her outside the bingo hall. 'When I came out, she would grab my arm and say, "Mummy, let on to my Daddy I was at bingo with you."

'One day she came in with an apple cake and said she was doing cookery in school. She was on the beak and was helping the apple cake man sell them.'

Her prized possession was a Timex watch she had received the previous Christmas. 'Every time she got her photo taken she was showing off that watch.'

The second eldest and oldest girl in a family of eight, her youngest sister, four-year-old Teresa, was Martha's shadow. 'Martha couldn't go out the door or Teresa would be crying after her.

'Geraldine was her best friend, and she and Geraldine used to fall out all the time because they both fancied this boy. Geraldine ended up marrying him.'

It had been a bad weekend in Ballymurphy. Following an explosion at Kelly's Bar on the Whiterock Road the previous day, there had been shooting from the IRA, loyalists and the British army, and Betty had kept the children inside for safety. Now Sunday evening, Betty thought Martha had gone to Scullion's sweet shop, where she regularly helped out; instead she had gone to call on her best friend Geraldine.

Martha was walking along Springhill Crescent when firing broke out. 'A man told her to stay where she was and he would come and get her, but Martha panicked and she ran towards him,' says Betty. 'She was shot and he put his hand out and pulled her over behind a wall. The one bullet hit her three times

– it ricocheted, and the last time it hit her it went in through her neck and out through her spinal cord and that's what killed her.'

Martha's family are certain the British army killed her; *Lost Lives* cites 'reliable loyalist sources' as stating she had been shot by the UVF. The Historical Enquiries Team found it was not possible to determine who killed her: 'At the time of her death she was caught between a three-way gun battle involving loyalist paramilitaries, republican paramilitaries and the Army.'[90]

Martha remains at the heart of her family. 'Our whole lives, growing up, Martha's always been in it,' says Teresa.

'If ever I'm down or depressed,' says Betty, 'I'll say a wee prayer to Martha to get me through.'

✳ ✳ ✳ ✳ ✳

Name: *Harold Morris*

Age: *15*

From: *Shankill, West Belfast*

Date of Death: *18 / 05 / 1972*

One minute Harold Morris was playing in the street; the next, he was dead.

The 15-year-old, from Court Street, had been playing with other children near the junction of Boundary Street and Cargill Street, on the so-called 'peace line' between the Protestant Shankill and Catholic Divis.

A friend who was with him later told the inquest into his death that they had been standing talking about a job.[91] Suddenly 'there were two bursts of automatic gunfire, said to have come from the direction of the Divis Flats complex'.[92]

Hit in the neck, Harold died almost instantly. When he heard his son had been killed, Harold's father collapsed and had to be taken to hospital.

'People at the scene said that the boy was hit in the first burst of shots and that the second was aimed at a man who ran to help him,' *The Irish Times* reported. 'A car near where the boy was playing was sprayed with bullet-holes.'

He had been shot by republicans: 'Witnesses were adamant that the fire was directed into the Shankill side of the line from the other side.'[93]

Harold died only hours after 1,500 Protestant workers held a city centre protest meeting about recent IRA killings.[94]

Shortly after his death, two Catholic teenagers were rushed to hospital with gunshot wounds following a burst of automatic gunfire from a car in the Springfield area. A 14-year-old was treated for an injury to his jaw, and a 15-year-old for a leg wound.[95]

'There was no mistake,' an RUC spokesman said. 'They wanted to hit children.'[96]

Harold's four brothers carried his coffin; among those who placed death notices in the *Belfast Telegraph* were the members of the Women's Defence, East Belfast and the Hopeton Street Football Committee.

✳ ✳ ✳ ✳ ✳

Name: Manus Deery

Age: 15

From: Bogside, Derry

Date of Death: 19/05/1972

Manus Deery was sharing a bag of chips with his friends. He was standing by an archway at the Bogside Inn when a soldier fired a shot from high up on Derry's Walls; it ricocheted off the archway wall and hit Manus in the head.

'He was a typical 15-year-old, funny and happy,' remembers his sister Helen, 'and up to all the mischief you could think of, raiding orchards and dobbing school.

'He was my older brother, I looked up to him. He'd just received his first wage packet and he was working as a fitter in a factory.

RTÉ reporter Kevin Myers heard the fatal shot, and described it as 'unlike any he had ever heard'. He said there was an enormous reverberation and he thought a bomb had gone off. 'There was a young man giving him the kiss of life. The chips were on the ground and the ricochet mark was on the wall.'[97]

The British army maintained that the soldier had been firing at a gunman, which the Deery family and witnesses in the Bogside had always denied. 'The most cruel thing,' says Helen, 'was the stain on his name and the stain on the witnesses' names and on the rest of the family.'

Following a long campaign by Helen, Northern Ireland's attorney general ordered a new inquest in to Manus's death. In 2017, the coroner ruled that Manus was 'totally innocent' and was not posing a threat to anyone.[98]

For Helen, it meant her brother could finally 'sleep easy'. 'I'm just proud to be his sister, and the reason I've stood and campaigned for so long is simply because I loved him. I just remember him smiling, and hope he still is smiling.'

✳ ✳ ✳ ✳ ✳

Name: *Joan Scott*

Age: *12*

From: *Oldpark, North Belfast*

Date of Death: *30/05/1972*

Joan Scott was homesick. The 12-year-old had moved to Liverpool with her parents the year before, but missed Belfast so much that she returned the previous weekend to live with her aunt in the Oldpark area of the city. She had been 'eating her heart out' to get back to Belfast, her mother Alice said.[99]

She and a friend had gone for a Sunday evening walk and were crossing the road on their way to get some sweets when she was 'cut down by a hail of bullets'.[100]

An RUC constable told the inquest into her death that two crowds of youths had gathered on opposite sides of the Oldpark Road. 'He spoke to two girls and asked them to move away. He then heard a burst of automatic gunfire.'[101]

Joan's death was raised in parliament, which was informed that 'a burst of automatic fire was directed at two RUC constables on duty … one of the constables was hit and two girls who were walking nearby received gunshot wounds'.[102]

According to *Lost Lives*, the IRA was 'almost certainly' responsible.[103]

Joan was taken to hospital and died two days later, her parents at her bedside.

She was buried from her aunt's house in Hillview Street; visibly in tears, her school friends walked behind her coffin.

✳ ✳ ✳ ✳ ✳

Name: *Joseph Campbell*

Age: *16*

From: *Ardoyne, North Belfast*

Date of Death: *11/06/1972*

Joseph - Josh – Campbell was a thinker.

'He was very intelligent from a very young age,' says his friend 'Martin'. 'He always wanted to be at the front of things and was good at organising. When we were kids, he would organise wee trips up around the caves on Cavehill.

'He had a great love of astronomy and talked a lot about the planets and the stars. He had his own telescope and would go out at night and watch the stars.'[104]

The eldest and the only boy, Josh had been named after his father and often acted as referee between his two sisters, Marion and Margaret. He loved going to stay with his grandparents on their farm near Lurgan, especially during the summer.

A neighbour, 'Bik', described Josh as 'a big, tall, wiry lad with this mass of hair flicked back'; Martin said Josh had always been in the 'A' classes – 'he read a lot of books' – and had just left school with a City and Guilds qualification in mechanical engineering.

He was also a member of the Fianna; he had joined, like many teenagers in his area, after the introduction of internment. According to Martin, who was also a member, Josh was an intelligence officer: 'That was no surprise, because he had leadership quality.'[105]

Josh was killed during a gun battle with the British army in Eskdale Gardens. The area had been in turmoil for much of the day. Trouble had flared after the security forces blocked a republican parade, and a 43-year-old shopkeeper, Hugh Madden, had been shot by the UDA on the nearby Oldpark Road.[106]

'I was told that he had opened fire on the army with a shotgun,' said Martin. 'He was hit in the head.' His friend was among those who formed the guard of honour at his funeral.[107]

His parents had no idea their son was in the Fianna. 'I still can't take what happened to my Joseph,' said his mother Patricia. 'A part of me died with him that day.'[108]

✳ ✳ ✳ ✳ ✳

Name: *John Dougal*

Age: *16*

From: *Ballymurphy, West Belfast*

Date of Death: *09/07/1972*

When he left school, John Dougal wanted to join the British army.

A member of the army cadets, he had been to the Isle of Man on manoeuvres, and his brother Jim remembers going to his passing-out parade. The eldest of eight, he and Jim – who was two years younger – were close. 'We shared the same bed up until he was killed.'

The Dougals were one of a few Catholic families on the predominantly Protestant Manor Street in north Belfast; Jim remembers himself and John collecting bonfire wood for 'the Twelfth'.

This all changed in August 1969; the Dougals were among many families forced to flee their homes. A few days later, the boys sneaked back to the house and climbed in over the back wall.

'They'd written slogans, "Fenians Out", above the fireplace, and John had this big army rucksack, like a kitbag, and we piled all the pots and pans and knives and forks into it to bring back for my mummy.'

The family were eventually rehoused in west Belfast; the following year, two plainclothes soldiers came to the house looking for John. 'They ran the cadets, and they wanted John to keep going, but my mummy said sure he could never get there from this side of town.'

By the time he was killed John had left school and was working in Casey's, a bottling company on the Falls Road. He had also joined the Fianna, and then the IRA.

That day there had been rioting in Lenadoon, where the British army had intervened to stop Catholic families moving into houses which had been abandoned by Protestants. Later that evening, as a ceasefire between the IRA and the British army faltered, an army sniper hidden in Corry's timber yard in the Westrock area of Ballymurphy opened fire on two cars.

John and his friend 'had their good clothes on, new clothes because they were going to see their girls', says Jim. When they heard shooting, and saw a friend of theirs lying on the ground, injured, John ran out to help.

'I was shot in the right arm,' says Brian Pettigrew. 'Both of us tried to make it back to my house when we were both shot in the back.'[109]

John was the first of three children to die in Westrock that night; five people were killed in total, including a Catholic priest, Fr Noel Fitzpatrick. The British army said they had hit six gunmen.

Jim remembers touching his brother's chest as he lay in his coffin and feeling the exit wound. 'There was just a wee tiny hole.'

✳ ✳ ✳ ✳ ✳

Name: *Margaret Gargan*

Age: *13*

From: *Ballymurphy, West Belfast*

Date of Death: *09/07/1972*

Margaret Gargan was the boss of the family. She and her twin sister Bernadette were the eldest, but she was closest to her brother Harry, who was a year younger.

'Margaret was a tomboy,' says Harry. 'She loved football, and we used to play her in our teams, she was that good. The other wee lads were afraid of her because they were afraid to fight with a girl in case she beat them.

'She hated wearing the school uniform, she used to wear a trousers and jacket to school and then get changed in school, and then get changed again before coming home.

'Only a few weeks before she was killed she was at a party, and she wore a dress, which would have been a rare thing for her.'

Margaret had recently taken up smoking. 'I used to fight with her over it,' says Harry.

Her life centred on the local community centre, where their father – who was the secretary of the local tenants' association – was the bingo caller on Sunday nights. Harry looked after the bingo balls and Margaret ran the shop. 'She wouldn't let you off with a penny,' says her mother Nelly.[110]

There had been trouble in Lenadoon earlier in the day, and Margaret had been sent home to check on the younger children. On the way, she stopped to talk to some friends.

'Next thing, she fell down. We never heard the shot. Within a couple of seconds, she was lying on the ground. It all happened so quickly. Then everybody started to scream.'[111]

'I was up turning the [bingo] cage for my father,' says Harry. 'Somebody ran in and said, "Margaret Gargan's been shot."

'My father grabbed me by the hand and we had to go out the back way, through the storeroom, and then we had to crawl to get to a neighbour's house, the shooting was so bad. When we got there Margaret was lying on a corrugated sheet, and there was just a wee mark on her head.'

Margaret had been shot shortly after John Dougal had been mortally wounded a few streets away; the shooting was so bad, ambulances would not come into the area.

'When there was trouble Margaret always wanted to go home,' says Nelly. 'That's what happened that night.'[112]

✳ ✳ ✳ ✳ ✳

Name: *David McCafferty*

Age: *15*

From: *Ballymurphy, West Belfast*

Date of Death: *09/07/1972*

David McCafferty loved animals and wanted to be a vet. He had a pet ferret, but according to his mother there were always other creatures about the house: 'If you went up to the bathroom, he had tadpoles or something floating about in the bath', and he kept a chicken up at the 'Rock Dam', a popular playing area for local children behind their house.[113]

He also liked art and working around the house, and did a lot of work for 'Mother Teresa's nuns', as they were known, after Mother Teresa and the Sisters of the Missionaries of Charity moved into Ballymurphy in 1971. 'He stole my paint – I didn't mind – and went round to paint the house,' remembers his father, also called David; he also made mass cards for the nuns.

David was the eldest and had just left school the week before he was killed. His father remembers him as 'a really good kid, there was no nonsense, no cheek or nothing off him'.

He had lots of friends, who were always in the family home in Springhill Avenue. 'He brought his mates in and they stole a couple of bottles of spirits off me and drank them. It was a bit of devilment, as kids do.'

A member of the Official IRA's Fianna – 'All his friends were probably in it,' says his father – he was killed when he went to help the dying Fr Noel Fitzpatrick.

British army snipers hidden in Corry's timber yard had already shot and mortally wounded two people; when young David heard the shooting he and a local man, Paddy Butler, went with two of the nuns and Fr Fitzpatrick to try and help one of the injured.

Instead, Fr Fitzpatrick and Mr Butler were themselves shot; young David grabbed the priest's arm and tried to pull him out of harm's way.

'When the first bullet hit the wee boy McCafferty he could not let go [of Fr. Fitzpatrick]. He was locked. He was then hit another several times,' an eyewitness recalled.[114]

Five civilians – including Fr Fitzpatrick and Mr Butler – died that night; three of them were children. 'My wife was never the same afterwards, and even my oldest daughter can't talk about it yet,' says David senior. 'They murdered those kids.'

※ ※ ※ ※ ※

Name: *Gerard Gibson*

Age: *16*

From: *Turf Lodge, West Belfast*

Date of Death: *11/07/1972*

Gerard Gibson was always drawing. If he had to take a message, he would sketch a little cartoon beside it; a big fan of T-Rex, he would draw T-Rexes and make doodles based on the band's song titles.

His heroes were Che Guevara, James Connolly and, most of all, the OIRA leader Joe McCann, who had lived near the Gibsons in Turf Lodge; Gerard would draw pictures of them or sketch their images onto handkerchiefs.

The 16-year-old had just left school and had made a test sketch of a design for a piece of stained glass, which had got him an interview with a stained-glass window company. 'They were in the process of looking at his work when he was killed,' says his brother Patrick.

The eldest in a family of five, Gerard might have been small for his age, but he was still 'our big brother'. The family's only photographs are of when Gerard was much younger; his brother Patrick describes him as having 'long black hair, collar length, with a wee bit of stubble, a wee bit of a moustache'.

'He thought he was Che Guevara with that moustache,' says his sister Margaret.

Apart from his brother Patrick, none of the family knew Gerard had joined the Fianna. 'He was doing guard of honour at Joe McCann's wake and my ma walked into the house and he had to get out,' says Margaret.

The night before he was killed, Gerard had been out manning the barricades in the area. He and Patrick – who was 12 – slept at opposite ends of the same bed. 'I was asleep when he got into bed, and there had been a few shots fired and I jumped and I remember kicking his hairy legs,' says Patrick.

'The next day I was in my aunt's house and his mates called for him and he came down the stairs, rushed into the kitchen and took a drink of orange juice and a piece of sponge cake, and that was the last I ever saw of him.'

A ceasefire between the IRA and the British army had ended two days previously, and there had been sporadic shooting in the area. For decades the army denied that they had shot Gerard, but during an inquiry by the Historical Enquiries Team, Gerard's family were made aware of an army briefing from the day of Gerard's death which stated that he had been killed by a soldier.[115]

Gerard was buried alongside his hero, Joe McCann. 'They're right beside each other,' says Patrick.

✳ ✳ ✳ ✳ ✳

Name: *David McClenaghan*

Age: *14*

From: *Oldpark, North Belfast*

Date of Death: *12 / 07 / 1972*

The evening before he was killed, Sally McClenaghan took her son David to see the Eleventh Night bonfires.

'He loved the big blazing fires and the coloured bunting and the wild atmosphere, and didn't feel its vicious edge,' wrote Susan McKay.[116]

Though he was a 'big, strong' lad of 14, David had a mental age of around five. 'He was anything but streetwise,' said his aunt Anne Larkey. 'He used to belt out "The Sash My Father Wore", and then he'd follow it with "The Soldier's Song".'[117]

David's mother was a Catholic who had married a Protestant; now a widow with three children, her new partner was also Protestant. According to *The Irish News*, Sally and her children were the only Catholics left on Southport Street.[118]

The younger children were spending the night with a relative; Sally and David were in bed when four loyalists broke into the house.

Sally's partner was allowed to leave after he produced his Orange sash – proof that he was a Protestant – but they insisted Sally was a 'Taig', and told David to get his mother's rosary beads.

'Sally tried to get David to stay where he was, but he went and got her handbag. They found the beads there, proof that she was a Catholic.'[119]

The men beat David, and raped Sally. Eventually she was ordered to lie on the bed beside her son. She pleaded with them not to touch David. 'He looked so afraid.'

David was shot three times in the neck and chest; when Sally tried to shield him with her body, she was shot in the thigh and hand.[120]

Two of their attackers were jailed for life, two others sentenced to 14 years in prison for their part in the crimes. The eldest was 23, the youngest 18.

'Even a community hardened by daily acts of violence must stand appalled at the human depravity manifested by this crime,' the judge said.[121]

✳ ✳ ✳ ✳ ✳

Name: *Alan Jack*
Age: *5 months*
From: *Ballymagorry, Co Tyrone*
Date of Death: *19/07/1972*

Alan Jack's family have no photographs of him. Born on 19 February 1972, baby Alan died exactly five months later, on 19 July.

In the absence of any pictures, Alan's square on a memorial quilt – entitled 'a patchwork of innocents' – represents his short life. An embroidered bib and Babygro are sewn alongside his rattle, Teddy bear and, in the centre, his pram.

Baby Alan was lying in his pram in Strabane town centre when his mother Barbara was told of a bomb warning. She was pushing him to safety, her other son Robert beside her, when the Provisional IRA car bomb exploded; a piece of glass just missed her, and went into the pram.

'My granny and grandfather used to say everybody else had their own personalities but that poor wee Alan never got the chance to get his own personality,' says Alan's cousin Scott Clark. 'I always remember my grandfather saying that he was a good little boy for five months old. There wasn't much bother with him.'[122]

Newspaper reports at the time showed Alan's father William cradling his tiny white coffin in his arms.

Alan's death devastated his family; they left Strabane and moved back to Cork, Barbara's home city, where they went on to have three more children.

His aunt, Mavis Clark, was living abroad when Alan was killed. 'I wasn't here, I was away working in Germany, and so I never got to see him at all. I always regretted that,' she says. 'I always remember Alan and wonder what sort of person he would have become, but he never got the chance to.'

✳ ✳ ✳ ✳ ✳

Name: *William Crothers*

Age: *15*

From: *Newtownards Road, East Belfast*

Date of Death: *21/07/1972*

It was Billy Crothers' first pay day. 'Mum said he came home as proud as punch for his lunch and gave her all his wage packet,' recalled his sister Janet.[123]

From Parker Street, the 15-year-old had left Ashfield Boys Secondary School three weeks before and was working as a messenger boy at the parcel office in the Ulsterbus station in Oxford Street in Belfast city centre.

Billy's life revolved around football – he had played right back for his school team, and trained with Bob Bishop, the Manchester United scout who had first discovered Billy's hero, George Best. 'The only thing Billy was interested in was football,' said Janet. 'That was his life, with Bob Bishop who ran the football training place. They were just like two old mates together.'[124]

Billy's widowed mother, Everal, had wanted her son to stay in school; 'Billy said no, he wanted to get a job to help Mum,' his sister said.[125]

Billy gave his mother his wage packet; after lunch, a neighbour saw him running back to work for the afternoon. At 3.02 p.m., the bomb exploded – one of 22 planted in Belfast by the Provisional IRA. The day became known as Bloody Friday. The IRA commander, Brendan Hughes, later described it as 'a disaster'.[126]

Billy was one of four Ulsterbus employees – and two soldiers – to die in the explosion at the bus depot. Eyewitnesses recalled the sound of screaming. Smoke was everywhere, and there was 'a horrible smell and a lot of blood on the pavement'.[127] Graphic television images of the police and army putting body parts into plastic bags would stay with many people.

When Billy failed to arrive for soccer practice that evening, Bob knew something was wrong. 'He was a good footballer and would have done very well here,' he told the *Belfast Telegraph*, tears in his eyes. His whole life seemed to revolve around football. I just do not believe that this has happened.'[128]

'He was a good boy, and completely dedicated to me,' said Everal. Neighbours spoke of 'a quiet, blond-haired boy who looked after his mother so well and lived for football'.[129]

Billy had been hoping for an apprenticeship in Harland and Wolff shipyard; it came through three days after his death.

✳ ✳ ✳ ✳ ✳

Name: *Stephen Parker*

Age: *14*

From: *Cavehill Road, North Belfast*

Date of Death: *21/07/1972*

Stephen Parker was 'a complete extrovert, full of life and fun, always playing jokes'.[130]

The 14-year-old was known as 'cheerful and helpful' and was a member of the Boy Scouts. He also had a part-time job at Cavehill shops, near his home in Tokio Gardens, where he would wash cars and run messages on a Friday afternoon.

He had a keen interest in music and was a member of the City of Belfast Youth Orchestra, where he played the French horn.

At breakfast that morning, Stephen had told his mother, Dorothy, of his fear that 'something awful' was going to happen at the shops, and that he had a premonition that a bomb would be left there.'[131]

That day would become known as Bloody Friday. Twenty-two bombs left by the IRA exploded across Belfast, shrouding the city skyline in a pall of smoke, killing nine people. At the shops Stephen noticed the bomb in the back seat of a car; he ran from shop to shop, shouting, 'Bomb, bomb'. It exploded.

Stephen's father, Reverend Joseph Parker – who was senior chaplain of the Belfast Mission to Seamen – was helping in the rescue efforts in the city centre, unaware that his own son had been killed.

At the mortuary, it was Stephen's love of jokes and his Scout belt that allowed his father to identify him. 'I asked [the attendant] to look in the pockets, and he pulled out a box of matches. I looked – Stephen had fooled me two nights before, he was always buying these trick games, and they were joke matches.'[132]

At the inquest into his death, the Coroner's Court was told that Stephen's bravery had been in stark contrast to the cowardice of the bombers.[133] Stephen was posthumously awarded the Queen's Commendation for Bravery; a memorial trust at the City of Belfast School of Music still awards an annual prize in his name.

His father set up the Witness for Peace movement, which organised marches for peace and held a three-day fast and vigils in Belfast and Dublin; disillusioned by the response, he emigrated to Canada in 1975.

He died in Vancouver in 2018, aged 89; his final wish was that his ashes be returned to Belfast and interred alongside his son.

'Stephen lived every minute of his life,' said Dorothy. 'He never sat still. I would say, "Oh for God's sake, sit still now."' I wish he was here making all that noise again, so I could say, "Stephen, be quiet."'[134]

❋ ❋ ❋ ❋ ❋

Name: *Daniel Hegarty*

Age: *15*

From: *Creggan, Derry*

Date of Death: *31/07/1972*

Daniel Hegarty was 'small, funny, very witty, and adored the ground my mother walked on', says his sister Margaret.

'He would always buy my mother a bar of Fry's Chocolate Cream, he called it her dark secret,' adds his sister Kathleen.

The eldest and the only boy in the family, 15-year-old Daniel used to collect copper wire and scrap and sell it; he used the money to buy ornaments for his mother.

Daniel loved comics and drawing, and would draw cartoons, as well as playing jokes and games. He also loved animals, and his kind-hearted nature meant he wouldn't think twice about bringing them home.

'Our house was full of strays, and you'd come in and they'd all be lying in front of the fire,' says Kathleen. Margaret recalls how one dog was named Peggy, after the next-door neighbour; fed up of coming running whenever Daniel called the dog's name, the neighbour eventually told Daniel's father, 'Either he renames that dog, or I'll do something about it.' He also caught frogs and kept them in his mother's sink, and got himself bitten by a rat.

He was also kind-hearted. 'He used to leave so early for school, and we wondered why,' says Margaret. 'He was stopping by the pensioners' bungalows and seeing if they needed anything from the shop and lighting the fire for them.'

Daniel was also a devout boy. 'Someone came into the house and they were saying the Lord's name,' says Margaret. 'Daniel would say, "I don't mind the cursing, but why do you have to keep saying the Lord's name?"'

Family holidays were taken at Kerrytown, in County Donegal. When he was 11, 'he saw Our Lady … he talked about seeing a beautiful lady on a cloud', remembers Kathleen

He was determined to protect his family from the Troubles that were going on around them. 'He wore scapulars round his neck, and he hung miraculous medals all round the house,' says Margaret. 'He said, "No bullets will get this house."'

The month before he died, he had been on a peace rally with his father, Alec; Alec had cradled a soldier, who had been shot outside their house, and comforted him as he died.

Early that morning, British army vehicles thundered into Creggan. The aim of Operation Motorman was to remove the 'no-go' areas in Derry and Belfast; it was the biggest British military operation since Suez.

Daniel and his cousins went 'to see a tank'.[135] Daniel was shot twice in the head by a British soldier; his cousin Christopher was also shot in the head but survived.

Daniel's mother later had a mass said for the soldier who had killed her son.

In 2011 an inquest found that Daniel had posed no risk when he was shot.[136] In April 2019 Northern Ireland's Public Prosecution Service announced that a former soldier, known as Soldier B, is to be charged with Daniel's murder.

In Margaret's house, Daniel's fishing rod hangs on the sitting room wall; she still keeps his Wrangler jeans, and the coins he kept in his pocket for playing pitch and toss – 'his lucky money'. 'Memories are all we have.'

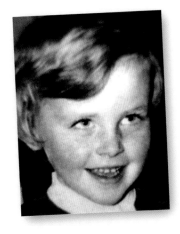

Name: *Kathryn Eakin*

Age: *8*

From: *Claudy, Co Derry*

Date of Death: *31/07/1972*

Kathryn Eakin had only arrived back home in Claudy that morning. She and her 12-year-old brother Mark had spent July with family friends in the seaside village of Castlerock.

A tomboy, the eight-year-old was mad about animals, and loved playing with her brother's friends and going fishing with them.

'She liked to knock about on her bicycle,' said Mark. 'Sometimes she'd go next door to a neighbour's house … she'd spend hours helping her bake scones and pancakes. That was her idea of a great day, footering about at the baking. The month before she was killed in 1972 had been one of the best the pair of us had together.'[137]

The Eakin children earned their pocket money, helping out with odd jobs in the family's shop on the village's Main Street; as soon as they returned from the seaside they were hard at work.

Kathryn was up on a set of steps, cleaning the window, while Mark was sweeping the yard. 'The pair of us were always fooling around,' said Mark, 'and I reached for the Windolene and squirted some on a bit of the window that she had already cleaned. She went mad at me … and next thing, boom.'[138]

The first bomb exploded. Mark was blown off his feet; when he looked around, Kathryn was lying on the footpath, unconscious. The IRA had planted three bombs in the village; in total nine people were killed, including three children.

Mark's parents received £56 in compensation for Kathryn's death. 'It didn't even pay the funeral costs, though Adair's [the undertakers] didn't charge my father. They were doing two and three funerals a day in Claudy at one stage.'

The family eventually moved to Castlerock in 1984. 'It got to the point where my mother couldn't take it anymore,' says Mark. 'We had to walk over where Kathryn was killed every day.'

In 2010, an investigation by Northern Ireland's Police Ombudsman found that detectives in 1972 had concluded that a Catholic priest, Fr Chesney, was an IRA leader in South Derry and was suspected of involvement in the bombing. He was never arrested; instead, following discussions between the then Primate of All Ireland, Cardinal Conway and the Secretary of State, William Whitelaw, he was moved to a parish in Donegal.

The Police Ombudsman found that the failure to arrest Fr Chesney had 'compromised the investigation' into the Claudy bombings and 'failed those who were murdered, injured and bereaved'.[139]

In recent years Mark spoke to the former IRA leader and Northern Ireland's deputy first minister, Martin McGuinness, about Kathryn's death. 'He did apologise for Claudy. He called it "an indefensible act".'

Mark has two daughters; his eldest is named Samantha Kathryn in his sister's memory. 'I can't help but think how they have outlived Kathryn,' he said. 'Kathryn is always eight years old.'[140]

❋ ❋ ❋ ❋ ❋

Name: *William Temple*

Age: *16*

From: *Donemana, County Tyrone*

Date of Death: *31/07/1972*

William Temple loved life. 'He enjoyed the crack,' says his brother David. 'He was a good man to have in a crowd because he was a good mixer, he could chat to everybody. He could have walked into a room and got on with any conversation, that was the kind of person he was. A lot of people liked him – he had a bubbly personality and enjoyed carrying on with the girls.'

William – or Billy as he was known to the family – had just left school in Strabane, where he had done well; he had also played cricket for the school and was hoping to play for the local team in Donemana.

He liked fishing too, and football; the four Temple brothers would play football in the back garden. 'Two against two, us in the garden like it was a wee pitch, and our mother would have looked out the back door at the four of us slogging it out,' remembers David.

'He was only a young boy, only starting out,' he adds, but he knows his brother would have been a success. 'He would have had a brilliant life.'

William had already found a good job at Leckpatrick Co-Op, where he worked on a bottling machine. 'When somebody else didn't turn up, the foreman needed a volunteer to go out with the lorry on deliveries. Billy put his hand up.'

On their round was the County Derry village of Claudy. 'He stepped out of the lorry a wee bit above the hotel and the first bomb went off. It missed him completely, but when the next one went off he was hit in the hand – he went down to the lorry driver and told him. Then he walked straight into the centre of the third bomb. He was about eight feet away from it when it went off.' David pauses. 'That was a tough time.'

Nine people were killed. Nobody has ever been convicted of the Claudy bombings; in 2010 a Police Ombudsman's investigation found that police had suspected a Catholic priest, Fr Chesney, of being an IRA leader who was involved in the bombing, but he was not arrested.

'Nobody wants to touch Claudy, nobody wants to lift the lid to see who's to blame,' says David, 'because it would be opening a can of worms. I have fought all my life to get answers for my brother's death. I'll not last forever, I want to see it out in the open. I'll keep fighting for it.'

His mother died in 2017, aged 93. 'She kept a photo of him [William] above her bed, and she always looked up every night and said, "Some day, Billy, we'll meet again." She got her wish. I'd say the two of them's happy now together.'

✳ ✳ ✳ ✳ ✳

Name: *Patrick Joseph Connolly*

Age: *15*

From: *Claudy, Co Derry*

Date of Death: *08/08/1972*

Patrick Joseph Connolly was never called Patrick. He was always Joe.

The 15-year-old was the youngest of seven from a farm just outside Claudy, and helped out on the family farm as well as working for a neighbour. 'That was the way it was in those days,' says his sister Maureen McElhinney. 'Everybody helped everybody else.'

Joe had just left school and was looking forward to starting work at Desmond's clothing factory in Claudy, where he was to work in the cutting room. Every night, he would call round to Maureen's house to see his sister and his young nephews before returning home.

'He was just a fantastic young fella,' she remembers. 'He loved football, and he was always reliable. He'd have gone into Claudy at night to get cigarettes for my father and if Joe told him he'd be back at nine, he'd have been back at nine, or even fifteen minutes before. He was never home any later, and then he would have made the supper for everyone.'

That morning, Joe had gone into Claudy to see the youth employment officer about his job in Desmond's. He was in McLaughlin's shop on Main Street when the first of three IRA bombs exploded. He was hit by flying metal and was flown to Altnagelvin Hospital in Derry; he died eight days later.

'He never returned home,' says Maureen. Joe was the ninth person to die in the Claudy bombings, and the third child. 'I don't think anybody will ever be held responsible, not at this late stage now,' she says. 'Over the years you learn to live with a lot of things.'

Her memories are of standing with Joe at her front door, of him playing with her baby son, of his amazement as he returned home down the family's dark lane late one night. 'He said, "Mammy, there's a moon in Derry and there's a moon out here too,"' says Maureen. 'He was that innocent.'

Family Snaps and Memorabilia

Damien Harkin on holiday in Buncrana.

James Morgan with his GCSE project.

Claire and Alan Radford.

Kevin McCauley.

Paul Maxwell with his younger sister Lisa.

Michael Turner (back left) with his father and siblings.

Stephen Bennett on holiday in Bundoran, buried in the sand.

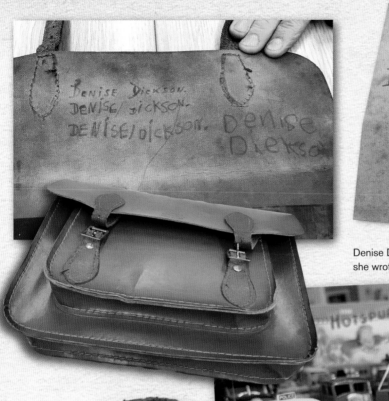

Today is monday I am a good girl. I talk to God

Denise Dickson's school satchel and the copy book she wrote in on the day she died.

A dinky car collection like the one Anthony McDowell treasured.

Patrick Toner's teddy bear.

Thomas, You'll be missed forever, we dont know how this could happen to such a nice guy!! You'll ALWAYS be our Harry Potter Love you loods Aisleen + Katie xxxxx

Message from friends of Thomas Devlin.

Name: *James Boyle*

Age: *16*

From: *Glen Road, West Belfast*

Date of Death: *27/09/1972*

James Boyle had left to go to a party. He failed to return home; his family realised he had been killed when they read a newspaper report that a body had been found.

The Irish Press described it as a 'mystery killing'. 'Police investigating shots near Flush Lane, in the Springfield area of west Belfast, found the body of a young man … lying on the pavement. He had been shot in the head.'[141]

'A spent cartridge was found beside his body, and people living nearby said they heard a number of shots in the area.'[142]

According to *Lost Lives,* Jimmy was an apprentice heating engineer.[143] He was also wearing a green scapular around his neck, and carrying a St Christopher medal and a small cross – all of which would have marked him out as Catholic.

Lost Lives quotes 'reliable loyalist sources' that Jimmy had been killed by the UDA.[144] Locally it was believed that he had been arrested by the British army and then handed over to loyalists, who killed him.

In his death notice in *The Irish News* he was described as a 'beloved son'; his friends Dermot, Gerard, Gerry and Eamon were among other pals who placed notices regretting his loss.

✳ ✳ ✳ ✳ ✳

Name: *Alex Moorehead*

Age: *16*

From: *Newtownstewart, Co Tyrone*

Date of Death: *07/10/1972*

Alex Moorehead was taking a shortcut home when he was shot.

The youngest in the family of four boys and three girls from Davis Crescent in Newtownstewart, County Tyrone, Alex – who was partially deaf – had been working at the Mid-Ulster Meat Packing Company's abattoir in Doogary in Omagh.

It was nine o'clock on a Saturday night. Local residents 'heard a number of shots in quick succession'; they rushed outside, and found Alex lying on the footpath.[145] He had been shot in the chest by a UDR patrol; he died without regaining consciousness.

A British army statement said that Alex had been attempting to climb a fence at the rear of the Gorey Cinema while carrying an 'object', and had failed to stop when challenged; local people disputed this, saying that: 'As a local boy he would have known that part of the fence was broken down and that one could walk through the gap. It would have been a short cut to his home from the cinema.'[146]

Among the members of the UDR unit was Alex's uncle.

Local residents later met with the British army's General Officer Commanding in Northern Ireland, General Tuzo, to express their 'extreme concern at the events surrounding the death'.[147]

His father Jack said he would like to meet the man who had shot his son. 'I want to put his mind at ease. I do not blame him in any way … he [Alex] was practically deaf. I feel sorry for the lad on the patrol concerned because he was in no way to blame.'[148]

Name: *Jim Doherty*

Age: *6*

From: *Turf Lodge, West Belfast*

Date of Death: *15/10/1972*

Ena Doherty's last memory of her son Jim is his laugh. The six-year-old was playing in the garden with his brother and sister; Ena had only let the children outside because there were no police or soldiers in Turf Lodge that Sunday morning.

'I heard him laughing that day in the garden,' Ena said in a 2010 interview with Relatives for Justice. 'I shouted out, "What's he up to?" [His sister] Anne shouted back, "We're cutting roses, he's got a surprise for you," but he was murdered with the wee surprise in his hand, the wee roses.'[149]

Anne – who was a year older – ran into the house screaming, saying that Jim had fallen; Ena rushed out. 'Jim was lying there unconscious and his blond hair covered in blood, he was lying there in the garden with the wee flowers he had picked crushed in his wee hand.'[150]

His parents did not realise what had happened until a doctor told them there was a bullet in his head. Shot on 8 October, he died in hospital a week later.

Jim had been a Christmas Day baby: 'A lovely baby with blond hair, blue eyes, absolutely beautiful,' remembers his mother. He loved the 25th of December 'because it was like two special days for him, his birthday and Christmas as well'.

He was preparing for his First Communion the following May, and was 'an awful happy wee child, always laughing, always singing and messing about,' remembers Ena. 'He loved playing with wee cars and he loved school, and his wee friends, he played with the wee boys next door.'

'Whenever the teacher brought down his school photos – they were taken just about six weeks before Jim was shot – I couldn't even look at them,' says Ena. 'I was taking them out of the envelope bit by bit, the hair and then the eyes and then the nose and then the smile. It took me weeks to really take a good look at his wee photo.'[151]

The IRA issued a statement denying responsibility; in 2011 the Historical Enquiries Team concluded that 'more likely than not' he had been shot by republicans. Ena believes her son was shot by the UVF.

Each year, she puts a memorial notice in the paper on the anniversary of Jim's death; she hopes that one day she will be able to add who was responsible. 'After all those years, I'd be able to put in the truth.'[152]

* * * * *

Name: *William Warnock*

Age: *15*

From: *Newtownards Rd, East Belfast*

Date of Death: *17/10/1972*

In the space of a month, William Warnock's mother buried two sons.

Fifteen-year-old Billy, as he was always known, was 'very popular', according to his best friend and cousin John Conlane, 'especially with the girls'.

'We had nothing,' says John. 'There wasn't even a park to kick a ball in. All we had was Billy's small tape recorder to listen to pop music and his dog – a brown and white collie who lived to 19, older than Billy.'

Both Billy and his older brother Robert, who was 18, were members of the UDA.

Robert died that September, shot by an off-duty officer while he was attempting to rob a bar. A few weeks later, John, who was 14, remembers calling to see Billy and finding his Aunt May – Billy's mother – with her head in the gas oven; he had the presence of mind to turn off the gas and run for help.

They had no idea that Billy would be killed shortly afterwards, knocked down by a British army Saracen on Templemore Avenue; another UDA man, John Clarke, had died the night before when a similar vehicle crashed into a house and pinned him to a wall during disturbances in nearby Hornby Street.[153]

About 1,000 people attended Billy's funeral; men in camouflage jackets and black berets flanked the cortege, and shots were fired over his coffin.[154]

Billy was the youngest member of the UDA to die during the Troubles; both his name and that of his brother appear on the UDA's East Belfast Brigade Roll of Honour.

Among the death notices in the *Belfast Telegraph* was one to a 'dearly loved boyfriend'. Pauline Graham wrote: 'Heartaches in this world are many, but losing you, Billy, was worse than any.'

✳ ✳ ✳ ✳ ✳

Name: *Tony Diamond*

Age: *12*

From: *Creggan, Derry*

Date of Death: *23/10/1972*

Tony Diamond and his younger brother Neil shared the same birthday. Both had been born on 19 May, but ten years apart.

'Tony would have been close to me,' says Neil. 'He would have been the babysitter at times, and he would have pushed me about in the pram.'

One of a family of eleven, 12-year-old Tony and his friends were always in the middle of everything. 'The Troubles were bad when Tony was growing up,' says Neil. 'He was always collecting bullet shells or rubber-bullet casings. If there was a gun battle Tony would have been near at hand, and even with the soldiers, he would have talked away to the soldiers.'

Tony was 'a character', says Neil, recalling how his father had been out for a walk one day when he caught sight of a group of boys in the River Foyle on top of a car bonnet. 'It was Tony and his friends,' says Neil, 'out paddling – and he was meant to be in school.

'All the girls in the street fancied Tony and would hang around outside the house hoping he would chat to them.'

He and his brother Ken were 'always trying to make a few bob'. They sold the 'Tilly' (*Belfast Telegraph*) on a Friday and Saturday night, and on a Tuesday and Thursday went to the cattle and sheep market on the Lone Moor Road. 'He was just one of those people who wouldn't have done you a bad turn,' says Neil. 'He was a likeable person.'

When the family dog, Rover, was killed – run over by a British army Saracen – his sister Louise recalls how Tony and his friends went down to the fields to bury him. 'He came back to tell Mum that he'd said a prayer for Rover, with big tears in his eyes.'

The night Tony was killed, he and a friend had sneaked in to look at a gun they knew was hidden in a pensioner's house in nearby Iniscarn Road. 'They were going up to mess about or whatever, and as far as I know Tony was pulling the blinds and the other fella hit the gun off accidentally,' says Neil.

Tony was shot in the head; he died shortly after arriving in hospital.

'I've never met that other fella,' says Neil. 'I'm sure he feels terrible – after all, he was his friend.'

⁕ ⁕ ⁕ ⁕ ⁕

Name: *Michael Turner*

Age: *16*

From: *Cavehill, North Belfast*

Date of Death: *29/10/1972*

Michael Turner and his younger brother Peter were 'best buddies'.

One of eight siblings, 16-year-old Michael and Peter, who was 13, shared a bedroom; the brothers spent their days 'playing football, listening to the radio – we had no TV or anything – talking about football, going raiding orchards, or playing conkers'.

They would go to watch Cliftonville FC play, and afterwards 'minesweep' the stands, looking for lemonade bottles to take back to earn a few bob; if anyone was going to an away match, the brothers would have offered to buy their train tickets for them, at half fare, in return for a few pennies.

Known as 'a bit of a messer', Peter remembers Michael playing a practical joke on their mother in the city centre. 'He ran up and pretended to take her handbag and she nearly had a heart attack.'

Michael had had a Saturday job working for a butcher; as Catholics delivering in a Protestant area, Peter remembers he and his brother having to 'run for their lives' when they were chased by a Protestant gang. 'Luckily enough he had juice and apples out of the shop, and that's what we started to throw. They stopped to pick them up, so that's how we survived that day.'

A former pupil of St Gabriel's Secondary School, Michael left school at 15 and was working in Stewart's supermarket, where he would bring home the damaged tins for his mother.

Michael had just turned 16 the previous month. 'He was as bright as anything,' says Peter. 'He could have done poetry – I used to have competitions in school for poetry and he would have written the poems for me.'

A cherished family photograph shows Michael wearing a paisley shirt. 'He would have had a cravat as well,' says Peter. 'He liked his style. He was just getting into girls and maybe having a drink of cider.'

Michael and a friend were walking along the street when a UVF gunman opened fire on them from a hijacked car; Michael was killed, and his friend injured.[155]

'It was a Sunday afternoon,' says Peter, 'and that's what you did in those days – he was out, probably mucking about, laughing and joking, and the next minute you're killed.

'Michael just happened to be walking along and the chances were 99 per cent he was a Catholic. They didn't know anything about him and didn't want to know anything about him. They just thought, *I'll kill him.*'

His family were awarded a 'death grant' from the government of £22.50; Peter believes his father sent the cheque back. 'He was disgusted.'

Peter still misses his 'brilliant big brother'. 'He was just a good kid. To me, he's still a kid.'

✳ ✳ ✳ ✳ ✳

Name: *Claire Hughes*

Age: *4*

From: *Sailortown, North Belfast*

Date of Death: *31/10/1972*

That Hallowe'en, Claire Hughes and her friend Paula Strong dressed up as witches.

The four-year-old was the youngest of eight children. 'We all adored her,' said her brother Kevin. 'She was a lovely bubbly and happy girl. She had curly blonde hair, and she always clung to her Mum wherever she was.'[156]

Claire's sister had organised a fancy dress competition for the local children; Claire was wearing her costume when Paula called for her to ask if she wanted to go out and see the bonfire.[157] 'The bonfire was just across from Mrs Hughes' house,' said Paula's brother Tony, 'where she could keep an eye on us.'[158]

As the children played outside, three members of the UDA drove up to the local bar, Benny's. They abandoned the car outside; a 100 lb bomb was inside.

Teenager Brian Quinn, who lived on Ship Street, saw it explode. 'The two little girls, dressed as witches, were warming their hands on the bonfire. Suddenly they were blown backwards.'

'It was raining bricks, and bottle tops were ricocheting around the place,' said Kevin. 'I was running up the street in shock. My mother lifted Claire and brought her into the house.'[159]

Nine years later three UDA members were sentenced to life imprisonment for the girls' murders. 'It wasn't intentional,' said one. 'I'm sorry it happened,' said another.[160]

'The men who planted the bomb must have seen the two little girls,' Claire's father James said. 'It was a callous act.'[161]

'It is clear you intended killing someone, if not the children,' Lord Justice O'Donnell said during sentencing. 'This will haunt you for the rest of your lives.'[162]

Name: *Paula Strong*

Age: *6*

From: *Sailortown, North Belfast*

Date of Death: *31/10/1972*

Paula Strong was full of excitement. Dressed in a witch's hat and cloak, the six-year-old ran in and out of neighbours' houses with the other local children, enjoying the parties, fancy dress competition and bonfire which had been arranged to mark Hallowe'en.

'She was the joy of my Mum's life,' said her older brother Tony. 'She was a loving girl, she would do anything for you. She was something special. You couldn't help but smile when she was around.'[163]

Paula was from Marine Street; her best friend, four-year-old Claire Hughes, lived on Ship Street, right opposite the bonfire. Paula called on Claire to ask her if she wanted to go to the bonfire.

'I didn't go with her,' said her brother Tony, 'so in a way I blame myself. I was in the house when the bomb went off. There was a massive explosion and the pictures fell off the walls. Our house was in the next street and the whole house shook.'[164]

A car bomb left by the UDA had exploded outside the Catholic-owned Benny's Bar; three men were later sentenced to life imprisonment for the murders of Paula and Claire.

Paula was found lying on the pavement; as her father tried to dig out survivors from the wreckage, he was told his daughter had been injured. She died in her mother's arms.

The friends had a double funeral. Their tiny, pale-blue coffins were carried side by side through the narrow, terraced streets, which were packed with mourners. Among them were Paula's classmates from Holy Family Girls School, and members of the Liam Reid Girls' Accordion Band.

'Black flags flew from many houses in the district,' *The Irish News* reported, 'and a large number of dockers, all members of the Irish Transport and General Workers' Union, left their work to attend the Requiem Mass.'[165]

Paula and Claire were buried together; their exact ages – 6½ and 4½ – are inscribed on their shared headstone.

＊ ＊ ＊ ＊ ＊

Name: *Rory Gormley*

Age: *14*

From: *Lisburn Road, South Belfast*

Date of Death: *27/11/1972*

Every evening, shortly after five o'clock, the ten Gormley children would take their set positions at the table in the long, narrow working kitchen of their home in Windsor Park in Belfast – boys on one side, girls on the other – as their mother Doreen served out the dinner.

The fifth boy born into the busy household, 14-year-old Rory was fascinated by nature. 'He built a bird table in the back garden and he saved every little creature that crawled all around him,' says his sister, also called Doreen. 'He actually joined the World Wildlife Fund and was very proud of it – he wanted to be a vet when he grew up.' But with ten children, the only pets allowed at home were rabbits and goldfish.

Rory's father, Peter, was an eye surgeon in Belfast's Mater Hospital and was involved with the civil rights movement; both parents were keen that their children get a good education, and Rory and his brothers were sent to St Malachy's College on the Antrim Road.

Holidays were spent in the family cottage in County Donegal. 'We absolutely loved the holidays,' remembers Doreen. 'They were so carefree. Rory would swim in the sea every day at Carrickfinn beach, play hurling and run around the sand dunes.'

A 'slim, fit, quiet boy', Rory had been an altar boy and was learning to play the piano accordion. He loved playing soccer with his friends and following his favourite team, Everton, and never missed *Match of the Day* on Saturday night.

Each morning Peter would drive three of his sons, their friend and Doreen to school on his way to the Mater. Having dropped Doreen off first, at St Dominic's on the Falls Road, Peter took a shortcut through the loyalist Shankill area as their usual route had been closed by the British army. As he did so, UVF gunmen opened fire.

Rory was killed; his father and his brother Paul were injured. 'Mr Gormley lifted out his dying son, and as he ran down the street calling for help he was fired on again.'[166]

It was believed the family were targeted because their school uniforms identified them as Catholics.

From then on, there was an empty place at the dinner table. Rory's month's mind fell at Christmas – his presents were to include an encyclopaedia, some books on animals, and an Everton annual.

✳ ✳ ✳ ✳ ✳

Name: *Bernard Fox*

Age: *16*

From: *Ardoyne, North Belfast*

Date of Death: *04/12/1972*

After the Troubles began, Bernard Fox and his friends learned a new game: 'Snatch Squad'. 'There were two sides,' his friend Bernard Glennon recalls. 'One took on the role of rioters and the others were a Brit snatch squad.'[167]

One of eight children from Etna Drive in the Ardoyne area of north Belfast, 16-year-old Bernard – who was known to his friends as Bocky – was gifted at football, handball and snooker. 'Everybody wanted to be on his team,' says Bernard Glennon. 'At handball he was unbeatable. He was fiercely competitive but in a fair way. He was a natural leader.'

He was also 'an extremely active member' of the Fianna, who 'was never far from the action'. Bernard was often on 'standby' keeping watch for loyalist attacks on the area. 'He would be the first one out on the street if something needed to be done,' said another friend, Seamus Clarke.[168]

Bernard's leadership qualities were quickly noticed, and at the time of his death he was O.C. of the Fianna in Ardoyne. 'When we were asked who we wanted to take over as O.C. of the Fianna, we all said there was nobody else but Bocky because he was always fair with people.'[169]

Another friend, 'Dutch', recalls how he and Bernard and another Fianna member made their way to the junction of the Crumlin and Woodvale roads where a 'military operation' was to take place; Bernard was killed during a gun battle between the IRA and the British army.

'When the shooting started, I looked to my right and saw Bernard fall. I remember looking at him. He was silent. I immediately wanted to help him and instinctively began to reach out to him. But I knew he was dead.'[170]

Bernard's family had no idea of his involvement until they were approached by republicans and asked if they wanted a military funeral.

His friend Dutch was among those who formed the guard of honour. 'Everyone wanted to be involved,' says Seamus. 'In the end it was a mix of Fianna boys and members of the Cumann na gCailíní. The funeral itself was really massive, and a real tribute to Bernard.'

He often wonders what his friend might have become. 'I have come to the conclusion that he would have ended up in the leadership of the [Irish Republican] Army.'[171]

❋ ❋ ❋ ❋ ❋

Name: *James Reynolds*

Age: *16*

From: *Shore Road, Newtownabbey*

Date of Death: *15 / 12 / 1972*

It was ten o'clock on a Thursday night. Sixteen-year-old James Reynolds was standing talking to a group of friends on the Shore Road; his home in Mount Street was a few minutes' walk away.

As the friends chatted, they noticed the motorcycle. The vehicle and its two riders – one driving, one riding pillion – had passed them, then turned. When two of James's friends went to investigate, the motorcycle came towards them. The pillion passenger fired, wounding them both. The driver kept going, heading towards the rest of the group; the passenger fired again.

James was fatally wounded; he died in hospital in the early hours of the next morning.

According to *Lost Lives*, his cousin – who had been with him – said James had received sectarian threats at the training college he attended and had been warned 'the next bullet would be for him'. Loyalists are believed to have been responsible.[172]

A former student of Stella Maris Secondary School in Newtownabbey, he was the fourth past pupil from the school to die violently that year. Twenty-seven of the school's pupils, including four children, would die in the Troubles; the best-known was the hunger striker Bobby Sands.[173]

The author Padraig O'Malley recalls asking the then vice-principal Tom Cunningham how many of the school's students had died in the Troubles.

'He opens the drawer of his desk and takes out a bundle of passport-sized photographs – photographs of the faces of young boys, twelve or thirteen years old, reflecting the self-consciousness and awkwardness of adolescence.

'He flips through them, arranges them in order, and then starts to put one after another on his desk, naming the boy in each photograph.

'On he goes, tears streaming down his cheeks, as he matches each picture with a name.'[174]

Name: *Geraldine O'Reilly*

Age: *15*

From: *Belturbet, Co. Cavan*

Date of Death: *28 / 12 / 1972*

Geraldine O'Reilly loved fish and chips. It was three days after Christmas; the fifteen-year-old's older brother, Anthony, had agreed to drive her into town to the chip shop.

The youngest of eight, Anthony remembers his sister as 'a typical, fun-loving teenager. She loved going out with her friends.'

Geraldine loved her pet dog Spot – a black Labrador – and was a fan of Thin Lizzy; that summer, she had seen them play at a festival in Cavan.

She was also an Irish dancer – for years afterwards, her mother left her dancing costume and her school uniform hanging on her bedroom door.[175]

A student at St Bricin's Vocational School, Geraldine had done well in her Inter Cert, Anthony recalls, and was 'keen on becoming a teacher or a nurse'. She also babysat her one-year-old niece, Anthony's daughter Caroline, and worked part-time in her Uncle Michael's shop in Bridge Street.

Anthony had double-parked on Belturbet's main street, and waited in the car while Geraldine went into Slowey's fish and chip shop.

The car opposite was one of three which had been stolen by loyalists in Enniskillen. They placed bombs inside each vehicle, then drove them across the border – to Pettigo, County Donegal; Clones, County Monaghan; and Belturbet.

Geraldine was just about to leave the shop when the 100 lb device exploded. Anthony's car, riddled with shrapnel, lifted off the ground. He remembers falling out of the car 'as if waking from sleep'.

The centre of the town was ripped apart; photographs show wreckage strewn across the street, and cars turned into twisted piles of metal.

Geraldine was one of two children killed in the explosion; the other, Patrick Stanley, had been calling his mother from a phone box when the bomb went off.

Nobody has ever been convicted of the atrocity but according to *Lost Lives*, 'reliable loyalist sources' attribute the bombings to the UVF. [176]

Geraldine's Uncle Michael – who was also the town's fire chief – found his niece's body; Anthony, dazed and injured, was brought to identify his sister. He did so by her blue skirt, her cardigan, and one of her tan knee-length boots.

Geraldine had been hit on the head by a piece of metal from the car. She died instantly, her chips still in her hands.

＊ ＊ ＊ ＊ ＊

Name: *Patrick Stanley*

Age: *16*

From: *Clara, Co Offaly*

Date of Death: *28 / 12 / 1972*

Patrick – Paddy – Stanley was a hard worker, and a great sportsman. Even though it was only three days after Christmas, the 16-year-old had gone back to work for Jennings' Truck Company because he was saving for a new pair of football boots.

He loved sport. 'It didn't matter what, so long as a ball was involved,' says his sister Susan. Paddy won medals for soccer, Gaelic football and the Community Games in his home town of Clara, County Offaly, but his prize possession was the hurling All-Star he'd received earlier that year, which sat 'framed on the sideboard for all to see'.

The eldest of nine, 'Master Pat', as he was also known, loved swimming with his brothers, sisters and cousins in the local pond, and also the family's annual 'holidays' – day trips to Galway or Bray – or evenings spent having sandwiches and custard creams on the river bank.

Paddy loved sitting with his mother Teresa each evening, remembers Susan, eating his favourite dinner – sausage and chips. His weekly pay packet went straight to his parents – so when the opportunity came to help with the delivery of gas cylinders he jumped at the chance to earn some extra money.

Their last delivery was in Belturbet, County Cavan. When they arrived the shop was closed; they would have to wait until the morning. Paddy went to find a phone box to let his mother know he wouldn't be home that night.

Back in Clara, the family learned on the news that there had been an explosion in Belturbet and interrupted their nightly Rosary to pray for the families of the victims. At 3 a.m. the next morning, the parish priest told them that Paddy had been killed.

Paddy had been about to put the coin in the slot to call home when a loyalist car bomb exploded outside. He never got through to his mother; he died in the phone kiosk.

The bomb killed two people, both children; Paddy and 15-year-old Geraldine O'Reilly are now remembered with a memorial in Belturbet.

His parents were later buried with their eldest child; on his deathbed, Paddy's father Joseph implored the family to keep up the annual visit to Belturbet on 28 December, 'the feast of the innocents'.

* * * * *

2

War on the Streets

'The first thing my father did when he left the house every morning was drop to his knees with a mirror and put it under his car.'

Brothers Peter and Johnny Watterson loved comics. In their bedroom above the family newsagent's on the Falls Road in Belfast they would read the *Beano*, the *Dandy* and, sent from America, *Batman*; outside their bedroom window was their own version of Gotham City.

'Belfast at the time, it was entirely lawless,' remembers Johnny. 'There were people being killed all the time, there was violence every day, and unless someone was killed it wasn't mentioned on the news.

'There were riots all the time and the road was constantly half melted with bits of bus sticking up or melted into the road and there was glass everywhere and the lights were broken.

'At night it was like a sort of Gotham City because it was all shadows, there was no light coming from anywhere, just the chipper or the shops that were open. People walked around in this crunching glass and melted road and zebra crossings with the white bits burnt.

'You got used to it. There were other people dying, but they weren't people you knew particularly. Then your brother dies, and you step into a new world where you can't understand anything, and you can't explain anything.'

Peter was killed in January 1973, shot dead by loyalists who fired at him and his two friends as they stood chatting outside his mother's shop. It was purely sectarian; his killers had driven onto the Falls because they knew they would find a Catholic.

'My 12-year-old world was very small,' says Johnny. 'It was my mum, my school, my brother, and what happened up the street. It all revolved around the street.'

For children like Peter and Johnny, the Troubles had brought a war onto the streets where they lived. Peter was one of many children killed as they stood at a corner, simply chatting to friends or watching what was going on. They died in circumstances typical of childhood: Angela Gallagher was going to the shop for sweets; Rosaleen Gavin was running a message; Joseph McGuinness was getting chips.

They speak of childish curiosity – Tony Diamond was shot accidentally as he and his friend were playing with a gun; Pat Smith had gone to investigate a booby-trapped motorbike.

Best friends Claire Hughes and Paula Strong died together, dressed in witches' costumes as they enjoyed a Hallowe'en bonfire; Jim Doherty, Paul Crummey and Gordon Gallagher all died in their own gardens.

Nine-year-old Patrick Rooney, the first child to die as a result of the Troubles, was killed inside his own home. 'They can't say to me he was in the wrong place at the wrong time,' said his father Neely. 'He was in his home when he was shot dead.'[1]

Of the 186 children who would be killed between Patrick's death, in August 1969, and that of Michael McIlveen in May 2006, 18 of them – 10% – were fatally injured in their own homes. A further three died in their gardens, and a further one in his back yard. Many more died only minutes from their front doors.

Locals drop to the ground during a gun battle, west Belfast, 1972.

CHILDREN OF THE TROUBLES

Areas like Divis Flats in west Belfast, where Patrick lived, changed with the advent of the Troubles. From August 1969 the British army were on the streets; so too were the IRA and loyalist paramilitaries.

'It was like Syria, but without the [aerial] bombings,' says Margaret McGuigan. Her younger brother Francis was just a month away from his second birthday when he died in April 1970; his family believe it was from the effects of breathing in CS gas.

The McGuigan family lived in 'the end house' in the Bullring in Ballymurphy – also in west Belfast – which meant they were always at the centre of any trouble. 'We grew up with a lot of gunfire, with the army just coming in, the doors banging, the bin lids going, bombs up the street.'

'My kids can't get it into their heads that we played in the street and when the shooting started you ran into the house and then when the shooting stopped you came back out,' says Karen McAllister. Her younger sister, four-year-old Siobhan McCabe, was shot and killed in 1975 as they ran home from their granny's house across the street.

'In the park, they'd be shooting through the railings so everybody would lie under the roundabout, and when it stopped you got back up and got back on again. Imagine that nowadays. We didn't know anything else. It was just the way it was.'

Urban, economically deprived areas like the Lower Falls in west Belfast, where the McCabes lived, were disproportionately affected; so too were Catholic ones. Of the children killed during the course of the Troubles, 80 per cent were Catholic. Just over a quarter were girls, and three-quarters were boys. More than 60% were teenagers and almost 30% were 16 years old. 29% of deaths took place in west Belfast, and 24% in north Belfast; together they represent 95 fatalities, more than half of the children killed as a result of the Troubles. 66% – two-third of children's deaths – took place in Belfast and Derry.

In Belfast, the names of areas such as Ardoyne, Ballymurphy and the Falls became part of the geography of the Troubles; in Derry it was Creggan and the Bogside. Similarly, Protestant working-class districts like the Shankill in west Belfast, or interface areas in north Belfast, were more sharply affected than middle-class parts of the city.

'If Brian [Stewart] had been born in the Malone Road he wouldn't be dead,' points out his sister Marie Duffy. The 13-year-old from Turf Lodge died after he was shot with a plastic bullet in 1976. 'If my mummy had married my uncle Billy instead of my da and we lived in Ballybeen he wouldn't have been dead.'

Born in 1962, Brian would have barely remembered a time before the Troubles. The British army, the IRA, the loyalist paramilitaries; the rioting, the petrol bombs, the plastic bullets; all this would have been commonplace, a new form of normality which had been quickly absorbed into the fabric of childhood.

In his memoir of growing up in Derry, Tony Doherty – then six years old – described how, in August 1969, the soldiers and their newly constructed 'sangar' became the centre of attention in his street.

'We played football at the bottom of the street next to it, instead of up the street. Women, including me ma, brought them tea, buns and sandwiches in relays … the soldiers allowed us to look down the sights of the SLRs [guns], picking out people as targets.'[2]

This quickly changed. 'Within a year of me bringing the Brits – who were outside the front door with their sandbags – a Penguin and a cup of coffee from my mum, we were making paint bombs and chucking them at Saracens,' says Johnny Watterson.

War was on the streets of many parts of Northern Ireland; the children who lived there suddenly found themselves on the front line. A total of 17 children – or 9% – were killed in Derry; nine of them in the initial three-year period between the arrival of the British army in August 1969 and the removal of the IRA 'no-go' areas in Operation Motorman on 31 July 1972. All but one of them was from the Brandywell, Bogside or Creggan; all died in or near their homes.

Of the three shot by the British army, one had gone to watch a riot and the other an army tank; the third was eating chips with his friends. Two were IRA members who were shot accidentally; two girls died in a house fire caused by a bomb-making accident in the kitchen below. Two were knocked down by British army vehicles – one while playing in the street, the other was walking home from the cinema.

'The Troubles consumed everything,' says Jim Dougal. His 16-year-old brother John was shot dead by the British army in 1972; both brothers were members of the Fianna, though it had no bearing on John's death. 'We might have played the odd game of handball but that was about it, in between rioting. It was all the Troubles, the rioting, the Brits.'

For a child, it could be exciting. 'It was great,' says Ted Healey. 'You had all the freedom, throwing stones, which children loved to do, and when you got chased by the army your adrenalin was going. We didn't go to school – you were given a "by ball" because of the Troubles, you weren't forced to go, so for weeks on end you'd hear there was a riot down in such and such a place, Andersonstown, say, so you'd go down and join in.'

Ted's twin brother Dessie was shot and killed during a riot in Lenadoon on the afternoon of the introduction of internment in August 1971. Among Dessie's friends was Martin Livingstone, whose younger sister Julie died after she was hit by a plastic bullet in 1981.

'Martin and his friend Mickey were there the day Dessie was shot,' says his sister Elizabeth Livingstone. 'When it was Dessie's fortieth anniversary they got together and raised some funds to have a wee plaque put up, because nobody ever talked about Dessie.

'Every time we were talking about Julie, Martin would always talk about Dessie, and I think what we've discovered is the ripple effect their deaths had on their contemporaries, on the kids that went about with them.'

Of the 186 children who died as a result of the Troubles, countless more were physically injured, and more again were left with mental scars. They survived the deaths of mothers and fathers, brothers and sisters, best friends; they saw friends and relatives interned, or imprisoned; they were themselves 'lifted', beaten, jailed.

Patrick Crawford had already lost his mother, Martha, caught in the crossfire of a gun battle three years before he was killed in 1975. David Devine's beloved older brother Hugh was interned and badly beaten; the family home was raided repeatedly. A year later, Hugh died in front of David; their sisters believe his death and the treatment of the family persuaded David and their other brother Michael to join the IRA.

Seamus Mallon, who later became Northern Ireland's deputy first minister, recalled teaching English at St Catherine's College, a girls' school in Armagh, during the 1970s. 'I had one small class, and every one of those girls had somebody belonging to them killed.'[3]

In 1972, Eimear O'Callaghan, a 16-year-old from Andersonstown in west Belfast, wrote in her diary of her fear at what was happening around her. Her

After riots, west
Belfast, 1976.

entry for 9 June read: 'Watched special edition of "24 Hours" about UDA plan to burn Andytown, Ballymurphy etc. to the ground. Say they will take on the Army – modern arms and plenty of them ... Shooting started. Lay in terror in bed for two hours listening to it. All I could do was pray.'[4]

John Lyttle's father Tommy was the brigadier of the West Belfast Brigade of the UDA. 'Every day of my childhood, and I do mean every day, from the age of about nine until I left at 18, I expected to die. I thought about death every day. Getting on the bus, it's going to blow up. Walking past Unity Flats, is a sniper going to take me out?

'The first thing my father did when he left the house every morning was drop to his knees with a mirror on a stick and put it under his car to see if a bomb had been placed. In the house, I couldn't sit with my back to the front window, because every time a car would pass, the blood would drain from me.'[5]

Julie Livingstone was terrified of soldiers; her sister Elizabeth dates it from when the family was burnt out of their home in 1969. Julie was only two: 'My daddy carried her across the Falls Road when there was shooting going on from both sides.'

Eventually rehoused in Lenadoon, Elizabeth remembers their house being raided 'constantly'. 'I remember sunbathing out the back and opening my eyes and seeing a big soldier standing over the top of me. I would have been about 18 but Julie was only a wee one and them coming into the house and up the stairs when she was in bed, she was really bothered by that.'

Johnny Watterson stopped going to the youth club because he was 'so frightened' of the Saracens. 'They'd be creaking up the road and then they'd stop and all the soldiers would jump out and start searching people.'

After his 13-year-old sister Margaret Gargan was shot and killed, Harry – who was a year younger – 'went a wee bit off the rails'. Caught throwing stones at an army Saracen, he was thrown in the back of the vehicle. 'All these Scottish soldiers were calling me "Irish scum" and kicking me and slapping me, and saying they were going to take me and drop me over on the Shankill. Suddenly they pulled in, threw me out and shouted, "There's a Taig."'

He was beaten up by a group of boys but managed to get away; had they been older, he is well aware he could have been killed. 'When I got back there was a crowd outside our house and my father said to me, "You have to stop this, your mother's already lost one." That was the end of my rioting days.'

Some families became used to harassment. 15-year-old Seamus Duffy was killed by a plastic bullet fired by a member of the RUC in 1989; after his death, his mother Kathleen says the security forces 'used to come down and do a three-point-turn in the street and deliberately shine their lights into the front room.

'They would have said to [my daughter] Bronagh, she was only ten, "is Seamus not coming out to play'?"'

In Belfast, the city's sectarian fault lines had hardened in August 1969. The burning of Bombay Street in west Belfast and the attendant violence that summer was the beginning of a pattern by which previously 'mixed' areas were redefined as either Catholic or Protestant as families were either forced to leave or chose to move.

Professor Marianne Elliott, in her evocative memoir of the White City housing estate in north Belfast, describes this as a 'sectarian reordering of space'; that year 3,570 families fled mixed areas in the west and north-west of Belfast, and yet more left in the weeks following the introduction of internment in 1971. By 1973, Elliott states, 'the Community Relations Commission estimated that between eight and 15,000 families (6.6–11.8 per cent of the Belfast urban area) had been intimidated out of their homes'.[6]

The Dougal family lived in Manor Street in north Belfast; they were one of a few Catholic families in the predominantly Protestant street. 'We played with Protestants,' says Jim, 'and we knew around the Twelfth they didn't talk to us much, but we used to have bonfires and everything. I remember when my sister was born in July 1968 me and [my brother] John were out collecting bonfire wood for the Twelfth.'

On 16 August 1969 they were told to get out. 'It was the middle of the night, and I remember we were all brought downstairs and dressed. Me and John were looking out of the window and we saw the people knocking doors and I remember saying to John, look at those policemen, they're not stopping those bad people.

'Eventually they knocked on our door and told us to get out and my da said, "I've seven children, where am I going to go at this time of night?"' The next morning, the family piled into his uncle's car. 'That was the last we saw of Manor Street.'

A few days later, John and Jim sneaked back, climbing over the back wall; 'Fenians Out' had been scrawled above their fireplace.

Often families had nowhere to go. Some crammed into relatives' houses; others were given refuge in schools or church halls where they would sleep in rows on the floor. At times of particular danger, such as around Internment, thousands fled to refugee camps in the Republic of Ireland. At its worst, houses were deliberately burned or destroyed to prevent 'the other side' moving in.

'We probably had more Catholic and Protestant churches per head of population than any other city in Ireland or Britain,' wrote Eimear O'Callaghan in 1972. 'We had Catholic schools and Protestant schools, Catholic pubs and Protestant pubs, Catholic streets and Protestant streets. Working-class territories were demarcated by bunting and flags, and kerbs painted red, white and blue or green, white and orange ... as a rule it was considered wisest and safest to stay among "your own".'[7]

'I know we never saw each other or mixed, and we used to throw stones at each other across the M1 every weekend, but I'd no animosity or hatred for Protestants,' says Johnny Watterson. 'It was just a bit of fun, good fun and it was almost like gangs, we could be the Crips and the Bloods.'

The death of his brother Peter was one of many in the litany of purely sectarian murders. So too was that of Rory Gormley, who had been killed two months previously after UVF gunmen fired on his father's car as he took them to school. His St Malachy's College uniform had marked him out as Catholic.

Eimear O'Callaghan knew the family; Rory's father, a surgeon, had removed her tonsils when she was six. 'I suddenly understood – with brutal clarity – why my school friends who lived in North Belfast were exempt from having to wear our drab St Dominic's overcoats.'[8]

Children – particularly those living on what would now be termed interface areas – could be verbally or physically attacked on their way to school. Anne Magee's family had lived in the predominantly Protestant Cregagh estate until

they were 'put out of our house', her brother JJ remembers; on her way home from her Catholic school she had been tied to a tree and hit.

Geraldine McKeown and her friend Angela Willett were pupils at Our Lady of Mercy in Ballysillan in north Belfast. 'The school was situated in a predominantly loyalist area and pupils were regularly attacked on our way to and from school. However, the odd bomb scare was welcomed as it meant we were sent home early.'

Eimear O'Callaghan recalled her resentment at the nuns' apparent refusal to recognise what was happening outside the school walls. 'When we managed to arrive in time for morning assembly, the nuns appeared to show no interest in whether we might have had to walk a couple of miles to get to school that day. They didn't openly acknowledge that we had possibly run a gauntlet of rioters and burning vehicles on the way home the previous evening. They seemingly made no allowances for the impact that a night-time backdrop of shooting, bin-lid banging, sirens and army helicopters might have had on our studying, nor did they blink when dozens of girls were recorded as absent during the morning roll call.

'The regimented school day, the focus on exams and the insistence on full uniforms were the only constants in our otherwise turbulent lives. School provided us with a rare but secure anchor in a very unstable world, but the wisdom to see that eluded us in Lower Sixth.'[9]

Inevitably, children dressed in school uniforms became a familiar sight at funerals. Among them were the friends of 11-year-old Lesley Gordon from Maghera in south Derry. She was killed in 1978 along with her father Willie, a school welfare officer and part-time member of the UDR, as he was about to drive her and her brother to primary school. The IRA bomb had been hidden in a cavity in the car.

Children of security forces grew up used to parents always checking under their car; they knew, even from a young age, that they could not tell their friends what their father's – or mother's – job was.

'I always told the children I was looking for cats until one day my then 12-year-old-son said, "You're not looking for cats, are you? You're looking for bombs",' said Mark Lindsay, a former RUC officer who is now chairman of the Police Federation. 'Another young child asked, "If you are a fireman why are you always driving into police stations?"'[10]

Yet for children who lived outside the worst-affected areas, the Troubles were a backdrop to their lives, something overheard on the radio or observed by chance as their parents watched the television news; its physical manifestation came, most frequently, in army or police checkpoints, or in bomb scares.

Shoppers in Belfast had to pass through a so-called 'ring of steel' to get into the city centre; bags – and even children – were searched. Families avoided the centre of Belfast because of the frequency of explosions; bomb scares were commonplace.

One child recalled how a wobbly tooth fell out as she and her family were evacuated from a café in Ballymena, County Antrim one Saturday lunchtime. 'Everybody was rushing along the street, and I stopped and said to my mum, "My tooth fell out." She grabbed me by the hand and pulled me down the street, and I felt really annoyed because she wasn't paying attention to my tooth.' As an adult, she reflects: 'It shows how normal it was. My tooth falling out was unusual, but the bomb scare wasn't.'

Another child's image of the centre of Belfast was of a city shrouded in darkness, a combination of security force uniforms, checkpoints, steel gates and apparently constant rain which lent it an air of damp menace.

Youth clubs and discos, run by community centres or by local churches, aimed to keep children off the streets; newspapers carried appeals – sponsored by the Northern Ireland Office – warning parents to keep an eye on their children.

An advertisement in the *Irish News* in May 1981 included a photograph of children throwing stones. 'The worry is yours, the sentence is theirs', it wrote. 'Save tears … Save time … Check on your children.'[11]

That same month, Roberta Guiney – whose son Desmond and husband Eric were killed after Eric's milk lorry was attacked by rioters in the New Lodge in North Belfast amid disturbances following the death of hunger striker Bobby Sands – pleaded with other mothers. 'Their mothers should not have let them out on the streets,' she said. 'I would never have let any child of mine out on the streets doing something like that – the kids are just being used by the perpetrators of violence.'[12]

Project Children, founded in 1975, took 23,000 young people, Catholic and Protestant, away to America for the summer and, quite literally, a better life. One of their success stories, Charles Love, had been twice to New York State and had planned to return to go to high school there; the day he was killed, he should have been in the States, not in Derry.

Project Children and others still exist; many would argue that the need to combat sectarianism is as relevant as ever. The images of girls crying as they walked past loyalist protestors and police in riot gear to get to school at Holy Cross in Ardoyne, north Belfast in 2001 are seared into the collective memory; two children, 16-year-olds Thomas McDonald and Glen Branagh, died in north Belfast before the protests were resolved.

In Northern Ireland, the majority of children are still educated in schools which are split along religious lines. Integrated schools, which deliberately bring together staff and pupils of both Protestant and Catholic faiths, as well as other religions and none, were attended by 7% of students in 2014/15.[13]

Divisions are also physical: In Belfast in particular, so-called peace walls which continue to separate communities living along 'interfaces' are testament to the continued division in Northern Ireland.

In the 50 years since the death of Patrick Rooney, the streets of Northern Ireland have changed. For the most part, they are now at peace; yet most would agree that much remains to be done. A 2019 report by Ulster University found that 'latent sectarianism persists in Northern Ireland … we now have to ask if the capability exists to provide solutions to these problems or whether we must

simply hope that with the passage of time they will somehow just go away.'[14]

Before Peter Watterson was killed, his mother Nuala's ambition in life was that her two sons would themselves get away. She wanted them to go to university – most likely, Queen's; this would be their passport out of Belfast. The day after Peter's funeral, she and Johnny packed up and moved to Dublin.

'Peter loved the Falls Road,' remembers Johnny. 'We loved our friends, he loved his friends, and he had a great group of people, twenty kids who lived in three streets, and he'd walk around owning the place, knowing everything and knowing everybody.

'The Falls Road was a community of parents and older brothers and younger kids and they all looked out for each other and it was always safe and there was no fear. There was no fear until your brother gets killed.'

Old Bailey bombing, 8 March 1973.
Opposite: The Sunningdale Agreement
is reached.

1973

- The UK and the Republic of Ireland join the European Economic Community, the forerunner of the EU

- An IRA bomb in Coleraine kills six people, four of them pensioners

- The IRA takes its campaign to England, as bombs explode at the Old Bailey and in Whitehall

- The UUP and the SDLP sign the Sunningdale Agreement, paving the way for the establishment of a power-sharing executive

- German industrialist Thomas Niedermayer, managing director of the Grundig factory in west Belfast, is kidnapped and murdered by the IRA

- Glam rock dominates the singles chart and provides the soundtrack for Northern Ireland's teenagers.

Name: *Peter Watterson*

Age: *14*

From: *Falls Road, West Belfast*

Date of Death: *29/01/1973*

Johnny Watterson's day began and ended with his big brother Peter. 'I followed him,' says Johnny. 'I didn't know what I was going to do, I didn't have any plan. I just walked after him up the street, and that's where my day started and that's where my day finished.'

Johnny (12) and 14-year-old Peter shared a bedroom above the family's newsagent's shop. Their father George – who had famously captained the Antrim GAA team to an All-Ireland semi-final in the 1940s – had died a few years before, and their mother Nuala now ran the family business.

'We both loved sport,' says Johnny, 'and in our bedroom one side of the walls was Celtic posters and we had Man United on the other, and George Best was everybody's God.'

Much time was spent playing football in the street – 'Our team was the Rockville Street team, which used to play against the Whiterock team' – or watching *Match of the Day*.

The brothers also loved comics – they read all the comics in the shop, for girls and boys, as well as Marvel comics sourced by friends who had relatives in America.

Peter excelled at school and passed the eleven-plus to go to St Mary's Grammar School. 'He was two years ahead of me and the teachers would keep saying to me, "You're good, Watterson, but your brother's much better."'

In the evenings, the only place to go was St John's Youth Club. Peter and his friends would play table tennis until ten o'clock, and then walk home.

That night Peter was standing chatting outside the shop. 'The chipper across the road was open,' says Johnny, 'and you could guarantee there would be loads of kids out talking.'

Johnny was inside and heard the shots. He ran out and saw that his friend Jim Toner had been injured; he tried to help him, not realising Peter had also been hit.

'I turned around and he was right behind me,' remembers Johnny. 'I hadn't seen him when I ran out, so I went over to him and I was about to bend down and people just pulled me away.'

Peter died in hospital; it's believed the UDA was responsible. That same night a UDA leader, Francis 'Hatchet' Smith, was killed by the IRA, who claimed that Smith had been involved in the murder of Peter and others in the area.[177]

The same UDA group is also believed to have abducted and killed 14-year-old Philip Rafferty the following night. 'It was part of a pattern of killing kids that had been apparent and that kept going after Peter was killed,' says Johnny.

The day after Peter's funeral, Johnny and his mother moved to Dublin.

'He was my older brother,' says Johnny. 'He looked after me all the time, and I'm sure I annoyed him by following him around. Sometimes he did mind, but most of the time he didn't, and that was magic.'

✳ ✳ ✳ ✳ ✳

Name: *Philip Rafferty*

Age: *14*

From: *Andersonstown, West Belfast*

Date of Death: *30/01/1973*

'Philip had brains to burn. He wanted to be an architect, and he told me he was going to build me a house,' remembers his mother, Maureen. 'He played the violin and the flute, and the house was always full of music.'

Philip had just turned 14. 'His birthday was 17th January and his birthday cards were still up. I said to him, "When are you taking those down?", and he said, "At the end of the month." He was just so chuffed with all his cards.

'He'd wanted me to buy him wellies so that he could help clear the snow from the pathways outside the pensioners' houses. That was Philip,' remembers Maureen.

Philip had just joined the James Connolly Youth Band. 'He was delighted, absolutely thrilled to pieces. I couldn't have said to him, don't you go.'

Maureen bought her son a new coat – 'with a hood on it, so he would be warm' – for the walk to band practice. 'I told him to avoid the main roads because they were shooting out of cars, and he said, "Nothing'll happen to me, Mum."'

One night, Philip didn't return. When it reached half past nine, Maureen went out to look for her son. At the police station, they asked her for a photograph of Philip.

'I went home and got this one we'd got at a festival in the Botanic Gardens [where] they took pictures and put them onto badges, and Philip had said to me, "I don't look too bad in that one." I said, "Ah, you're lovely, son," so I went looking for it because it was a photo he liked.'

Philip had been abducted from the street by the UDA. He was taken to the Giant's Ring – a beauty spot several miles away on the southern outskirts of Belfast – where he was beaten and then shot in the head. That same night, another teenager, 17-year-old Gabriel Savage, was also abducted and shot by the UDA; the previous night, the gang believed to be responsible for Philip's murder had shot and killed another 14-year-old, Peter Watterson.[178]

'They took Gabriel Savage that night too, and they tried to take another two wee boys, but they fought back and got away,' says Maureen.

A policeman came to Maureen's door to break the news; earlier, when she had reported Philip missing, he had said he was probably just out late. 'He knelt down in front of me and said, "You know what I'm going to say," and I said, "Yes, my son's dead, because he wouldn't be out at this time otherwise."'

She remembers seeing Philip's new coat at his inquest. 'It was in a plastic bag, saturated with blood. They took a child off the road, put his hood over his head and murdered him,' says Maureen. 'I think the world should know these things.'

✳ ✳ ✳ ✳ ✳

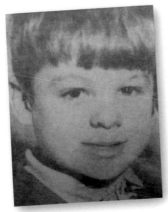

Name: *Gordon Gallagher*

Age: *9*

From: *Creggan, Derry*

Date of Death: *25/02/1973*

Gordon Gallagher was rarely allowed to play on the street. Instead, his mother Pat thought it was safer to keep him and his siblings in the back garden of their home in Leenan Gardens in the Creggan area of Derry.

'He'd a wee twinkle in his eye,' remembers his father Billy. 'He was full of devilment, and his hair – you can't see it in the photos but it was nearly yellow, bright corn-coloured. I took him everywhere with me when he was young.'

That Christmas, Gordon had received a cowboy outfit; Paul, a year younger, got an Indian costume. Gordon's new passion was karate – his uncle was the captain of the Irish karate team and had just started to teach his nephew.

It had been snowing, and that morning the nine-year-old had pleaded with his father to be allowed to go to an earlier mass than usual so that he and his brother Paul could get back home to build a snowman.

'The two of them were playing in the snow,' says Pat, 'and I remember thinking that would be a beautiful photo to take.'

Gordon and Paul were playing cowboys and Indians when the bomb exploded. Gordon had unwittingly upset a tripwire and triggered the device which had been left by the IRA in an attempt to target the British army.

His mother Pat saw Paul running down the garden. 'The fear on his face, I'll never forget it. Gordon was lying, and I thought he had just fallen, so I ran out and shouted to him, "You're alright, you're alright," and I went to lift him. That's the last I remember.'

Pat remembers four soldiers in civilian clothes who came to the wake and stood at Gordon's coffin. About a thousand people attended his funeral, and hundreds of his schoolmates from St John's Primary School lined the route of the cortege.

For months afterwards, Billy recalls, he would continue to call Gordon in for his dinner with the rest of his brothers. 'I keep thinking did we do anything wrong? Why Gordon? That's the way your mind goes.'

At the time, the IRA said it had planted the device but claimed the army had added a detonator. In 2012 republicans admitted full responsibility for Gordon's death and apologised to his family.

The Gallagher family are still angry. 'It's amazing that they would leave a bomb in someone's garden,' says Pat. 'If they had even sent the priest or somebody down to warn us, but they couldn't even do that.'

✳ ✳ ✳ ✳ ✳

Name: *Kevin Heatley*

Age: *12*

From: *Newry, Co Armagh*

Date of Death: *28/02/1973*

Kevin Heatley was a 'jovial, outgoing boy who was always full of crack, wit and stories'.[179]

A pupil at St Joseph's Secondary School in Newry, the 12-year-old was one of a family of six children from the town's Derrybeg estate. Kevin – who was known to his friends as Beansy – was out on the street watching a British army patrol which had come into the area.

Kevin was sitting on a wall when the single shot was fired. An eyewitness said, 'There was this crack which I knew was a rifle shot. When the boy fell I thought he had just lost his balance but someone coming from behind said he was shot.'[180]

The British army claimed a shot had been fired at the patrol and 'a gunman was hit when fire was returned'.[181] Patrick McCloskey was nearby; he ran over and lifted Kevin up, and saw blood pouring from his head. 'The boy had no gun,' he said. 'The child would not know how to use one if he had.'[182]

By chance, a TV engineer who lived across the road had been recording a programme at the time. On the tape is the crack of the single shot which killed Kevin.

The funeral of Gordon Gallagher,
February 1973.

The *Newry Reporter* recorded that Kevin's funeral was one of the largest ever seen in the town. 'Thousands of men, women and children walked in the funeral procession .... Black flags hung from many homes in the town. School pals of the dead boy formed a guard of honour alongside the hearse. In front walked more pupils headed by a young man carrying a black flag.'[183]

In Newry, there were immediate calls for an inquiry into Kevin's death. The soldier who had fired the fatal shot was charged with unlawful killing – the first time since the beginning of the Troubles that such a charge had been brought against a serving member of the British army.[184]

The 22-year-old corporal was convicted and jailed for three years; the judge said he was 'satisfied that the soldier had fired an unaimed shot without cause or justification'.[185]

The conviction was quashed three months later, after three Appeal judges 'found irregularities in Crown procedures at the no-jury trial'.[186]

Kevin's father Desmond, who had suffered from depression after his son's death, took his own life shortly afterwards.

Kevin's parents were given £750 compensation; the Ministry of Defence regarded this as 'the acceptable rate for a minor'.[187]

'Who could have been so cruel and heartless?' asked Kevin's brother Martin. 'This was the final blow for my parents. The MoD offered us about £60 for each year Kevin lived. What an insult.'[188]

✳ ✳ ✳ ✳ ✳

Name: *Alan Welsh*

Age: *16*

From: *Beersbridge, East Belfast*

Date of Death: *12/03/1973*

As a young teenager, Alan Welsh would have watched the huge crane taking shape above the east Belfast skyline.

Nicknamed 'Goliath', it was part of an ambitious expansion plan at the Harland and Wolff shipyard – a £16 million modernisation programme which had seen the world's largest building dock installed on nearby Queen's Island. The towering structure was in stark contrast to the narrow streets where Alan was growing up.

From Tamar Street, Alan was the only boy in a family of three children. Described as 'very outgoing', he was a member of the Pride of the Raven Flute Band.

He excelled in all sports, especially snooker and soccer, and had been due to go on trial with Tottenham Hotspur FC.

A former pupil of Euston Street Primary and Orangefield Secondary School, Alan had left school and was serving an apprenticeship in the shipyard.

A member of the UDA, he was fatally injured when his own bomb exploded prematurely in a vacant shop on the Woodstock Road; he died a week later.

He is listed on the UDA Roll of Honour as a member of the Cregagh 4th battalion; his name is among those engraved on a memorial in Dee Street commemorating the members of the organisation's East Belfast Brigade.

Above it, the two famous shipyard cranes still stand sentinel over east Belfast; 'Samson', Goliath's partner, was not installed until after Alan's death.[189]

✳ ✳ ✳ ✳ ✳

Name: *Bernard McErlean*

Age: *16*

From: *Grosvenor Road, West Belfast*

Date of Death: *20/03/1973*

It was a Tuesday night. Sixteen-year-old Bernard McErlean – from Durham Street off Belfast's Grosvenor Road – had been in his friend Kieran Nugent's house in nearby Merrion Street.

The two teenagers left Kieran's and walked towards Grosvenor Road with a dog;

they were standing at the corner when a Ford Cortina did a U-turn beside them.

Kieran later recalled the car pulling up alongside them, and someone shouting his name; a man with a machine gun started firing. Bernard 'fell to the ground and while still lying on the ground the gunman fired another shot into his body'.[190]

'I ran but I got hit in the leg and fell,' Kieran said. 'The fellow with the sub came up to me and stood over me. He stopped to put in a new mag and I got up and ran. He fired a second burst at me.' Kieran managed to stagger home. 'I remember the ambulance coming, and someone saying, "It's no good, this one's [Bernard's] dead."'[191]

Kieran had been shot six times. He later went on to join the IRA, and in 1976 became the first republican prisoner to be convicted after the withdrawal of Special Category status. His refusal to wear the prison uniform – vowing that 'they would have to nail the clothes to my back' – began the 'blanket protest' which led ultimately to the hunger strikes of 1981.[192]

The car sped off towards Sandy Row; according to *Lost Lives*, the UDA was responsible.[193]

The same car was believed to have been involved in an earlier incident, when shots were fired at a group of boys playing off the Antrim Road. 'A masked gunman stepped from a Ford Cortina which pulled in close to them and opened fire,' said an eyewitness. 'It was a miracle there were not half a dozen bodies.'[194]

The newspaper also reported that a group of about ten Protestant youths escaped injury in Roden Street when a blast bomb was thrown at them.

An RUC spokesman said, 'Children seem to be the targets for terrorists tonight.'[195]

✳ ✳ ✳ ✳ ✳

Name: *Patrick McCabe*

Age: *16*

From: *Ardoyne, North Belfast*

Date of Death: *27 / 03 / 1973*

Patrick McCabe had just got engaged. The 16-year-old, who was known as Pat, had been going out with his girlfriend Geraldine for two and a half years, and had proposed on her birthday.

The second eldest in a family of seven children, Pat had a twin brother, Gerard, who had died at birth.

A former altar boy, Pat had been studying for the priesthood, but had left the seminary at 13 and enrolled at St Gabriel's Secondary School. A member of the local youth club, he loved judo and cars, and was training to be a mechanic.

He was also in the Fianna and was 'eager to play a role in the conflict', his sister Marian recalls. 'Like many of the young lads in the district then he was constantly being harassed and arrested,' she said. 'It seemed to be nearly every other night my mum and me were down in Tennent Street RUC station bringing him home. My father tried to curb his enthusiasm by sending him up to his room. But once in his room Pat was away out the window and down the drainpipe.'

In 1972, their mother, Bridget, died; Pat's younger brother, also called Gerard, remembers Pat reassuring him. 'After my mother died Pat actually told me that I had nothing to worry about and he would look after me.'

'He was a tower of strength to the rest of the family,' says Marian. 'On that morning before he left home he went to my father, put his hands on his face and said, "Daddy, you know that I love you."'

By now Pat was a member of the IRA's Third Belfast Battalion. 'It was the first time I had been out on an IRA operation with Pat,' says his former comrade 'Jamesy'. 'He had a .38 automatic …. I was told he was going to do cover with the pistol …. We were intending to go up Alliance Avenue where there was a British army post.'

Pat was shot by a member of the British army's Parachute Regiment as they walked along Etna Drive in Ardoyne.

Joanie Clarke cradled Pat's head in her lap as he was driven to the Mater Hospital. 'He was badly wounded and I did my best to comfort him.' He died minutes after arriving at the hospital.

His fiancée, Geraldine, later married Pat's friend, Martin McClenaghan. In their home, a picture of Pat is displayed along with their other family photographs; their youngest son Pádraig is named after him. All five of their sons know about 'uncle Pat'.[196]

✳ ✳ ✳ ✳ ✳

Name: *Martin Corr*

Age: *12*

From: *Grosvenor Road, West Belfast*

Date of Death: *30/03/1973*

Martin Corr and his friend were out looking for scrap when they were 'lifted'. The boys – who were 12 and 13 – were bundled into the back of a British army Saracen and taken to Mulhouse barracks, in west Belfast.

Martin lived in nearby Distillery Street; the family had been bombed out of their former home in Roden Street less than a year earlier.

'The area was feral,' says Martin's brother Tommy. 'It was an interface area, and all of the kids would have been out on the street. They would have been rioting out on the street, throwing stones, and the modus operandi for soldiers is that they would have lifted children of that age, thrown them into the back of Saracens, and questioned them.'

In the barracks, they were questioned about the contents of their bag – containing copper and lead – and asked about IRA activity. 'I'd a brother in Long Kesh at the time and they knew the family,' says Tommy. 'They gave them a bit of a slap about.'

Martin's friend, Joseph McCusken, told *Republican News/An Phoblacht* the boys had been kicked by the soldiers.[197]

When Martin got home, he asked his brother Brendan to help him sneak back into the house. 'I was playing on a swing at the corner, and he came and asked me to let him in the landing window on the stairs,' remembers Brendan. 'Obviously being a wee brother, I said no until a bit of bribery – half a tin of Coke and half a bar of chocolate – got me to do it. I ran up the stairs, opened the window, checked where my ma was and gave him the all-clear.'

Martin went straight to their room and went to bed. 'He started to feel a bit sick,' says Brendan, 'but we thought it was all the Coke and chocolate he had eaten. Later that night he felt worse but wouldn't go to our ma as he thought he was in trouble after what had happened that day.'

The next morning, Martin's mother found him dead in his bed. 'He died of a brain haemorrhage,' says Tommy. He made a complaint to the RUC; two weeks later, according to Tommy, detectives came to the door and told him they couldn't take it any further.

'It was traumatic. Nobody would ever talk about it,' he says. 'We could never do anything when my mother and father were alive. That's why we just let it go.'

Tommy is in no doubt Martin was a victim of the Troubles. 'He should be remembered.'

✳ ✳ ✳ ✳ ✳

Name: *Tony McDowell*

Age: *12*

From: *Ardoyne, North Belfast*

Date of Death: *19/04/1973*

Tony McDowell had just got his first passport. The 12-year-old – who was a member of the Knights of Malta – was looking forward to going with his grandparents on the parish trip to Lourdes that June.

The eldest in his family, Tony lived with his Granny Sadie – who he called Mummy – and his Grandad Bobby, who had the house next door to his parents. It was not uncommon for children to be raised by close relatives, particularly in large families; Tony's mother would go on to have 11 children.

His grandparents idolised him. 'He got a Chopper bike from my mummy [Granny Sadie] and I think it was his life,' remembers his uncle Michael. 'He just loved that bike.'[198]

Tony loved comics – Granny Sadie bought him the *Topper*, *Beano*, *Dandy* and *Beezer* every week – and he kept them safely in their own drawer. He was also mad about Dinky cars, which he arranged in a circle in the bay window. He looked after his cars so carefully, his uncle Joe remembers, that he wouldn't even crash his Dinkys into one another.

He was also well-known for looking after people. When there was rioting outside, Joe remembers that 'instead of getting caught up in the excitement Tony ran back into his house to sit with his Granny Sadie and help keep her calm'.

He ran messages for his next-door neighbour, Patsy McArdle, and joined the Knights of Malta because Patsy was a member. 'That was reason enough for Tony to join as he went everywhere with me,' says Patsy.[199]

It was Holy Thursday. There had been firing in Ardoyne between the IRA and the British army's Parachute Regiment – a not uncommon occurrence. Tony had been helping his uncle Michael move into his new house in Craigavon, and Michael was driving him home.

Tony started to cry; he said, 'Uncle Michael, I'm hit, I'm hit.' Michael said, 'Don't be silly, son,' and then he said, 'No, no, get my mummy, get my mummy.'[200] Michael stopped the car; when he put his hand around Tony's back, he could feel the blood.

At the inquest into his death, the coroner said that 'gunmen, by causing a gun-battle with the army, caused this boy's death'.[201]

A report by the Historical Enquiries Team concluded that the forensic details 'strongly indicate that the shot which caused Tony's death was fired from the [British] Army observation post'.[202]

At his funeral, Tony's coffin was draped in the flag of the Knights of Malta. He never got to use his new passport; his Chopper bike was donated to an orphanage.

❇ ❇ ❇ ❇ ❇

Name: *Eileen Mackin*

Age: *14*

From: *Ballymurphy, West Belfast*

Date of Death: *17/05/1973*

Eileen and her friend Lucy had gone out for a walk. There had been rioting in Springhill Avenue earlier in the day, but by nine o'clock that evening the area was quieter.

A pupil at St Rose's Secondary School, she was also a member of Cumann na gCailíní, the girls' equivalent of the Fianna. A neighbour described her as 'one of the most popular lassies in this street. She would have done anything for you, and many a time ran errands for me.'[203]

According to *The Irish News*, the two girls were on the pavement when 'four high-velocity shots were fired at an Army Saracen'.[204] Eileen was hit in the stomach, and Lucy in the leg.

The newspaper quoted local residents who said the shots had come from the Protestant Springmartin estate; according to *Belfast Graves*, which commemorates the republican movement's dead, Eileen was killed by loyalist gunmen.[205]

The inquest into her death heard that she had been shot by gunmen who were firing at soldiers, and the *Belfast Telegraph* reported that the bullet which killed her had been fired from an Armalite rifle, a weapon which was used 'virtually exclusively' by the IRA.[206]

That evening Eileen had been due to go to a disco. 'The disco session was not on,' her grandmother said. 'If it had, Eileen would have been alive today.'[207]

✳ ✳ ✳ ✳ ✳

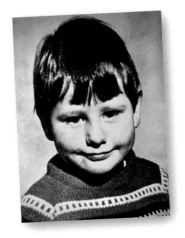

Name: *Paul Crummey*

Age: *4*

From: *Finaghy Road, West Belfast*

Date of Death: *26/05/1973*

Paul Crummey couldn't wait to start school. The four-year-old was to go to St John the Baptist Primary School – directly across the road from his home on Finaghy Road North – that September.

'He was my brother's first child,' says his uncle, Peter Crummey. 'He was a beautiful, loving boy.'

Paul would stand at the front gate and watch the other children going to school – among them, the writer Philip MacCann. 'Sometimes a four-year-old watched us walk to school from behind the front gate of Crummey's house,' he later wrote. 'We made it in safely the day Paul was shot at by gunmen aiming at passing British troops.'[208]

Paul was playing in the garden of his home when shots were exchanged between the IRA and a British army foot patrol. He was hit in the head and died later in hospital.

Both sides denied firing the fatal shot, but Paul's family believed the IRA was responsible. 'We are all stunned,' Paul's uncle Frank said after the funeral. 'There is no one to blame except the Provos.'

His great-uncle, the Rev. Sean Crummey – who concelebrated the requiem mass – described how he had been 'dangling him on my knee a couple of weeks ago at an uncle's wedding. He was a shy, loveable little child. We were trying to get him to dance with his cousin, but he wouldn't.'[209]

'Paul was such a young child that he had no chance to develop hobbies, interests and so on,' says Peter. 'I have no doubt that, like his siblings, he would have become a high achiever, very interested in sports and, in time, a loving and caring father.'

✳ ✳ ✳ ✳ ✳

Name: *David Walker*

Age: *16*

From: *Belvoir, South Belfast*

Date of Death: *21/06/1973*

David Walker was last seen getting into a car with three men near Shaw's Bridge in Belfast. It was half past eight in the morning; just before midnight, his body would be found lying in an entryway in O'Neill Street, off the Lower Falls. He had been shot in the head and chest.

Sixteen-year-old David had been walking to work. An apprentice on a government training scheme for school leavers who had been unable to find employment, he was described in newspaper reports as 'educationally sub-normal'.

According to the journalist Kevin Myers, David had boasted 'emptily' that he had been responsible for the UDA murder of a 17-year-old Catholic, Daniel Rouse, not knowing that one of the boys on the training scheme was a Catholic and a member of the Official IRA.

David was abducted and taken to the Lower Falls, where he was interrogated and, according to Myer, 'confessed to a murder he was innocent of.'[210]

According to *Lost Lives*, a man who was subsequently jailed for David's murder said he thought the teenager was a loyalist paramilitary. 'He told police he had been approached by a man in Leeson Street who asked him if he was 'man enough to shoot a member of the UFF murder gang'. The man said he would do it 'if there was proof that he was killing innocent Catholics', and was told David had been involved in the murder of Daniel Rouse.[211]

David was not a member of any paramilitary organisation and was not involved in the teenager's death.

Four days later the SDLP senator Paddy Wilson and a civil servant, Irene Andrews, were stabbed to death in Paddy Wilson's car in a 'frenzied' attack; a man later phoned the *News Letter* to say they had been killed in retaliation for David's murder.[212]

Among the many notices of sympathy posted in the *Belfast Telegraph* was one from David's parents and his brother and sisters: 'We did not have a last farewell or even say goodbye, for you were gone before we knew and only God knows why.'

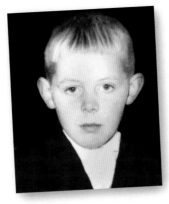

Name: *Henry Cunningham*

Age: *16*

From: *Carndonagh, Co Donegal*

Date of Death: *09/08/1973*

It was a sunny August evening. The Cunningham brothers – 21-year-old Robert, Herbie (20), and Henry, who was only 16 – and their three co-workers were on their way home to Donegal from Glengormley, just outside Belfast, where they had been working on a building site.

Herbie was driving; due to play in a band that evening, Robert took the opportunity to sleep in the back of the van, while Henry sat in front. The 16-year-old had just started going to dances, and had a date with his girlfriend in the Lilac Ballroom in Carndonagh that night.

Henry was the youngest son in a hard-working Presbyterian family of eight boys and five girls; Henry's father would hire a car on Sunday to bring his children to church.[213] 'If the weather's good and you've your work done round the house, you up and play football,' says Herbie.[214]

In the summer, the siblings would be 'out to the hill to work at peats'. The brothers had been working for a construction firm in Derry, but when work dried up, they undertook the 170-mile round trip to Belfast.

As they drive west along the M2, the sun is beaming down on the brothers' Bedford van.[215] 'We passed a slipway and saw three men up on the flyover ahead of us,' recalled Herbie. 'Next thing, I heard a noise like a shower of hail and I could see the flames coming flying from their guns. Henry cried out, "I'm hit."'[216]

The van is hit by more than 30 bullets; in a panic, Herbie manages to keep driving on burst tyres for three miles. 'I think they're all dead in the back. I'm roaring, turning round, roaring not knowing as none of them's answering me. I keeps m'foot to the pedal, I'll get as far away as possible.'[217]

It is thought the van was targeted by the UVF because it had Republic of Ireland number plates and their killers presumed its occupants were Catholic.

The family had no idea loyalists were responsible until Herbie read it in *Lost Lives*; an investigation by the Historical Enquiries Team found evidence of collusion in relation to the 'theft' of the weapon from a UDR base.[218]

Every year, an essay prize is awarded in Henry's honour to 16-year-olds in Inishowen. 'We can never bring Henry back,' say his brothers, 'but his name will forever be associated with the need to protect human rights and that's a good thing.'[219]

✳ ✳ ✳ ✳ ✳

Name: *Patrick Quinn*

Age: *16*

From: *Dungannon, County Tyrone*

Date of Death: *16/08/1973*

Patrick – Patsy – Quinn was the eldest in the family; a 'quiet lad, thoughtful by nature with a talent for sport'.[220] He and his younger brother Frankie, who was almost 12, did everything with each other. 'We were great mates. We boxed together, played football together, went to school together.

'I used to follow him about – you know, like younger brothers do. He was a very good-hearted lad.'

Both boys were members of St Anne's Boxing Club in Dungannon; the family – which was originally from Tyrone – had moved back to Dungannon after they were forced out of their home in Finaghy North in Belfast.

The Quinns were one of only two Catholic families left on their street, says Frankie; they were threatened by loyalists, and the words 'Patrick Quinn is next' appeared on a bridge near their home.

The final straw came in 1972, when the UDA marched to their house and smashed the front door and all the windows. 'We went up the road [to Tyrone] in cattle trailers like refugees,' remembers Frankie.

In Dungannon, Patsy joined the IRA's East Tyrone Brigade. He was arrested with a weapon and spent three months in Belfast's Crumlin Road Gaol before being sent to a training school. He escaped, and fled over the border to Monaghan. Patsy and another IRA member, Dan McAnallen, were killed when a rocket launcher exploded prematurely as they attacked the RUC station in the village of Pomeroy, County Tyrone.

The rocket launcher had been mounted on the back of a lorry; other IRA members drove the blood-stained vehicle containing their bodies for ten miles to a crossroads near Ballygawley, where they left their remains by the roadside, covered in sheets.[221]

At home in Dungannon, Patsy's parents, Alfie and Rose, waited; it was their seventeenth wedding anniversary.[222]

'I'll never forget the morning the priest told my mother at the front door,' says Frankie. 'All you could hear was a blood-curdling scream.'

✳ ✳ ✳ ✳ ✳

Name: *Anthony McGrady*

Age: *16*

From: *Donegall Road, West Belfast*

Date of Death: *25 / 08 / 1973*

The birthday card was dated 19 August 1973. 'Hope the whole year through / will be a bright and cheerful one in every way for you,' the verse read.

Anthony – 'Anto' – was 16. According to his brother Liam, Anto and his best friend had spent much of their school days in the Bog Meadows, and he had been delighted to leave school that June.

His favourite subjects had been art and singing: 'He used to race home from primary school all excited when he had learned a new song,' remembers Liam. 'He'd throw his schoolbag down, grab a kitchen chair and demand all our attention while he would stand on the chair and sing for all of us. His favourite song of all time was "The Unicorn".'

Anto was also a good athlete – 'the high jump and the long jump were his specialities' – and loved keeping pigeons, fishing, his Meccano set, Fleetwood Mac and *Top of the Pops*. He was a 'dapper dresser', says Liam. 'He even wore a dickie bow on his confirmation day, and regularly sported a cravat.'

Outside the family home sat his Morris 1100. 'Anto loved cars,' remembers Liam. It had come as no surprise when he found a job as an apprentice in a car repair garage on the Cliftonville Road in north Belfast; an animal-lover, Anto would bring the garage's mascot, a mongrel dog, home every weekend.

That Saturday, he was due to join his six siblings in their holiday cottage in Omeath, County Louth; instead, he died along with his employers, brothers Ronald and Sean McDonald, when the garage was attacked by the UVF.

The loyalists shot them and then bombed the building; one newspaper report said that their attackers threw the body of one of their victims on top of the bomb before they left. When it exploded, the premises were engulfed in flames; the dog was the only survivor.

The McDonald brothers had opened their garage on the Cliftonville Road after being forced out of their former workshop by loyalists.[223] One man was later jailed for seven years for his part in the killings.

Anto's family still have his birthday card. Inside is written, 'To Anthony, with love and best wishes. God bless, Mother and Father and all the family, XXX.'

✳ ✳ ✳ ✳ ✳

Name: *Bernard Teggart*

Age: *15*

From: *Ballymurphy, West Belfast*

Date of Death: *13 / 11 / 1973*

When Bernard Teggart and his twin brother Gerard were born, they made the paper.

'They were the biggest twins in the city,' says their older sister Alice Harper. 'My mother was in the *Irish News*, because one was 7 lbs 12 and the other was 7 lbs 8.' Identical twins, their sister remembers them as 'two wee imps, two real wee boys'.

Bernard had a beautiful singing voice; a favourite song was 'Bridge Over Troubled Water'.

The twins hated school. 'My daddy used to put them in the front door of St Kevin's [Primary School] and they would wait until they saw him moving off, and then they would go out the back door,' remembers Alice. When they were nine, they were sent to St Patrick's Training School on Belfast's Glen Road, where they stayed during the week.

Their father Danny had been shot dead two years before, one of 11 civilians killed by the British army in Ballymurphy in west Belfast between 9 and 11 August 1971. Alice and her other married sisters helped their mother raise their younger siblings.

'The very last words Bernard said to me were, "Alice, can I come to your house?", the way a child would say it. He said, "They're letting us out on Wednesday, Princess Anne's getting married, can I come to your house and watch it?"'

Instead, 15-year-old Bernard – who had a mental age of nine – was abducted from the school by the IRA. Unable to tell which twin was which, both boys were taken. Eventually Gerard was released and given his bus fare home; Bernard was shot in the back of the head and his body dumped outside the Floral Hall, in the grounds of Belfast Zoo. A cardboard placard bearing the word 'tout' had been hung around his neck.

'A drinks lorry had been held up when Bernard was on his way home and one of the gunmen had a gun at the driver's head, and our twin is supposed to have said, "Mister, leave that man alone,"' says Alice.

At Bernard's wake, Gerard had to be watched constantly. 'It was awful; you couldn't keep your eyes off Gerard. Any time there was nobody in the room he would take Bernard out of the coffin and put him on his knee. When Bernard was killed, part of Gerard died.'[224]

Alice and her family later fought for, and eventually received, an apology from the IRA. She also continues to campaign on behalf of Bernard and their father.

In 2015 the report of Northern Ireland's Historical Institutional Abuse Inquiry identified failures in the school's handling of the abductions and their aftermath as 'negligent and constituted systemic abuse'.[225]

Alice can't help but smile when she looks at her photograph of Bernard. 'I looked after him, and I have really lovely memories. Those are things you'll have until the day you die. Every time you look at Gerard, you can just picture Bernard.'

Name: *Kathleen Feeney*

Age: *14*

From: *Brandywell, Derry*

Date of Death: *14 / 11 / 1973*

Among Kathleen Feeney's prized possessions was a signed photograph of Eurovision Song Contest winner Dana.

Like Dana, 14-year-old Kathleen was a Derry girl. From Quarry Street in the Brandywell, Kathleen loved music and dancing, especially T-Rex and Suzi Quatro, and discos at the Long Tower Youth Club, which were run by her brother Danny; her favourite song was Michael Jacksons 'Ben'.[226]

She could also be mischievous – she often borrowed her younger brother John's shoes – and had just started smoking, though she took care to hide it from her parents.

A pupil at St Cecilia's College, the previous summer she and her friends from the youth club had gone to stay with families in Monaghan, part of a scheme to bring them away from the Troubles. Two weeks before she died, she wrote her Monaghan family a letter: 'I wish I was back in Monaghan again as I enjoyed myself so very much.' It was never posted.

That evening, Kathleen's sister Mary, who was a year older, had rushed home from school to watch Princess Anne's wedding. Kathleen, who was 'more militant', according to her brother Harry, told her off: 'What are you watching that for?'

Kathleen was chatting to a friend on the street when a British army mobile patrol drove across the Lecky Road. Shots were fired and Kathleen fell; she had been hit in the neck. Her brothers rushed out. John realised immediately it was his sister. 'He saw his shoes on her feet, and he knew it was her,' says Harry.

At the time, the IRA denied responsibility: 'We say categorically now that the shooting of young Kathleen Feeney was the work of the British Army and not of the Republican movement.'[227]

In 2005, following a campaign by the Feeney family, the IRA apologised and said it had killed Kathleen. 'Our failure to publicly accept responsibility for her death until now has only added to the hurt and pain of the Feeney family,' the statement said.[228]

Kathleen's family still keep her photograph of Dana, the clothes she was wearing the night she was killed, and the single cigarette that had been in her coat pocket.

Aftermath of Dublin bombing, May 1974.
Opposite: Celebrations in east Belfast
at the collapse of the Sunningdale
power-sharing assembly.

1974

- A two-week strike by the Ulster Workers' Council leads to power cuts, food shortages and road blocks that bring the Sunningdale power-sharing assembly crashing down

- Loyalist bombs in Dublin and Monaghan claim 34 lives, while IRA bombs in Britain kill 38, including pub bombings in Guildford and Birmingham and an attack on a military coach on the M62

- In December the IRA calls a truce that would last, in an imperfect form, for over a year

- Tartan outfits are all the rage as the Bay City Rollers enjoy huge chart success, while five teenagers from Derry's Bogside and Creggan form The Undertones.

Name: *Lee Haughton*

Age: *5*

From: *Manchester*

Date of Death: *04/02/1974*

It was just after midnight. Five-year-old Lee Haughton and his two-year-old brother Robert were dozing on the back seat with their mum and dad, Linda and Clifford, beside them; earlier they had been sitting on their parents' knees. The coach drove on through the night.

The family were on their way back to the British army base in Catterick where Clifford, a corporal in the Royal Regiment of Fusiliers, was stationed. They had been back home in Manchester for the weekend, vising friends and relatives; the bus had been specially hired for soldiers and their families. Clifford had only recently returned from Northern Ireland.

Lee 'loved doing exercises with his dad in front of the telly', says his aunt Kath Moores. Like most young boys, he also liked playing football, and took good care of his younger brother Robert.

'They were lovely, sweet children,' says another aunt, Jean Whittle. 'Lee loved Robert, he always had his arm round him to protect him. Lee would get into mischief where Robert wouldn't.'[229]

By 12.20 a.m. the coach was on the M62 near Bradford. John Barry Clark was driving about 500 yards behind. 'Suddenly there was an immense flash and I was running into wreckage.'[230]

A 50 lb bomb had been left in the luggage compartment underneath the coach. It exploded, ripping the bus virtually in half. On the back seat, Lee, Robert and their parents were right above the blast. They died instantly.

One of the first reporters on the scene, Neil Mackwood, wrote: 'The skeleton of the 49-seater coach, laid bare in the stark glare of the arc lamps was the grim reality. Behind it, stretching for more than 200 yards, was a trail of destruction …. I counted seven bodies, some covered with blankets hastily thrown over them before ambulancemen carried them away.'[231]

Twelve people were killed, including nine soldiers; the youngest of the soldiers, Paul Anthony Reid, was 17.

The IRA was believed to be responsible. Later that year a 25-year-old woman was sentenced to 30 years in jail for the bombing, though the IRA denied she was a member. In 1992 her conviction was quashed after it was accepted she had been wrongly convicted and that she had confessed to IRA involvement while suffering from a personality disorder.[232]

The family were buried together. There were 'two big coffins and two small ones'.[233]

✳ ✳ ✳ ✳ ✳

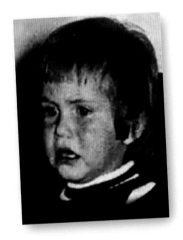

Name: *Robert Haughton*

Age: *2*

From: *Manchester*

Date of Death: *04/02/1974*

Robert Haughton's favourite song was 'Tie a Yellow Ribbon Round the Ole Oak Tree'. 'A neighbour tied yellow paper around an old oak tree nearby and he loved it,' remembers his aunt, Jean Whittle. 'He thought it was for him.'

The two-year-old was 'a shy little boy', but very funny; his five-year-old brother Lee was more mischievous. 'Robert was a little beggar, he was into everything, he used to make you laugh and he was very handsome,' says Jean. 'They both were.'

Another aunt, Kath Moores, remembers Robert was very particular about chocolate, and would only eat white chocolate.

Robert's parents, Clifford and Linda, had met when they were 15 and married at 18. Now 23, Clifford was a corporal in the Royal Regiment of Fusiliers and had completed three tours in Northern Ireland.

'He was injured a number of times,' says Kath. 'He was attacked when he was separated from his patrol in Belfast, bashed in the face, and he was run over at a checkpoint. But his proudest moment was when he delivered a child in Belfast. I remember him remarking that he was grateful his own two boys weren't living in Northern Ireland.'

That night, the family were on a bus carrying service personnel back to their base in Catterick after a weekend in Manchester. They took the coach at the last minute after Clifford's car failed to start. As it travelled along the M62 near Bradford, a bomb – believed to have been planted by the IRA – exploded, leaving bodies and debris strewn across the motorway. Robert and his family – his brother Lee and their parents Clifford and Linda - were among the 12 people killed.

The driver, blood running down his face, managed to steer onto the hard shoulder. Torch in hand, he got out and walked towards what had been the back of the bus. 'It wasn't long before he found the first of the bodies. It was that of a child who he reckoned was no more than two.'[234]

The next morning, the devastation became all too apparent. 'Amid the carpet of glass and twisted metal which covered part of the M62 carriageway lay broken gramophone records and a man's shoe. A little further on was a Fusiliers' cap and a child's abandoned toy.'[235]

※ ※ ※ ※ ※

Name: *Thomas Donaghy*

Age: *16*

From: *Rathcoole, Newtownabbey*

Date of Death: *11/02/1974*

Thomas Donaghy was the heart of his family. Known as Tucker to his friends, he was always Thomas at home. 'My mummy used to tell people off, "You don't call him Tucker, you call him Thomas,"' says his sister Marian.

'He was always tired at night when he came in,' says his brother Jim. 'And he always liked his wee cigarette and drink at night, which my mother didn't know,' adds another brother, Joe.

He loved football – Thomas was a Liverpool supporter – and fishing; a former pupil of Stella Maris Secondary School, he had gone on fishing trips to places like Donegal.

Thomas could be daring – when he was eight or nine, he and his friend went missing. They had decided they were going to Butlins; instead they were brought home in a police car.

As a teenager he was 'mad about his clothes', says Joe, particularly his favourite bomber jacket, and was proud of his hair. 'His sister was the same, always saying, "Don't touch the hair, don't touch the hair."'

'He was so full of life,' adds Marian. 'He loved going out with his mates, going to the dances at Stella Maris school or going down to the chippy. When Thomas died, they brought us down a lot of food from the chip shop.'

An apprentice butcher at Abbey Meats, Thomas had been working there for a year when he was killed. Every morning, he got a lift with his co-workers; when their car arrived at the premises, UDA/UFF gunmen opened fire. The vehicle was riddled with bullets; trapped in the back seat, Thomas was unable to get out. 'Apparently the two wee girls in the back tried to save him, because he was the youngest,' says Joe. 'One of them lay across him.' One of them, Thomas's 18-year-old neighbour, Margaret McErlean, died later.

The five in the car were all Catholics from the Bawnmore area of Rathcoole - a Catholic enclave in a predominantly Protestant area.[236] The Donaghys are in no doubt they were targeted deliberately.

The Donaghy siblings still live in the family home. Nearby, a Tricolour flutters over a memorial to those from the Rathcoole area who lost their lives in the Troubles; among them, the hunger striker Bobby Sands. When Marian visits, she runs her fingertips over Thomas's name; she goes to his grave 'most days'. 'It's just part of the past to some people, but not for us.'

⁎ ⁎ ⁎ ⁎ ⁎

Name: *Michael McCreesh*

Age: *15*

From: *Dromintee, Co Armagh*

Date of Death: *10/03/1974*

Michael McCreesh carried his hand-held four-track cassette player with him everywhere he went.

The 15-year-old – from Dromintee in the heart of the Mourne Mountains in south Armagh – loved listening to all kinds of music, his only sibling Sean recalls.

He also 'loved anything to do with wheels and a motor', says Sean. 'He spent his evenings and weekends tinkering with old motorbikes and cars.' His best friend, 18-year-old Michael Gallagher, had a Ford Zephyr. 'The Gallaghers were a large family and myself and Michael just loved hanging around with them,' Sean recalls.

Michael was tall for his age, and was already six foot; in his final year at St Paul's High School in Bessbrook, he wasn't particularly interested in school, and helped out at his father's pub – the Three Steps Inn – at weekends; Captain Robert Nairac would be abducted from the same pub three years later. He also worked on the family farm – 'especially if it had anything to do with tractors', laughs Sean.

The green Morris 1000 van had been abandoned near the church when the two friends, along with Michael Gallagher's brothers, Owen and Pat, went to investigate. It was a Sunday evening; the boys were in Michael Gallagher's car. 'Paper Roses' – the Marie Osmond hit – was playing on Michael McCreesh's cassette player.

'Michael was just crazy about cars and vans and had probably gone to the van out of curiosity to investigate,' his father Desmond said.[237]

When he opened the door, the van exploded. His body was blown across the road; only four wheels remained of the van.

His friend Michael Gallagher died of his injuries four days later; his brother Owen, who was 14, was blinded.

The bomb had been left by the IRA; local assembly member Seamus Mallon criticised the British army for failing to deal with it before it exploded. 'This is not the first time they have ignored a suspicious vehicle with fatal consequences,' he said.[238] An army spokesman said the bomb disposal officer in the area was one of the busiest in Northern Ireland.[239]

At Michael's funeral his fellow students from St Paul's formed a guard of honour, and local schoolchildren carried wreaths.

'Parents must realise that any of the children who carried wreaths in today's cortege could have been the innocent victims,' the parish priest said.[240]

※ ※ ※ ※ ※

Name: *Baby Doherty*

Age: *Unborn*

From: *Sheriff Street, Dublin*

Date of Death: *17/05/1974*

Colette Doherty's baby was to be born that evening. She was hoping for a boy.

The 21-year-old and her two-year-old daughter Wendy had gone to Dublin's Rotunda Hospital earlier that day, where Colette was diagnosed with pre-eclampsia and high blood pressure. The hospital told her the baby's arrival was imminent, and she was instructed to take Wendy home and return immediately.

But Colette had always loved shopping, Wendy explains, and couldn't resist going for a few last-minute baby purchases. By 5.30p.m. they were heading home, towards John's grocery shop on Sheriff Street, Wendy walking between her mother and her pram. They were on Talbot Street when the bomb exploded.

'Mammy was blown one way and the pram was blown the other way,' says Wendy. 'I was shielded. When the bomb went off, I was just left standing.'[241] Lost and wandering the streets, Wendy was found an hour later by a fireman.

Her mother and unborn sibling were among 34 victims of the Dublin and Monaghan bombings. Carried out by the UVF, it was the deadliest day in the history of the Troubles. Wendy has no conscious memory of the day, but has tried for years to put together a story of what happened.

Years later, when Wendy herself was in the Rotunda giving birth, the gynaecologist remembered her as the little girl who had been brought by her mother to the hospital. The doctor told her how she and her husband had gone to help after the explosion. 'He saw a silhouette of a pregnant woman and travelled with her in the ambulance. He noticed there was not a scratch on her, but she was dead – she had died of a heart attack.'

Wendy's father John was 'a broken man'; after Colette's death, John discovered that she had already bought clothes to fit Wendy until she was five.

At the inquests in 2004, Baby Doherty was officially listed as the 34th victim of the Dublin and Monaghan bombings. The baby's gender was never recorded.

✳ ✳ ✳ ✳ ✳

Name: *Jacqueline O'Brien*

Age: *16 months*

From: *Lower Gardiner Street, Dublin*

Date of Death: *17/05/1974*

Jacqueline O'Brien loved playing on the swings in Mountjoy Square. Only 16 months old, the toddler lived with her parents, John and Anna O'Brien, and her baby sister Anne Marie, in Lower Gardiner Street in Dublin's north inner city.

'Her favourite food was baked beans,' remembers her uncle Thomas O'Brien. 'She loved her teddy bear.'

John and Anna were pushing their two babies in a pram past the Welcome Inn on Parnell Street when the car, a green Hillman Avenger, exploded. There had been no warning. 'The car was parked outside,' says Thomas. 'They got the full blast.'

The bomb was one of three that went off almost simultaneously in Dublin that Friday evening; there was another explosion in Monaghan. 'The dead and injured lay on the pavement, in the roadway and inside shop windows,' one reporter wrote.[242] Twenty-six people and an unborn child were killed in the Dublin explosions and seven died in Monaghan in what was the greatest loss of life in a single day during the Troubles.

The 'grimmest place in Dublin' was the city morgue; the maimed bodies of Jacqueline and Anne Marie lay there, unidentified. According to *The Irish Times*, it was almost 48 hours after the explosions before staff had 'the realisation that both their parents had died too'.[243]

Anna's father Paddy Doyle was brought to the morgue by Gardaí. 'Jesus, when I looked, all bodies, just legs, they weren't even their own legs … the two grandkids, I seen them, they were all in a small box, foot to foot.'[244]

'When we told me ma, I'll never forget the screaming,' says Thomas. 'She was saying, "The two kids." I just remember her screaming the roof off.'

Nobody has ever been convicted of the killings. Loyalist paramilitaries – the majority of whom were members of the UVF – were responsible. The 2003 Barron Report concluded that a finding that members of the security forces in Northern Ireland could have been involved was 'neither fanciful nor absurd', and that it was likely that members of the UDR and RUC 'either participated in, or were aware of' the preparations for the attacks.[245]

The families of the victims continue to campaign on behalf of their loved ones. The U2 song 'Raised by Wolves' is about the atrocity; the O'Brien family's only photograph of Jacqueline was displayed as a tribute during the band's 2015 world tour.

'I always wonder,' says Thomas, 'if they'd been alive today, would they be married and have their own families?'

✳ ✳ ✳ ✳ ✳

Name: *Anne Marie O'Brien*

Age: *4½ months*

From: *Lower Gardiner Street, Dublin*

Date of Death: *17/05/1974*

Anne Marie O'Brien was born on her sister Jacqueline's first birthday – 2 January 1974. She was so young – only four and a half months – that her family have no photographs of her.

Unlike her older sister, Anne Marie was a very quiet baby, their uncle Thomas O'Brien remembers.

The baby died in her pram along with her sister. Their parents, John and Anna, were pushing the pram along Dublin's Parnell Street when a no-warning bomb exploded; they were also killed. 'The whole family was wiped out,' says Thomas. 'Two generations gone.'

The O'Briens were among 33 people and an unborn child killed in UVF explosions in Dublin and Monaghan, the greatest number of fatalities of any single day of the Troubles.

The family were buried together in Glasnevin Cemetery; the girls' tiny white coffins were so small it took only one person to place them into the grave. They are remembered in the memorial garden at Glasnevin. 'We have a little spot and we planted a tree there,' says Thomas.

When the family's home, a flat in a tenement in Lower Gardiner Street, was pulled down, one of the replacement buildings was named O'Brien Hall in their memory.

The O'Briens are part of the Pat Finucane Centre's 'In Their Footsteps' legacy campaign, in which bereaved families donate a pair of shoes to represent a loved one lost in the Troubles. Jacqueline is represented by a pair of navy sandals; in place of a photograph, a pair of pink knitted baby bootees are all that is left to remember Anne Marie.

Their note reads: 'We were murdered with my Daddy and Mammy ... we were blown up in the Dublin bombings in Parnell Street. Please get us justice so we can rest in peace.'

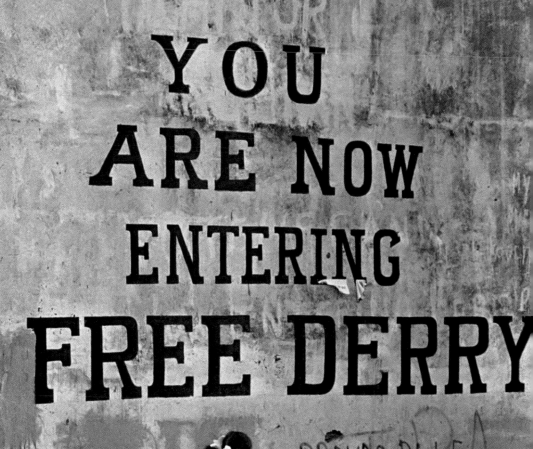

Name: *Michelle Osborne*

Age: *12*

From: *Ligoniel, North Belfast*

Date of Death: *09/06/1974*

Michelle Osborne's school photograph shows a smiling girl with long, blonde hair. 'She was a sweet wee girl,' recalls Angela O'Connor, a classmate of Michelle's at Our Lady of Mercy Secondary School in Ballysillan, north Belfast. 'She was quiet, and on the shy side.'

That Sunday the 12-year-old was out with her father, Michael, and brother and sister, John and Karen, on a family trip to a greyhound track near Hannahstown in west Belfast. Michael was a well-known billiard player who also kept and ran greyhounds, and often went out to the Ballymacward greyhound kennel club to give the dogs a trial run.

About a hundred greyhound racing enthusiasts and their families had been at the track 'for a sunny afternoon out'.[246] The 'hare' had broken down, and when a sunshower came on, the family returned to their van.

A 200 lb bomb had been left in another vehicle in the car park; it exploded just as the Osbornes were about to leave. 'I tried to get John out and saw that he, Karen and Michelle had been injured,' Michael later told the inquest into Michelle's death. 'I spoke to Michelle as she was being taken away in an army helicopter but she could not answer me.'[247]

Michelle's had been a difficult birth, said her mother Eileen. Speaking of the bombing, she remarked, 'She had a terrible death … Her daddy took her for a day's outing and then this is what happened …. I don't know why they picked on us. We were very quiet.'[248]

The family had been due to go on holiday in two weeks; the trip, to a holiday camp, was to be their first break in years.

The UFF – a cover name for the UDA – admitted responsibility. In a call to a Belfast newsroom, a 'Captain White of the UFF' said the van, containing 200 lb of explosives, had been left in the club's car park 'for collection'. He said they 'regretted' Michelle's death.[249]

Her father, brother and sister were unable to attend her funeral as they were still in hospital. Her schoolmates formed a guard of honour; dressed in their school uniforms, their hands clasped before them, they escorted her coffin to Milltown Cemetery.

Her simple white headstone reads: 'In loving memory of our darling daughter Michelle.'

✳ ✳ ✳ ✳ ✳

Name: *Michael Browne*

Age: *16*

From: *Bangor, Co Down*

Date of Death: *12/07/1974*

At 16, Michael Browne was the eldest of four brothers; the youngest, Brendan, was 13. 'Michael was very streetwise,' says Brendan. 'He would have got up to mischief.'

A good footballer – he had played for his school teams – Michael 'liked his snooker and card school'. Brendan recalls Michael coming up with a scheme when playing cards: Brendan had to keep watch, and when Michael had won a few hands he had to interrupt, and claim Michael had promised to take him to the cinema.

'I started to do that – he would say, "Lads, I have to go, I've promised him," and then he'd say to me, "Ah for God's sake, I was making a fortune there," and it meant they never got the chance to win the money back.'

A Catholic family living in a predominantly Protestant town, the majority of their friends and neighbours were Protestant. As the boys got older, 'You started to feel the atmosphere,' says Brendan. 'You felt second-class. You knew which bars not to go to.'

Michael had just left school, and was working as a car sprayer. He was also hanging around with a rough crowd and was the only Catholic among a group of Protestants. 'Michael was up to no good at times as well,' says Brendan. He recalls catching sight of Michael's tattoo: it was a red hand of Ulster.

Michael had just returned from holiday in Scotland and went out to the 'Eleventh night' bonfire just before midnight. His body was found on playing fields just over an hour later; he had been shot in the head. The artist Charlie Whisker cradled Michael's body. 'He was alive and fighting for breath, even though unconscious, so I did everything to try and help him.'[250]

Two 21-year-olds were later jailed for life for his murder. As they were led from the dock, one of the men shouted, 'Up the UVF.'[251]

'They were told to go out and shoot a Catholic,' says Brendan, 'and they didn't really know any Catholics in the estate. They couldn't find the one they wanted, and the only other person they knew was our Michael, so they shot him.'

Brendan later met one of his brother's killers, who apologised. 'He said, "I'm terribly sorry."'

Brendan named his own son Michael, after his brother; the boy, who had special needs, died when he was seven years old. He was 'the spitting image' of his uncle Michael.

✳ ✳ ✳ ✳ ✳

Name: *Joseph McGuinness*

Age: *13*

From: *New Lodge, North Belfast*

Date of Death: *15/08/1974*

Joseph McGuinness 'hardly left the corner of the street', said his mother Ellen.[252] The 13-year-old was one of four children. A pupil at St Aloysius' School, Ellen said he took 'a keen interest' in the local Artillery Youth Club.

'I'm heartbroken,' said Ellen. 'Just before ten o'clock he came into the house and asked me for the money to get chips and then he went off with his friends.'

A 15-year-old who was with him said that he and Joe – as his friends called him – and two others had been on their way to a chip shop in York Street when 'a crowd of Protestants started shouting at us from the corner of North Queen Street and Brougham Street'.

The boys ran. 'They were shouting "Fenian bastard" at him and he shouted at them to come up and fight. Then the shooting started and I saw Joe hitting the ground. I couldn't do anything because there was still shooting.'[253]

Joseph managed to stagger back to his own street; he was taken to hospital, where he died early the following morning. A UDA commander was later jailed in connection with Joseph's death.

'He wasn't a bad boy,' said his mother Ellen. 'These Troubles affect all the children. It makes them aggressive and wild. It changes them. They just can't settle down.'[254]

✳ ✳ ✳ ✳ ✳

Name: *Patrick McGreevy*

Age: *15*

From: *New Lodge, North Belfast*

Date of Death: *19/09/1974*

Patrick McGreevy was shot dead as he stood outside a café in north Belfast. 'A gunman in a moving car sprayed the entrance to the Pacific Café, in Clifton Street, with a hail of bullets.'[255]

A pupil at St Patrick's College, Bearnageeha in north Belfast, Patrick had been among a group of nine people fired on by the gunmen.

'I saw the two young chaps leave the café,' said one eyewitness. 'Then there was a burst of gunfire and we all threw ourselves to the ground. When the car passed I saw one of the boys still lying on the ground. His head was covered in blood.'[256] According to *Lost Lives*, Patrick had been killed by the UVF.

Patrick's father, a seaman, had just departed on a six-week voyage to South Africa.

A death notice placed in the Irish News described him as a Volunteer in the 2nd Battalion, Official Fianna Eireann, who had been 'murdered by sectarian thugs'.[257]

Name: *Michael Hughes*

Age: *16*

From: *Newry*

Date of Death: *18/10/1974*

In the Derrybeg estate, everyone knew Michael Hughes. Most people knew him by his nickname, Sticky; according to his sister Kathleen, the 16-year-old made friends easily, and was popular.[258]

Instantly recognisable because of his 'distinctive ginger hair', Michael enjoyed his social life, and was often at the local community centre. He also liked football and reading books about Irish history. At school, he was 'quiet and noted for being a bright pupil'.[259]

Eldest of seven children, Michael had been only 14 when his father, Patsy – an IRA volunteer – died, one of nine people, including three customs officers and three IRA members, killed when an IRA bomb exploded prematurely at the customs clearing station at the Killeen border post.

Michael had to grow up fast; the family home was frequently raided by the British army, and his mother – who had been pregnant with her youngest daughter when her husband was killed – needed her eldest son's help to raise his brothers and sisters.[260]

He had just left school and had completed his second week at work in the nylon factory in Newry; he had also joined the IRA. Michael was shot dead by a British army soldier; according the army, he had been among a group of armed youths who had tried to hijack a bus and had refused to throw down his weapon when challenged.[261]

This was disputed by local people and by representatives of the SDLP and the Republican Clubs, who said Michael had no gun, and had been shot in the back.

One witness told the *Newry Reporter* that the young people, who were unarmed, were approaching a bus when soldiers rushed from a concealed position in a field and raced across the road. 'The youths turned and fled and as they ran one soldier opened fire, hitting Hughes,' the eyewitness said, adding that as 'a local woman tried to place a crucifix on the dying youth's lips and breathe a prayer into his ear she was ordered away by troops'.[262]

SDLP, Alliance and Independent members on Newry and Mourne District Council later called for a public inquiry into the circumstances of Michael's death. Councillor Thomas McGrath said he had spoken to Michael ten minutes before he was shot 'and he had not the attitude of a person who was about to embark on any illegal activity'.[263]

＊＊＊＊＊

Name: *Michael Meenan*

Age: *16*

From: *Shantallow, Derry*

Date of Death: *30/10/1974*

Michael Meenan was always known as Ben.

At a fortieth anniversary commemoration in Derry, his brother Joe described the 16-year-old as a 'relentless Volunteer in the Shantallow area, who along with his comrades showed not only military capability but also community action'.

During the Ulster Workers' Council strike earlier that year he had helped collect water from an old spring well and deliver it to homes.[264]

He was killed instantly when a bomb exploded prematurely as he sat inside a car on a garage forecourt on Derry's Strand Road. According to the *Derry Journal*, the driver had got out and asked the attendant for petrol. 'As the attendant was going to get the petrol, the car suddenly exploded and went on fire.' After the fire was extinguished, 'the body of the youth was found in the back seat'.

A British army spokesman said an explosives charge of about 3 lbs had been in the back seat 'and it was obvious the dead youth had been killed instantly in the blast'.[265]

Death notices placed by the IRA described Michael as a lieutenant in the IRA's Second Battalion, Derry Brigade, and said he had 'died on active service'; his family said his death was the result of an accident.[266]

Name: *John McDaid*

Age: *16*

From: *Strand Road, Derry*

Date of Death: *07/12/1974*

It was only the start of December, but John McDaid had already bought his younger sister Anne her Christmas present.

That was typical of John. 'He was just a perfectionist', remembers his sister. 'He was into all his music and loved heavy metal bands – Black Sabbath, Led Zeppelin, Deep Purple. There wasn't a square inch of his bedroom that didn't have a poster on it, and he was mad about Leeds United, and just fanatical about keeping everything.'

John could also be stubborn: 'He could huff for Ireland,' says Anne. 'When he was smaller, he used to go off and sit on the bottom step. I don't remember that, but if somebody did something on him, he was so thick and stubborn, he just would not give in.'

'He was very determined', remembers his brother Paul. 'If he was arguing with my father, if he didn't get his way or he didn't like something he would have huffed, and my father used to tempt him. He enjoyed the craic with him and he enjoyed the cut and thrust with him.'

The family ran a bakery in the Bogside; John and Paul helped out at weekends, or during school holidays. 'John eventually reckoned he wasn't being paid enough by my father and he went on strike,' says Paul. 'My father thought this was hilarious and he sort of argued it out with him a wee while and then he gave in, so John got his pay rise.'

John had left St Columb's College after completing his O Levels; 'he had a few run-ins with the priests about his hair,' says Anne.

'He had this mad curly hair – I suppose it was the style in the day - but he was sent home from school one day to get his hair cut so he went in and he brushed it and he wet it and he went back in again and they were none the wiser. There was no way he was getting his hair cut.'

His friend Seamus Soal recalls John's comic side. At school, the desks were arranged in rows; 'as the priest turned to walk down the aisle … John got out behind him holding his own book and mimicked him the whole length of the class. The whole class fell apart laughing.'

John's determination had also led him to join the IRA: "We were growing up in that period of time from the start of the civil rights movement through to internment, and we were becoming more and more politically aware,' says Paul. 'Bloody Sunday was the watershed for everybody in Derry.'

That night Anne had been Christmas shopping; she was wrapping John's Christmas present in the living room when he came in.

'He said, 'what's that, what is it?' and I said, 'you're not allowed to look at it'. Away he went, and I never saw him again.

'We heard the explosion a few hours later, then the knock came to the door. It was Father Mulvey, and our lives just changed completely.

John was killed instantly when a bomb exploded prematurely in a derelict house on Bridge Street.

A member of the 1st Battalion of the Derry Brigade of the IRA, John was buried on the same day as another young Derry IRA member, 22-year-old Ethel Lynch, who had been fatally wounded in another premature explosion.

That Christmas, Anne opened her present from John; it was a Timex watch. 'He had written the card for it. I still have it to this day.'[267]

✳ ✳ ✳ ✳ ✳

Families bereaved by the Troubles donated shoes representing their loved ones to the 'In Their Footsteps' campaign by the Pat Finucane centre.

Patrick Barnard

Hillcrest Bar, Dungannon

17 March 1976

WHY

Jacqueline O'Brien

Marie O'Brien

3

Families

'They took a child off the road, put his hood over his head and murdered him. I think the world should know these things.'

'Nobody knows my Philip's name.' A thin, frail-looking woman in her eighties, Maureen Rafferty's eyes sparkle as she describes her son. 'He had brains to burn, you know. He wanted to be an architect, and he said he was going to build me a house.'

A widow, Maureen now lives alone in what was once the family home in west Belfast. Her two other children, a son and a daughter, both live in England. She encouraged them to go away, because then she would know they were safe.

'When Philip was murdered I didn't lose one son, I lost my whole family, because I was afraid for them and I encouraged them to go away so they would be safe. I'm still scared, that'll not go away.' She leans forward in her chair, her voice strong and determined. 'I want the world to know my Philip's name.'

On 30 January 1973, 14-year-old Philip Rafferty was abducted by the UDA as he walked to band practice. When he didn't return home, Maureen went to look for him. She gave the police a favourite photograph, taken at a festival in the Botanic Gardens.

'They took pictures and put them onto badges. Philip had said to me, "I don't look too bad in that one," and I said, "Ah, you're lovely, son." I went looking for it because it was a photo he liked.'

Philip had been taken to the Giant's Ring, a beauty spot on the outskirts of Belfast. He was beaten, then shot in the head. When his clothes were returned to Maureen, the duffel coat she had bought him to keep him warm as he walked to band practice was saturated with blood.

'He loved music, you know. The house was always full of music. When he got into the James Connolly Band, he was so delighted. I couldn't not have let him go,' Maureen remembers.

'They took a child off the road, put his hood over his head and murdered him. I think the world should know these things.'

At its most fundamental, Maureen's desire is simply for acknowledgement – that her son lived, and was loved, and should not have died. Her appeal is one that has been repeated time and time again by families who have lost children as a result of the Troubles.

The death of a child is an unimaginable tragedy; for those, like Maureen, who are forced to live with this reality, then it is imperative that their children's lives are recognised, the truth is told, and the record is set straight.

For many, knowledge is a vital part of that acknowledgment. They need to know what happened to their loved one, to find out how or why they died, or to have their name cleared, or somebody held accountable.

It has turned many relatives into campaigners, fighting for the truth, or justice, or an apology, even as they continue to live with the trauma occasioned by their loss.

Police search for evidence following the discovery of the body of Philip Rafferty.

The landmark volume *Lost Lives* is the only work in existence which comes close to a full list of all those who died as a result of the conflict in Northern Ireland. Compiled by David McKittrick, Seamus Kelters, Brian Feeney, Chris Thornton and David McVea, it is perhaps the most significant book ever written on the Troubles. As such, it represents both a valuable body of research as well as an important acknowledgement of the more than 3,700 lives lost to the Troubles, and it is unlikely to ever be surpassed in either scale or scope.

The authors' criterion was that they would include 'all deaths directly related to the Troubles.' [*Lost Lives*, p18]. We have chosen to include nine children who do not have an entry in *Lost Lives*; in each case, their families believe that they too were killed as a result of the conflict in Northern Ireland.

These include children like two-year-old Francis McGuigan, who died after his home was filled with CS gas; Kevin McCauley, 13, a Fianna member who was killed while building a barricade; 12-year-old Tony Diamond, shot and killed accidentally while playing with a gun; Martin Corr, also 12, who was found dead in bed after being arrested and beaten by the British army; three-year-old Gary Gormley and eight-year-old Damien Harkin, knocked down and killed by British army vehicles outside their homes in Derry within six weeks of each other in 1971. In effect, these children have never been officially recognised as victims of the Troubles.

'He is a person,' says Margaret McGuigan of her younger brother Francis. 'He was there, and he did die during the Troubles.'

'Damien was never mentioned,' says his mother Lily Harkin. The eight-year-old was largely forgotten, remembered only by his family and in the local area,

Jim Doherty's family are still searching for answers.

Funeral of Annette McGavigan.

until a memoir by one of his former classmates, Tony Doherty, brought his name to a wider audience. 'It means a lot, now that he's being remembered.'

The passage of time – and the advent of a more peaceful Northern Ireland – means that siblings who were often preoccupied with raising their own young families or simply surviving the Troubles are now able to reflect, while the advent of relative peace has created the space for a multiplicity of projects which encourage people to tell their stories through oral history, the arts or initiatives aimed at promoting peace and reconciliation.

Damien has since featured in newspapers, online, and in a play telling the stories of six families of children killed in the Troubles. *The Crack in Everything*, by Jo Egan, premiered in November 2018, the first production to come out of a new Peacebuilding Academy based at Derry's Playhouse Theatre; both Lily and Tony took part.

'We should have been quoted saying our lad was killed in the Troubles, not that it's a road accident,' says Lily's character. 'It wasn't a normal road accident really, you know.'[1]

'Damien's death is never acknowledged as a death of the Troubles,' says Tony. 'If you read *Lost Lives,* and in the chronology of the Troubles, there's no mention of Damien at all. Without acknowledgement, what do you have? You have humiliation, you have loss.'

The Harkin family still live in Derry's Bogside, within walking distance of the area's famous murals. Among them is an image of a girl in a green school uniform – Annette McGavigan. Shot less than two months after Damien was killed, she was the hundredth civilian to die in the Troubles.

Each day, tourists take photographs of Annette's mural, or buy souvenirs bearing her image. She has become a powerful – and highly public – symbol of loss and remembrance; for her family, it is a way of keeping Annette's name alive. 'We cannot forget about our loved ones and never will,' says her brother Martin. 'There isn't a day when I don't think about Annette but I suppose it's good to think that way too.'

His father spent hours standing at the railings in front of his daughter's mural; each day, Martin and his siblings would come home from school to find their mother crying on the landing, Annette's clothes and newspaper clippings about her death spread out in front of her.

In interview after interview, the brothers and sisters of victims have recounted, often through tears, how their sibling's death had destroyed their mother.

Alice Harper's mother Bella Teggart had already lost her husband Danny, who was one of 11 civilians killed in Ballymurphy between 9 and 11 July 1971. Two years later, Bella's 15-year-old son Bernard was abducted and killed by the IRA.

Mural of Annette McGavigan, Bogside, Derry.

'She said to me, "Your Daddy was my best friend and he was my husband,"' says Alice. "But I carried Bernard for nine months, he was part of me."'

'The night he died my mummy might as well have been shot with him,' says Maureen Griffin, the older sister of 16-year-old Michael Neill. 'She died that night.' Mrs Neill did die soon afterwards, only a year and seven months after her son; it was a pattern that was repeated time and time again.

Many have been unwilling – or simply unable – to speak about their loss until now; others still cannot.

'For years there was never even a photograph up in the house,' is how one woman described the family reaction to her sister's death. 'It was just shut down, nobody spoke about it. No photos went up. It was as if, *"you don't talk about, it goes away"*. But it doesn't, it doesn't.'

Nine-year-old Gordon Gallagher died in his own garden; a bomb left by the IRA exploded while he was out playing with his brothers. His parents, Billy and Pat, moved away from their home in the Creggan area of Derry as soon as they could; the trauma of Gordon's death meant Pat can recall little of her baby daughter's development. 'I remember her in a wee dress sitting on the carpet, and the next time I remember seeing her she was running out the sitting room door, she was walking.'

Mollie Barrett's daughter Tina was only seven when her older brother Danny was killed, shot by a soldier as he sat on the wall outside their home in Ardoyne in north Belfast in 1981. Unable to cope, Mollie had Tina's long hair cut short. 'I was always a woman able to run my home, but I couldn't wring a dishcloth out, couldn't make food,' Mollie remembers. 'Tina had the most beautiful long ringlets and I got them cut so she'd be able to comb her own hair. To comb Tina's hair was out of the question, I couldn't do it.'

'When I think back to childhood it's just tears and sadness and mummy being in bed, but you always knew this wasn't normality,' adds Tina.[2]

A 2014 report by the Belfast-based WAVE Trauma Centre described how families affected by such experiences 'develop unhealthy methods of communication which can range from silence to intrusive attempts to discuss the traumatic events and imposing their interpretations of those events on other family members, including children'.

Parents may no longer be able to effectively function in their parental role, and families experience 'changes in how they function, changing domestic routines, financial situations and the potential loss of former friendships and social networks'.[3]

A 2015 study carried out by Ulster University found that almost 30 per cent of the population of Northern Ireland suffer from mental health problems, and nearly half of those are as a direct result of the Troubles.[4] The prevalence of mental health problems are greater in Northern Ireland than in the rest of the UK, and are exacerbated by unemployment, low educational achievement, and social deprivation. In 2018 Together for You - a group of Northern Ireland's mental health charities – warned that 'Northern Ireland has a 25% higher overall prevalence of mental illness than England – 1 in 5 adults here have a mental condition at any one time.' It also has the highest suicide rate in the UK.[5]

Of the almost 100 families interviewed during the research for this book, there is scarcely one which has not been touched, to a greater or lesser degree, by such issues. Parents such as Desmond Healey, whose 12-year-old son Kevin was shot by the British army in Newry in 1973, have taken their own lives; so too have siblings. Many died young, broken by their loss. Others turned to alcohol in order to cope.

'His reaction to it all was drinking,' was a typical response. 'In the pub. I think that was his way of dealing with it – just not be there, and then he wouldn't have to deal with it.'

'I always put on a front because you don't want to upset your mummy and daddy.'

Brothers and sisters were sent to bed – in some cases, a bed they had shared with their dead sibling. Often there was no explanation. 'There was no counselling in those days,' was an oft-repeated statement. 'You just had to get on with it.'

Parents, siblings, friends, neighbours blamed themselves. 'My father took it real bad,' said Tony Diamond's brother Neil. Twelve-year-old Tony died after being shot in the head when he and another boy went to play with a gun in Derry's Creggan estate in 1972. 'My father went missing one night and we found him, he had climbed the cemetery wall and he was sleeping at the grave. He sort of blamed himself. It was hard on the family.'

Jimmy Dempsey recalls going to the republican plot in Belfast's Milltown Cemetery – where his son John was buried – after it was reopened ahead of another burial. 'I knew it was John's grave, it was about ten feet down … I slept in that grave until eleven o'clock that night. This is the way your mind goes.'

John had been shot by the British army; Jimmy later went to the barracks. 'Three or four in the morning I was attacking that on my own, climbing up on top of it, but they wouldn't shoot me. They shot my son, but they were torturing me, they wouldn't shoot me. You do these mad things.'

In some cases, families broke up as parents blamed each other for their child's death; the surviving children were left with a single, often highly traumatised, parent; others lost homes or schools as they were sent to live with older siblings, or families moved completely.

Oliver Tristan Barker keeps a folder entitled 'Ripples'. He was only three when his older brother James was killed in the Omagh bomb. 'I have no memory of my brother – well, I have one memory, which I'm pretty sure is false,' he says. 'I've simply had to live with the consequences thereafter. I have no grief because

I never knew him, but I certainly have observed what it's done to my family.'

The Barkers moved from Buncrana, County Donegal, back to England; his parents – Donna-Maria and Victor – separated.

'The folder is called "Ripples" because that's the way it affects families. It has had a profound effect on my family and on my family life in that it set my parents on diametrically opposed paths.'

These ripples are still felt by many in Northern Ireland. It is virtually impossible to quantify how many people have been affected – directly or indirectly – by the Troubles, and to what extent. In 2011, Northern Ireland's Victims Commission estimated that the Troubles created 500,000 'victims' in the North. Today's population is approximately 1.8 million; at a rough estimate, one in four people. It is worth bearing in mind that this figure covers only those 'directly affected' by bereavement, physical injury or trauma.[6]

Within these statistics are families who have been bereaved multiple times; incredibly, entire families have been erased from existence. Among them were the Dempseys – 22-year-old Joe, his 19-year-old wife Jeanette, and baby Brigeen, who was ten months. The family died when their home in Hillman Street in the New Lodge area of north Belfast was petrol bombed by loyalists; asleep upstairs, they were unable to escape the flames.

'That was a complete family wiped out by the Troubles and there's been very

Joe, Jeanette and Brigeen Dempsey died together.

little said or written about them,' says Joe's brother Hugh. 'They always seem to have been in the background, as if it never happened. It did happen. It was one of the worst atrocities, that a complete family could just vanish into thin air.'

'Time doesn't heal,' adds his sister, Eliza McGurk. 'People say it heals, it doesn't. We all still remember them.'

Families find different ways of remembering. The parents of Tim Parry, Colin and Wendy, set up a Peace Foundation in memory of their son and Johnathan Ball, who were killed in the IRA bombing of Warrington in 1993; Thomas Devlin's parents, Penny and Jim, award a music bursary each year to young people who would like to study or pursue a career in the creative arts.

Sometimes, just to speak their loved one's name is enough. John McCabe goes regularly to his daughter Siobhan's grave. 'I went three days in a row just trying to psych myself up for this interview,' he admits. It is his first. 'It's 43 years, but talking to somebody again now, it's as if it was last night.'

In Milltown Cemetery in west Belfast, children are buried side by side, or together. Their names are recorded on memorials, or spoken in commemoration ceremonies; increasingly, they are remembered through projects such as oral histories or memorial quilts.

Five-month-old baby Alan Jack is among those commemorated on the South East Fermanagh Foundation's (SEFF) quilt. His family have no photographs of him; instead, his square on the quilt with its images of a pram, a rattle and a teddy bear must serve to represent him. The IRA bomb which killed him 'denied his family the right to even have a photograph', says Kenny Donaldson from SEFF. 'Think about the impact of that on a family.'

In Bernie Doherty's living room in Buncrana, County Donegal, a familiar picture of her son Oran hangs on the wall.

Bernie recounts how eight-year-old Oran was a thoughtful child, who paid attention and who would ask questions her other children wouldn't.

'When the Good Friday Agreement was signed, he knew I was happy, and asked me what that meant. I told him it means that there won't be any more killings in the North.'

Four months later, Oran was killed in the Real IRA bombing of Omagh.

The image on display in his mother's living room is the same photograph, of a smiling, blond boy in his school uniform, that was given to the media in the wake of his death. It has been reproduced in newspapers for the 21 years since.

'You always want him to be remembered,' says Bernie. 'It's the scariest feeling thinking that people will forget. It means a wild lot when somebody says, maybe out of the blue, that they always remember that day and that wee boy. You just have this thing in you, you think they should be thought about.'

Maureen Rafferty would agree. In Belfast, she leans forward in her chair, hands clasped together. Briefly, her eyes flick up, towards the ceiling, as if in a moment of private communication with her son. When she speaks, she looks straight ahead. 'I want the world to know my Philip's name.'

Memorial quilt for Alan Jack.

The scene of the Miami Showband killings in County Down, 31 July 1975.

1975

- The IRA's truce is only fitfully observed, with the organisation killing over 40 people this year

- Loyalist paramilitaries kill over 70, among them three members of the Miami Showband in an attack that raised questions of collusion between loyalist paramilitaries and the security forces

- The counterproductive policy of internment comes to an end in December

- The unionist-dominated 'constitutional convention' advocates a return to unionist majority rule

- Steven Spielberg's summer blockbuster *Jaws* has children cowering behind cinema seats.

Name: *Patrick Toner*

Age: *7*

From: *Forkhill, Co Armagh*

Date of Death: *19/01/1975*

'Wee Pat' Toner loved Mandy, Isabelle, Jean and Snowball. They were the family cows, which he looked after every day; the seven-year-old also loved his imaginary friend, 'Mister Watson'; his eleven older brothers and sisters; his mammy and daddy, Penelope and John; his toy cars and his pet dog, Bruno.

'You could not imagine anyone as simple as Wee Pat in the things he loved,' remember his sisters.

Every day 'Wee Pat' – to distinguish him from his older uncle Pat – would help move the cattle to their field; he also helped out in the piggery. His older sisters Mary, Pauline and Ann had to wash him every time he came in from the farm.

Even in school, Pat was obsessed with the farm, and wanted to be a vet when he grew up. Ten days before he was killed he wrote: 'The present I liked best at Christmas is my vet set. There is a thing to listen to a cow's heart. There are two small boxes for giving to sick cows. There is a needle for giving injections. I play with it every day.'

Four years earlier, the family had moved north from Dungooley, County Louth, across the border to Forkhill in Armagh, where their father had inherited the family farm. There were only three miles between them, but in their new home their old lives seemed worlds away. 'It was the worst thing that ever happened to us,' the sisters recall. 'Our lives changed forever – different schools, we left our friends behind, and then Wee Pat was killed.'

The new house in Forkhill was opposite the heavily fortified RUC station. Attacks on the station were commonplace; a rocket had previously landed on the Toners' roof. 'Wee Pat dived under the table in fright.'

Every Sunday, Pat and the farmhand would herd the family's cattle up Main Street at around 3p.m.

Earlier that day, the IRA had left a booby-trapped car outside the RUC station. The army carried out a controlled explosion and towed it away. As Wee Pat drove the cows home, one of them triggered a landmine.

Pat died instantly; so too did one of his pet cows, Isabelle. The family heard the explosion. 'I dropped the tray of tea I was carrying with the fright,' says Pauline.

Forkhill came to a standstill for his funeral. 'It is a crime to kill a child,' the parish priest, Fr Brendan O'Neill, said, 'and this is not lightened by listening to lame and fatuous excuses that this was not meant to happen.'[268]

The inquest into his death heard that there had been a command wire leading across the border, 500 yards away.[269]

The following weekend 6,000 people took part in a peace rally in Newry in response to Pat's death; his parents and other relatives were among those present. *The Irish Times* said the attendance was 'almost four times as large' as any previous peace rally in the town.[270]

Years later the Toner family donated a field to the local church as the site for a new chapel. Inside, 'Wee' Pat is commemorated with a stained-glass window of a shepherd.

✳ ✳ ✳ ✳ ✳

Name: Eddie Wilson

Age: 16

From: Cavehill, North Belfast

Date of Death: 26/01/1975

Eddie Wilson had always loved cars and aeroplanes. 'He was just mad about cars, from when he was no age,' remembers his mother Betty. 'He loved the wee model cars, the Dinky cars and Matchbox cars. I still have a whole pile of them, and there's not a mark on them.'

He was also fascinated by planes and was an air cadet in the RAF's Air Training Corps (ATC). 'When he was younger, one minute he would have said he was going to be a pilot, and the next he would have said he was going to be a steeplejack.'

From Mountcollyer Road, Eddie had been helping out in the family steeplejack business ever since he was old enough, and had just started working there when he was killed.

'The first time that he went with his daddy to work and he got his pay, that was a big deal,' says Betty. 'He went up to the shop at the corner, and he bought my mother – we lived next door to each other – he bought my mother a quarter of sweets and me a quarter. That happened every week, he came in with the sweets. That's the type of boy he was.'

The eldest in the family, and the only boy, his grandmother 'doted' on Eddie; his mother remembers him as a quiet and gentle boy, who hated to see others shouting or fighting.

A member of the Anchor Boys – a junior version of the Boys' Brigade – he loved anything to do with the outdoors, especially playing football, going sailing in his father's boat, and his role as a corporal in the Air Cadets.

The group met in the ATC hut in the grounds of Cavehill Primary School. An IRA booby-trap bomb had been left inside, wired to an inside door; when Eddie opened it, it exploded, killing him instantly. 'It could have been any of the boys that day,' says his mother. 'His life was just taken in the flick of a switch.'

His love of cars meant Eddie had been looking forward to passing his driving test. 'He kept saying to me, "Mum, I can't wait until I learn to drive." He would have been thrilled to bits – he used to say, "I'll go here, I'll go there." Just after Christmas he said to me, "Mummy, just think, another six months and I'll be able to get my licence to drive," but he never made it.'

※ ※ ※ ※ ※

Name: *Robert Allsopp*

Age: *15*

From: *New Lodge, North Belfast*

Date of Death: *23 / 03 / 1975*

Robert Allsopp was a keen footballer and, like many 15-year-olds, enjoyed going to dances and youth clubs. A student at St Patrick's Secondary School, Bearnageeha, he had been given his nickname, 'Swab', at school.[271]

He had joined the Fianna in 1969, when he would have been only nine or ten years old. Questioned by a British army foot patrol about an IRA badge he was wearing, he replied that it meant 'I'm Robert Allsopp'.[272]

That evening, Robert's mother had gone to work, leaving him money to go to a local disco.[273] Instead, he was found lying at the back door of his house by a neighbour. He had been shot in the head.

According to the *Irish News*, a neighbour told the inquest into his death that 'there was a smell of burning and a fog or smoke in the house', but she said that 'at no time' did she see a gun.

The inquest heard that the shooting had been reported by a 13-year-old girl, who was never traced. 'It is quite mysterious what happened,' the deputy coroner said.[274]

According to *Belfast Graves*, Robert had been shot accidentally during an 'arms training lecture'.[275]

A flute band in north Belfast is named in his memory.

✳ ✳ ✳ ✳ ✳

Name: *Baby Bowen*

Age: *Unborn*

From: *Killyliss, Co Tyrone*

Date of Death: *21/04/1975*

'A wee baby girl with black hair like her mother,' Baby Bowen never had a chance at life.

Marian Bowen was eight and a half months pregnant when she was killed. She died along with her two brothers, Michael and Seamus McKenna, and her unborn daughter in an explosion in the house she and her husband Thomas had been renovating in preparation for the baby's arrival.

Marian (21) and Thomas (23) had been living with his mother while they were doing up the Bowens' former family bungalow at Killyliss, near Dungannon.

Marian had been busy painting the walls, and picking out curtains; that day, she and her brothers had gone to check a new hot water cylinder which had just been installed.

The family had no idea a bomb had been placed inside. 'As soon as they opened the door it exploded,' says the baby's aunt, Maura Martin. 'Mammy was out at the line and she heard the bang, and she ran the whole way there, it was about a mile, because she knew Marian was there.'

She arrived at a scene of devastation – the house had been destroyed, and the debris littered the surrounding fields.

The bodies of the adults were taken to Dungannon; when the pathologist examined Marian, he realised she had been heavily pregnant. 'They went out to search for the remains of the baby and they found the wee girl, fully formed, underneath the rubble,' says Maura.

Marian had been due to give birth just over two weeks later, on 7 May.

At the time the so-called Protestant Action Force – a cover name for the UVF – claimed responsibility; their deaths have been subsequently attributed to the loyalist 'Glenanne Gang', which – facilitated by RUC and UDR collusion – murdered 120 civilians in the 'Murder Triangle' of south Tyrone and Armagh between 1972 and 1978.[276]

Maura Martin has no doubt they were killed simply because they were Catholics who were upwardly mobile and setting up home near a predominantly

Protestant area. 'The intended victims were my brother Thomas and Marian. They wanted to wipe out the new wee family.'

'The night before Marian was killed, Thomas carried her up the stairs to bed in our house because her wee ankles were swollen,' says Maura. 'They got into bed and Thomas said she turned to him and said, "This time next month we'll have another wee person in this bed with us." But that wasn't to be.'

✳ ✳ ✳ ✳ ✳

Name: *Michelle O'Connor*

Age: *3*

From: *Ormeau Road, South Belfast*

Date of Death: *13/06/1975*

Michelle O'Connor was on her way to playschool. There had already been a hunt for her father John's car keys that morning, which the mischievous three-year-old had hidden.

Michelle and John had then waited for her friend Nuala, who usually came with them, but that morning Nuala insisted on staying at home to watch her mother bath their new baby. Finally ready to leave, John put Michelle in the front passenger seat and then opened the driver's door. The car exploded.

The only trace of the little girl left in the car, *The Irish News* reported, was 'a scrap of her dress where the front seat had been. Her pink hair ribbon was found on the roof of a nearby car.'[277] Michelle's mutilated body was found underneath another car.

Her mother Nora screamed, 'Where's my baby, my baby?', and collapsed as she ran towards the wreckage. 'Although he had terrible injuries, John still shouted for neighbours to search for Michelle. When he knew she died in the explosion he pleaded with a policeman, "Shoot me, shoot me."'[278]

Michelle's father was the owner of a bar in south Belfast which had previously been attacked by loyalists. In 1973 one of its patrons had been shot dead by the UVF as he played darts inside the bar.

'Michelle was murdered deliberately,' a family friend said. 'Whoever planted that bomb knew that her daddy took her to playschool every morning before he went to work.'[279]

In the death notice placed by her parents in *The Irish News*, Michelle was described as a 'beloved only child'.[280]

Two boys and two girls carried Michelle's small white coffin from the church following Requiem Mass. 'Then some of Michelle's little friends from nursery school walked behind, paying their own tribute to their lost playmate.'[281]

✳ ✳ ✳ ✳ ✳

Name: *John Rolston*

Age: *16*

From: *White City, North Belfast*

Date of Death: *28/06/1975*

John Rolston had just left school. Friday had been his final day at Stella Maris Secondary School; Saturday nights were spent at his friend's house in Rathcoole.

The youngest of a family of five from Fairyknowe Park in the White City, an estate to the north of Belfast, the Rolstons had previously lived in Rathcoole, where John was still a member of Star of the Sea Youth Club on the Shore Road.

A friend of the Rolston family told the *Irish News* that just before midnight, when there was no sign of John, his father phoned the other boy's home, but was told that John had already left to walk back.[282]

In her memoir of life on the White City housing estate in Belfast, Marianne Elliott writes that as John walked back, 'he was followed by two Rathcoole teenagers, members of the UVF youth wing, who knew him. He was murdered just as he reached the Throne Hospital.' A passing motorist saw him lying on the roadway as two men ran away; he had been shot.[283]

A police spokesman said it was 'the usual act of despicable cowards who are bent on keeping sectarian trouble going at all costs. I don't know who they are or where they are, but this brutal murder will live with them for the rest of their lives.'[284]

According to *Lost Lives*, a teenage member of the Young Citizen Volunteers was ordered to be detained at the secretary of state's pleasure for the killing. 'He was said to have told police that he and another youth followed John Rolston, whom they knew to be Catholic, to tell him to keep out of the Rathcoole estate.'[285]

John is remembered on Stella Maris Secondary School's website as one of 27 of the school's past pupils to lose their lives during the Troubles. Twenty of them were, like John, killed by loyalist paramilitaries.[286]

✳ ✳ ✳ ✳ ✳

Name: *Charles Irvine*

Age: *16*

From: *Divis Flats, West Belfast*

Date of Death: *13 / 07 / 1975*

Charles Irvine and his friend Arthur McDonnell were having a great time. They had bought an old banger for £15, and were driving it around west Belfast, 'backfiring like mad', said Charles's brother; he and his mates had 'cheered at it' as they drove past.

The British army claimed a shot had been fired at them from the car after it failed to stop at a checkpoint. Charles's brother told the inquest into his death that he heard 'a dull noise as the car backfired, but nothing like a shot'.

'The next thing I knew two soldiers were down on their knees and firing away. The car swerved, hit a car coming up the Falls and finished up on the footpath ... Charlie was slumped over the wheel with blood pouring from his head and his mate had been thrown through the windscreen.'[287]

Eyewitnesses said the boys had been unarmed, and the IRA said Charles was not connected with any branch of the republican movement. A spokesman for the Northern Ireland Office said a member of the security forces had narrowly escaped injury.[288]

Charles died later in hospital. Arthur survived, but died of his injuries in 1994, some 19 years later. The state pathologist said that 'due to old bullet wounds' clots in his right calf had travelled to his lungs and killed him. 'There is no doubt there was a direct link between the shooting 19 years earlier and his death,' he told the coroner.[289]

Among the many death notices inserted in *The Irish News* by relatives, friends and neighbours, there were also messages of sympathy from his brother Sean's friends 'and all the lads in Cage 4, Long Kesh', the IRSP in Divis Flats, and Charles's 'comrades' in Clonard Youth Club.[290]

✳ ✳ ✳ ✳ ✳

Name: *Patrick Crawford*

Age: *15*

From: *Glen Road, West Belfast*

Date of Death: *10/08/1975*

Patrick Crawford was everyone's blue-eyed boy. 'Everybody loved Paddy,' remembers his sister Maggie.

The third eldest in a family of ten children from Ramoan Drive, 15-year-old Paddy was six feet tall but was still 'a big softie'. 'He was really, really funny,' remembers Maggie, 'and he loved his clothes. One of his mates, Tucker, called him Shiny Shoes because his red DMs were always shining.'

A skinhead, he 'loved all the skinhead dances'; told to take his younger brother John to get his hair cut, he turned him into a skinhead too. 'My dad was going to strangle him,' says Maggie.

She remembers Paddy 'torturing my mummy to give him money to buy a pigeon'. He got his pigeon on condition that it was kept secret from his father; the pet lived in his friend Brian's shed. 'I loved animals and I was so happy he had it, and he used to take me down and show me it.'

Paddy was 'a real worker'; always whistling, he loved tinkering with cars and lorries. He had already left school and worked as a truck driver for a group of Travellers. After Paddy was killed, they made a point of bringing his wages down to his father.

His mother Martha had been shot dead three years previously, caught in the crossfire during a gun battle. Paddy helped look after his siblings, 'especially us younger ones', says Maggie, who was nine.

That evening, Paddy was on his way home to babysit. There was rioting going on in the area, and he decided to cut through the grounds of the Royal Victoria Hospital where it felt safer. 'He waited until two women came and he said, "Can I walk up with you?", says Maggie. He told them about Mummy, and he said that if he didn't get home, "It'll kill my Da." They were linking arms, and the next thing he went down on one knee and he says, "I'm shot."'

In 1979 the inquest into Paddy's death heard that there had been shooting between the IRA and the British army, and that the shot which killed him had come from the Falls Road direction; the year previously, a court had been told that there had been a feud between the Official IRA and the Provisionals, and that Paddy had been a member of the Official IRA.[291]

This has always been disputed by Paddy's family. In 2015, the attorney general for Northern Ireland granted a fresh inquest into Patrick's death; at a preliminary hearing the following year, the Crawford family learned that Paddy may have been killed by the British army, as ballistics evidence suggested he had been shot by a bullet fired by high-velocity rifle.[292]

The family is currently awaiting an inquest date. 'I want his name cleared,' says Maggie. 'He was the best brother. He's not special to everybody, but he's so special to me and my family.'

※ ※ ※ ※ ※

Name: *Siobhan McCabe*

Age: *4*

From: *Lower Falls, West Belfast*

Date of Death: *10 / 08 / 1975*

Siobhan McCabe couldn't wait to be five.

'I'm nearly sure she was getting a goldfish for her birthday,' remembers her sister, Karen McAllister. 'That's why she was so excited about it.'

Siobhan – who was from McDonnell Street in the Lower Falls area of west Belfast – was also looking forward to starting school, because it was another opportunity to follow in six-year-old Karen's footsteps. 'Siobhan always wanted to be with me because obviously I was the older sister, so if I was going out with my friends she was just stuck behind me.'

If she wasn't with Karen, she was with her father, John. 'She was lively and full of life,' he remembers. 'It's hard to talk about it, because I took her most places with me.'

The day Siobhan was killed, she and Karen had been out playing in the street outside their home. When shooting broke out between the IRA and the British army, they sought refuge in their granny's house across the road.

'When the shooting stopped my granny said, "Go over home now." I had Siobhan by the hand, and we were two doors away from our house and I didn't know what happened, only that she fell. I had her by the hand. I turned round, and she'd been shot.' Karen dragged her sister into a neighbour's hallway.

'My daddy came back, hours and hours later, from the hospital, with a bag full of her clothes and we were all sitting on the settee waiting and he just said, "She's gone."'

The post-mortem result showed that Siobhan had been hit in the chest, 'probably by a bullet nearly spent, or which had ricocheted'.[293] A local member of the IRA was subsequently charged with her murder;[294] the McCabes knew his family.

Karen has a vivid memory of seeing him as the girls left their grandmother's house. 'He was crouching down at the side of my granny's wall.'

Neither she nor her father blame him for Siobhan's death. 'It was just an accident,' says John McCabe. 'If somebody shot anybody belonging to me deliberately, I'd be pursuing it, but it was a different thing altogether, it was a tragedy.'

'He was young,' adds Karen. 'I'm sure he was traumatised for the rest of his life too, I know I would be if I killed a child.'

Karen remembers seeing photographs in the newspapers of her sister lying in her coffin. 'She had wee green ribbons in, and two ponytails.'

Siobhan had been killed on 10th August; she would have turned five a week later.

✳ ✳ ✳ ✳ ✳

Name: *James Templeton*

Age: *15*

From: *Ormeau Road, South Belfast*

Date of Death: *29/08/1975*

'Cropped fair hair, bright blue eyes in a round baby face, and a tall slim body on the verge of getting taller.' For Arthur Fegan, James Templeton will always be fifteen years old.

The friends had met when they started at St Augustine's Secondary School. 'Like me, he had no love of school,' Arthur wrote in a tribute in *An Phoblacht*. 'Both of us spent more days investigating the world outside than attending classes.'[295]

Known as 'Temp' to his friends, he was Jim at home, and lived with his parents and two sisters in Peveril Street, off Belfast's Ormeau Road.

For the past two summers Temp and Arthur had gone camping 'without a tent, and very little money either'. The friends went to all the discos, venturing further afield to areas like the New Lodge and Andersonstown 'only to find the talent as elusive and non-committal as in our own wee areas'.[296]

Jim also loved 'to be well turned out'; this meant 'short coloured trousers, black socks and well polished DMs. He especially liked the "ould Wrangler suit".'[297] He was, says Arthur, 'an ordinary teenager'.[298]

Jim had joined Na Fianna Éireann two years previously; Arthur recounts how they twice had to run for cover when a loyalist gunman opened fire.

That night, Jim and another friend had planned to go to a disco in Andersonstown in west Belfast, but when their van broke down they decided to walk up the Ormeau Road to buy chips.[299]

Outside the Rose and Crown – which had just reopened after a UVF bomb killed six of its customers – the friends stopped to talk to the doorman. Shots were fired from a passing car; Jim was hit in the chest and stomach. According to *Lost Lives*, the UVF was responsible.[300]

As Jim lay on the footpath, he asked for his mother. She found him in the hospital, about to be wheeled into theatre, and was able to speak briefly to him before he died. 'I couldn't believe it,' she said. 'It was something I always dreaded.'[301]

✳ ✳ ✳ ✳ ✳

Name: *Stephen Geddis*

Age: *10*

From: *Divis Flats, West Belfast*

Date of Death: *30/08/1975*

That summer, Stephen Geddis had had his first taste of peanut butter, root beer and sunburn. 'Peanut butter and root beer he loves,' the local newspaper wrote. 'Sunburn he can live without.'[302]

Ten-year-old Stephen had just returned from six weeks with the Owen family on their ranch in South Shore, South Dakota. He had been one of 33 children – Catholic and Protestant – brought to the USA by the NSPCC in order to take them away from the Troubles.

The local paper, the *Watertown Public Opinion*, interviewed 'Steve' that July. 'One of his most memorable experiences here was riding his bike, decorated with the colours of his country, in the South Shore Fourth of July Parade. He has also ridden a horse for the first time here. "I like all the horses here," he said, "and the cowboys!"'[303]

In Belfast, Stephen had been a quiet child who preferred to stay indoors playing with his toys and learning the guitar and the mouth organ. When he returned from the US, he was distraught. 'He lay in bed crying for three days, refused to go out and pleaded with his parents to be allowed to go back to America.'[304]

Afraid he would be teased over his American accent, Stephen insisted on staying inside for three weeks. Eventually, his father William insisted he go out to play.[305] Soldiers were attempting to remove a burning barricade from the street; the British army claimed they had fired plastic bullets after they were stoned by a crowd of children. Stephen was hit in the head and died in hospital two days later. He was the first person to die after being shot with a plastic bullet in Northern Ireland, and also the youngest.

William told the inquest into his son's death that Stephen had been 'walking along the street eating a lollipop' when he was 'hit at point-blank range'.[306] A subsequent investigation by the Historical Enquiries Team found that Stephen had not been involved in rioting but was 'playing innocently with friends and became caught up in events'. [307]

In 2014 Northern Ireland's attorney general ordered a fresh inquest into Stephen's death. Then aged 82, William told the *Irish News* that he still welled up every time his son's name was mentioned. 'I talk to my child every night, the photo I have in the living room.'

Stephen's dream had been for his whole family to see America. 'Steve says he likes it here and would like to return some day – "And bring my family with me".'[308]

＊ ＊ ＊ ＊ ＊

Name: *Eileen Kelly*

Age: *6*

From: *Beechmount, West Belfast*

Date of Death: *30/10/1975*

Eileen Kelly's school photograph shows a dark-eyed little girl, her school tie and blouse smartly buttoned, her long, dark hair tied in bunches and framing her small face.

It was a typical evening in the family home in Beechmount Grove. Six-year-old Eileen and her younger brother Sean, aged two, were playing with their father John.

'Eileen was with me on the settee and we were playing about, wrestling and generally engaged in horse-play,' John told the *Irish News*. 'Suddenly the front door was kicked in. I looked up and saw a man with a hand gun. He started blazing away at us. I don't know how many shots were fired because my only concern was for the children.

'I pushed Sean flat on the floor and threw Eileen into the corner of the settee. I then jumped up to attempt to tackle the gunman. Then I looked round and saw that Eileen had been shot.'[309]

The bullets had been meant for her father, John, the result of a violent feud between the Provisional and the Official IRA. 'The Provisionals ... are clearly concentrating on known Republican sympathisers in the knowledge that Republican Club members have taken full precautions against attack,' the chairman of the Republican Clubs, Malachy McGurran, told the *Irish News*.[310]

Two IRA members – who had been aged 18 and 19 at the time of Eileen's killing – were later jailed for life for her murder.[311]

Eileen was buried on the same day as another feud victim, Seamus McCusker, a 40-year-old father of three, who ran a Sinn Féin incident centre in the New Lodge. According to *Lost Lives*, he was reported to have been the IRA Northern Command's intelligence officer at the time of his death.[312]

Eileen and Seamus 'had little in common until yesterday', the *Irish Independent* wrote, 'when they were buried in an almost simultaneous funeral at Milltown Cemetery.'

For Seamus, there was 'a full military-style turnout, with shots fired over the coffin'. 'Only relatives and family friends attended the burial of Eileen.'[313]

Name: *Kevin McCauley*

Age: *13*

From: *Andersonstown, West Belfast*

Date of Death: *06/11/1975*

Kevin McCauley was 'a Celtic fanatic.' When Kevin was about ten, explains his brother Paddy, he was given the whole strip – top, shorts and socks. He posed for a photograph like a footballer, one foot resting on top of the ball, a wide smile on his face.

The eldest of four children from Ladybrook Park in west Belfast, Kevin was a pupil at De La Salle Boys School. Paddy – who was five years younger – remembers playing Monopoly with his brother, and the fun of going away together on holiday; their last had been to Killarney that summer.

His nickname was 'Yippy' – 'I don't know where he got that from' – and he was always playing football, usually in the driveway with his friends. 'Unfortunately, the Troubles kicked in,' says Paddy, 'and as he got older the football took a back seat.'

Kevin's grandfather, James McCauley, had been a member of the Old IRA in Cavan during the 1920s and had been interned in the Curragh, Co Kildare. Later, during the Troubles, Paddy remembers going to visit their aunt, who was a republican prisoner in Armagh Jail. 'He was a big Irish republican,' says Paddy. 'He would have known our granda and his stories, and probably this was what he wanted to be – like many kids at the time.'

Kevin joined Na Fianna Éireann; Paddy remembers being asked to keep watch while Kevin collected money for republican prisoners' dependents outside St Michael's church every Sunday. 'I had to stand beside him and if the soldiers came, we had to run.'

That evening, Kevin was among those trying to build a barricade across the Andersonstown Road. 'What I've been told about that night,' says Paddy, 'is that Kevin was a section leader of the Fianna and he was looking down the road, watching for the [British army] while they were getting all this stuff out onto the road.'

Among the building materials was a dumper truck, which was being rolled towards the barricade. 'Tragically, it all went wrong,' says Paddy. 'This dumper got out of control. Kevin didn't see it coming, and it came down from behind and it crushed him. It came out at the inquest that a soldier tried to help him. He went in the ambulance with him.'

The family still meet people who remember Kevin. 'They have fond memories of him. He was a likeable child.'

When Ireland played Italy in the quarter-finals of the World Cup in 1990, Paddy watched the match with a friend. 'He started crying. "Your Kevin was one of the best footballers I've ever seen", he said.'

✳ ✳ ✳ ✳ ✳

Name: *Michael Donnelly*

Age: *14*

From: *Silverbridge, Co Armagh*

Date of Death: *19 / 12 / 1975*

That year, Michael Donnelly had a part in the Christmas play at St Joseph's College in Crossmaglen: he had to die on stage.

14-year-old Michael loved performing. His favourite television programme was *Daktari* – about a vet in an animal sanctuary in Africa – and he would act out scenes at home, jumping from chair to chair in the house as his mother laughed at his antics, his older sister Deirdre recalls.

Deirdre remembers her brother as "funny and annoying, handsome, with a lovely smile and a good nature – and a great hit with the girls."

He and his friends Peter and Joseph were inseparable and would go fishing in the nearby Cully river, or hanging about in the orchard behind the family's pub, where they would also hide their Woodbine cigarettes.

Donnelly's pub, shop and petrol pump was the heart of the village of Silverbridge in South Armagh. Michael's parents, Gerry and Marie, had been running it for twelve years; the family lived above. On Sunday mornings, the four children would crowd into their parents' bed and enjoy tea and a full loaf of hot buttered toast before Mass.

The siblings had no choice but to help out, but Michael especially loved the banter with the customers. His family are in no doubt that he would have been the one to take over the business.

That evening Michael was serving at the petrol pump when a car drove up. A man opened fire: his customer, Patrick Donnelly (no relation) was shot in the head and killed instantly; as Michael ran into the bar to warn the customers, the gunman followed him inside and sprayed the room with bullets, killing another man, Trevor Bracknell.

Behind the gunman came a second man, who threw a bomb into the bar. As they ran out it exploded with 'a blue flash … the bar was plunged into darkness'. Michael was hit on the head by fragments of rubble and killed. His father found a flash lamp and searched through the debris for survivors; he found his son's body.[314]

The Red Hand Commandos – part of the UVF – later claimed responsibility; the Silverbridge murders are among more than 120 which have been linked to the Glenanne Gang, which between 1972 and 1978 killed 120 civilians in the 'Murder Triangle' of South Tyrone and Armagh, facilitated by RUC and UDR collusion.

Michael could not be waked at home. The family's home and livelihood had been destroyed by the explosion. 'We fell out with God after Michael was killed,' says Deirdre.

Instead, Michael's remains were brought directly from the hospital in Newry to St Brigid's, Glasdrummond; Deirdre remembers a British army helicopter swooping low over the hearse and scattering the wreaths.

'We never celebrated Christmas afterwards.'

✳ ✳ ✳ ✳ ✳

Betty Williams and Mairead Corrigan of the Peace People lead a rally through Belfast calling for an end to violence. Opposite: Funeral of Joanne, John and Andrew Maguire.

1976

- Almost 300 deaths, the second-highest total in the history of the Troubles

- In January the UVF shoots dead six Catholics in their homes; the following night the IRA carries out the Kingsmill massacre, killing ten Protestant workmen

- The loyalist 'Shankill Butchers' kill their first victim

- The proposed ending of 'special category status' for prisoners leads to the 'blanket protest' over republican refusal to wear prison uniforms

- The deaths of the three young Maguire children in Belfast prompts the formation of The Peace People, a cross-community movement in which women from both communities unite in marches against violence; its founders, Mairead Maguire and Betty Corrigan, are awarded the Nobel Prize the following year

- During a scorching hot summer the cinema blockbuster is the horror movie *The Omen*, while Swedish band Abba dominate the music charts.

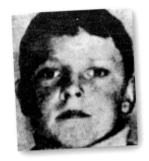

Name: *Thomas Rafferty*

Age: *14*

From: *Portadown, Co Armagh*

Date of Death: *07/02/1976*

Thomas Rafferty was missing.

That Thursday afternoon the 14-year-old had gone home for lunch as usual, but had failed to return to St Malachy's High School.

An explosion had been heard in the Derryall area of Portadown that day, but according to the *Belfast Telegraph* its location could not be traced.

Thomas's body was found two days later, lying near a bombed shed behind a row of derelict cottages.[315]

'The police theory is that the boy was probably killed when he pushed open the door of a garden shed,' the *Irish News* wrote. 'His body was found 20 feet from the scene of the blast, and may have lain since soon after he left home on Thursday.'[316]

The INLA booby-trap bomb had been intended for the security forces; the *Craigavon Times* reported that the house was situated on Thomas's route to and from school.

'The terrorists responsible must know the area and must surely know that children are attracted to vacant houses and frequently play among them,' said Chief Superintendent Jack McConnell.[317]

In 1979 a 29-year-old Portadown man was jailed for life for Thomas's murder.[318] Thomas's headmaster and many of his school friends attended his funeral. Thomas's older brother, John, had drowned in 1973 after he fell from a boat into Lough Neagh on Christmas Day.

※ ※ ※ ※ ※

Name: *Robert McLernon*

Age: *16*

From: *Stewartstown, Co Tyrone*

Date of Death: *07/02/1976*

Sixteen-year-old Robert and his sister Rachel (21), were driving into Cookstown with friends when they saw a car in the hedge. Thinking there had been an accident, they stopped and got out to see if they could help.

But Rachel's boyfriend, Robert Nethercott, became suspicious 'when he discovered there was no sign of injured people or any traces of blood, *The Mid-Ulster Mail* reported.

'He shouted at the others to be careful and get out of the field as it could be a booby-trap bomb. He had just got back onto the road when there was a vicious explosion, throwing him onto his back.'[319]

The occupants of another car saw the brother and sister 'hurled into the air'.[320] One of them had unwittingly set off a pressure plate wired to explosives.[321]

The car had been hijacked in Cookstown an hour and a half earlier. The IRA were thought to be responsible; the police said they believed 'the fake accident was staged as a trap for members of the security forces'.[322]

Among those who condemned their murders was Fr Denis Faul, who said he 'failed to understand the mentality of people who would use large quantities of explosives with murderous intent in an area of highly sensitive community relations which required stability and peace'.

Robert and Rachel's cousin, the Reverend Willie McCrea, told a loyalist rally that 'two innocent young Ulster children willing to help their fellow man had been taken from them without even a farewell.'[323]

On the front page of the *Irish News* was a photograph of a large crater – the width of a country road – which marked the scene of the explosion that had killed Robert and Rachel. Beside it was a warning from the Primate of All-Ireland, Cardinal Conway, to the 'men of violence' that they would be 'haunted for as long as they lived by the memory of their deeds'.[324]

Robert and Rachel were buried together in a double grave. Among the wreaths was one from Rachel's boyfriend, also called Robert, to whom she was due to have become engaged that weekend.[325]

✳ ✳ ✳ ✳ ✳

Name: *Anthony Doherty*

Age: *15*

From: *Turf Lodge, West Belfast*

Date of Death: *14/02/1976*

Anthony Doherty had been on his way home. That afternoon the pupils at St Peter's Secondary School in west Belfast had been let out of school early because of rioting following the death of Frank Stagg on hunger strike; among them were Anthony – Tony – Doherty and his 14-year-old cousin, Anthony Hagans.

The teenagers had gone to the youth club, then to the younger boy's house to get something to eat. Anthony Hagans later told the inquest into his cousin's death that he had been seeing Tony to a taxi when they came across the burnt-out lorry – which had been hijacked earlier – on Leeson Street.

Anthony 'turned towards the lorry and saw a flash and put his hands over his face. He started to run up the road and felt his hands sting'.[326] The lorry's petrol tank had exploded; Tony had been showered with burning petrol.

Another teenager told the inquest that he had seen the boys running up the Falls Road. 'Tony Doherty was on fire,' he said, 'so they ran over to him and put the fire out with their coats.'[327]

He died in hospital the following morning; he had suffered burns to much of his body.

Anthony Hagans recalled at the inquest how passers-by had 'grabbed' them and put them into a taxi. 'We were both taken to hospital and I was released the next day, but Anthony died.'[328]

✳ ✳ ✳ ✳ ✳

Name: *James McCaughey*

Age: *13*

From: *Dungannon, Co Tyrone*

Date of Death: *17/03/1976*

It was St Patrick's night. James – Jim – McCaughey was on his way to a disco in a local school with his best friend, Patrick Barnard.

The 13-year-olds had already called for another friend, who told them he couldn't come – he was too busy watching *The Magnificent Seven* on television.[329]

Undeterred, James and Patrick walked to the disco. They were almost there, standing outside the Hillcrest Bar, opposite the school, when the UVF car bomb exploded.

John Fee, the manager of the Hillcrest Bar, said he had smelled something burning and had gone to an upstairs lounge to check when 'the building seemed to crumble around him'.[330]

Four people were killed – James, Patrick and two men aged 62 and 57. A member of the UVF was later jailed for life for six murders, including those at the Hillcrest Bar. The explosion has been linked to the Glenanne Gang, which is believed to have been responsible for 120 killings in the Tyrone/Armagh area.

James's father Norbert – known as Nory – identified his son from the Pioneer pin on his lapel. Shown his body in the morgue, at first he did not recognise James. 'Then I saw that the Pioneer pin was attached to his jacket upside down – just like James' always was, despite Molly telling him to put it on the right way up.'[331]

From that day until her death in 2008, James's mother Molly slept with her son's photograph under her pillow. Later, when they travelled to Lourdes, 'James was always there with us,' said Nory.[332]

They never celebrated another St Patrick's Day.

✳ ✳ ✳ ✳ ✳

Name: *Patrick Barnard*

Age: *13*

From: *Dungannon, Co Tyrone*

Date of Death: *18/03/1976*

Patrick Barnard had had a busy St Patrick's Day. He had already been to the parade in Coalisland, County Tyrone, and had rushed home for dinner before going out to meet his friend James McCaughey.

Thirteen-year-old Patrick was from Fairview Park in Dungannon where, in 1964, local families had famously squatted in protest at anti-Catholic discrimination in the allocation of housing; as a baby in his pram, Patrick had been taken on the marches of the Homeless Citizens' League, a forerunner of the civil rights movement.

The youngest in the family – only 'a cub', said his brother Eddie – Patrick liked hanging around with the older boys as they played in the fields and hills around Dungannon. 'He was a copycat,' says Eddie. 'Everything we did he wanted to do as well. If we were making bows and arrows, the next thing was he'd come out of the hedge with a stick, wanting it sharpened.'[333]

Known as 'Paddy Whack', he was the pet of the family, and was 'always in the middle of everything', whether that was selling holly round the doors at Christmas, or doing his milk round.

'A dog adopted Patrick,' said Eddie, 'an old black and white spotted dolly mixture of a thing …. It would come down and bark at the house and then we'd hear Patrick going out and talking to it. Everywhere he went the dog was with him.'

The disco was only round the corner from Patrick's house. He and James were just across the road, outside the Hillcrest Bar, when the UVF car bomb exploded. Patrick was fatally injured and died in hospital the following day; his friend James and two others – a patron in the bar and a man who was walking home from mass – were also killed.

A local UVF man was later jailed for six murders, including those at the Hillcrest Bar – the aforementioned member of the Glenanne Gang, which has been linked to 120 killings in the so-called 'murder triangle' of Tyrone and Armagh.

His mother, Mona, slept with her son's school jumper under her pillow every night; it was there when she died.

Patrick's dog came looking for him. It would stand outside the house and bark, said Eddie; eventually, Mona let it in. 'It sniffed about the house, realised he was no longer there, and never came back.'[334]

* * * * *

Name: *Joanne Maguire*

Age: *8*

From: *Andersonstown, West Belfast*

Date of Death: *10/08/1976*

Joanne Maguire was riding her bike. Beside her, her mother Anne was pushing new baby brother Andrew in his pram. Two-year-old John was toddling beside them; another brother, seven-year-old Mark, was walking ahead.

The young family, from Ladybrook Crescent, was just passing eight-year-old Joanne's school, St John the Baptist Primary on Finaghy Road North.

The car was already speeding down the road towards them. British soldiers were chasing two IRA men; they opened fire, killing the driver, Danny Lennon. Out of control, the car mounted the pavement and crashed through the Maguire family and into the school railings.

Joanne's aunt, Eilish O'Connor, who was nearby, said there had been shooting between the IRA and the British army. 'My sister and the children ran up Finaghy Road North to get away from [the shooting] and they must have just crossed the road when they were hit by the car,' she told the *Irish News*.

'I grabbed my son, who was with me, and ran with him behind a garage at the corner. I was shocked and all I remember was being put into an Army Saracen and being taken to the hospital with two young children and a baby. It was only then that I saw it was my sister's two children who had been killed.'[335]

'It is terrifying to think that a young mother and her family, just walking along happily together, could be cut down like this in a matter of seconds,' a neighbour said.[336]

The front page of the *Irish News* showed a group of children standing, heads bowed, at the wreckage of Joanne's bicycle and Andrew's pram; beside it was a picture of Joanne in her First Communion dress.

Andersonstown came to a standstill for the children's joint funerals, and thousands lined the route of their funeral cortege, which was led by members of Joanne's Girl Guide troop.

Newspaper photographs showed her coffin in Milltown Cemetery, piled high with wreaths, and surrounded by her friends and classmates.

The following year, Anne had another baby girl, whom she named Joanne in her daughter's memory.

❋ ❋ ❋ ❋ ❋

Name: *Andrew Maguire*

Age: *6 weeks*

From: *Andersonstown, West Belfast*

Date of Death: *10/08/1976*

Baby Andrew Maguire's last glimpse would have been of his mother, Anne. She was wheeling the six-week-old infant along Finaghy Road North in west Belfast, his brothers and sister walking and cycling alongside.

Moments later, a car crashed into the family, pinning them against the railings of his sister's school.

The *Irish News* reported that the baby was hurled from his pram by the impact.[337] Andrew died instantly.

His eight-year-old sister Joanne was also killed; another brother, John (2), died in hospital the following day.

An IRA member, Danny Lennon, also died; he had been shot by the British army as they chased the car he was driving, sending it careering out of control.

Afterwards 'a silent crowd stood looking at the wrecked bicycle and the squashed pram that lay beside the caved-in railings of the school'.[338]

Seriously injured, Anne was too ill to attend her children's funerals. She took her own life in 1980.

The family are buried in a single grave in Milltown Cemetery. The inscription reads: 'They died that others may live in peace.'

✳ ✳ ✳ ✳ ✳

Name: *John Maguire*

Age: *2*

From: *Andersonstown, West Belfast*

Date of Death: *11/08/1976*

Two-year-old John Maguire was fatally injured in the crash that killed his sister Joanne and brother Andrew.

The family were struck by an out-of-control car which careered onto the pavement and hit the family, pinning them against the railings of his sister's school.

The car had been driven by Danny Lennon, an IRA member who had been shot dead as he was being chased by the British army.

John died in hospital the day after the crash. His father, Jackie, said he held the IRA responsible for the deaths of his children.

Within a week, the *Irish News* reported 'peace groups springing up all over the city' and said that more than 10,000 had gathered outside Joanne's school for a peace rally.[339]

Joanne's aunt, Mairead Corrigan, said, 'They have taken three of our children, but these deaths will not have been in vain if they stop one kid from taking a gun and running out with it.'[340]

Mairead and another local woman, Betty Williams, founded the Peace People movement in the aftermath of the children's deaths. At its height, 10,000 people attended a rally organised by the Peace People in London's Trafalgar Square;[341] the pair were awarded that year's Nobel Peace Prize.

✳ ✳ ✳ ✳ ✳

Name: *Majella O'Hare*

Age: *12*

From: *Ballymoyer, Co Armagh*

Date of Death: *14/08/1976*

Every summer, Majella O'Hare went to stay with her sister Marie on the Isle of Man. The 12-year-old would be joined by her mother and another sister, Margarita, and would babysit for Marie's young daughter.

'She was only 12, but she was very mature, intelligent, and would do any housework that was needed,' says Marie. 'She was a lovely wee person, a special little child.'

Majella had been a 'late arrival' – there were seven years between her and her closest sibling, Margarita – and was treasured by the household. She loved music, especially singing, and was taking piano lessons; Marie is adamant that she would have ended up in a showband with her older brother Michael.

Majella also loved school and had just completed her first year at St Paul's Secondary School in Bessbrook. Her school report shows excellent results in her summer exams, and her form teacher described her as pleasant and well-mannered and a 'keen, hard-working girl'.

'She was very mature for her age,' adds Marie. 'If anyone would swear at a British solider she would interject, reminding everybody that he was "somebody's son".'

Majella had great fun on the Isle of Man that summer. For a laugh, she and her family even went to get their tea leaves read by a local fortune teller; she did not want to read Majella's cup, as it had turned up empty. 'Then two nights before she was killed, Majella woke from a nightmare telling her parents that she dreamt the British army were after her,' says Marie.

Majella returned home on 9 August, because she wanted to spend the last of the summer with her friends.

Majella and a group of friends were walking down the narrow country lane on their way to confession before that day's trip to the seaside. 'Then there was a bang and some stones started flying in front of us,' said her friend Caroline Murphy. 'Then she fell.'[342]

A 13-year-old said: 'I heard one single shot, sounded to be from behind us. I heard Majella scream … I had already jumped off my bicycle in fright and I saw her fall on the road.'[343]

Majella had been shot in the back by a soldier; a member of the British army's Parachute Regiment, he was later tried for manslaughter and acquitted. In 2011 the British government formally apologised to Majella's family.[344]

The morning of her death, Majella's father James had got up early and given her cornflakes in bed. She had been at the sea at Gyles' Quay, County Louth, the day before, he said, 'and had brought me home some mint sweets and a stone from the beach. She said: "You want to see it, Daddy, when it is wet, it turns brown" … She was going to the sea again with Mrs McGivern and did I want more sweets.'[345]

✳ ✳ ✳ ✳ ✳

Name: *Brigeen Dempsey*
Age: *10 months*
From: *New Lodge, North Belfast*
Date of Death: *27/08/1976*

A treasured family photograph shows baby Brigeen Dempsey on her father's knee. Joe is holding his daughter's tiny hand; her mother Jeanette holds the other.

Their house in the New Lodge area of Belfast was one of three attacked by loyalists, who threw petrol bombs through the front window while the family was asleep upstairs. The flames tore through the house, trapping them in the bedroom. Rescuers who tried to reach them saw Joe and the baby at the window, and heard Jeanette's screams.

'Joe was standing at the window, trying to get the child out,' says Brigeen's uncle Hugh, 'and the flames were coming up. The next thing, he was gone.'

Overcome by smoke, Joe was found lying on the ground, baby Brigeen in his arms. Brigeen was only ten months old; Jeanette was 19, and Joe was 22.

'He really idolised her, she was the light of his life, that wee baby,' says Brigeen's aunt Eliza. She remembers her niece as 'a gorgeous wee thing. Our Joe and Jeanette were both really dark, so you didn't know was she more like him or more like her. She had our Joe's eyes, brown eyes.'

Esther Dempsey had made her niece a rag doll in school which was kept in the baby's cot. 'You can see it still, in the photos,' says Esther.

The Dempseys are in no doubt the attack was purely sectarian. Nobody has ever been charged with their murders.

The family had only recently moved into Hillman Street, and had been starting to do the house up. 'That's where they were that day,' remembers her uncle Paddy. 'They'd been in town getting wallpaper and paint.'

'The hardest thing is what might have been,' says Hugh.

'Walking, talking, all those things you watch out for and see happening, all that was taken away,' says Eliza. 'Would she have had wee brothers and sisters? You often think of it.'

'They were happy,' says Hugh. 'They hadn't much, but they were happy.'

Name: *Brian Stewart*

Age: *13*

From: *Turf Lodge, West Belfast*

Date of Death: *10/10/1976*

Brian Stewart was the joker of the family.

His sister, Marie Duffy, remembers her 13-year-old brother as 'a very likeable kid' who was known by everybody. 'He laughed easy, always had a smile on his face, joked and pranked,' she says. 'He had dyslexia, so school wasn't his favourite place. He loved being up on the mountains, lighting campfires.

'Brian had these big, blue eyes with long eyelashes and long blond hair. He was just coming to that point where girls were interested, and there were a lot of girls interested in Brian.

'All his schoolfriends liked him, and his teachers. Even if he did something wrong, he just kind of looked at you and smiled, and he got away with it.

'The day Brian died maybe sums up a wee bit of his personality. He came home for lunch that day and my mum was minding my daughter, and he was playing with her.

'He was singing that song, "Save All Your Kisses for Me" – he did like singing – and then he put her on his shoulders and ran around with her on his shoulders, giggling.'

After school Brian came home and watched television, then got out his school books and began doing his homework. Marie was helping her brother while their mother prepared dinner for the family.

'Then my mum said, "Marie, your tea's ready," and I walked up the hall but Brian had went round to the shop. He had a cigarette and he was asking for a light off two wee girls that he knew.'

Within minutes Brian had been fatally injured, hit by a plastic bullet fired by the British army. A neighbour, Clara Reilly – who would become a campaigner against plastic bullets – saw what happened. 'Suddenly I heard a bang and saw a white object strike Brian Stewart on the head.'[346]

At the time, the army claimed they had been attacked by young people throwing stones, and then by a crowd of about 500 people. This was refuted by numerous local eyewitnesses and by members of the media.

Kept alive by a life-support machine, it was turned off after six days. Brian was buried on his fourteenth birthday.

His family and others have spent years campaigning to have his name cleared, and took his case all the way to the European Court of Human Rights.

'My mum used to always call Brian the joker,' says Marie. 'He was the one who messed about and told stupid jokes and sometimes did wee stupid things. That kind of died in our house when Brian was murdered.'

❋ ❋ ❋ ❋ ❋

Name: *Anne Magee*

Age: *16*

From: *Cliftonville Road, North Belfast*

Date of Death: *11/10/1976*

Anne Magee was the Bay City Rollers' biggest fan. The eldest of a family of seven, every inch of the bedroom the 16-year-old shared with her sisters, Marie and Catherine, was covered in posters, articles, photographs – and tartan.

'She had all the gear,' says her brother JJ. Anne wore tartan trousers, a red jumper and a 'Rollers' scarf; her favourite was lead singer Les McKeown. 'She loved them and lived them.'

The previous December, she had queued with 4,000 other teenagers to see them perform in the ABC in Belfast's Great Victoria Street, and she had tickets to see them again in September.

Originally from the Cregagh estate in south-east Belfast, the Magee family had been forced out at the start of the Troubles, and had eventually found a home in Harcourt Drive, off the Cliftonville Road.

A pupil at Our Lady of Mercy Girls' School in Ballysillan, Anne had just completed her O Levels, and had gone back to school to take her A Levels. She was 'always studying', remembers JJ, and was also learning shorthand typing, competing with her sister Marie to see how many words they could type per minute.

She also loved netball and swimming and had a part-time job in Hughes' shop on nearby Manor Street. Due to go to Newcastle, County Down for the weekend with the youth club, JJ headed to the shop to buy an apple from Anne 'for a bit of banter,' he says. 'It was the last time I saw her.'

The Magees lived on an interface area. 'We were very conscious of the Troubles,' says JJ. 'We weren't allowed out at night. We even dreaded going to the chippy on a Friday night, beside Anne's shop. We all knew people who had been killed.'

Anne was working in the shop when she was shot in the face during a UDA robbery. She was taken to hospital and had been doing well – 'she was up and talking and walking around' – when, three weeks later, her condition suddenly deteriorated.

A 16-year-old later pleaded guilty to her murder and was ordered to be detained indefinitely. Three others were sentenced to ten years in prison for their part in the robbery; the eldest had been only 17 at the time of the attack.[347]

Four days after Anne was shot, the Bay City Rollers were back in Belfast; Anne had tickets to see them. Her friends tried, unsuccessfully, to get the band to her bedside.

In December 2018 Anne's hero, Les McKeown, was back in Belfast performing two sell-out Bay City Rollers shows. Anne's family are certain she would have been in the audience.

✳ ✳ ✳ ✳ ✳

Name: *Carol McMenamy*

Age: *14*

From: *New Lodge, North Belfast*

Date of Death: *06/11/1976*

That Friday night, Carol McMenamy and her cousin had plans. They were on their way to a disco; the 14-year-old would call for her cousin and then they would make their way to the dance in the local church hall.

A fellow pupil at Our Lady of Mercy Girls' School, Angela O'Connor, remembers how Carol had stood out in the class. 'There were some big personalities in our class and Carol fell into that category. She was tall and skinny with mousey hair in a feathered cut. Carol always had an answer for the teachers, even if it wasn't the expected one.'

Carol was standing at the door of her cousin's home in Newington Street in north Belfast when she was shot in the head and neck. 'Two youths fired ten shots from across the road. They then escaped in a blue car.'[348] Carol died the following day.

According to *Lost Lives*, the UVF was responsible. A detective told the inquest into her death he believed she had been murdered in retaliation for the killing of a Protestant woman, Georgina Strain, in north Belfast a few days before.[349]

Carol's 17-year-old brother Martin had been shot and killed the previous year. The year before, her cousin, Michelle Osborne, died when a loyalist bomb exploded at Hannahstown greyhound track.

Carol's mother, Charlotte McMenamy, said, 'I thought I would never get over Martin's death and now this has happened. Carol was just an ordinary schoolgirl.'[350]

The Sunday after Carol was shot, the annual Witness for Peace commemoration took place in the grounds of Belfast City Hall. Set up by the Reverend Joseph Parker after his 14-year-old son Stephen was killed in the Bloody Friday bombings in 1972, a total of 1,159 white crosses were placed in the ground to remember every victim of the Troubles.

At the last minute, according to the *Irish Press*, 'three extra crosses had to be found'. Between Saturday night and Sunday morning three more people had died – a barman, Eugene McDonagh, who had been shot outside the premises where he worked in Newtownabbey, Ronald Bond, a part-time UDR soldier who had been shot in Derry ten days before, and Carol McMenamy.

* * * * *

Name: *Philomena Greene*

Age: *16*

From: *Lurgan, Co Armagh*

Date of Death: *28/11/1976*

Philomena Greene did not have to worry about adding the trademark Bay City Rollers tartan to her jeans and jackets. Her mother Marie was an outstanding dressmaker and made all the alterations for her 16-year-old daughter.

One of eight children, Philomena – or Philly, as she was known – had loved drawing in school, but 'was keen to get working', Marie remembers, and had just started a job at Warp Knitters in Lurgan.

The Greene family were close, especially the six girls, who all shared a bedroom; Philomena had 'a wee habit' of borrowing everyone else's clothes. The house backed on to a large playing field, and six of the family played camogie for St Peter's.

With Marie as coach and goalkeeper, Philomena would play outfield with her sisters while baby Angela sat in her pram on the sidelines with her camogie stick in her hand; Angela would later go on to play for Armagh.

Philomena was sporty – 'loved camogie, athletics, hurdling and the long jump', says Marie, and she won medals for Irish dancing. She also helped the sacristan at the local church, St Peter's, an older man who lived alone. Philly washed and ironed his shirts every week. 'All of the family did something like that,' said Marie; through her, the family received the Lord Mayor's Community Award.

Cooking was not Philly's strong suit; cooking chips one day, she realised she didn't have enough oil so ran to the local shop for more. 'By the time she came back the whole family were battling the blaze with dishcloths,' remembers Marie.

That Sunday night, Philomena was on her way home from the local disco with her friends Joanne O'Hagan and Nuala Burke, when they noticed a light on in an unoccupied house owned by Joanne's father and went to investigate.

'I went upstairs to see if there was anybody in bed,' Joanne told the *Irish News*. 'Then I went downstairs and I was in the living room when the explosion happened. Philly had gone into the kitchen and could not find the light switch. Her last words were, "How do you get this door open?"'[351]

The booby-trap bomb had been left by the IRA; in a statement, the organisation sent its 'deepest sympathy' and said the bomb had been intended for the security forces.[352]

Marie was driving a relative home and heard the explosion. As usual, Philomena had been wearing something borrowed; one of her mother's pleated skirts.

✳ ✳ ✳ ✳ ✳

Name: *Geraldine McKeown*

Age: *14*

From: *Ardoyne, North Belfast*

Date of Death: *08/12/1976*

Geraldine McKeown loved music. She and her friend Kate McCurdy spent most of their time in her bedroom listening to records. Fourteen-year-old Dina – as her friends called her – loved ABBA and The Eagles. 'She used to get the tennis racket and pretend she was playing the guitar while I sang into the hairbrush,' says Kate.

One day the friends set up Dina's red Dansette record player on the street corner. When it began to rain, Dina ran to get an umbrella to shelter it. 'Then me and her stood dancing with it raining, like we were two eejits. Every time I hear "Dancing Queen" I think of her.'[353]

Another friend, Angela O'Connor, lived in a house which backed onto the McKeowns' in Mountainview Gardens. 'Dina loved the Bay City Rollers ... the tartan-trimmed parallels were the thing to own and wear. I wasn't allowed them but Dina had two pair, a red pair and a pair of electric blue which I would change into at hers and off we'd go.'

The youngest of four and the only girl in the family, Geraldine was 'adored' by her parents. 'She was just a great kid,' says her older brother Ciaran. 'Friendly, lively, chatty with loads of friends.'[354]

She was a pupil at Our Lady of Mercy Girls' School in Ballysillan. Three students from the school had already lost their lives to the Troubles; the most recent, Carol McMenamy – who was also 14 – had been killed only a month before, and according to Ciaran had been a friend of Geraldine's.

Geraldine was also well aware of the violence going on around her. Ciaran had been arrested and was on remand in Crumlin Road Gaol, and the family had already been threatened by loyalists. 'I found these letters of Geraldine's saying, "I'm afraid to die, I'm afraid,"' said Kate.[355]

If there was a knock at the door, Geraldine had a habit of peeping through the Venetian blinds to see who was there. That evening, when loyalist gunmen arrived, 'that's exactly what she did', said Ciaran. 'The fellas saw the blinds opening and they just fired through the window. It could have been anybody.'[356]

Kate McCurdy recalled that 'her mummy and daddy said later that when the door rapped she said, "That's Kate." She thought it was me.'[357]

At Geraldine's wake, her open coffin was placed in the bay window where she had been shot; Geraldine had planned a concert for her schoolfriends to raise money for the missions; it was cancelled, and instead they sang at her Requiem Mass.[358]

Kate recalls how Geraldine would stay at her house on a Saturday night; they would stand outside a club and listen to the groups because they were too young to go in. 'She used to say she couldn't wait until she was old enough.'[359]

✳ ✳ ✳ ✳ ✳

PLASTIC
BULLETS
KILL

BAN THEM

Clara Reilly and
Theresa Rowntree
protest against the
use of plastic bullets.

4

Rubber and Plastic Bullets

'How can they justify shooting children? You hit anybody in the head
with one of those, it's going to kill them.'
From *They Shoot Children: Use of Rubber and Plastic Bullets
in the North of Ireland*

A rubber bullet is the size of a child's fist, and twice as long. A plastic bullet – or
baton round – is only slightly smaller, and lacks the tapered, bullet-shaped tip.
Held in the hand, it is clear there is a weight to them – the sort of projectile that,
fired with any sort of force, is capable of causing serious injury or death.

Every day, John Kelly shows the bullets to school groups in the Museum
of Free Derry. He passes them round, allowing the children and teenagers to
hold them in their hands. Two boys, he tells them, Paul Whitters and Stephen
McConomy, were killed by these nearby. He can see the shock on the pupils'
faces. Suddenly, the Troubles are made real. 'They're imagining what it would be
like to be hit by one of these things, and the damage it would do.'

Of the seventeen people killed by rubber and plastic bullets in Northern
Ireland, eight of them were children. The first, 11-year-old Francis Rowntree, was
hit in the head by a rubber bullet fired by a British soldier in Belfast in April 1972;
the last was Seamus Duffy, 15, who died after his heart was crushed by a plastic
bullet fired by a member of the RUC in August 1989.

Rubber and plastic bullet (left); Brian Stewart, featured on the cover of a 1976 pamphlet (right).

'They were beautiful children, all slaughtered,' says Clara Reilly. A lifelong campaigner against the use of plastic bullets, she and her friend Emma Groves – who had been blinded by a rubber bullet when a soldier shot her in the face in her own living room in west Belfast in 1971 – founded the United Campaign Against Plastic Bullets in 1984.

Eight years before, Clara had witnessed the shooting of 13-year-old Brian Stewart; now 80 years old, she points out Brian's photograph on the front of a campaign pamphlet. 'Look at that lovely face,' she says. 'They're horrible weapons, and it's such a horrible death.'

Clara was on her way to a neighbour's when she 'heard the bang ... I saw the child falling'. She and a neighbour lifted Brian and brought him into a nearby house.

His older sister Marie Duffy knew he was seriously injured. 'The ambulance man lifted Brian and he went limp, so when he walked past me Brian's big blue eyes were level with mine and he was staring, and he wasn't seeing nothing. I knew Brian was dead. I had to go and tell my mummy.'

Developed by the Hong Kong police in the 1960s, a 'baton round' was a teakwood cylinder, just over an inch long, which could be fired into crowds. These first baton rounds were used against anti-colonial protestors; they killed a girl and caused serious injuries through impact and splintering.[1]

Winners of a fancy dress competition in Creggan, Derry, 1970s.

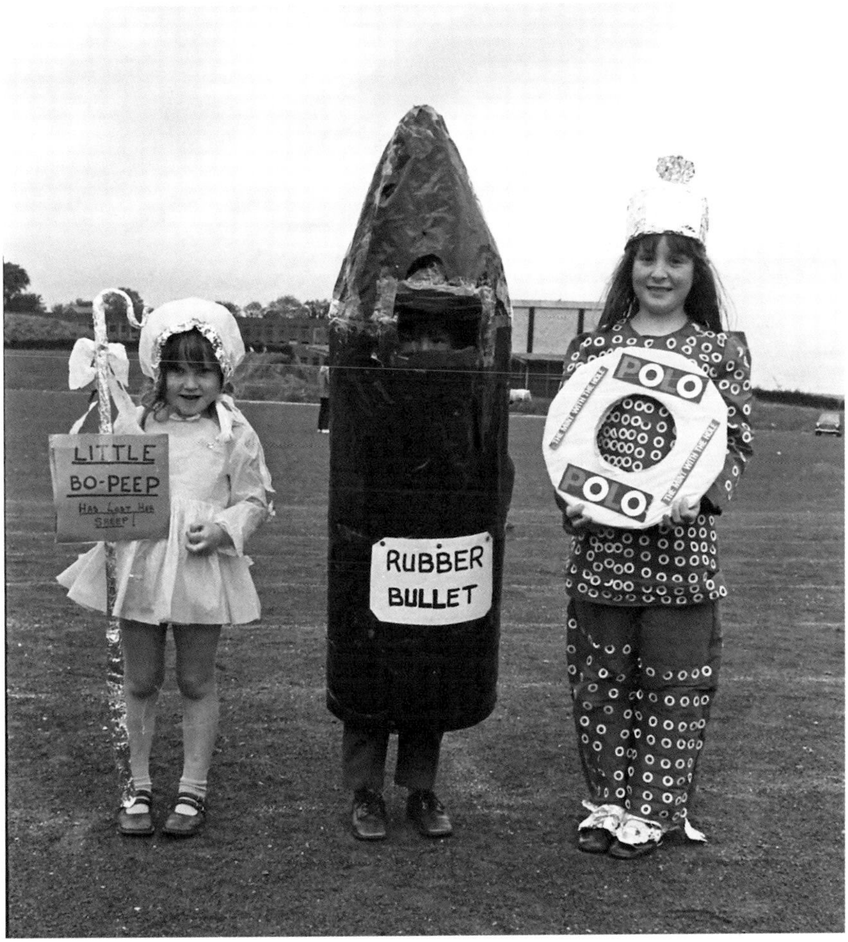

Rejected for use in riots in Northern Ireland on the grounds that they were 'too dangerous', British scientists instead developed a rubber version.[2]

Army Captain Roderick Young unveiled the new weapon to the press in August 1970. Rubber bullets, he explained, were not to be aimed at a specific target but should be fired in front of a crowd so that they would ricochet off the ground and into the group. 'The rubber bullet was not designed to give an open wound, but would give a thump equivalent to a hard blow or a smack with a truncheon.'[3]

The rubber – and later, plastic – bullet was to be a defensive rather than offensive weapon, a 'non-lethal' method of riot control which, in theory, would create a 'sterile area' between security forces and rioters.

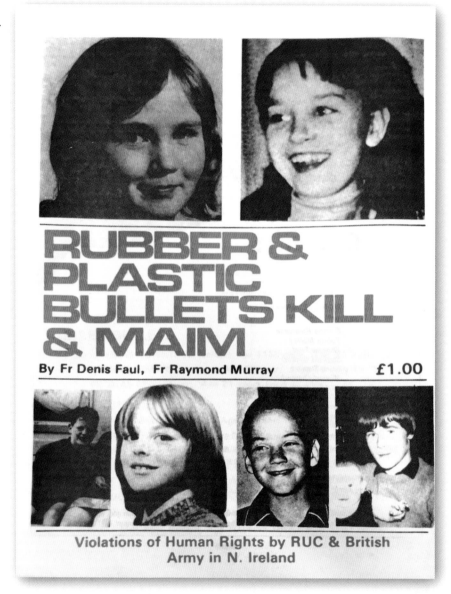

Part of the attraction of rubber bullets was their almost comic-sounding name. One journalist described them as 'soft and squidgy things' and credited a fellow reporter as saying 'soon they'll be lobbing grenades full of confetti'. The aim, said one of the manufacturers, was 'to get a "slightly humorous" image … Looking back, it does seem as if that aim was achieved.'[4]

Some 16,000 rubber bullets were fired in 1971, and over 23,000 in 1972; following Bloody Sunday, nearly 4,000 were fired in February 1972 alone.[5] Yet as early as 1970, concerns were being raised on the ground that the rules governing their firing were being routinely broken and that the weapon was causing severe injuries.

Between 1970 and 1972 four surgeons at the Royal Victoria Hospital in Belfast studied 90 patients treated at the hospital for rubber bullet injuries. Eighty per cent of inpatients had head injuries and one, Francis Rowntree, had died.[6]

There was also evidence that rubber bullets were being doctored. According to eyewitnesses the rubber bullet that killed Francis had a torch battery inserted inside it.[7]

Plastic bullets were introduced in 1973, and by 1975 had completely replaced rubber bullets. The RUC began to use them in 1978. Language was important: officially, they were described as plastic batons, or simply, baton rounds, which sounded less dangerous than plastic bullets.

The attraction of plastic bullets was, according to the army, their greater accuracy. Rubber bullets were unstable in flight, and it was impossible to control their bounce, whereas plastic bullets were to be aimed at selected targets – rather than indiscriminately into a crowd – so that 'they strike the lower part of the target's body directly'.[8]

The British army's Rules of Engagement for PVC Baton Rounds (August 1980) stipulated that they could be used to disperse a crowd 'whenever it is judged to be a minimum and reasonable force in the circumstances'. Rounds should not be fired at a range of less than 20 metres 'except when the safety of soldiers or others is seriously threatened'.[9]

The Committee on the Administration of Justice (CAJ) and others argued that plastic bullets were in fact more dangerous. Their pamphlet of 1990 compared the statistics: one person killed for every 18,000 rubber bullets fired, as compared to one for less than every 4,000 plastic bullets fired.[10]

Bob Harker, a former British soldier who became a campaigner against plastic bullets, said the security forces on the ground did not realise the damage the bullets could do. 'During our training you could see that they were simply unstable,' he told the BBC in 2001. 'Someone would fire at the target and completely miss. We were told they were just these little rubbery things that weren't lethal. You'd see them fired all over the place, soldiers firing them willy-nilly, especially at night.'[11]

Campaigners on the ground, including Clara Reilly and Emma Groves and priests Fr Denis Faul and Fr Raymond Murray, compiled a list of injuries. Often accompanied by photographs of the bandaged casualties, or the circular bruises left on their skin, it makes for difficult reading: fifteen-year-old Paul Lavelle, whose head was so badly damaged he had to be put on a life-support machine; Paul Corr, 12, who lost part of his nose and needed emergency surgery for a shattered palate; four-year-old David Madden, who received six stitches for a head wound.[12]

The nature of the injuries were such that victims tended to survive for a time on life-support machines; when they died, it was days later in hospital.

Scientist Jonathan Rosenhead argued that political reasons were behind the switch from rubber to plastic bullets. 'It is preferred that onlookers do not get the impression that police are using excessive force or that the baton has an especially injurious effect on the targeted individuals. A flow of blood and similar dramatic effects are to be avoided,' he wrote. The effects 'should look harmless enough on the TV news and yet still be unpleasant to those who experience it.'[13]

1981 was the worst year. Clara Reilly, who was living in Turf Lodge in west Belfast, recalls how plastic bullets were fired into groups of people who had gathered to say the Rosary at street corners as the hunger strikers were dying.

She had been hit in the arm by a rubber bullet years before – 'I was lucky I had my arm up otherwise I would have got it in the face' – and for a long time afterwards was nervous every time she passed a British army jeep. 'I was just waiting for a bullet to come out. They were driving about in their jeeps and the plastic bullets were being fired like confetti, it was very frightening.'

In May 1981 – the month of the death of the first hunger striker, Bobby Sands – a total of 16,656 plastic bullets were fired;[14] during the hunger strikes at least 54 people were injured by plastic bullets, 16 of them children.[15]

Seven people, including three children – 15-year-old Paul Whitters, Julie Livingstone (14) and Carol Ann Kelly, who was 12 – died between April and August 1981 after being hit by plastic bullets. Julie and Carol Ann were shot by the British army, Paul by a member of the RUC.

The Ministry of Defence (MoD) – and British government – position had always been that plastic bullets were necessary given the unrest in Northern Ireland, and that their use was consistent with the principle of minimum force and was subject to strict controls. If they did not use plastic bullets, they warned, they would be forced to use lead.

Days after the death of Carol Ann, their use was defended by the RUC chief

Mural in Falls Road remembering seventeen people killed by plastic bullets.

constable, Jack Hermon. 'It is the considered and professional judgement of the security forces that the plastic baton round is an indispensable and reasonable response to the violence with which the security forces are confronted,' he said.

'The plastic baton round is certainly not used with any intention to kill. It is used against rioters who are themselves determined to kill or wound or to cause destruction. It is an alternative to more severe measures.'[16]

Both Julie and Carol Ann were shot on their way home from the local shop. Carol Ann had a carton of milk in her hand. Despite the denial of multiple local witnesses, the British army claimed that the girls had been shot during rioting.

The pattern was familiar: in 1976, following the death of Brian Stewart, journalist Fionnuala O'Connor described how the army's story had changed.

'The first Army statement said two patrols had been attacked by stone-throwing youths, at first a few, then a crowd of about 400, and had fired "a number of baton rounds" to extricate themselves. "Unfortunately, one baton round hit a thirteen-year-old boy," said the spokesman. Yesterday the unfortunate boy became a leading stone-thrower according to the officer commanding the regiment involved. Not an impressive change in the story.

'In the meantime, local people maintained that there had been no crowd and no riot and the boy had been standing at the corner with a few friends when the soldiers began firing. They admitted that people gathered angrily after that.'[17]

This was repeated time and time again. Opponents of plastic bullets maintained that most of those killed had not been involved in rioting and the fatalities and injuries were inconsistent with the principle of minimum force. The 'strict controls' regarding their use were either inadequate or not applied. In any

Grandson of Clara Reilly, one of the founders of the United Campaign Against Plastic Bullets.

case, it was argued, there were other options for riot control and the suggestion that lead bullets replace plastic ones in a riot situation was contrary to the law.

'Evidence ... has shown that many of those killed and injured had no part in rioting,' the CAJ pointed out. 'Rioters, most of whom are young people, now run the risk of a penalty of death or life-changing injury. This is a situation which, critics argue, is inconsistent with the principle of minimum force and should not be tolerated by any society aiming to maintain democratic and human rights standards.'[18]

'The penalty for rioting is, at most, six months, not death,' said one resident

CHILDREN OF THE TROUBLES

of Divis Flats. 'The penalty for ten-year-olds throwing stones at heavily armoured vehicles should be a clip on the ear, not death. But we now have the situation that the penalty for being a Catholic ... and walking in your own street or even standing at your own window is now death.'[19]

Politicians, clergymen, trade unions, teachers and parents were among those who protested. They argued that the weapon was being used overwhelmingly against the Catholic community, and that the use of plastic bullets was both a moral and a human rights issue.

The vast majority of those killed and injured by rubber and plastic bullets were Catholic; Keith White (20), who was shot and killed by a plastic bullet fired by a policeman in 1986, was the only Protestant fatality.

The Organisation of Concerned Teachers [OCT] was inspired by Fr Raymond Murray, who called on 'all responsible adults to make public their opposition to the use of plastic bullets'.[20]

"The ghosts of these children are asking," Fr Murray told the OCT in 1982, "you people who took responsibility for our growth, why are you not speaking publicly and effectively about the way in which the growth of our young lives was cut off?"[21]

'We are alarmed,' the OCT wrote in the same year, 'that there have been no prosecutions despite the fact that 14 innocent people have been killed by rubber and plastic bullets and more than 60 seriously injured. Their right to life is being viciously disregarded. The fact that the only crime committed by these children was to be out of doors makes it impossible for responsible adults to be silent.'[22]

Fr Murray described what he had witnessed at the International Tribunal of Inquiry into deaths and serious injuries caused by plastic bullets, which was held in August 1981. Among those who gave evidence was an injured child. 'I will never forget the 14-year-old boy who moved like a crab across the floor to testify at that tribunal,' Fr Murray said.

'The teachers of Belfast and Derry have seen ten of their children killed by the state in a hostile and brutal fashion .... Some people give the impression that a child is expendable – "only a child, they say", as if the children of the city streets do not count, as if their lives were less valuable. To teachers this is doubly hurtful because they realise the potential that is there.'[23]

Among those who had attended the tribunal were senior British scientist Dr Tim Shallice, who admitted he was 'astonished by the widespread and indiscriminate use of plastic bullets and by the negligible official response'.[24]

'The conclusion seemed inescapable to members of the commission,' he later wrote. 'The Northern Ireland authorities were knowingly allowing widespread, indiscriminate and illegal use of a weapon whose lethal potential was well known.'[25]

In 1982, the European Parliament voted by 100 to 43 to ban the use of plastic bullets throughout the EEC.[26]

The same year, the US House of Representatives passed a motion calling on the British government to terminate its use of the weapon in Northern Ireland.[27]

Clara, Emma and other campaigners, including the families of some of the children killed by plastic bullets, took their campaign to the plastic bullet manufacturers in the UK and the United States. 'We spoke to the workers as they were coming out and told them what the bullets were doing. They had no idea, because they were always described as non-lethal,' says Clara.

In 1988 the then principal plastic bullet supplier for the UK, Standard Fireworks, announced it would not be renewing its contract with the MoD.[28]

Yet the British authorities had been aware, years before, of the dangers of rubber and plastic bullets. Declassified documents, which were uncovered by the Pat Finucane Centre (PFC), have demonstrated that the MoD was concerned that the use of rubber bullets might be 'exposed in court'.

In 1977 it sought legal advice over the compensation case of Richard Moore, a ten-year-old Derry boy who was shot and blinded by a rubber bullet in 1972. As to whether the rubber bullet was a 'suitable and safe weapon for riot control purposes', the MoD was advised that 'if this line of questioning was pursued, it would have a potential for embarrassment'.

The documents also revealed that the MoD was aware that, because the army needed a riot control weapon 'urgently', testing had been carried out 'in a shorter time than would have been ideal'.[29]

Testing was the responsibility of scientists at the British military research laboratories in Porton Down; based on their research, a Medical Committee would evaluate the results and advise the government.

In the archives, the PFC discovered 'newspaper clippings but little official data'; a declassified letter from the former scientific officer to the British army's General Officer Commanding (GOC) in Northern Ireland warned that the Medical Committee 'feel they are being thwarted by the MoD'.

It was dated 10 May 1982, just weeks after the death of Stephen McConomy; the

former scientific officer wrote again in July, stating that the committee 'have not been given any meaningful data on actual wounding but each time they meet they comment on the reports in the press and journals about injuries caused by baton rounds. Our excuse for not providing them with data ... is wearing a little thin.'[30]

The MoD was also aware that the type of plastic bullet gun used to shoot Stephen was faulty; the same claim was made about the gun which killed Paul Whitters.

The majority of families later received compensation. In 1990 the CAJ wrote that the total figure paid out by the Northern Ireland Office, Police Authority and MoD was 'well over £1 million'. 'In no compensation cases have the police or army admitted liability.'[31]

The use of plastic bullets continued into the 1990s.

Only one prosecution was ever brought, in relation to the death of Sean Downes in 1984. Shot by a plastic bullet fired by an RUC reservist during an anti-internment rally in west Belfast, the moment of impact was captured on television and shown around the world; the reservist was later acquitted of his manslaughter.

Often, there was simply no investigation, and witnesses who tried to complain or to give evidence were told they could be charged with rioting. 'Mrs Toner, who rang the RUC to say she was willing to testify about the death of Carol Ann Kelly, had her house shot up with plastic bullets the same evening.'[32]

'A child died at the hands of a grown man and the police didn't do anything about it,' says Stephen McConomy's brother Emmett. 'They said they asked the soldier and he said it was an accident, and they left it at that. That's the value that's placed on a child's life. How can you turn a blind eye to that? It's rotten to the core. I believe that went right through the heart of the army and the judicial system as well as the police. There were questions that were never asked.'

In an exhibition in Derry in 2018, Mary Kay Mullen recalled the 'sombre mood' in the city in April 1981 as she returned from a rally calling on the British government to meet the hunger strikers' demands.

'Three young boys in bright T-shirts arrived throwing stones at the empty offices next door to the bakery. A sudden flash from the small door in the heavy bakery gates – a plastic bullet fired by a heavily-armed policeman. One young boy lies prostrate in the middle of an empty street.

'Our babysitter phones for an ambulance. More policemen emerge and shelter behind a small wall taunting a group of young people …. They seem to laugh. They drag the boy's body inside.'

Mary Kay and a friend give witness statements to a local solicitor, but the police do not come to talk to them. She gives evidence at Paul [Whitters'] inquest. 'Our eyewitness evidence is not accepted at face value. It is twisted to make the young boy the leader of a mob of dangerous rioters posing "serious threat to life and property". Thus the policeman suddenly emerging from a closed doorway firing, without warning, a plastic bullet at close range was "protecting lives".'

'I often think of Paul Whitters, that young boy of fifteen in a bright T-shirt, severely brain-damaged lying alone in the middle of Great James Street surrounded by heavily armed RUC – we witnesses too stunned and afraid to step forward to comfort him.'[33]

At the time, the Director of Public Prosecutions recommended 'no prosecution'.

In 2007, a report by the Police Ombudsman, Nuala O'Loan, found that it had been 'wrong and unjustified' to fire at Paul, and the shooting was 'clearly not consistent with RUC rules'. She also found that his death had not been properly investigated.

As the peace process gathered strength, the use of plastic bullets declined. Increasing political stability meant there was less call for their use, though there were exceptions, in particular the unrest which accompanied the Drumcree protests in the 1990s.

In 1998, the United Nations Committee Against Torture would recommend their abolition, and the 1999 Patten Report into policing recommended discontinuing their use 'as soon as possible'.

'If you're facing a crowd who won't go home and are intent on rioting, you have to know that you can defend yourself and the area you are protecting,' said one RUC officer. 'That sometimes means that you have no choice but to up the ante – go on the offensive and clear an area so that you can prevent destruction of property and therefore the endangerment of lives. You're stuck between the devil and the deep blue sea. But what would happen if we weren't there with our equipment? A lot more injuries to our officers.'[34]

The latest version of the plastic bullet, the 'less lethal' Attenuated Energy Projectile (AEP), continues to be used sporadically in Northern Ireland, most recently in 2018, when a total of four rounds were fired at 'two males who were responsible for throwing petrol bombs and IEDs at police lines' during rioting in Derry.[35]

Yet for the families of the children killed by rubber and plastic bullets, there are still questions to be answered. In April 2019 it was revealed that there are named files about Julie Livingstone and Paul Whitters in the National Archives in London – the file on Julie is to be kept closed until 2064, and that on Paul until 2059. Another file on plastic bullet deaths is sealed until 2071.

Paul Whitters' mother Helen made a direct appeal to the Northern Ireland secretary of state, Karen Bradley, to release the file to Paul's family.

'I brought Paul into this world,' she wrote. 'When this file is opened on January 1 2059 I will not be alive. No one will still be alive who actually knew Paul as the lovely, handsome, caring, intelligent young man that he was. Your Government does not have the right to withhold this from my family. You do not have the right to withhold this from his two brothers and sister. What could there be in this file about a 15-year-old schoolboy? Is it because there's stuff in the file, nothing to do with Paul perhaps, that they don't want publicised?

Paul Whitters' football boots.

Paul Whitters

These football boots are here to represent my son, Paul.

Paul was a popular boy with a generous nature. He was fond of his grandparents, always popping in to help out. He had a paper round and was particularly appreciated by his older customers as he was always happy to run errands. He loved fishing and football.

Paul was 15 when he was shot in the head from close range by an R.U.C. officer. He spent 10 days on life support and passed away on April 25th 1981. It was a senseless killing of a child.

I am here today to stand alongside families who have suffered a similar injustice. I am here today because the man who did this has never been held to account.

Helen Whitters

She now lives in Scotland. 'If we don't do our best to get these things opened up to the public people will never understand. Even people here, where I live, haven't a clue about what happened in Northern Ireland – they wouldn't believe the half of it. It's important that they know.'

Each year, a vigil against the use of plastic bullets is still held at the site of the former Andersonstown police barracks in west Belfast. In 2019 it was renamed

Campaigners Clara Reilly (left), Emma Groves (middle), and Elizabeth Livingstone.

Groves Reilly Corner in recognition of Clara and Emma, who campaigned there for decades.

'The line of placards on the road beside the barracks was and is a familiar August site,' said Julie Livingstone's brother Robin, 'and my family can think of no better place and no better way to celebrate the inspirational lives of two amazing women.'[36]

'Every year as many of us try and go as we can,' says Julie's sister Elizabeth. 'They have placards now, but we have this big picture of Julie that my mummy had hanging on the wall and before that we would have brought that down with us and the kids would have brought the prams and we would have stood there holding it.

'One year we went to get something to eat after the vigil and we just sat Julie on her own chair and we said, "What do you think she'd be doing now?"'

Opposite: Queen Elizabeth meets children at Hillsborough Castle.

1977

- A British proposal for a legislative assembly is quickly abandoned following a lack of nationalist support

- The SDLP declares its preference for 'an agreed Ireland'

- A feud between the Provisional and Official IRA leads to a number of deaths in Belfast

- Queen Elizabeth visits Belfast as part of her Silver Jubilee celebrations, her first trip to Northern Ireland in eleven years

- Children of all ages queue outside cinemas as *Star Wars* is released.

Name: *Graeme Dougan*

Age: *15 months*

From: *Glengormley, Co Antrim*

Date of Death: *01/01/1977*

The previous summer, baby Graeme Dougan had his first holiday. The family – Graeme, his older sisters Wendy and Jennifer and their parents Alan and Maureen – had gone to the seaside, staying in Helen's Bay, County Down.

At the family home in Harmin Park, New Year's Day was marked by a bomb scare.

Police had received a warning that an IRA bomb had been left in a hijacked car and had begun evacuating the area. The family were the last to leave; Graeme was on his mother's lap in the front seat of the car when the bomb exploded.

According to *The Irish Times* a 40-minute warning had been given, but the bomb exploded 15 minutes early.[360] The car which had contained the bomb was turned into a mangled heap of wreckage; newspaper photographs also showed a small hole in the passenger door of the Dougans' car, left by a fragment of metal which blasted through the door, killing Graeme and injuring his mother.

The *Evening Herald* reported that the explosion had been the result of a 'massive IRA intelligence blunder' because the area had once been mainly occupied by the families of policemen and prison officers, but that had been several years ago, and most had moved out.[361]

The following year a 22-year-old Belfast man was convicted of manslaughter and sentenced to 20 years in prison for Graeme's killing; he was also sentenced to a minimum of 30 years for the murders of two policemen, three soldiers and a civilian. Two other men were sentenced to 16 years in prison in connection with Graeme's death.[362]

Family home video of Graeme's only holiday was shown on television in Northern Ireland after his death. His grandmother, Caroline Dougan, said she wanted viewers to see the pictures of the baby enjoying himself at the seaside.

'Maybe it will prick the consciences of those responsible and if it contributes to saving someone else's life, possibly that of another baby, then that at least will be of some consolation to us,' she said.[363]

Name: *Kevin McMenamin*

Age: *7*

From: *Ballymurphy, West Belfast*

Date of Death: *10/04/1977*

Kevin McMenamin loved to dress up and dance.

'Kevin was a wee character,' says his mother Susan. 'His teacher would say he would push the tables and chairs back in the classroom so he could dance and entertain the class. He loved music so much, we bought him a transistor radio, and he used to walk around with it on his shoulder and sing.'

Seven-year-old Kevin was one of a family of nine children from New Barnsley Crescent. He had just made his First Communion, and his family always said he would become a priest. 'We had two sets of bunk beds,' remembered Susan, 'and Kevin would always say, "turn the lights on, I want to say my prayers".'[364]

It was Easter Sunday – the day republicans commemorate their dead. Two parades had been organised, one by the Provisionals, the other by the Officials. The Officials' parade was about to set off; Kevin's father Paul, a Workers' Party sympathiser, was near the front. Kevin – who had not been allowed to go – slipped out with his ten-year-old brother, Sean.

The bomb had been left in a parcel on a windowsill. 'There was a hell of a bang,' said Charles Begley. 'I rushed into the street, where there were a lot of people waiting for the parade to start. There was a cloud of smoke down the street where the bomb had gone off and many windows were broken. I ran down and found a wee boy lying on the pavement. Half of his head was blown off … he was covered in blood. I cradled him in my arms to say an Act of Contrition in his ear.'[365]

As panic swept through the crowd, scuffles broke out as many assumed – wrongly – that the bomb had been left by the (Provisional) IRA and that the explosion marked the resumption of feuding between the Officials and the Provisionals. Kevin's uncle, John Short (49), was shot dead later that day by the IRA, as he went to tell relatives that Kevin his nephew had been killed.[366]

The bomb had been left by members of the UVF Shankill Butchers gang;

one of them was later convicted of murder and three others of other charges in connection with Kevin's death.[367] Kevin was their youngest victim.

The McMenamin family moved to Downpatrick, but found it difficult to escape the legacy of Kevin's death. 'He left a mark on you, and the house seemed empty without him,' says Susan.

'I always remember that morning, I was downstairs getting all the kids' clothes ready for Easter Sunday mass while they were all sleeping. I could see someone behind me and when I turned around, it was Kevin. He just smiled and said, "Happy Easter, Mummy."'

✳ ✳ ✳ ✳ ✳

Name: *Paul McWilliams*

Age: *16*

From: *Springhill Avenue, West Belfast*

Date of Death: *09/08/1977*

Paul McWilliams was easy-going. 'He was very laid back and saw the funny side of everything,' remembers his brother Thomas. 'Nothing really fazed him, he just took it in his stride and got on with it. He was so easy-going at times our mother used to call him Paul Stall, because if you asked him to do something he would always have said, "Stall."'

A student at St Thomas's Secondary School, as a teenager he also had a part-time job collecting and washing glasses in a local men's club.

One of Paul's favourite pastimes was playing pool, and he also enjoyed football and other sports. He loved music too, and had diverse tastes, says Thomas – 'everything from sounds of the 60s and 70s to Irish music, country and Elvis. There's a song Dickie Rock sang called "Back Home Again", it always reminds us of him.'

The outbreak of the Troubles changed the family's life. By the time he was 12, Paul had witnessed the internment without trial of three brothers and his 17-year-old sister. 'Our family home became the subject of constant early-morning raids by the army,' says Thomas, 'which caused Paul a lot of stress and resentment.'

Paul became involved in street protests and riots, and joined the Fianna; his father Charles died when Paul was 14. 'Paul was very protective of our mother and always worried about her.'

Sent to St Patrick's Training School on Belfast's Glen Road after he was arrested for riotous behaviour, he had been allowed out to attend his grandmother's funeral.

Due back on 8 August, the day after was the anniversary of internment, which was marked by bonfires in nationalist areas. 'Paul begged our mother to let him stay out [for an extra day] and he promised he would go back the following day,' says Thomas.

'It's something that my mother regretted very much, for the remainder of her life, letting him stay out. If he had gone back to the home, he would have been very much alive.'

On the morning of the 9th, Paul and his brother Christopher were on their way home with an errand for their mother.

'They were taking a short cut through a gap in the wall when 'Christopher said a single shot rang out from Corry's Timber Yard,' says Thomas. 'He looked round and saw the soldier. Christopher had run in one direction and he thought Paul had gone in the other direction, but then he saw him on the ground.'

The British army claimed Paul had been throwing petrol bombs, which his family has always denied; they cite forensic tests which were carried out on Paul's hands to check for flammable liquid, and which came back negative.

Christopher – Crip – was later jailed for the murder of a Belfast bar owner, Colm Mahon. In 1997, while in prison, he shot dead the LVF leader Billy Wright.

Thomas still campaigns on Paul's behalf. 'For over 40 years now our family has been denied the truth. We will never stop campaigning until the truth is told, and maybe then our brother Paul can rest in peace.'

✳ ✳ ✳ ✳ ✳

Name: *Michael Neill*

Age: *16*

From: *Unity Flats, North Belfast*

Date of Death: *24/10/1977*

Michael Neill never got his first pay packet. The 16-year-old had just completed his first week's work at a firm in the city centre which made hessian sacks and coal bags.

'He was ecstatic when he got that job,' says his sister Patricia. 'It was like he was a big boy now, I'm a working man, I'm the man of the house.'

Known as Mousie to his friends, he was Michael at home. 'His friends used to call to the door and say, "Is Mousie there?" and my mother would say, "Who?" until they said Michael and then she'd go, "Yes. Michael, you're wanted at the door."'

The second youngest, and the youngest boy in a family of six, his brother Harry remembers him as 'a comedian, always messing about'.

'He was full of life,' adds his sister Maureen.

Michael could get away with anything. He and Patricia – who was two years younger – used to skip school together. 'We went on the beak and I was always the one caught, never him. Even in the house, he used to keep my mummy going, saying, "Hi, have you any butts for me, have you any fags for me?" She used to save up the butts for him.'

'He was the only one of us could have got away with that,' adds Maureen. 'The rest of us weren't allowed to smoke.'

Michael had 'seen a lot as a kid', says Maureen. 'Because Michael was one of those kids you didn't know he was there until you knew he was there. Unity Flats at that time, there were lots of corners, lots of nooks and crannies, and lots of hidey holes, and Michael could have been in any one of them.'

One day he was beaten by soldiers on his way home, yards from his front door; it came as no surprise when he joined the IRA.

Michael was shot by the British army on the Cliftonville Road in north Belfast. The army said that two youths, one carrying a gun, had hijacked and burnt a bus, and that they had then shot the gunman. This was disputed by Michael's family, who continue to campaign for a full investigation into his death.

'He didn't reach his adulthood,' says Maureen. 'He didn't have a girlfriend or have his own family. There's not a whole lot you can say about Michael because he didn't get to live life.'

⁎ ⁎ ⁎ ⁎ ⁎

Name: *Marcia Gregg*

Age: *15*

From: *Ligoniel, North Belfast*

Date of Death: *16/11/1977*

Even today, Wolfhill Road is remote. A long, narrow lane running through the north Belfast hills, it boasts beautiful views over both the city of Belfast and the surrounding countryside.

A pupil at Everton Girls' School in north Belfast, Marcia was one of ten children of Albert and Anne Gregg; the eldest was 23, the youngest only six years old.

When the fire broke out in the family's farmhouse early that Wednesday morning, 15-year-old Marcia helped save the lives of her brothers and sisters; trapped at an upstairs bedroom window, she was too frightened to jump herself.

Fourteen-year-old Catherine Hodgkins and her sister Ellen (12) – who lived nearby – later told the *Belfast Telegraph* how they watched their friend disappear from the window.

'She kept shouting for her father to save her as I watched the fire and smoke all around her,' said Catherine.

'One moment she was there crying and frightened while we waited for her to jump,' said Ellen. 'It was horrible.'

Catherine had raised the alarm. She had heard something smashing through the window of the Greggs' house, and woke her parents; her father Wesley pleaded with Marcia to jump to safety as he sprayed the burning window frame with a hose.

She described how Marcia's older sister Jean grabbed her hand in a vain attempt to pull her from the burning house. 'But Jean lost her grip and leapt out of the window on her own,' said Catherine.[368]

Regular firefighters were on strike; it took British army firefighters about 20 minutes to reach the blaze. One RUC officer said he believed Marcia would have survived had there not been a strike, but the Fire Brigades Union said the fire caught hold so quickly it would have made no difference.

In the aftermath of Marcia's death, police launched a murder inquiry and said petrol bombers were suspected of starting the fire. Nobody was ever convicted of her death.

A detective inspector told her inquest that the family had been 'dogged by fires'. A car parked in the garage at the farmhouse had previously been set alight, and a fire had been started in a shed. After Marcia's death the family had moved to a new house, where there had been another blaze.

'They were the kind of fires,' a policeman said, 'that would appear to have been started by children or someone of little sense.'[369]

※ ※ ※ ※ ※

THINK OF THEIR TOMORROWS

JOIN

ALLIANCE

TODAY

Write to ALLIANCE PARTY H Q
6 Cromwell Road, Belfast BT7 1JW

Telephone Belfast 24274/5

Published by THE ALLIANCE PARTY of NORTHERN IRELAND   Printed by SIGN SERVICES

1978

- An IRA bomb at the La Mon restaurant near Belfast kills 12 Protestant civilians

- David Cook of the Alliance Party is appointed Belfast's first non-unionist mayor

- Reports by the European Court of Human Rights and by Amnesty International condemn British treatment of detainees in Northern Ireland

- Production of the futuristic DeLorean sports car begins in Belfast

- *Grease* is the year's movie blockbuster, while *Grange Hill* becomes the first soap opera aimed specifically at children.

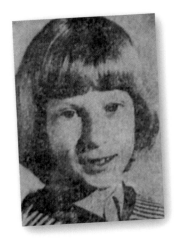

Name: *Lesley Gordon*

Age: *11*

From: *Maghera, Co Derry*

Date of Death: *08/02/1978*

Lesley Gordon loved school, Showaddywaddy, and going to Brownies. The eldest of three children, the 11-year-old was always trying to help – especially with her younger brother and sister.

'I look at the photographs and she is sitting with her arms so protectively around [her younger sister], who was just four,' says Lesley's mother Georgie.

'She was a very quiet child for a long time and she was just beginning to develop and come out of herself. She was really lovely. I suppose every mother thinks that, but I thought she was gentle. She was just an ordinary child – but very special to us.'[370]

A pupil at Culnady Primary School, Lesley and her seven-year-old brother Richard were always driven to school by their father Willie – a school attendance officer and part-time member of the UDR.

As he always did, Willie had checked for explosives underneath the car and in the boot before driving off. But an IRA bomb had been hidden in a cavity in the car. It exploded, killing Lesley and her father instantly.

A neighbour found Richard lying on the pavement. 'Whoever did this must have known that he [Willie] took the children to school at the same time every day,' the neighbour said.[371]

Their deaths were widely condemned, and sparked protests in Derry and outside the Provisional Sinn Féin headquarters in west Belfast. Members of the police, UDR and the British army used helicopters and sniffer dogs to search a 120 square mile radius for their killers, and police went door to door in the town distributing leaflets headed 'Child Murder in Maghera'.[372]

In a joint statement, Archbishop Tomás Ó Fiaich and the Bishop of Derry, Dr Edward Daly, said, 'The fact that the attackers must have known they were putting little children at risk before planting a lethal booby-trap makes their act all the more repulsive.'[373]

The day after their joint funerals, the headline on the front page of the *Belfast Telegraph* read: 'Town of Grief'. The newspaper also wrote of Lesley's empty desk, and her painting of a monster which still hung on the classroom wall; an award is made at Culnady Primary School every year in her memory.

One of her teachers wrote a poem remembering Lesley's 'sweet and gentle nature'. 'The world was a better place for having heard her merry laughter.'[374]

⁂ ⁂ ⁂ ⁂ ⁂

Name: *Michael Scott*

Age: *10*

From: *Oldpark, North Belfast*

Date of Death: *12 / 02 / 1978*

Oldpark Avenue was Michael Scott's world. The ten-year-old lived on the north Belfast street, off Cliftonville Road, with his widowed mother; his granny, 70-year-old Mary Smyth, also lived on Oldpark Avenue, as did his uncle Michael.

He had been spending the weekend at his grandmother's; in the early hours of Sunday morning, there was an explosion.

'It was like setting light to a box of matches,' one neighbour, Marie Loughlan, said. 'The blast blew off the front door and the stairs were blazing in no time at all. The men got a ladder up to the front window, but it would have been suicide to try and get into the house.'[375]

Michael's uncle, who had been sleeping in the back bedroom, was awoken by his mother shouting his name. 'When I went out onto the landing there was a wall of flame between me and my mother's room at the front,' he said. 'I broke my bedroom window and jumped down 15 feet or so into the yard.'[376]

Among those watching the rescue efforts on the street was young Michael's mother. 'It was heartbreaking to see her,' said Marie. 'First of all she was screaming, "My mother is in there," then it must have hit her that Michael was in the inferno too, and she started screaming, "My son is in there too."'[377]

Photographs on the front page of the *Irish News* showed a smiling Michael, wearing a bow tie, as well as the gutted house, a ladder still propped against one of the blackened windows where neighbours had tried to rescue the boy and his grandmother.

Members of the family said the fire had been started by an explosive device described as 'two gas cylinders possibly attached to petrol' and hung on the front door with a meat hook.

Lost Lives quotes 'reliable loyalist sources' as saying the UVF was responsible for their murders.[378]

✳ ✳ ✳ ✳ ✳

Name: *John Boyle*

Age: *16*

From: *Dunloy, Co Antrim*

Date of Death: *11/07/1978*

John Boyle lies buried in one of Dunloy's graveyards; he was killed in the other. One of a family of nine – eight boys and one girl – from the village of Dunloy, County Antrim, John was a few weeks away from his seventeenth birthday.

His brother Vincent was a year older. 'I would have come in at night and kicked John's bed and said, "Are you awake?" If he had come in after me he would have kicked the bed and said, "Are you awake?" and I would have said, "What were you at tonight, and did you have any luck with the girls?"'

Each of the brothers helped on the family farm, and they all enjoyed sport, particularly football. John loved hurling – he played minor hurling for Dunloy – and snooker. A snooker trophy is still awarded annually in the village in his memory.

John's nickname was 'Heaven', after the lyric in the Seekers song 'We Shall

Not Be Moved'. 'He was always humming or singing it,' says his oldest brother, Hugh. 'That Seekers record got a lot of playing.'

The day before, he had gone to investigate an old family headstone, and instead found a hidden gun. That evening he told his father, who went to the police. 'He told me how he had cut a hole in the bag and seen what looked like a gun, bullets and masks,' says another brother, Brian. 'He sounded very excited about it all.'

The next morning, John jumped at the chance to help Hugh, who was working in a field opposite the graveyard. 'I think he was keen to get driving the tractor as he was just learning to drive that summer,' says Brian. 'I remember him driving up the lane on the tractor. That was the last time I saw John alive.'

In the graveyard, the SAS had been lying in wait. John was shot three times – once in the back of the head and twice in the back. Two soldiers were later acquitted of his murder.

Years later, his mother told Vincent that after John was killed, she would be downstairs saying the Rosary at night, and she would hear him upstairs in the corner of his bed, crying.

Vincent believes his brother always wanted to travel. 'I would have been going to dances with him, and I always had the notion that he would have gone to work abroad, only he never got the chance.'

The family have never received an apology for John's death. Vincent remembers asking his father about his decision to go to the police. 'I said to him, "If you could do the same again, would you do it?" He said, "If it saved lives I would."'

✳ ✳ ✳ ✳ ✳

Name: *Graham Lewis*

Age: *13*

From: *Woodvale, North Belfast*

Date of Death: *14/10/1978*

Graham Lewis was over at his friend's house listening to music. It was a typical Saturday evening. The 13-year-old, from Leopold Street off the Crumlin Road, and another boy had gone round to see their friend, who lived less than ten minutes' walk away in Enfield Parade.

His friend's parents were at the cinema, so the boys had the house to themselves. When they found the gun – wrapped in a handkerchief and hidden inside a gas heater – there was nobody to stop them taking it out, and having a good look.

As the teenagers played with the revolver, it went off accidentally; Graham was shot in the head.

His friend's father was later fined £90 on charges of possessing the weapon and UVF membership. According to *Lost Lives* he admitted in court that he had belonged to the UVF since 1972 and had been involved in welfare work for the organisation.

'He said he had been approached [by the UVF] to keep the weapon in his home and had been afraid to refuse them. It was said that since the incident he had received poison-pen letters but had kept in regular contact with the family of the dead teenager.'[379]

At the inquest into Graham's death, the coroner described it as a 'horrible and ghastly incident', calling it 'a tragic case with all the elements of a nightmare'.[380]

Among those who placed messages of sympathy in the *Belfast Telegraph* were the neighbours and children of the nearby Montreal Street; his brother Jim's football club, Ballygomartin FC; the Montreal Street Ladies' Club; the Ohio Darts Club – where Graham's father Robert was a member – and Graham's friends Roy, Tom, David, Sammy and Andy.

✳ ✳ ✳ ✳ ✳

Belfast street life, 1970s.

Remains of the car
belonging to Airey Neave.
Opposite: Warrenpoint massacre.

1979

- The 'blanket protest' among republican prisoners escalates into the 'dirty protest' against the ending of political status

- Airey Neave, Conservative spokesman on Northern Ireland (and close friend of soon-to-be prime minister Margaret Thatcher) dies in an INLA bomb explosion in a House of Commons car park

- British royal Lord Louis Mountbatten and three others – including two children – are killed when an IRA bomb explodes on his boat in County Sligo. Later that day another IRA bomb kills 18 British soldiers at Warrenpoint in County Down

- The DUP's Ian Paisley tops the poll in Northern Ireland's first European election, followed closely by the SDLP's John Hume

- The visit of Pope John Paul II to Ireland sees thousands flock south to open-air masses in Dublin, Knock and Drogheda

- Village People's 'YMCA' is the sing-along hit of the year, while the 'Strawberry Shortcake' doll becomes one of the most sought-after toys this Christmas.

Name: *James Keenan*

Age: *16*

From: *Darkley, Co Armagh*

Date of Death: *24/02/1979*

James Keenan was off to see his first showband. 'He had just taught me how to tie my shoelaces,' remembers his younger brother Eddie. 'I gave him a big thumbs up as he headed off.'

James – who was known as Jim – helped out in his mother Molly's shop in the village of Darkley, County Armagh. On Saturdays he would dole out the paraffin oil, and on Sundays he delivered the papers. 'He loved anything mechanical,' says Eddie. 'He drove diggers in our father's quarry, where he also raced his Hillman Imp and Austin Cambridge in the back fields with his best friend Martin Mulligan.'

The pair spent a lot of time on Mulligans' farm. They loved horses and fishing, and would mitch off school and spend the day fishing for trout. 'We would skip the school bus, get our hidden rods, and go fishing in Tullynawood lake,' remembers Martin. If the bailiffs appeared, it didn't matter. 'We loved the chase.'

Jim won a jennet and cart in a local raffle, and could often be seen parading up and down Darkley's main street with the cart full of children. He was well known for his sweet tooth, and always had sweets in his pocket for them from his mother's shop, as well as bottles of lemonade, recalls his sister Diane.

Jim had pestered his mother all week to allow him to go to Carrickmacross to see the Dublin showband The Memories. He had never been allowed further than the parish disco on Saturday morning. Molly relented.

Jim borrowed his father's brown leather jacket, and was wearing his 'Christmas clothes' – plum-coloured flares and platform boots. 'He was very handsome,' says Eddie. 'He looked great, like he was John Travolta.'

Before he left, he set five-year-old Diane on top of a new Mother's Pride stand in the shop. 'He was an awful messer,' remembers Diane. 'He left me there, and he said, "See you later."'

Jim and his friends – brothers Martin and Ray McGuigan, Martin Mulligan and Tony Nugent – decided to save money by walking the three miles to Keady to get the bus to the dance. Shortly after nine o'clock, as they walked past an abandoned cattle trailer on the 'low road' to Keady, the IRA detonated a booby-trap bomb.

The explosion hurled them across the road and blew a crater in the road five feet deep. Jim was killed instantly; Martin McGuigan survived for a few hours in hospital. His brother Ray was left paralysed and in a wheelchair for life. Martin Mulligan lost his right arm.

The IRA later apologised for their deaths and said the boys had been mistaken for a British army foot patrol. A 20-year-old Keady man was later found not guilty of their murders; a 19-year-old was jailed for five years for conspiring to pass on information about police patrols and being a member of the IRA.[381]

Jim and Martin were given a double funeral; virtually all of Darkley's 300 inhabitants walked behind the two hearses.

＊ ＊ ＊ ＊ ＊

Name: *Martin McGuigan*

Age: *16*

From: *Darkley, Co Armagh*

Date of Death: *24/02/1979*

Martin McGuigan loved music. The 16-year-old's favourite band was Status Quo, and he had even copied guitarist Rick Parfitt's long hairstyle.

Marty – as Martin was known – was the eldest in the family from the village of Darkley in south Armagh; he had left St Patrick's High School in nearby Keady the previous summer.

A keen Gaelic footballer, Martin played for Granemore GFC; he also supported Arsenal and played soccer for Darkley FC. 'He was a great goalscorer, he really stood out on the pitch,' remembers his friend Martin Mulligan.

That Saturday night, he and his younger brother Ray, who was 15, were looking forward to the Saturday night dance in Carrickmacross. The Dublin showband The Memories were playing, but they also did covers, and Marty hoped they might play some of Quo's hits.

With them was Martin Mulligan and Jim Keenan; Ray remembers calling for another friend, Tony Nugent, and sitting in his kitchen listening to Rod Stewart while they waited for him to get ready.

Ray still remembers the 'starlit night' as the friends walked to Keady to catch the bus to Carrickmacross. At home, another brother, 14-year-old Christopher, was watching *Starsky and Hutch* when the massive explosion shook the family home.

As the brothers passed an abandoned trailer, the IRA detonated a bomb. Martin and Jim were killed; Martin Mulligan lost an arm, and Ray was paralysed. He has been in a wheelchair ever since.

'I remember the explosion, but I'd rather stay away from that part,' Ray says. 'I was talking to Martin on the road. When the ambulances arrived, I had a lot of external injuries, and they thought I was worse because of the amount of blood. Martin had very little blood but had internal injuries, and he was dead by the time he got to hospital.'

The police said the IRA fired about a dozen shots at the injured teenagers as they lay on the road.

The IRA later apologised. 'Tragically the youths and their position on the road were mistaken for the movements of soldiers and the bomb was set off.'[382] A 19-year-old from Keady was later jailed for five years for conspiring to pass on information about police patrols and being a member of the IRA.[383]

At their joint funerals, the Archbishop of Armagh, Dr Tomás Ó Fiaich, said the IRA's intention had been to kill, 'and the fact that the victims were innocent young people from the area makes their crime more repulsive in the minds of people'.[384]

Martin and Jim were buried side by side.

✳ ✳ ✳ ✳ ✳

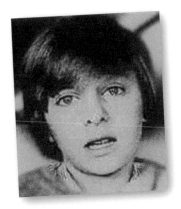

Name: *Nicholas Knatchbull*

Age: *14*

From: *Mersham, Kent*

Date of Death: *27/08/1979*

Nicholas Knatchbull and his twin brother Timothy were never more than a few feet apart. The twins were identical; their only distinguishing feature was a mole under Tim's chin.

Even their mother, Countess Mountbatten, couldn't always tell the difference between the two 14-year-olds. 'They were bright little boys bound up in each other,' she remembers.[385]

'It felt like being in a two-boy club all of our own,' says Tim.[386]

The pair often switched places to fool teachers and friends. When Tim was struggling at a doubles snooker competition at school, Nicky knew what to do. 'I looked at Nick and without a word he knew what was in my mind. From that point on he stepped in and took all my shots.'[387]

Their favourite album was that year's 'Hot Hits' compilation. 'Twinhood was fun, constant companionship and total empathy,' wrote Tim. 'It was central to our lives and we were each other's closest friend, protector and partner.'[388]

The youngest of a family of seven, the twins grew up in the family home in Kent. Their grandfather was Lord Louis Mountbatten, the last British Viceroy of India and Queen Elizabeth II's cousin; Prince Charles, the Prince of Wales, was their godfather.

The twins had left home at nine years of age to board at the Dragon School in Oxford, and both had won scholarships to Gordonstoun, the Scottish public school attended by Prince Charles. Summer holidays were spent in Ireland at their grandfather's castle at Mullaghmore, on the Sligo coast, where the twins and their siblings and cousins would fish and swim.

That morning, the boys and their parents and grandparents set off on Lord Mountbatten's boat, the *Shadow V*. The boat had just left the harbour when an IRA bomb, which had been planted on board overnight, exploded.

Nicholas and another boy, 15-year-old Paul Maxwell, were killed, as was the twins' grandfather, Lord Mountbatten, and their grandmother, Lady Doreen

Brabourne. Tim was seriously injured. Later that year a 31-year-old man was sentenced to life imprisonment for their murders.

On a visit to Mullaghmore in 2015, Prince Charles said that his personal loss had helped him understand 'in a profound way the agonies borne by so many others in these islands, of whatever faith, denomination or political tradition'.[389]

'Where is Nick now?' asks Tim. 'Free and gone. Wherever he needs to be. Maybe in a place where I will meet him again.'[390]

∗ ∗ ∗ ∗ ∗

Name: *Paul Maxwell*

Age: *15*

From: *Enniskillen, Co Fermanagh*

Date of Death: *27/08/1979*

Paul Maxwell loved boats, fishing and the sea. Every year, the family – from Enniskillen, County Fermanagh – would go on holiday to their cottage in Mullaghmore, County Sligo; that year, 15-year-old Paul was delighted to have secured a job as a boat boy on Lord Mountbatten's boat.

'I am having a great time working at the castle,' he wrote on a postcard to his grandmother. 'The food is great. The weather has been very bad. I have brought Lord Mountbatten out about six times and I find him very nice.'[391]

'He was always getting jobs,' says his younger sister Lisa, who was 12. 'He was a real wee entrepreneur.'

'He was working, and he would lend me money and never ask for it back,' adds Donna, who at 17 was the oldest in the family. Paul was 'generous, kind and funny', she adds, but he also enjoyed winding her up. 'I had my first boyfriend and we were walking round the headland and Paul was tracking me, following me round the headland. I was furious.'

'He would bring me on the back of his bike to the circus,' says Lisa, 'and he would make go-karts. He was also very mischievous – I remember a time in Enniskillen he had me in the ditch throwing stones at cars.' On another occasion, Paul painted a white cat blue.

He was also generous, Lisa remembers, and used to buy her little animal-shaped soaps. At Halloween he would build massive bonfires, which he would spend weeks preparing.

On a good day, the beach at Mullaghmore is a golden yellow and the sea sparkles bright blue. Paul had just left the harbour in Lord Mountbatten's boat, the *Shadow V*. One of Lord Mountbatten's grandsons, Timothy Knatchbull, later recalled that Paul had asked him the time. Tim looked at his black Casio watch and announced 'jokily' that it was '11.39 and 30 seconds.'[392]

An IRA unit had been watching the boat from across the bay. Donna and Lisa heard the explosion. 'I remember a man scything a field,' says Donna, 'and I yelled over and I thought, Paul's on it. I went down and I could see the bits of the boat just floating in the water.'

The girls went down to the harbour. 'I have an image of my father staggering,' says Lisa. 'Not walking, but staggering. He knew.'

Gerry Moriarty, then a young reporter with the *Donegal Democrat*, was one of the first journalists on the scene. He recalls watching Paul's father John waiting for his son's body to be brought back to land. 'When the boat came alongside he cried repeatedly, "Look what you've done to him, look what you've done to him. I'm an Irishman, he's an Irishman. Is this the sort of Ireland you want?"'[393]

Timothy's twin brother Nicholas was also killed, as was his grandfather, Lord Louis Mountbatten, and his grandmother Lady Doreen Brabourne. A member of the IRA was later sentenced to life imprisonment for their murders.

Donna and Lisa still return to Mullaghmore every year with their own children. 'This is where Paul was,' says Donna, 'and he loved it here, and it makes me feel closer to him. I don't want this place to be overshadowed by this traumatic event.

'I wonder what he would have been like as a man,' she says. 'I think he would have been a good man.'

✳ ✳ ✳ ✳ ✳

Rioting in Belfast.
Opposite: Margaret Thatcher
in Dublin.

1980

- An IRA land mine kills three UDR soldiers near Castlewellan in County Down, while loyalists shoot dead prominent republican Miriam Daly and INLA leader Ronnie Bunting

- A sex abuse scandal engulfs the Kincora Boys Home in Belfast

- The ending of 'special category' status sees seven republican prisoners go on hunger strike at the Maze prison; the action is called off two months later

- Margaret Thatcher becomes the first serving British PM to visit the Republic of Ireland; there is talk of Anglo-Irish co-operation on security and economic matters

- A Thin Lizzy concert at Belfast's King's Hall is one of the musical highlights of the year, while 'Hungry Hippos' proves one of the most popular games for children.

Name: *Doreen McGuinness*

Age: *16*

From: *Grosvenor Road, West Belfast*

Date of Death: *01/01/1980*

For Doreen McGuinness, it was the start of a new year, and a new decade. The 16-year-old was one of a family of nine children from Distillery Street; before the night was out, she would be in Belfast's Royal Victoria Hospital with gunshot wounds.

She and a 17-year-old boy – who had a serious foot injury – were dropped off at the hospital in a bullet-riddled car about 25 minutes after a vehicle as fired on by British soldiers at a vehicle checkpoint on the Whiterock Road in west Belfast.

An RUC spokesman said the car was reported to have refused to stop at a checkpoint, and soldiers fired shots after it as it sped through.[394] *The Irish Times* reported that police believed the car had been stolen, and the couple may have been joyriding.[395]

A Republican Clubs spokeswoman, Mary McMahon, said that the soldiers involved had made no attempt to stop the car, and said they should be charged with Doreen's murder. 'This latest tragedy is grim evidence that capital punishment for the offence of joy-riding is very much in effect.'[396]

Doreen's death prompted a campaign to get stolen 'killer cars' off the streets. According to the *Irish News*, joyriders – who were mostly young people – were stealing up to 100 cars a month in one part of west Belfast, and two lives had already been lost as a result. The previous year a woman had been knocked down and killed by a stolen on the Falls Road.

'The most distressing features are the moral implications of joyriding and the physical dangers to themselves and others which don't seem to register with the young people,' said Fr Vincent McKinley. 'In fact, the physical danger seems to be part of the thrill of it all,' he added.[397]

Republican Clubs/Workers' Party councillor Jim Sullivan said it was the result of social deprivation and teenagers having grown up amid ten years of violence. 'The identification of socio-economic deprivation with juvenile delinquency has long been established,' he said. 'There is no easy, no cheap solution to the problem; if it is to be tackled at all it must include a massive attack on the chronic unemployment, male and female, young and old, that these teenagers are growing into.'[398]

✳ ✳ ✳ ✳ ✳

Name: *Hugh Maguire*

Age: *9*

From: *Ballymurphy, West Belfast*

Date of Death: *10 / 02 / 1980*

Hugh Maguire was 'the fun one in the family'. 'He brought the laughter in the house,' says his older sister Ann. The youngest of three children, nine-year-old Hugh loved being outdoors.

The back gardens in New Barnsley Crescent were wide open; the 'Rocky Dam', at the bottom of Black Mountain, was right on Hugh's doorstep. 'Hugh loved that – he'd come in with his shoes muddy, hands muddy,' says Ann. 'If he was late coming in for dinner, we knew where to find him.'

Farm animals used to wander down from Rogers' farm. 'Hughie loved the cows. You could have come down and opened the back door and there were cows standing there, and he thought it was amazingly funny, he laughed at that. The horses would come down, and you could give them apples while you were standing in the garden – we have a photograph of him giving the horses apples.'

He also loved trips to the beach. 'He would be the one with his bucket and spade out. He wasn't afraid to get dirty.'

When it was time to come indoors for the evening, 'Mummy would always have sensed with Hughie, he's in now, he's a wee bit sad.' A drink of Ribena and a biscuit cheered him up. 'Hughie used to say, "When's the sun coming back?" or "When are the lighter nights coming back?", because that meant he could be out longer. If Mum wanted a message, he would have said, "I'll go," because it was another reason to step out of the house … it was just to be out in the world.'

Hugh's favourite toys were his 'wee cars and trucks'; he had no interest in Ann's dolls 'because they weren't fun enough'. 'He liked anything that made a noise or that was loud. Mummy sometimes bought him things deliberately that were loud, because she knew he would like it.'

His older cousins made him a 'glider' – a go-kart built with old pram wheels. 'They knew, a boy like that, he'd love it, and oh he did. He went up and down the street on it.'

That Sunday, Hugh had burst into Ann's room early in the morning. 'He shouted, "Get up, get up, everybody get up." I told him to go away, I was still sleeping. That was the sort of thing he would have done, shouted, "What are we doing today?"'

Hugh was with his friend, who was going to get a bag of coal for his mother; Ann still does not know exactly what happened next. He was found lying injured on the Upper Springfield Road. The British army said he had been hit by an iron bar which had bounced off a Saracen during a riot; local people said there had been no riot, and Hugh had been hit by the armoured vehicle.

Ann and her other brother, Vincent, talk of Hughie often, and try and guess what he would be doing now. 'I always imagine he'd be doing something mechanical, or engineering, something that involved building or putting things together,' says Ann. 'Something creative, with his hands.'

✳ ✳ ✳ ✳ ✳

Name: *Paul Moan*

Age: *15*

From: *Glen Road, West Belfast*

Date of Death: *31/03/1980*

Paul Moan died on the same street where he lived. From the Glen Road, he was a pupil at the Christian Brothers school there, and was killed at the British army checkpoint at the junction with Shaws Road.

He and three others were speeding along the road in a stolen car; when they came to the checkpoint, they kept going. The soldiers opened fire: Paul was killed, and another young person critically injured.

'Soldiers at the checkpoint, at the corner of Shaws Road and Glen Road … claimed the driver of the car had tried to run down two of them. The RUC said the red Ford Escort, which crashed at the checkpoint after four shots were fired into it, had been stolen.'[399]

Fr Colm Campbell, who comforted Paul's parents, Patrick and Helen, pleaded with children to 'stop playing this game of stealing cars'.[400] 'If Paul's death is to mean anything,' he said, 'hopefully it will be that other people will realise this is not a game.'[401]

The education programme set up in Catholic schools in west Belfast following the death of 16-year-old Doreen McGuinness on New Year's Day had included campaigns against vandalism and car theft, and stressed pride in the community. 'With all its good intentions the programme is not working,' wrote the *Irish Press*. 'On Monday night, the night Paul was killed, nine cars were stolen in Andersonstown.'[402]

Fr Des Wilson, from Ballymurphy, said, 'There are hundreds of cars being stolen every week in Belfast, but the Catholic area of west Belfast is the only area where summary execution is the penalty for doing so.'[403]

✳ ✳ ✳ ✳ ✳

Name: *Michael McCartan*

Age: *16*

From: *Lower Ormeau, South Belfast*

Date of Death: *23/07/1980*

The last time Molly Lyttle saw her son Michael alive, he had a scone in one hand and a paintbrush in the other.

The family home was full of activity. Michael's father, Charlie, had knocked through the partition wall and was trying to get the work finished before Michael's 15-year-old brother Sean arrived home from America.

'Michael had a paintbrush in his hand, and I said, "You're not going out anywhere until that skirting board is finished,"' says Molly. 'I was baking, and I remember him taking a couple of scones.

'A couple of fellas came for him at the back door and he said, "I'll be back in a minute," and it seemed only about five minutes later that [his brother] Dermot came in and said something had happened to Michael.

'I said, "Sure he's just away out there." Then I heard everybody screaming around me.'

Michael was the eldest in the family: 'I think he thought he was the boss, he was the oldest and he thought no matter what, his word went,' says Molly. He had been an altar boy when he was younger, though he managed to drop the wine the first time he served mass.

He was also responsible for dyeing himself and his brother's jeans bright green by jumping into a vat of dye even though Molly had them all dressed up for Easter in sailor suits sent from America. 'They were like wee green men,' she remembers. 'I didn't laugh at the time, I could have killed them.'

The family went to Butlins every year, and Michael loved being away on holiday. At home, he was popular: 'There were more girlfriends than enough at the door for him.'

He was a Bay City Rollers fan. 'I'd say, "Michael, you're not going out in those trousers," and he would say, "If you buy me a good pair of Wranglers."' Molly saved for weeks to get Michael his jeans; he was wearing them when he died. 'They had to cut them off him.'

Michael was shot by the RUC after painting 'Provos' on a gable wall; the constable said he had mistaken the paintbrush for a handgun. He was tried for murder and acquitted.[404]

'I couldn't hold anything against him,' says Molly. 'I couldn't have any bitterness. If I did, I just thought of Michael and I thought, what would he think?'

✳ ✳ ✳ ✳ ✳

Support for hunger strikers.
Opposite: Students from Lagan College.

1981

- Ten republican prisoners die on hunger strike. Each death is followed by widespread disturbances in nationalist areas

- Bobby Sands is the first to die, on 5 May; he had been elected an MP the previous month

- The hunger strike leads to the rise of Sinn Féin as a major political force and its adoption of the so-called 'Armalite and ballot box' strategy

- MP Bernadette Devlin and her husband are seriously wounded in a loyalist gun attack on their home

- Ian Paisley's support for a 'third force' blurs the lines between political unionism and its loyalist counterpart; by year end, Paisley claims the force has over 15,000 members

- Northern Ireland's first integrated secondary school, Lagan College, is established in Belfast

- The Rubik's Cube is the year's puzzle sensation, while The Human League's 'Don't You Want Me' and Adam and the Ants' 'Stand and Deliver' are huge chart hits.

Name: *Paul Whitters*

Age: *15*

From: *Bishop Street, Derry*

Date of Death: *25/04/1981*

By the time he was ten, Paul Whitters had almost died twice. When he was born, the second eldest in his family, complications during his birth meant his mother Helen couldn't bring him home from the hospital with her; nine years later, he developed encephalitis and spent ten days on a life-support machine.

'It was horrendous, absolutely horrendous,' Helen recalls. 'We were told he might not survive.'

But Paul pulled through – and as a teenager showed no signs of his previous ill-health. Instead the 15-year-old was always out and about, helping relatives and neighbours near the family's home in Belview Avenue, or taking his cousin or baby brother to the shops. Above all, he loved people – his friends, his uncles, and all the neighbours.

'He knew everybody, all the old people in the district,' says Helen. Paul had a paper round in Ferguson's Lane, and – unknown to his mother – he would also deliver the shopping for some of his older customers. 'Half of it I didn't know about, I was only told after he died.' He also helped his grandfather to light the fire and do the dusting – though Paul's idea of dusting was to lift an ornament, blow away the dust, and replace it.

'He was into music, and The Boomtown Rats,' remembers his mother. 'He had a black cassette box with a lid and he had all of his cassettes in it, and the whole box was covered with his punk badges. He had a girlfriend, Rosemary, and she used to come down to the house. She was a lovely wee girl.'

Paul was 15 when he was shot by a plastic bullet during rioting in Derry. Fired by a policeman at point-blank range, it hit Paul in the temple. 'It was exactly a rerun of what had happened before,' recalls his mother. This time, the life machine had to be switched off. 'Do you know what I thought? I wished it had happened when he was nine. You can accept illness easier.'

More than 1,500 mourners, including Paul's friends from St Brecan's Secondary

School, followed his funeral cortege as it made its way through the city.

Nobody has ever been charged in connection with Paul's death. In 2007 the Police Ombudsman found that it had been 'wrong and unjustified' to fire at Paul, and that the shooting was 'clearly not consistent with RUC rules'.[405]

'You miss him all the time,' says Helen. 'Even little things like technology – Paul was always curious about new things, new innovations. He would have loved to see how the world has developed.'

✳ ✳ ✳ ✳ ✳

Name: *Desmond Guiney*

Age: *14*

From: *Rathcoole, Newtownabbey*

Date of Death: *08/05/1981*

Desmond Guiney loved horses. The 14-year-old belonged to a riding club and wanted to be a jockey when he grew up. 'He just didn't want to grow any bigger,' said his uncle Billy Johnston.[406]

He also loved helping his father, Eric, on his milk round, and was extremely popular with the customers. 'Everyone loved Desmond – he was always such a jolly wee boy and would have given you the coat off his back,' said his mother Roberta. 'Once, when they changed part of the milk round, the customers phoned up Dale Farm to ask them to put Desmond back,' she added.[407]

The youngest of four children, Desmond was a pupil at Ardmore House School in Downpatrick, but had been home over the May bank holiday. The family had spent the day in Carrickfergus; when they got home, Desmond and his sister Alison, who was a year older, went out with the family's horse.

Bobby Sands had died on hunger strike on 5 May. As the news spread, rioting broke out in nationalist areas, including the New Lodge in north Belfast, part of Eric Guiney's milk round. Desmond was due to catch the nine o'clock bus back to school – 'He had his good clothes in the back of the van,' said his uncle David Guiney – but first, he would help his father deliver the day's milk.[408]

'Eric had the window down – he always drove with the window down,' said Roberta. 'The stones came through the window and hit him on the head.' The milk lorry went out of control and crashed into a lamp post. 'Desmond went through the front window.'[409]

Both suffered severe head injuries; Desmond died in hospital three days later. Eric never regained consciousness and died the day after his son was buried. A 26-year-old man who was described in court as having the mental age of a child was charged with Desmond's manslaughter.[410]

About a thousand people attended Desmond's funeral. The funeral cortege was led by two ponies, Flash and Sabre; Flash had been Desmond's favourite.

✳ ✳ ✳ ✳ ✳

Name: *Julie Livingstone*

Age: *14*

From: *Lenadoon, West Belfast*

Date of Death: *13 / 05 / 1981*

The youngest of 13 children, Julie Livingstone was a 'bright sparky presence' in the family home.

'Everybody adored her because she was the baby,' remembers her older sister Elizabeth. 'She would have got up and danced and annoyed the boys, and my daddy would have encouraged her. He would have said, "Show us your wee dance, Julie," and then she'd have been blocking the TV and the boys would have been shouting but she would have been more than able for them.'

Julie loved singing and dancing. She and her sister Bernadette and her best friend Nuala had formed a group, The Sweet Roses, and practised in the alleyway beside Julie's house. 'I think they thought they were The Nolan Sisters,' says

Elizabeth. 'When Julie died her favourite song was Stevie Wonder's 'Lately'; she knew all the words and would have sung it from start to finish.'

Julie and Nuala, who lived around the corner, went virtually everywhere together. They loved going to discos – the 'Olly bop', as it was known, at St Oliver Plunkett's School, or the dances at local youth clubs. 'They just wanted to enjoy themselves,' says Elizabeth.

They also loved children and spent a lot of time babysitting; when they were older, they planned to move to Bangor, Co Down – 'because nobody was ever shot in Bangor' – and earn enough money to go to America and become nannies.

Julie was terrified of soldiers. Elizabeth recounts how the family had been burnt out of their former home in 1969, and Julie had been carried across the Falls Road by her father amid a hail of bullets; the British army often raided the family home, and Julie would awaken to find soldiers in her bedroom. 'I think that's why she and Nuala had this plan that they would get away from all this,' says Elizabeth.

On 12 May 1981, Francis Hughes died on hunger strike. As the news filtered back to Lenadoon, groups of people gathered outside to say the Rosary. Julie and Nuala had been to the shop to do a message for Nuala's sister, and were crossing the road when they saw the army vehicle approaching at speed.

The pair jumped into the hedge to avoid it; it opened fire. Julie was hit by a plastic bullet. 'Get those cigarettes out of my pocket,' she said to Nuala. 'I don't want my mummy to see the cigarettes.'

Julie was taken to hospital, and died the next day. When she was told her daughter had passed away, Julie's mother 'fell down on her knees and she just said, "I offer her up to God."'

Elizabeth remembers walking with her mother through a corridor in the hospital which was decorated with sea creatures. 'It felt as if everything was coming in on top of you, like you were underwater,' she says. 'Then we were told the pope had been shot.'

Julie had died at virtually the same time Pope John Paul II had survived an assassination attempt; for the rest of her life, Julie's mother would believe her daughter had been taken in the pope's place.

The Livingstone family still talk about their sister all the time. 'Any time we get together we ask, Who do you think she would have been like? What would she be doing now, if she was out with us? What do you think her drink would have been?

'I think she'd still be smoking, and she'd probably have five kids by now.'

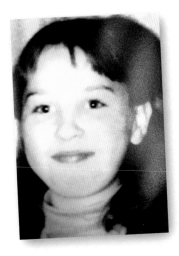

Name: *Carol Ann Kelly*

Age: *12*

From: *Twinbrook, West Belfast*

Date of Death: *22/05/1981*

Carol Ann Kelly loved babies. She and her older sister Eileen were window shopping in Lisburn when Eileen told her she was pregnant and looking for baby clothes. 'I told her it was "our secret",' Eileen recalls.

Carol Ann – who had turned 12 just two weeks previously – was one of 11 children, and she was particularly fond of her neighbour's new baby. Every day, she would take the little girl out in her pram and insisted on going in to say goodnight as she was being put to bed.

She loved being out and about – especially with the family dog, Rocky – and had 'a real thirst for life', says Eileen. 'She was always smiling, and she sang all the time. She could hear a song once and she would know all the words.'

Carol Ann always wore leggings, never a dress, says her brother Mark, and cut her own hair – 'as you can see from her Confirmation photograph'. 'She was active, very helpful, loved running messages to the shops,' Mark remembers, and 'was always smiling – she would talk to everybody'.

She was in her first year at the nearby St Colm's High School, where Mark – a year older – was already a pupil; he was caught smoking when 'Carol Ann squealed on me'.

Bobby Sands – who had been living in the same estate – had died on hunger strike earlier that month; the fourth hunger striker, Patsy O'Hara, died on 21 May. The deaths were followed by widespread rioting in nationalist areas.

As usual, Carol Ann had run across to say goodnight to the baby; the neighbour asked her to get some milk from the shop. She was on her way back, the carton of milk in her hand, when she was hit on the back of the head by a plastic bullet. Mark was standing beside her. 'She had no chance,' he says. She died in hospital three days later.

The RUC press office said soldiers stationed at Carol Ann's former primary school had been attacked by youths and had 'fired baton rounds to disperse them'; local people were adamant there had been no rioting.[411]

Speaking on behalf of the 'Mothers of Twinbrook', Kathleen Robinson said they wanted the facts made known so that there would be 'no more Carol Ann Kellys'. Since Bobby Sands' death, she said, the British army and the RUC had been 'coming into the area and firing plastic bullets at our children from speeding Land Rovers'.[412]

At Carol Ann's funeral, hundreds of her schoolfriends watched as her brothers carried her white coffin from St Luke's Church, the same chapel from which Bobby Sands had been buried three weeks previously.

Four months later, her sister Eileen gave birth to a daughter, Carol Ann.

✳ ✳ ✳ ✳ ✳

Name: John Dempsey

Age: 16

From: Turf Lodge, West Belfast

Date of Death: 08/07/1981

John Dempsey took after his father. 'He was like I was when I was young,' recalls Jimmy. The 16-year-old loved sport – 'weightlifting, bodybuilding, football, swimming' – and played football and hurling for Gort na Móna GAC and soccer for Corpus Christi FC; his younger brother and sister used his football socks for their Christmas stockings.

A Celtic fan, a precious family photograph shows John with some of the team's players; Jimmy remembers John's excitement at a trip to Parkhead, Celtic's home ground in Glasgow, with his uncle.

John's older sister Angela remembers her brother sitting on the doorstep of their house talking about music and the start of the summer holidays. 'We were made the same lunch every day by our mother, Tayto crisp sandwiches and a custard bun.'

They used to go jogging together at night then 'stuff our faces' when they got home, 'watching *Top of the Pops* together and laughing at *The Kenny Everett Television Show*'.

Another sister, Diana, remembers John out on the street playing with the family dog, Jess, or 'jumping over the wall because he was "on the beak" from school'.

Diana recalls how John and a friend 'dressed up like Adam Ant and painted white stripes across your faces,' she says. 'Off you went down to St Theresa's disco. What a sight, but you thought you were gorgeous.'

John had joined the Fianna the previous autumn. He was shot by the British army amid the rioting and disturbances which followed the death of IRA man Joe McDonnell on hunger strike early that morning. John had been among a group of Fianna members who had hijacked a minibus, loaded it with petrol bombs, and attempted to drive it into the bus depot on the Falls Road.

John's youngest sister, Martina, was only 13. 'I remember him buying a green ska jacket with his first "Bru" money. The last time I saw him alive he was wearing it along with his turned-up Wranglers and his Doc Marten boots. He was smiling.'

✳ ✳ ✳ ✳ ✳

Name: *Danny Barrett*

Age: *15*

From: *Ardoyne, North Belfast*

Date of Death: *09/07/1981*

Danny Barrett was 'a real wee lad', says his mother Mollie. 'Loved the girls.'[413]

The second eldest in a family of four, 15-year-old Danny and his friends were skinheads. 'We went to the disco in Ardoyne youth club,' said his friend Thomas Stewart, 'and we got banned from the John Paul youth club a few times for being too rowdy … it was all harmless fun. Once we pinched all the records out of the youth club, but we brought them back again.'[414]

'We wore the skinhead type clothes,' said another friend, George McErlean. 'We wore our jeans turned up right over the DM boots and we wore the big cromby [sic] coat. We thought we were great.'[415]

'He always had the music up dead loud, and you'd always be saying, "Danny, lower that," and he'd have had his head away under the thing getting the full blast of the music,' remembers Mollie.

He also loved his food. 'When he was taking his dinner he would have said, "Mammy, what are you making tomorrow night?" and I'd have said, "Danny let us get the night over."'[416]

Danny and his older sister Susan had been due to go on holiday the next day to Greystones, County Wicklow with the youth club; their father Jimmy had got their money changed into punts, and Mollie had all Danny's things sitting out ready for the trip.

The hunger striker Joe McDonnell had died the previous day, and there was some rioting nearby. 'Danny never got out to a riot,' says his mother. 'He would have loved to, but he wasn't allowed.'[417]

He was sitting on the wall outside the family home in Havana Court; Jimmy was standing at the front door. 'There was one shot,' said George, 'and the next thing, all I saw was Danny's feet going up in the air; it was a gradual thing, it was like slow motion … and his Daddy running over.'[418]

'Jimmy took his clothes off and he made a wee pillow for him at the door and he said an Act of Contrition into his ear,' said Mollie.[419]

Danny had been shot by a British soldier firing from an army observation post; at the inquest into his death the soldier's colleague claimed that Danny had a rifle, but the jury concluded that Danny had not been armed and was 'an innocent youth shot by a soldier as he sat on the garden wall'.[420]

Mollie recalls her youngest daughter Tina, who was only seven when Danny was killed, asking, 'Do you think they've given our Danny his breakfast in Heaven?'

'I'm sure they did, aye,' said Mollie.

'What would they give him?', asked Tina.

'Do you know your first Holy Communion that you made?' Mollie said. 'Well, I think that's what Danny'll be getting in Heaven for his breakfast.'

'Mammy,' said Tina, 'you'd better go back to Heaven and get him, for he hates that Holy Communion.'[421]

✳ ✳ ✳ ✳ ✳

Aftermath of the Hyde Park bombing.
Opposite: Debris from the Droppin' Well bombing.

1982

- IRA bombs in London's Regent's Park and Hyde Park kill 11 soldiers and seven horses, 20 July 1982

- An INLA bomb kills 11 off-duty soldiers and six civilians at the Droppin' Well pub in Ballykelly, County Derry

- The IRA kills Lenny Murphy, the leader of the Shankill Butchers

- Three unarmed IRA men are killed at a police checkpoint in County Armagh, fuelling suspicions of a shoot-to-kill policy by the security forces

- Assembly elections see increased representation by the DUP and Sinn Féin

- Northern Ireland cause a World Cup sensation by beating the hosts Spain 1-0; *ET: The Extra-Terrestrial* is the year's movie blockbuster, Michael Jackson's *Thriller* album is a massive hit, while the BMX bike is a Christmas favourite.

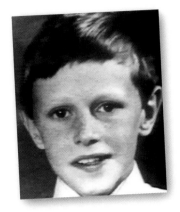

Name: *Alan McCrum*

Age: *11*

From: *Loughbrickland, County Down*

Date of Death: *15/03/1982*

Alan McCrum had just finished his Monday evening piano lesson. A pupil at Banbridge High School, Alan would make his way to Watson's Jewellers on Bridge Street, where his neighbour, Mary McMullan, worked; she would give him a lift home.

The 11-year-old was one of five siblings – three older brothers and a younger sister.

It was half past five – time to go home. As Mary put away the last few trays of jewellery, Alan was chatting to the owner, Rodney Watson, about a watch Rodney had given him a few months before. 'I said, "Well, you've still got the watch. How's it going?" "It's going great," said Alan, and then there was this huge bang. I hit the floor. The noise was fierce. I looked over the road and it was a mass of black. And then Mary said, "Oh my God, Alan's been hit."'[422]

An IRA car bomb had exploded without warning. Thirty-four people were injured; Alan was killed when he was hit by a piece of flying debris. Mary held Alan in her arms until the ambulance came, and then drove, cut and shocked, to his parents' house to tell them what had happened.

His mother Eleanor said she did not hold any hatred towards the bombers. 'What is happening in Northern Ireland is very sad and terribly tragic,' she said. 'All we can do now is pray. Alan was just in the wrong place at the wrong time.'[423]

A memorial service was held at Alan's school, where the principal, David Elliott, described him as a 'bright, cheery pupil who was popular with everyone in the school'.[424]

On the day of Alan's funeral Banbridge High School was closed, and his classmates formed a guard of honour as his coffin was carried into Banbridge Baptist Church.

'Alan was very jolly all the time and enjoyed himself,' said one of his classmates, Bryson McClelland. 'We will miss him very much.'

'I played football with him at lunchtime,' said another school friend, Gary McAuley. 'It's all very sad.'[425]

Name: *Stephen McConomy*

Age: *11*

From: *Bogside, Derry*

Date of Death: *19/04/1982*

When Paul Whitters was shot by a plastic bullet, Stephen McConomy came running to tell his mother.

'Stephen had a soft heart,' said his mother Maria. The eldest of three boys, Stephen had stepped into his father's role in the house after his parents separated.

'For a wee boy of 11 he took over the role of the Da,' said Maria. 'Me and him used to share secrets that I wouldn't share with the other two. When I was sick, he was always the one who was beside me.'[426]

Stephen was a daydreamer. 'I saw him many a day standing on the street and I would say to him, "What are you doing there?" "Nothing, Ma." He used to stand for hours looking out the window.'

He loved cleaning his teeth – 'If he ate a sweet, he would clean his teeth,' said Maria – and played the flute in the Mickey Devine Band. 'I think the only reason he joined was to get the uniform. I said this to him, and he started to laugh.'[427]

A pupil at St John's Primary School in Creggan, he was due to start at St Joseph's Secondary School in September. He had just made his Confirmation: absent from the celebration was his godmother, Annette McGavigan, who had been shot and killed by the British army in the Bogside in 1971.

That evening, Stephen had gone out to play. An eyewitness, Elaine McGrory, saw him standing on his own, and a group of children around a British army Saracen.

'Stephen turned his back with his two hands in his pockets as if he was coming away from it … the next thing [my boyfriend] Martin shouted to me "the flap is down. They are going to shoot somebody". At that the gun came out – I saw it coming out – I heard the bang and I saw Stephen falling.'[428]

Stephen had suffered serious brain damage; he survived on a life-support machine in the Royal Victoria Hospital in Belfast for three days before it was turned off. Serious rioting broke out once news of Stephen's death reached

Derry; there were calls in the city for the soldier who had shot him to be charged with murder.

More than a thousand people attended his funeral, and the *Derry Journal* reported that workers from many of the city's factories walked out in order to pay their respects.

The family home was raided several times after Stephen's death; his younger brother Emmett, who was only seven when Stephen was killed, remembers passing soldiers in the street, or being stopped and having his schoolbag searched, 'and asking myself, was it you that killed my brother?'

Emmett continues to campaign on his brother's behalf. He still keeps one of his brother's favourite toys, a 'big army Action Man truck'; their other brother, Mark, has his Stiff Little Fingers LP.

✳ ✳ ✳ ✳ ✳

Name: *Patrick Smith*

Age: *16*

From: *Lower Ormeau, South Belfast*

Date of Death: *02/06/1982*

Patrick – Pat – Smith was just starting out in life. The youngest of five children from Rutland Street, the 16-year-old had left St Augustine's High School at Easter and had only started work three weeks previously.

He and his friends, Brian Molloy and Paul Sykes, had spent the evening playing football. They then decided to ride their bikes round to Fr Denis Newberry to collect some photographs of the pope's visit to Britain.

They were cycling along Rugby Road when they spotted the motorbike. The Yamaha had been hijacked at gunpoint in west Belfast and had been left propped against a hedge.

Pat went over to have a look; he was holding onto the handlebars and appeared to have been trying to mount it when it exploded.[429]

'The next thing I remember was Brian lying beside the bike screaming for someone to get an ambulance,' said Paul. 'Pat was blown over the hedge.'[430] The INLA said it had planted the bomb, which had been intended for the security forces.[431]

Requiem mass was celebrated by Fr Newberry, who described Pat as 'a happy, sensitive lad, extrovert yet sensitive and loved by the whole community'.[432] He said that the pope had learned with 'deep sorrow' of Pat's death and said he would include his family and friends in his prayers.

Pat's mother, Alice, said she found 'great strength and comfort in the Pope's words'.

'I have the consolation that Patrick was an innocent young boy who was never in trouble and loved by all his family, friends and young people round here,' she said. 'But I pity the men who committed this atrocity. They will have to live with this for the rest of their lives. They will have to meet God some time.'[433]

＊ ＊ ＊ ＊ ＊

Name: *Stephen Bennett*

Age: *14*

From: *Divis Flats, West Belfast*

Date of Death: *16 / 09 / 1982*

Stephen Bennett could charm the birds off the trees. The eldest of four and the only boy, the 14-year-old 'loved the girls – from when he was no age', remembers his mother Irene. 'I remember him sitting his pram and putting his hand out to this woman, and I says, "Oh my God, you're going to be a quare heartbreaker."'

A pupil at 'Barney' – St Patrick's College, Bearnageeha – Stephen 'hated authority' and used to 'beak' school. Irene remembers the school board coming to her door. 'I looked out and who's slinking up the street with his schoolbag, the boul' Stephen, so I ran one way and he ran the other but Stephen couldn't be caught.'

He was 'full of devilment,' says Irene. One Easter Stephen opened all the

Easter eggs, took out the sweets, and then closed them up again. 'He was caught red-handed standing out in the hall' – Irene mimes him making an innocent face – 'practising his "innocent me" face.'

Stephen and his friends loved music, especially Madness, and had started their own band – Face to Face. Stephen was the drummer. 'That was their road to fame,' says Irene. 'They thought they were going to be famous.'

He and his sister Mairead, who was a year younger, were particularly close. The pair secretly adopted a hamster and kept it in the cupboard under the stairs. 'They were feeding it and I knew nothing about it, until it got out,' says Irene.

Stephen also smoked – though he wasn't supposed to. That evening he had called round to the shop to get two cigarettes – one for himself, and one for Mairead, to smoke while they watched *Top of the Pops*.

Stephen was killed when an INLA bomb exploded in a drainpipe near a British army foot patrol. Another boy, 11-year-old Kevin Valliday, died the following day of his injuries, and a soldier, Kevin Waller, died four days later. 'A priest told me that soldier, God help him, was trying to see to the kiddies, and he was dying.'

Among those who had been with Stephen was 14-year-old Felix Rooney, whose older brother Patrick was the first child to die in the Troubles.

'I had just passed the drainpipe when it blew up,' Felix told the Irish News. 'The explosion threw me forward and, when I got up, I staggered round to the house.'

Felix identified Stephen's body: 'He had just got a new pair of boots and that's how I recognised him.' Felix later named his baby son Stephen, after his friend.[434]

A 25-year-old local man, Martin McElkerney – who had acted as look-out while the device was planted - was given three life sentences for his part in bombing. He died in hospital in May 2019, after shooting himself in the head at the Republican Plot in Belfast's Milltown Cemetery.[435]

Irene treasures her photographs and her memories of Stephen. She remembers coming downstairs late one night to find 'Stephen sitting, the chair pulled right over in front of the TV, the legs up crossed, and the smoke. I've never seen a bigger cigarette in my life. Everybody was in bed and there he was king of the castle. I've never forgotten that. That was him. That was Stephen.'

✳ ✳ ✳ ✳ ✳

Name: *Kevin Valliday*

Age: *11*

From: *Divis Flats, West Belfast*

Date of Death: *17/09/1982*

Kevin Valliday was just about to turn 12.

One of 17 children, Kevin was the fourth youngest in the well-known family from Divis Flats in west Belfast; his mother Lena would eventually have more than 200 grandchildren and great-grandchildren.

Kevin and his friends Stephen Bennett and Felix Rooney were on a second-floor walkway on the flats when an INLA device hidden in a drainpipe exploded. Stephen was killed, and Kevin was seriously injured.

Kevin's father Paddy said he and his wife were at their son's bedside facing a horrible dilemma. 'The chief surgeon at the hospital has told me that if they operate my son Kevin will die and if they don't operate, he will die anyway. I will be spending the night at the hospital counting the hours – but without much hope,' he said.[436] Kevin died the following day.

The bomb had been intended for a British army patrol; a solider, 20-year-old Kevin Waller, also died. 'We were all very moved at the time of the explosion,' Fr Buckley said, 'when the injured soldier said, "see to the children first."'[437]

Kevin's brother Danny said those who had planted the bomb were 'utter madmen who don't give a damn. They are psychopaths. I am very bitter. It's dangerous to say more than that,' he added.[438]

The INLA later apologised for the boys' deaths; local people marched on the offices of the INLA's political wing, the IRSP, in west Belfast and pinned a 'notice to quit' to the INLA on the door. The *Irish Independent* subsequently reported that two members of the INLA had fled to the Republic of Ireland following the outcry.[439]

A man who was identified in court as the lookout for the INLA bomber who detonated the device was subsequently jailed for life for his part in the three murders.[440] Fr Pat Buckley said they had the 'blood of innocent children on their hands'.[441]

Each of Kevin's brothers took turns carrying his coffin at his funeral. 'Kevin would have been 12 years old in a few days' time,' said his father Paddy. 'I can't believe he won't be here for his birthday.'[442]

Unionist protests against the Anglo-Irish Agreement in Belfast.
Opposite: The Brighton bombing.

1983-5

- The future Sinn Féin president Gerry Adams defeats former SDLP leader Gerry Fitt to become MP for West Belfast

- An IRA bomb at the Grand Hotel in Brighton kills five and injures many more; prime minister Margaret Thatcher, the prime target of the bomb, escapes unharmed

- The New Ireland Forum – backed by the Irish government and the SDLP – is established, though it is boycotted by unionists and the Alliance Party

- A controversial Orange Order parade along the Garvaghy Road in Portadown leads to a stand-off and clashes between nationalist protestors and the RUC

- The Anglo-Irish Agreement – which gives the Irish Republic a consultative role in Northern Irish affairs for the first time whilst re-affirming the principle of consent in regard to any change in the North's constitutional status – is signed by prime minister Margaret Thatcher and taoiseach Garret FitzGerald

- 100,000 march in protest against the Agreement in Belfast

- At the cinema, 1985 is the year of *Back to the Future*, while thousands of teenagers flock to see Bruce Springsteen perform at Slane Castle.

Name: *David Devine*

Age: *16*

From: *Strabane, Co Tyrone*

Date of Death: *23/02/1985*

David Devine was 'the baby of the house and spoilt rotten'. The youngest of a family of six – three boys and three girls – from Courtrai Park in Strabane, County Tyrone, David 'got up to everything', according to his sisters Antoinette and Sheila.

He played football and loved fishing – 'did a bit of poaching too', says Sheila – and was into CB radio and punk rock, even starting his own band.

David was also kind-hearted. 'When he met the older people in town, he would have carried their messages home for them, or sat and chatted to them outside their houses. Every time he went out, before he left the house, he would always have given my mother a hug and kissed her,' says Sheila.

A student at St Colman's High School, his sisters remember him as a very diligent pupil. 'He was very intelligent – he could have been anything. We still have the bike he got for passing his eleven-plus.'

The death of David's oldest brother, Hughie, had a major impact. Hughie had only recently been released from Long Kesh, and his sisters say prison damaged his health. 'They'd been playing football and were in the changing rooms afterwards, and he just keeled over. Davy took it very bad. That's why both of them joined.'

A Fianna member since the age of 14, David and his other brother, 22-year-old Michael, were both members of the IRA. The brothers and another local man, 20-year-old Charles Breslin, had set up an ambush on the Plumbridge Road in Strabane. When the security forces failed to appear, the operation was abandoned; the three were making their way across a field to return their weapons to an arms dump when the SAS – who had been hidden in the field – opened fire.

'People living in the vicinity reported they heard one of the men plead not to be shot during the 15 minutes spell of gunfire,' the *Derry Journal* wrote. 'They said the firing ended with three single shots.'[443]

Their families believe it was part of a deliberate 'shoot to kill' operation. 'The guns had the safety catches and all on them, they were going back to the dump, and the SAS just opened fire. Each one of them was shot in the head,' says Antoinette.

'A witness supposedly heard them shouting, "Don't shoot, don't shoot," and Davy shouting for his mammy,' adds Sheila.

Several thousand mourners attended their funerals; Fr McCloskey described their killings as 'ruthless execution'.[444] A court judgement in 2002 ruled that the three presented no danger and had been shot without warning.[445]

'You miss that brotherhood thing,' says Antoinette. 'They always had people round the house and were always doing things like painting or mending things, but we lost that. All the brothers were gone.'

'My father had a bible with the family names in it,' says Sheila. 'When the boys died, he closed it. "That's the end of the Devine name," he said.'

* * * * *

Funerals of the three IRA
members shot in Gibraltar.
Opposite: Enniskillen bombing.

1986-8

- Eight IRA members and a civilian are killed in an SAS ambush at Loughgall in County Tyrone

- An IRA bomb at a Remembrance Day ceremony in Enniskillen on 8 November 1987 leaves 11 people dead

- Fourteen soldiers are killed in IRA bombings in Lisburn and Ballygawley

- Three unarmed IRA members are shot dead by the SAS in Gibraltar, 6 March 1988

- Three republican mourners attending one of the Gibraltar funerals are killed in a UVF gun and bomb attack in Milltown Cemetery in Belfast. Two British corporals caught up in a subsequent republican funeral are beaten and then shot dead by the IRA

- A number of meetings take place between SDLP leader John Hume and Sinn Féin leader Gerry Adams, paving the way for the eventual peace process

- The Teenage Mutant Ninja Turtles were the 1987 hit of the year for children.

Name: *David Hanna*

Age: *6*

From: *Hillsborough, Co Down*

Date of Death: *23/07/1988*

David Hanna had been looking forward to the holiday of a lifetime. 'David was all excited about going to California and to Disneyland,' said his next-door neighbour.[446]

The six-year-old was the youngest of three, and the only one of the Hanna siblings to make the trip to the States that summer. His brother Peter, who was 17, was in Tenerife with another family; his 19-year-old sister Pauline stayed at home.

David and his parents, Robert (45) and Maureen (44), spent three weeks in the USA; as they drove north from Dublin airport, Pauline was preparing a meal before a welcome home party in the local pub.

They had just crossed the border at Killeen when the IRA detonated a 1,000 lb landmine. The Hannas' car was destroyed and the explosion left a huge crater in the road. Newspapers later showed a photograph of two cars, which had been travelling behind, thrown sideways across the road, with the caption 'The Tunnel of Death'.[447]

The IRA's intended target had been a High Court judge, Eoin Higgins, who was also returning from America with his family. Another judge, Lord Justice Gibson, and his wife had been killed in virtually the same spot the year before.

Rumours of a 'mole' which had supplied the judge's travel arrangements surfaced almost immediately; in 2013 the Hanna siblings' solicitor called for a joint PSNI–Garda review into IRA killings along the Newry–Dundalk border.[448]

Shops and offices shut in Hillsborough for the Hannas' funerals; the Rev. John Dineen praised the orphaned Pauline and Peter for their 'courage and dignity'.[449]

'The pathetic remnants of a holiday of a lifetime were collected yesterday in a Border field by forensic experts, detectives, police and troops,' the *Irish Independent* wrote. 'Souvenirs and family gifts were detached from the shattered wreckage of what was once a family vehicle and what was left of three happy people homeward bound on the last stage of their dream vacation in America. Among them was a child's ticket to Disneyland, a treasured keepsake of six-year-old David Hanna, to remind him in the winter months of a great day out.'[450]

Name: *Emma Donnelly*

Age: *13*

From: *Benburb, Co Tyrone*

Date of Death: *23 / 11 / 1988*

Emma Donnelly was player of the year at her camogie club. The eldest of four sisters – her only brother, Ryan, had died of cot death as a baby – she played for both Naomh Mhuire Camogie Club in Blackwatertown and her school, St Catherine's College in Armagh.

'She had loads of friends, she was very popular, and a great camogie player,' remembers her mother Bernie. 'I would say she probably would have played for Armagh eventually.'

Benburb was just over the county border in Tyrone; a highlight of the year was Benburb Sunday, a festival held in the village's priory.

'She loved her pop music and she really loved her clothes, and I remember that Saturday before Benburb Sunday she was looking for something to wear and she bought herself a wee wool skirt and a wee jumper with three-quarter-length sleeves and she went to Benburb Sunday and she looked a million dollars,' says Bernie.

'She was always so proud of me, because I would have dressed very well if I was going out, and she'd say to me, "So and so said is that your mummy because that's a lovely thing she has on her."

'On the morning of her funeral [my husband] John said, "Bernie, you know the way Emma was always so proud of the way you looked? Well, she'd be so disappointed in you now." So I got up and took a shower and did my hair and I didn't feel any better for it but I thought, at least I'm not letting her down.'

Emma was killed with her grandfather – Bernie's father Barney Lavery – when an IRA bomb exploded outside the village's police station. They were on their way home from bingo – Barney was the bingo caller – and had just left an elderly Protestant neighbour home when the device exploded. The force of the blast was such that their car was blown into a nearby field. The IRA later apologised, and said their deaths were 'tragic'.

'It says on their gravestones, "innocent victims of violence",' says Bernie.

The year after Emma's death, she was again awarded player of the year. 'I'd love to have known how she would have turned out, what she would have done.'

Gerry Conlon leaves the Old
Bailey in London with his sisters.
Opposite: Lawyer Pat Finucane
(right) with client.

1989

- Belfast solicitor Pat Finucane is shot dead by loyalists less than a month after public criticism of his profession by a Home Office minister

- Northern Ireland secretary Peter Brooke states that the IRA cannot be defeated militarily, paving the way for further talks to try and reach a solution

- The Guildford Four, wrongly convicted of an IRA pub bombing in October 1974, are freed after their convictions are quashed

- Simple Minds' 'Belfast Child' is in the charts this year, a fusion of traditional and popular sounds accompanied by poignant images of children during the Troubles.

Name: *Seamus Duffy*

Age: *15*

From: *Oldpark, North Belfast*

Date of Death: *09/08/1989*

Seamus Duffy didn't walk, he bounced. The 15-year-old walked on his toes, and had a 'bounce in his step', recalls his mother Kathleen. A pupil at St Gabriel's Secondary School, he was no fan of school but loved his food, and liked to cook. 'He often said that he would like to be a chef,' she says.

Kathleen remembers how she used to buy jam doughnuts as a treat; there was one for each of her four children. 'I would have put them out of the way until they had their main meal, but there was always one missing. I discovered after Seamus died who had been stealing the jam doughnut.'

Seamus also loved football and music, especially UB40 and Bob Marley. When Kathleen and her husband Brendan were out, Seamus and his brother turned the music up. 'If me and his daddy went into town, when we came back the window would have been wide open and you could have heard the music down the street,' says Kathleen. 'Whenever we got near, the music went down.'

Kathleen remembers her son as a popular teenager, 'a happy-go-lucky fella, no different from any other child'.

He was also becoming interested in girls. 'He had started showering himself away into nothing,' says Kathleen. 'After he died I knew all about the girls he was with, for there was enough came to the door looking for his mass card.'

The anniversary of the introduction of internment was celebrated with bonfires in Catholic areas. Seamus's friend had called for him. 'I said to him, "Don't you be going down near the New Lodge," because the RUC had been giving off about the size of the bonfire and I knew there would be a confrontation of some sort. He was not to go.'

Like a typical teenager, Seamus went anyway; according to Kathleen, he and his friend were on their way home when they heard somebody shout, 'They're coming in.'

This meant the RUC; Seamus's friend Damien later told Kathleen that the pair had started to run. 'He shouted, "Duff, run." When he looked round Seamus was lying on the ground.' He had been hit by a plastic bullet fired by the RUC; the missile left two large, round bruises on his chest. 'Seamus was wearing a Celtic top because he was a Celtic supporter and that's what happened to him, the Celtic shirt on him made him a target.'

The RUC claimed they had fired only at petrol bombers; the inquest into Seamus's death found there was no evidence that he had been actively involved in rioting when he was shot.[451]

Northern Ireland's Director of Public Prosecutions had already ruled that no RUC officer should be charged in connection with Seamus's death.[452]

Seamus had been named after his uncle Seamus Cassidy, Kathleen's brother, an IRA member who was shot dead by the British army in 1972; Seamus was the first grandchild born into the family after his death. The Duffy family still have a child who walks on their toes. 'I have a grandchild now, does exactly the same thing,' says Kathleen.

✳ ✳ ✳ ✳ ✳

Name: *Nivruti Islania*

Age: *6 months*

From: *Wildenrath, West Germany*

Date of Death: *26/10/1989*

Baby Nivruti Islania was in the back of her parents' car. The six-month-old, who was known as Ruthie, lived on the RAF base in Wildenrath, West Germany, with her mother Smita and her father, Corporal Maheshkumar 'Mick' Islania, a supervisor in the communications centre on the base.

About a thousand people lived in Wildenrath, a village 'typical of those neat, ordered German villages where the studied calm is broken only by the pealing of the church bell'. By contrast, around 4,000 servicemen and their families lived on the RAF base, where there were 'hundreds of grey and white chalets, and all around there are English pubs, restaurants and video clubs where the British community lives a separate life'.[453]

That evening, Mick and Smita had driven out of the base to a nearby petrol station, and had stopped for food at a fast-food stand. Mick was on his way back to the car 'when two men emerged from the shadows to open fire'.[454] Mick and Nivruti were killed instantly.

Ruthie's mother Smita was unhurt. She snatched her daughter from the car and cradled her in her arms while her husband lay slumped in the passenger seat, 'dead from a dozen bullet wounds'.[455]

Erich Musebrink was out walking with his wife when he heard the shots. 'A very upset woman was holding the baby, she refused to let it go. She sat on the chair wrapped in a blanket just clutching the little child. It was horrific.'[456]

Their bodies were flown back to England by the RAF; Ruthie's tiny white coffin, draped in a Union Jack, was carried alongside her father's.

The IRA later expressed its 'profound regret' for the killing of baby Ruthie and said its members had been unaware of the little girl's presence when they opened fire.[457] An IRA member suspected of involvement in the attack was shot dead by the SAS in County Armagh the following year.[458]

'Until recently, a posting to West Germany was very much sought after,' *The Irish Times* wrote. 'Five IRA murders within five months has seen recruitment levels decline and an increased feeling that the streets of places like Wildenrath are not too dissimilar from those of Belfast or Derry.'[459]

✳ ✳ ✳ ✳ ✳

1990

- Files belonging to the Stalker Inquiry – set up in 1984 to investigate allegations of a 'shoot to kill' policy – are destroyed in a fire

- The IRA continues its campaign in England with a bomb attack on the London Stock Exchange and the killing of Conservative MP Ian Gow

- Peter Brooke states that Britain has no 'selfish economic or strategic interest' in Northern Ireland and would not oppose unification by consent

- *Ghost* and *Home Alone* are two huge movie hits, while Sinead O'Connor has a number one in Ireland, the UK and around the world with 'Nothing Compares 2 U'.

Name: *Charles Love*

Age: *16*

From: *Strabane, Co Tyrone*

Date of Death: *28/01/1990*

Charles Love might never have been in Derry that afternoon. The 16-year-old had already spent two summers in Norwich, New York State, with peacebuilding organisation Project Children, and had got on so well with his American host family, the Henzlers, that they had arranged for him to return for a full year to attend high school in the States.

He was due to start the previous September, but a visa mix-up meant his departure had been postponed while the paperwork was sorted out; in the meantime, he stayed at home in Strabane, County Tyrone, taking part in a local training scheme and working as a Republican Youth activist.

Known as Cha to his brothers and sisters – 'but always Charles or Charlie to my mum and dad' – his sister Anne-Marie remembers him as 'very easy going. You kind of had to really rattle him to annoy him,' she says. 'He never really fell out with anybody.'

He loved Coke and chocolate, willingly sharing his treats with everyone in the family. He and another brother bought weights and used to lift them at home – 'to build themselves up', says Anne-Marie – and he loved going out running, even competing in local marathons.

A heavy metal fan, Charles was into 'Bon Jovi, Def Leppard, Whitesnake, anything. He loved it. He had all the T-shirts.' He was also busy around Strabane, selling copies of *An Phoblacht*, collecting money for the Prisoners' Dependents Fund, and helping put up Sinn Féin election posters, and was a member of the Strabane Memorial Flute Band.

That Sunday, Charles and two friends took the bus to Derry for the annual Bloody Sunday commemoration march and rally. As they stood waiting to see the bands, there was an explosion high on Derry's walls. An IRA bomb, intended for British soldiers, sent masonry and debris flying into the Bogside. Charles was hit on the head.

'His two friends told me he went down straight away and he wasn't aware of anything, which we're grateful for,' says Anne-Marie. It [the bomb] wasn't meant for him. It was just unfortunate the debris hit him.' At the wake, the girls were 'crying their eyes out', she adds.

'He never would have told you if he was meeting a girl or anything like that because he didn't like any slagging. There was even one [girl] saying, "He was meant to show up to me last night and didn't". Apparently he hadn't been bothered,' says Anne-Marie. 'It was funny as well as devastating.'

Had Charles gone to America that September, Anne-Marie believes he would have stayed and made his life there. 'What would have happened if the visa had worked out and he had gone off to America? You do wonder.'

✳ ✳ ✳ ✳ ✳

Children taking part in a republican parade.

5

Young Combatants

'If you didn't become part of it, you were effectively
stepping outside of a complete culture.'

John Dougal had a plan. As soon as he left school, he was going to join the British army. He was already a member of the Army Cadets and had been to the Isle of Man on manoeuvres in the summer of 1969; John's younger brother Jim and their father had proudly attended his passing-out parade at the cadet base on the Antrim Road.

The start of the Troubles meant the end of the British army for John. His family was forced out of their home in north Belfast and was eventually rehoused in the west of the city. 'Your world is the street and your school and your friends,' says Jim. 'It's all gone, completely gone.'

The following year, two soldiers – in plain clothes – called to the family's new home on Springfield Avenue. 'They wanted John to keep going to the cadets,' explains Jim. 'My mummy said he could never get there from this side of town, so he wasn't going back.'

In the intervening year, much had changed in Belfast. 'I don't think there was a big leap to "I want to be a freedom fighter for Ireland,"' says Jim. 'At the time the Brits were in the streets and we were fighting with them and rioting.'

Both John and Jim joined the Fianna. At the time of John's death – aged 16 – he was a member of the IRA, though his membership had no bearing on his death.

The second child to die in the Troubles, Gerald McAuley, was a member of the Fianna; he was shot dead by a loyalist sniper in west Belfast in August 1969. The 15-year-old is celebrated as a hero who died defending his area, and whose death inspired other young people to join the Fianna in their turn. More than 30 years later, Glen Branagh – a 16-year-old member of the junior UDA organisation the Ulster Young Militants – was killed as he attempted to throw a pipe bomb during rioting in north Belfast. He was one of the last children to die.

Of the 186 children who died as a result of the Troubles, 31 – or just over 16 per cent – were members of paramilitary organisations. The vast majority were republican – members of either the IRA or its youth wing, Na Fianna Éireann, with one a member of the girls' equivalent, the Cailíní; two were members of the UDA and one was a member of its junior wing, the Ulster Young Militants.

Membership was greatest in urban working-class areas. Of the fatalities among child members of the Fianna or IRA, 20 – or 74 per cent – were from Belfast (west or north); four were from Derry City; and there was one each from Newry, Strabane and Dungannon. All three of the UDA fatalities were in Belfast (east or north).

Sometimes described as a republican equivalent of the boy scouts, the 'Fians' were organised into troops known as slua and were intended to act in a support capacity to the IRA by running messages, hiding weapons and acting as lookouts, as well as providing a guard of honour at funerals. In reality, the extent of their involvement varied widely.

'We firmly believed (and we were told so by members of the IRA) that we were their backbone; they couldn't operate without co-operation from the Fianna. Members of Na Fianna Éireann would have carried out operations alongside the army and would have been involved in military operations on many occasions,' says one former Fianna member, 'Martin'.[1]

'The Fianna of '71 and '72 were just as active as IRA volunteers,' said another former member, Seamus Clarke. 'The 'RA couldn't move in Ardoyne without the Fianna. They would be scouting, standing beside the volunteer if shells had to be lifted or involved in providing cover … through the Defence group the Fianna boys also started handling weapons.'[2]

Membership was particularly strong in areas like Ardoyne. A small, economically deprived part of north Belfast bordered by the equally deprived but loyalist Shankill Road, the burning of Catholic streets by loyalist mobs in 1969 – and the subsequent relocation of both Catholic and Protestant families

A photo journalist captures a scene on the Falls Road, west Belfast, in 1972.

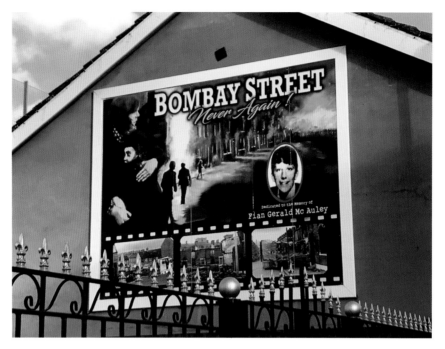

Mural commemorating 15-year-old Gerald McAuley overlooks a peace wall that still stands in west Belfast.

– hardened lines of segregation which still exist today as physical barricades, the so-called 'peace walls'. When the British army arrived, they too made their own mark on the landscape, with fortifications of sandbags, corrugated iron and barbed wire.

In her book on the Holy Cross dispute of 2001, Anne Cadwallader describes Ardoyne as a place where history is 'writ into brick, stone and metal'. 'Going down into the streets of Ardoyne, teeming with small children, there are murals, social clubs, republican memorials, a Sinn Féin advice centre and projects to create much-needed work.'

She speaks of the stories that 'every yard of pavement' has to tell: 'Gardens where gunfights ended in death and imprisonment. Streets where children learned to make petrol bombs. Pavements where British soldiers and IRA men bled to death.'[3]

In 1972, 496 people died[4] – the highest death toll of any year of the Troubles. The Fianna in Ardoyne lost four members; three of them – David McAuley, Josh Campbell and Bernard Fox – were 16 or under; the fourth, Joseph McComiskey, was 18.

Resentment at the British army, and the perceived need to defend the

community from loyalist attack, fuelled recruitment; so too did family affiliation and community loyalties, a sense of excitement and a desire to be involved. 'Rioting would have been his interest,' says David McAuley's sister Rita Alexander. He would have started a riot in an empty house. I suppose that was a reflection of the era he grew up in … that was his life, the Fianna.'[5]

David was shot accidentally; Josh and Bernard were on 'active service' when they were shot by British troops. David was OC of the Fianna at the time of his death; so too was Bernard Fox. Josh was an intelligence officer, explained his 'friend and comrade', Martin. 'He told them about things he had seen as regards the RUC and British army movements. He had us watching, timing, making notes and delivering them to him, then he would pass on the information that we gave him.'[6]

That February, Bernard Fox had been among the guard of honour at David McAuley's funeral; in December, his friends in the Fianna did the same service for him. For Bernard's friend Seamus Clarke, the effect of his death was 'shattering': 'When you lose four Fianna boys in an area like Ardoyne it affects the community as a whole.'[7]

The reality was that children as young as 11 or 12 joined the Fianna; two 13-year-olds, Sean O'Riordan and Kevin McCauley, were the youngest members to be killed during the Troubles. Sean was a Fianna section leader, though his death was not related to his membership; Kevin was killed accidentally as he and others tried to build a barricade across the Andersonstown Road.

'Back then the Fianna was sort of like joining the boy scouts,' says Margaret Gibson. Her brother Gerard, who was shot and killed by the British army in 1972, was a member; he had been out manning barricades the night before. 'If your friend joined it, you joined it,' says Margaret. 'I was in it myself where I lived down in Springfield, but I never told nobody. My ma would have killed me.'

In Derry in the 1980s, Cathy Nelis recalled how boys she and her friends hung around with were killed as IRA volunteers. 'Because you were losing friends at that age and you were losing other friends going to jail, you made that choice, whether you were going to become part of it; if you didn't become part of it, you were effectively stepping outside of a complete culture you were familiar with, including family and friends and the entire community.'[8]

Affiliation was fluid; it was sometimes a moot point as to whether some teenage rioters were members of the Fianna or not, or indeed whether they were full members of the IRA. In theory, 17 was the age limit for joining the IRA; in practice, this was not always adhered to. 'In all the memorials you'll see John referred to as Fianna,' says Jim Dougal, 'but when John was killed, John was in the IRA. A well-known republican came to the house and said, "We can't claim him as a volunteer, he's too young," so he was put down as Fianna.'

Internment, Bloody Sunday and the hunger strikes all led to significant spikes in recruitment. On the evening of Bloody Sunday, Denis Bradley – then a priest -

remembers the eeriness as he walked through the city with his friend and fellow priest Fr Tom O'Gara. 'We would have known young people who were either in or on the verge of or thinking about the IRA, and there was always this movement to be a counterbalance to that. Yet my memory of that night is that both of us knew that day had come and gone. While there had been maybe a small stream of youngsters, mainly young men, [joining the IRA] before this, in the following weeks they would have run over you, they would have walked over you to join.'[9]

That day, 30th January 1972, British paratroopers shot dead 13 unarmed civilians in Derry; a 14th dying later. Among the victims was Patrick Doherty; his nine-year-old son Tony was playing marbles on the street when he heard his father had been killed. In the late 1970s, Tony was sworn in to the Fianna in a house in Creggan: 'I held a folded Irish Tricolour in my hand and repeated an oath in the company of the Fianna Brigade Staff.'

Training involved 'an IRA veteran from the 1950s [who] ... patiently talked us through Irish history over the course of many evenings in a house in Carnhill. Another man ... talked to us about our responsibility as junior IRA men. He told us not to drink or make fools of ourselves, either through taking drink or while sober, and to become young men that others would respect. Keeping out of fights was another rule. He warned us that joining the IRA would likely result in death, imprisonment or going on the run, and that in all cases our families would suffer.'[10]

Commemorative hoarding in Strabane featuring three IRA members – including 16-year-old David Devine – who were shot and killed by the SAS in 1985.

Mural for the Ulster
Young Militants,
west Belfast.

Yet for all those who joined, far more did not. 'Bik' describes himself as a republican activist in Ardoyne. 'To be involved, as I was, meant you had taken a decision and if you came to grief then that is something you had to accept.'[11]

Of the child members of paramilitary organisations – republican and loyalist – and IRA children who lost their lives during the Troubles, a third – 12 – died as a result of an accident, usually involving a gun or a bomb that had exploded prematurely. Some were killed on 'active service', though again the distinction was often fluid. 'In those days, if things were bad you just reported. You knew where to go,' says Jim Dougal. Thirteen – 12 members of the Fianna/IRA and one UDA member – died in 1972 alone.

By the age of 16, Patrick – Patsy – Quinn, from Dungannon, County Tyrone, had already been arrested and spent time on remand in Belfast's Crumlin Road Gaol for transporting a weapon. According to his entry in the republican commemorative book *Tírghrá*, in August 1973 he was 'part of an Active Service Unit which attacked Pomeroy RUC barracks. The attack lasted for almost 20 minutes during which the barracks was raked with fire from three positions and pounded with mortars from a fourth. During the operation, a rocket launcher

CHILDREN OF THE TROUBLES

misfired and killed Patsy and Dan McAnallen.'[12] Aged only 13, Patsy's younger brother Frankie formed part of the colour party at his funeral.

'People may say that having young ones handling weapons was wrong but it was a fact of life in those days,' says Seamus Clarke.[13]

Just as children were killed, so too did children become killers. One of those responsible for the death of 14-year-old Rory Gormley was believed to have been just 15; the IRA member believed to have shot another 14-year-old, Kathleen Feeney, was 16.

Karen McAllister recalls, at the age of six, catching sight of the young IRA man who, moments later, would kill her four-year-old sister Siobhan. 'He was young. I literally came out of my granny's house and I looked at him. He was crouching down at the side of my granny's wall, she was in the end house, and I looked at him and I saw him. I don't know. Was he just trying to use us thinking the Brits wouldn't try and shoot back because we were in the street?'

Instead, Siobhan was hit; Karen was holding her hand. 'You don't blame that fella. I'm sure he was traumatised for the rest of his life too. I know I would be if I killed a child.'

Some families point out that a member of a paramilitary organisation had made a choice – a choice not afforded to their victims. In 2018 Colin Nicholl's father Jackie resigned from the Northern Ireland Victims and Survivors Forum after he discovered that a fellow member – whose grandfather had been killed in the UVF bombing of McGurk's Bar a week before his baby son Colin was killed – was a convicted IRA bomber. 'I couldn't sit with that man – and this is personal to me – because every time I'd be talking to him I'd be thinking about Colin,' says Jackie.

The death of Colin and two-year-old Tracey Munn in the bombing of the Balmoral Furniture Company showrooms on the Shankill Road in 1971 is often cited as the turning point that persuaded many young Protestants to join the UDA.

By the time he was 14 or 15, Billy McQuiston was already involved with 'vigilantes'. 'The area I came from was surrounded on all sides by republican areas. There was a siege mentality … as far as people were concerned the republicans were about to march in and burn us out of our homes.'

A barricade was erected opposite Billy's house. 'Being the age I was this was a big adventure. I was out scouting around and listening to the gunfire. It was like a John Wayne movie was happening just outside the estate.'[14]

He was also a member of the Ulster Boot Boys, one of the so-called 'tartan' gangs who would fight with Catholic teenagers; that particular Saturday, however, he and his friends were on their way into Belfast to buy records when they heard there had been a bomb on the Shankill Road. 'I didn't actually see the babies' bodies as they had them wrapped in sheets, but the blood was just coming right through them … there were people shouting at the back, "let's get something done about this",' he said. 'I just stood there and cried.'[15]

The following day he and his friends went to offer their services to the UDA; his father was a UDA commander. Billy recalls his swearing-in ceremony. 'There were three people sitting at a table. On it was an Ulster flag, a Bible and a gun. Two hooded men brought you in and stood in front of the table. You were asked, "Why do you want to join the Ulster Defence Association?" … there was an oath which you had to repeat with your hand on the Bible and your hand on the gun. I remember when I came out, my heart was swollen with pride that I was going to do something. I was going to fight back.'[16]

He was 15. Asked by the journalist Peter Taylor whether he was prepared to kill people, he replied: 'Whatever it took to defend the people of my area to make sure no more children's bodies were getting carried out of buildings, I was prepared to, yes.'[17]

The UDA had been formed from the amalgamation of local Protestant defence associations which had emerged at the start of the Troubles with 'the remit of defending the British and Protestant community, and Northern Ireland more generally'.[18]

For all their opposition to each other in identity and outlook, factors such as excitement, family and community links, and the desire to belong drew children in Protestant areas to loyalist paramilitary organisations as much as, in Catholic areas, these elements formed part of the attraction of the IRA.

David Stitt was taken to his first UDA 'show of strength' by his father when he was a toddler. 'I don't remember, but I was there with full combat gear on and my wee boots, walking with my da with his combat gear on and he held my hand.' Teachers would ask what he wanted to be when he grew up. 'I wanted to be a UDA man when I grew up. It's as simple as that. I couldn't wait until I was the right age to join a loyalist paramilitary organisation.'[19]

Like David, Billy Warnock and Alan Welsh were from east Belfast. Both 15-year-old Billy and 16-year-old Alan had joined the UDA; Billy was knocked down and killed by a British army Saracen in 1973; Alan died when his own bomb exploded prematurely. Both are remembered on the memorial to the UDA's

East Belfast Brigade in Dee Street; towering over it are the famous cranes of the Harland and Wolff shipyard, where Alan worked.

For almost 30 years they were the only young members of the UDA to lose their lives; Glen Branagh, a member of the Ulster Young Militants, was killed in 2001 after a pipe bomb he was about to throw at police – who were manning barricades separating Protestant rioters in Tiger's Bay from Catholic ones in the New Lodge in north Belfast – exploded in his hand. It says much about the changed nature of Northern Ireland that he was the first young member of a paramilitary organisation to die in more than 15 years.

In the intervening years, much has indeed changed. Yet paramilitary-style shootings and assaults continue; the deliberate wounding of a 16-year-old in the legs in Belfast in 2017 was described as 'child abuse' by the police.[20]

Teenagers only slightly older were believed to have been responsible for the killing of 29-year-old journalist Lyra McKee as she stood and watched a riot in the Creggan area of Derry in April 2019.

Conal McFeely was born and raised in Creggan and has worked there for more than 40 years. 'There's a problem for lots of young people of isolation, marginalisation and feeling completely abandoned. There are very low levels of aspiration.'

In areas like Creggan, such young people are vulnerable to older, 'dissident' republicans; some would argue that 'the bad old days' were no different.

In 1973 Alice Harper's 15-year-old brother Bernard Teggart – who had a mental age of nine – was abducted from a training school on Belfast's Glen Road by the IRA; he was shot in the head and his body dumped in the grounds of Belfast Zoo, a placard bearing the word 'tout' hung around his neck. For Alice, there are 'many murderers' responsible for her brother's death. 'They don't go out and do it on their own. Somebody had to give the order.'

Following the death of 16-year-old IRA volunteer John McDaid in a premature explosion, the RUC made a similar point. 'The IRA is training young people to handle explosives, which even experts treat with extreme care,' a police spokesman said. 'They are recruiting these teenagers for death – their own and that of others.'[21]

In contrast, the graveside oration for another 16-year-old (Official) IRA member, Gerard Doherty, who was shot and killed accidentally in Derry in 1972, laid the responsibility for his death on 'the people who force young men to take up arms.'[22]

The year after, the *Derry Journal* carried a report of a commemoration held

by 'about 80 members of the Official IRA, wearing black berets and paramilitary uniforms' who marched from Creggan to Gerard's grave in the City Cemetery.

At the graveside, an unnamed speaker described him as 'a credit to the struggle for the emancipation of the Irish working class … He was born into a repressive society dominated by imperialist Britain. His life was spent in the shadow of unemployment and exploitation. Is it any wonder then, that at the age of 14 years he entered the Republican movement through its youth section, Fianna Éireann?'[23]

More telling is the statement from Gerard Doherty's parents, issued in response to a similar commemoration in 1975. 'Like many boys of his age, he was caught up in the mood of the times. His present-day outlook would have been different. To describe him as a revolutionary socialist is far from the truth, as his family knows it.'[24]

John Dempsey's father Jimmy is similarly critical. A member of the Fianna, 16-year-old John was killed amid the rioting which followed the death of hunger striker Joe McDonnell in July 1981.

John had been one of a group of Fianna who had hijacked a minibus, loaded it with petrol bombs, and attempted to drive it into the Ulsterbus depot on the Falls Road; John was shot and killed by a soldier who had been on guard in the depot. 'They sent all them kids down to a fortified base where there were soldiers with guns, and they had not a gun among them. It's a miracle they all weren't killed,' says Jimmy.

From a republican family – Jimmy and a number of John's uncles spent time in prison during the boy's childhood – he had been 'hardened' by the Troubles, his father says. 'Consequently, he joined the Fianna. I took him out of it when I heard about it; he was only a kid playing on the street. I can understand adults getting killed – if you're involved in something you understand that risk – but kids, killing kids, it's a whole new dimension.'

Jimmy is proud of his son; without exception, so is every family. 'That's who he was and what he believed in,' says Kevin McCauley's brother Paddy.

A member of the IRA, 16-year-old Michael Neill was shot dead by the British army in disputed circumstances in 1977. Every Easter Sunday – the day republicans traditionally remember their dead – Michael's siblings carry his black-framed portrait as they march to the commemoration at Belfast's Milltown Cemetery. It is a day for families: pensioners sit on chairs specially laid out for them; teenage grandchildren listen attentively; young children play amongst the headstones. 'We do it for him,' says Michael's sister Maureen Griffin. 'It mightn't have been our belief but it was his, and we're proud of him as our brother.'

2010 Republican Easter commemoration in Derry.

Funerals of three people – including 16-year-old Katrina Rennie – killed in a loyalist attack on a mobile shop in Drumbeg, Craigavon. Opposite: Mortar attack on 10 Downing Street.

1991

- An IRA mortar attack on 10 Downing Street narrowly misses its target – new British prime minister John Major and his cabinet, who are holding a meeting at the residence

- The Birmingham Six – wrongly convicted for murdering 21 people in two pub bombings in 1974 – are released after their convictions are quashed

- Secretly, talks are already taking place between representatives of the British government and the IRA

- Bryan Adams' 'Everything I Do' tops the charts for 16 weeks, boy band Take That burst onto the scene, while the long-anticipated Game Boy console finally comes to Northern Ireland.

Name: *Katrina Rennie*

Age: *16*

From: *Craigavon, Co Armagh*

Date of Death: *28/03/1991*

Katrina Rennie was full of hopes and dreams for her life ahead. 'She wanted to travel the world and to live by the sea, and hoped one day there would be world peace,' her mother Mary remembers.

The teenager was one of three people shot dead by the UVF as she helped her friend, 19-year-old Eileen Duffy, who was working in a mobile shop in the Drumbeg estate in Craigavon. Both teenagers were killed, as was a customer, Brian Frizzell.

'Brian was a young man noted among old people for his kindness; Katrina, the friendly companion, and Eileen, the animated, vivacious, lively person,' said the parish priest, the Rev. Thomas McGuinness, at their joint funerals. 'Those three beautiful young lives – we can only guess at what they would have become.'[460]

It had been a deliberate policy to employ girls. 'The owners of the mobile shop … had felt that if there was any trouble in the area, nobody would harm young women.'[461]

At the time, Mary appealed for no retaliation. Nothing was going to bring her daughter back, she said, 'and I don't want any other mother to suffer like this'.[462]

Mary remembers Katrina as 'a bubbly girl, with a kind heart and a great personality that captured the hearts of those who loved her'. She had many friends and loved music. 'She would sing from morning to night, never without a smile. Her favourite time of year was Christmas. She loved to see people smile and so Christmas she classed as the happy holidays.'

Katrina's brother John – who was 15 when his sister was killed – founded a reconciliation group and was later named 'Young Person of the Year' by the National Children's Day Committee.[463]

Their memories remain a comfort to the whole family. 'I think about Katrina every day,' says Mary. She's my first thought in the morning and my last going to bed. Every day my other children will reminisce over old times, sometimes happy and sometimes sad, but knowing they still think about her every day lets me believe she'll never be forgotten.'

Name: *Colin Lundy*

Age: *16*

From: *Glengormley, County Antrim*

Date of Death: *09/11/1991*

Colin Lundy had lived with sectarianism all his life. A budding Gaelic footballer with St Enda's in Glengormley, the 16-year-old had grown up with his mother Kathleen and his 19-year-old brother Gerard on a predominantly Protestant estate and was the son of a mixed marriage.

Kathleen – who had been raised Protestant – had converted when she married a Catholic man; when her marriage ended she brought the two boys up on her own, raising them in their father's religion.

In their teenage years, the two boys had been subjected to taunting and sectarian attacks: trees Kathleen had planted outside their home had been cut down, she had been attacked on her way to mass, and their house had been painted with sectarian graffiti and UVF slogans. There was also a warning – on a nearby wall – that their home would be petrol bombed.

'Kathleen was frightened,' her mother Irene Bleakley said, 'but she was tough, and she wouldn't let them force her out.'[464]

Kathleen had just celebrated her fortieth birthday. 'They say life begins at 40,' she had told friends. 'I hope that turns out to be true for me.'[465] Less than a week later, while the family was asleep in bed, two teenagers poured petrol through their letterbox and set it alight. As the house burned, Gerard tried desperately to save his mother and brother, but was unable to reach them. He survived by jumping out a bedroom window; he insisted on leaving hospital in a wheelchair in order to attend their funerals.

The Reverend Ian Paisley was among the many who condemned the murders, describing it as 'a diabolical outrage to bomb people in their beds because of their political or religious beliefs'.[466] Among the death notices in *The Irish News* was a message of sympathy from 'the entire mixed community of the Harmin estate, friends and neighbours'.[467]

The two teenagers – who had been 16 and 17 at the time of the attack – were later jailed for 15 years for the murders of Colin and Kathleen. The judge told them that the mother and son had 'met a terrible death, screaming as they were burned alive and poisoned by smoke'.[468] Catholics in that area, the judge said, had suffered much from sectarian strife, adding that the attack was 'as frightening and cowardly as any of the killings'.[469]

Colin and Kathleen were among five members of St Enda's GAC to be killed during the Troubles; since the early 1970s, the club had suffered what *The Guardian* described as 'a catalogue of bombings, shootings and arson attacks, earning it the unenviable reputation as the most terrorised sports club in Northern Ireland'.[470]

In 2019, St Enda's won the Ulster club final and made it to their first-ever All-Ireland intermediate football final in Croke Park; at the club, their lost members were 'still in the mind's eye, smiling at the prospect'.[471]

✳ ✳ ✳ ✳ ✳

'Hands Across the Divide' sculpture
by Maurice Harron in Derry City.
Opposite: Teebane massacre.

1992

- An IRA land mine at Teebane, County Tyrone, kills eight Protestant civilians returning from work on a military base; in apparent retaliation, loyalists shoot dead five Catholics – including a 15-year-old – at Sean Graham's bookmaker's in Belfast

- Talks continue to take place between the British government and the main Northern Ireland parties; Sinn Féin are invited to attend if the IRA ends its campaign of violence

- The banning of the UDA in August – after more than two decades of killings under its own name and the pseudonym the Ulster Freedom Fighters – signals a shift in British government policy

- Grunge band Nirvana plays Belfast's King's Hall.

Name: *James Kennedy*

Age: *15*

From: *The Markets, South Belfast*

Date of Death: *05/02/1992*

There were five Kennedy brothers – enough for their own five-a-side football team. 'They called us the Kennedy five-a-sides,' says James's brother David.

From Hamilton Street, the boys 'played football at the front door, in the wee driveway. The windows were smashed every other day, and every day we were told we weren't allowed to play football. But sure within a few hours we were back out again.'

Football was 15-year-old James's passion. A striker, he played for Rosario Youth FC – as well as GAA for the local parish, St Malachy's – and took his school, St Augustine's, to the Northern Ireland Schools Cup final.

'It was unheard of for such a small school,' says David. 'They were up against Boys' Model, and James said to me, "We're going to beat them," but I said, "You've no chance." James scored two goals and they were beating them two-nil with five minutes to go and then Boys' Model equalised.'

Two years younger, David looked up to his older brother. 'He was a real jack the lad, had lots of friends and was a bit ballsy and cheeky – not cheeky to his elders, but he would have been daring. He loved to mess about. He looked after me and I looked up to him. In school nobody touched me – if anyone had hit me I wouldn't have told our Bosco – my oldest brother – I would have told our James.'

James was one of five people killed in a loyalist gun attack on Sean Graham's bookmaker's on Belfast's Ormeau Road. Two men entered the shop and sprayed it with bullets. James was dead on arrival at the hospital.

'I know my mammy never really recovered,' says David. 'She wouldn't leave the house, she wouldn't eat, she just gave up.' His mother Kathleen died of a broken heart two years later.

'The bullets that killed James didn't just travel in distance, they travelled in time,' her husband Jack told *The Irish Times*. 'Some of those bullets never stop travelling.'[472] It is inscribed on the memorial stone erected on the twentieth anniversary of the atrocity. 'We also got a banner made with it on it,' says David. 'It's true what he said, isn't it?'

David now has two sons of his own, aged ten and seven. The eldest is called James. 'I tell him, you were named after your Uncle James, and he's proud of you.'

✳ ✳ ✳ ✳ ✳

Name: *Patrick Harmon*

Age: *15*

From: *New Lodge, North Belfast*

Date of Death: *25/03/1992*

Patrick – Patsy – Harmon was 'a happy-go-lucky young fella, full of life and fun'.[473] On St Patrick's night, the 15-year-old was 'brutally beaten for playing the Good Samaritan'.[474]

His father Charles said Patsy had seen a boy being attacked and rushed to his aid, calling an ambulance and tending to him until it arrived. 'On his way home, the gang took their revenge, kicking and beating him. Some people tried to intervene, but someone forced them away.'[475] Patsy was beaten with sticks and baseball bats; he survived in intensive care for eight days before he died.

Patsy had been attacked by the so-called 'F' gang – described as a 'self-appointed vigilante group' – which, it was alleged, was linked to the IRA, who were 'attempting to control the district through the young people'.[476] The IRA denied any involvement in his death, and said Patsy had suffered 'a freak blow'.[477]

Residents in the New Lodge had previously raised concerns over fighting between rival teenage gangs in the area. 'Gangs armed with machetes, bats and hammers are fighting all over the New Lodge,' said Sinn Féin councillor Joe Austin.[478] According to *The Irish News*, the fights 'are apparently sparked off by arguments over partners, alcohol, football teams and varieties of music'.

Two teenagers – one of whom was a juvenile – were later charged with Patsy's killing. A lawyer said one of the accused was a member of the Republican

Youth movement, and it was thought the fighting had broken out because the two victims had refused to join.

One youth pleaded guilty to manslaughter and was jailed for six years, and the other admitted a charge of grievous bodily harm.[479]

＊ ＊ ＊ ＊ ＊

Name: *Danielle Carter*

Age: *15*

From: *Basildon, Essex*

Date of Death: *10/04/1992*

'Dad, whereabouts do you work? Can I come and see where you work?' pleaded 15-year-old Danielle Carter to her father, Danny.

A chauffeur based in the Commercial Union building in central London, Danny and his friend Wayne were due to return a car to the office; he couldn't say no to Danielle.

'She had a heart of gold,' he recalls. She loved her dog, Sly, and cat, Sam, and 'she would do anything for you – except go to school. She didn't like school – she would rather watch *Neighbours* with her friends. Once, when the truant officer called, Danielle pretended to be her mother and shouted out that her daughter had gone to school.'

She loved all kinds of music – 'from rhythm and blues to The Carpenters', says her brother Robert; she played both ice hockey and inline hockey, though he recalls that his sister was 'a better spectator than a player'.

The four children piled into the back seat of the Mercedes – Danielle, her 'sweetheart' Craig, friend Sarah and younger sister Christiane. Once the other car had been dropped back, the plan was to take the Mercedes and show the children the sights. 'London is really lovely lit up at night,' Danny had told them.

He had left the vehicle and was walking up from the underground carpark towards the Baltic Exchange building; the car containing Danielle and the others was sitting outside. 'The shock wave from the blast blew me backwards. I ran up the ramp and saw the loading bay was blown to bits. I ran through the dust and rubble, choking, hysterical, glass under my feet, debris still falling around me, a terrible smell of smoke, of burning. It was deadly quiet for a split second, then I started hearing the sirens, the screaming, the people shouting, "help, help", me shouting, "Danielle, Danielle".'

The car had been destroyed. 'All I could think of was the kids, and then I saw Christiane and the others smothered in blood. I shouted, "Danielle, Danielle", and ran round the car and found her, lying half out of the car, face down in a pool of blood.'[480]

The 100 lb bomb, planted by the IRA, killed three people; an ambulance man who cradled Danielle as she died in his arms later killed his girlfriend and attempted to take his own life. He pleaded guilty to manslaughter on the grounds of diminished responsibility and was remanded to a secure psychiatric unit.[481]

Eight-year-old Christiane was badly injured; two and a half pounds of glass was removed from her jacket. That Christmas, when she was asked what present she would like, she replied, 'Danielle.'

Each year Danielle's hockey team, Basildon Allstarz, hosts a tournament in her memory.

'Danielle loved life and she loved laughing, she was always laughing and smiling,' remembers Danny. 'She was only 15 years old – she didn't have much of a life.'

✳ ✳ ✳ ✳ ✳

Floral tributes at Warrington city centre.
Opposite: Prime minister John Major and
taoiseach Albert Reynolds agree
the Downing Street Declaration.

1993

- Loyalists kill four Catholic workmen in Castlerock, County Derry

- An IRA bomb in Warrington in England kills two children

- Ten people, including the bomber, die in an IRA attack on the Shankill Road; loyalist retaliation includes the slaughter of seven at a Hallowe'en party in the Rising Sun bar in Greysteel, County Derry

- Irish president Mary Robinson meets Queen Elizabeth in London, and later Gerry Adams in Belfast

- The Downing Street Declaration – issued jointly by the British and Irish governments – suggests a possible framework for peace based on consent and on arrangements involving representatives from Northern Ireland, Britain and the Republic

- Stephen Spielberg's *Jurassic Park* is the summer blockbuster, while Thunderbirds' Tracy Island and Beanie Babies are popular toys.

Name: *Johnathan Ball*

Age: *3*

From: *Warrington, Cheshire*

Date of Death: *20/03/1993*

Johnathan Ball loved his name. 'He would tell everyone, "My name is Johnathan with an H,"' remembers his aunt, Rose Latham. 'He was adorable and was a mummy's boy who loved kisses and cuddles,' she says. 'He loved his teddies and Thomas the Tank Engine, and music and playing outside.'

Fifty-seven years old when his only child was born, Johnathan's arrival transformed his father Wilf's life. '[His mother] Marie and the arrival of Johnathan took ten years off me,' he said.[482] 'He charmed everyone. He was mischievous as well. I once caught him ironing the carpet.'[483]

Johnathan had gone into Warrington that Saturday afternoon with his babysitter, 13-year-old Samantha Thompson, to buy Marie a Mother's Day card. The IRA had planted two bombs in litter bins in the town centre; Samantha and Johnathan saw the first explode without warning. 'We stood alongside the bin just looking up the street and it went off. Johnathan was still holding my hand.'

Samantha had no idea she had been badly injured. 'My instinct took over. I just got my hands under his armpits and dragged him into a shop doorway.' A passer-by came to help. 'He rolled Johnathan over and I remember him saying, "He's gone." His little eyes were half shut and I passed out – that is the last time I saw him.'[484]

Twelve-year-old Tim Parry was seriously injured and died five days later. Nobody has ever been convicted of their murders.

Marie Comerford died of a heart attack in 2009; the deputy coroner for Cheshire, Janet Napier, said that Marie's decline was linked to her son's death, and that 'in a way she died of a broken heart'.[485]

Wilf had died five years previously, in 2004; in an interview ten years after his son's death, he said he was certain Johnathan's spirit was still with him. 'I hear the floorboards creaking under his weight, just like they did when he was living.'[486]

Name: *Tim Parry*

Age: *12*

From: *Warrington, Cheshire*

Date of Death: *25/03/1993*

Tim Parry was 'a mad keen Everton supporter'. It was the family tradition – his older brother Dominic, father Colin, and even his paternal grandfather were all Everton fans, and Colin took his sons to matches as often as he could.

He played for his school football team and loved sports of all kinds, adds Colin. 'I introduced him to squash, in which he showed promise, and he was having golf lessons.' Tall for his age 'after a recent growth spurt', Tim was also learning to play the guitar and 'loved the outdoors'. 'He was a Sea Scout and had just passed his first solo sailing certificate.'

His mother Wendy remembers her son as outgoing, with lots of girlfriends. 'He was just a young boy who wanted to do everything.'[487]

Like three-year-old Johnathan Ball, Tim was in Warrington looking for a Mother's Day card, but also – more importantly, Wendy joked – a pair of Neville Southall (the Everton goalkeeper) football shorts.[488]

As he left the sports shop, Tim stopped to help a member of staff pick up some fallen footballs. Briefly, he was separated from his friends – and right beside one of the IRA's bombs.

When he failed to return home, his parents went to the local hospital to look for him. As he was transferred to Liverpool, Colin and Wendy drove behind the ambulance, trying to keep up with it as it sped through the traffic, its sirens blaring. 'I remember Colin saying, "It's a pity Tim doesn't know what's going on as he would have loved this."'[489]

Five days after the explosion, his life-support machine was switched off; Johnathan Ball had died at the scene. Colin and Wendy returned to the sports shop to buy the full Everton kit; Tim was buried in it.

They later founded the Tim Parry Johnathan Ball Peace Foundation, a charity which works in the UK and internationally for peace and non-violent conflict resolution.

'I do sometimes wonder what he would be doing,' says Colin. 'He could have been an Everton football star.'[490] If Tim had lived, 'we wouldn't have had four grandchildren. We'd have had 10.'[491]

❋ ❋ ❋ ❋ ❋

Name: *Michelle Baird*

Age: *7*

From: *Forthriver, North Belfast*

Date of Death: *23/10/1993*

Michelle Baird usually spent her Saturdays cheering on her daddy. Her father, Michael Morrison, played for Albert Foundry FC; seven-year-old Michelle was always on the touchline. 'The football team loved her, she was their little mascot,' remembered her aunt Diane Morrison.[492]

Michelle's grandfather had died unexpectedly, and Michelle – proudly wearing her new pink coat – had gone with her parents to the Shankill Road to order a wreath for the funeral. At one o'clock, the family was in Frizzell's fish shop. 'Michelle probably went to the fish shop to get crab sticks,' said Diane.[493] 'She always came back with those if they went onto the Shankill,' said her grandfather, Bobby Baird.[494]

Without warning, an IRA bomb exploded, demolishing the shop and trapping the customers underneath the rubble.

Michelle's great-uncle Charlie Butler was among those who ran to help. 'I looked over to where Frizzell's shop was, through the dust and smoke, and saw nothing except ruins. It just looked as if the whole shop had come down on top of anyone that was there. I, along with hundreds of other people, got on the rubble, climbed through it. Unfortunately, we knew there were fatalities because as I was digging I came across the body of little Leanne Murray.'[495]

The 13-year-old was one of ten people killed in the explosion, including one of the bombers; 57 people were injured. Charlie had no idea that Michelle and her parents, Evelyn and Michael, were among the fatalities. 'We never saw them again,' said Bobby. 'The coffins came home sealed.'[496]

The IRA later said it had been attempting to target UDA members who met in the office above the shop, and the bomb had exploded prematurely; the premises above were empty. Another IRA member, who had been badly injured but survived, was later given nine life sentences for the bombing. He was released early under the terms of the Good Friday Agreement.

Michelle's nine-year-old brother Darren and baby sister Lauren, who was only six weeks old, were orphaned; they were raised by Michelle's grandparents, Bobby and Evelyn Baird.

'All my friends have mummies and daddies and I don't,' said Lauren on the twentieth anniversary of the bombing. 'I have never been able to call anybody mummy or daddy.'[497]

Five years later, on the twenty-fifth anniversary, Michelle's colouring book was among the items in a memorial exhibition in Shankill Presbyterian Church. The words 'kiss and hugs' are written inside it in crayon.

'That was Michelle's,' said Charlie. 'She didn't want to leave the house that day but her mum promised she could finish colouring in when they got home. They never came home.'[498]

✳ ✳ ✳ ✳ ✳

Name: *Leanne Murray*

Age: *13*

From: *Shankill, West Belfast*

Date of Death: *23/10/1993*

Leanne Murray wanted to be a nursery school teacher or a nurse. She had just returned from a cross-community trip to Chicago and was keen to return to America to do work experience. 'She was a bubbly girl, a smart girl,' says her brother Gary. 'She knew what she wanted.'

There were two years between the siblings; Leanne was 13, and Gary 15. 'We would fight over who would do the dishes before our mum came in from work, and if I got up to anything, she used to squeal on me to my mum.'[499]

Leanne loved netball, and was 'very fussy' about her long, brown hair. 'I used to call her my brown-eyed girl, because she had brown eyes like me,' remembers her mother Gina.[500]

'She had just turned 13. We were as close as a mother and daughter can be,' said Gina. 'She was our baby. Where I went, she went.'[501]

Life had been tough for the Murray family. Leanne's father, Thomas, had died of a stroke eight months previously, and Gina had lost two boys – a stillborn baby, and five-year-old Paul, who had been killed in a road accident.[502]

Mother and daughter went shopping on the Shankill Road every Saturday. That afternoon, Gina was looking forward to the future. 'It was a nice day. I had got my children on a good track, both doing well in school. Life was going places.'[503]

Gina was about to go into a fruit shop when Leanne spotted her favourite, whelks, in the window of Frizzell's fish shop. 'I couldn't have stopped her going in,' says Gina. 'It's what she did when she was down there. The last time I saw her she was standing at the back of the fish counter. I said, "I'll see you in five minutes,", and it's the last image I have of her. She had a smile on her face.'[504]

When the IRA bomb exploded Gina ran outside, looking for Leanne; she later learned that a man lying on the ground, calling for help, had been one of the bombers.

Eamonn Ferguson, who was one of the first ambulance men on the scene, recalled moving a stone, 'and that's when I saw a child's face looking at me through the rubble. I could tell the child was dead but, for some reason, I just thought if we could somehow manage to free this child then we might be able to resuscitate them. We were digging and digging, trying to free the child … then I saw another arm underneath the child, which was another child.'[505]

Leanne and seven-year-old Michelle Baird were both killed in the explosion, along with eight others, including one of the bombers. The injured IRA man Gina had seen on the ground was given nine life sentences for his part in the bombing; he was released early under the terms of the Good Friday Agreement. He later apologised for his role in the atrocity.

'Like any 13-year-old, she had dreams,' says Gina. 'She was headstrong; I think she would have gone out and done what she wanted.'[506]

Name: *Brian Duffy*

Age: *15*

From: *Ligoniel, North Belfast*

Date of Death: *05/12/1993*

Brian Duffy was 'a Good Samaritan'. A pupil at St Gabriel's Secondary School, the principal, John McGartland, described him as 'a typical 15-year-old boy' who had played for one of the school soccer teams and had been concentrating on working for his GCSE exams.

A former altar boy, he had been due to take part in the school's annual distribution of food hampers to pensioners.[507]

He had been to his grandmother's, where he helped her put up Christmas decorations, and then went to the depot on the Ligoniel Road to catch a taxi home. Brian and the driver, John Todd, had just put on their seatbelts when the UDA/UFF gunmen riddled the car with bullets. They were both killed; the inquest into their deaths heard that the shotgun had fired ammunition normally used for big game hunting, and had 'exacted terrible injuries to both victims'.[508]

The murders were purely sectarian. At their joint funerals, the Bishop of Down and Connor, Dr Walsh, warned politicians and other leader that 'words can kill'.

'Who murdered John Todd and Brian Duffy?' he asked. 'Who left two families shattered? It was not just the man who pulled the trigger – oh no, a trail of people share the guilt, a trail going back to those who sharpened their tongues like swords, to those who aimed bitter words like arrows.'[509]

Among those who attended Brian's funeral were his school friends. 'We have all been crying,' one said. 'The other day we talked about getting the hampers ready for pensioners at Christmas and now the UFF have taken away his life. We're absolutely devastated.'[510]

✳ ✳ ✳ ✳ ✳

Ceasefire – soldier & child.
Opposite: Ceasefire – people
reading the news.

1994-6

- In 1994, the IRA declares a ceasefire; loyalist paramilitaries follow

- In 1996 the IRA declares its ceasefire is over with a bomb attack in London's Docklands which kills two people

- The Loyalist Volunteer Force (LVF) – an offshoot of the UVF – is formed; the organisation would carry out fourteen killings in the years to come

- Tensions continue over an Orange Order parade at Drumcree in Portadown, and a loyalist demonstration outside a Catholic church in Harryville, County Antrim

- US senator George Mitchell advocates that arms decommissioning should run parallel to any peace talks

- Elections to a new Northern Ireland Forum sees further progress for Sinn Féin

- The Spice Girls have huge chart success, while Buzz Lightyear from *Toy Story* is the must-have action figure.

Name: *Barbara McAlorum*

Age: *9*

From: *Skegoneill, North Belfast*

Date of Death: *15/03/1996*

Barbara McAlorum was her mother's 'eyes and speech'. The nine-year-old had learned sign language to help Margaret – who was deaf and dumb – communicate.

Mother and daughter were in the living room of their home in north Belfast; Barbara was sitting on the floor doing a jigsaw puzzle her father had made out of a picture of Pocahontas.

Earlier, Barbara had asked her father, Kevin, if he was still going out to buy her new clothes for St Patrick's Day and Easter, and said she wanted to come with him to buy something for Margaret for Mother's Day.[511]

When the shots were fired through the window, Margaret couldn't hear them; instead, she felt the vibrations as the glass shattered, and thought it was a bomb. Barbara and a 19-year-old friend of the family had been hit; a nurse, Donna Watters, who lived nearby, ran to help. 'The girl was unconscious, lying on her back. I put her in the recovery position and dressed her wounds. There was a faint pulse. I did what I could until the ambulance came.'[512]

Among the photographs released by Barbara's parents to *The Irish News* were an image of Barbara smiling on her First Communion day; beside it was a picture of her jigsaw, stained with blood.

The shooting was believed to have been the result of an INLA feud; Kevin said he did not know why the house had been targeted, and he had 'never had any dealing with that organisation'.[513] In 2004 Barbara's brother, also called Kevin, was shot dead outside a Belfast primary school.[514]

Children carrying wreaths in the shapes of cuddly toys and hearts led her funeral procession; her schoolfriends from Star of the Sea Primary School sang hymns and formed a guard of honour. Fr Adrian Brankin, who was also Barbara's school chaplain, spoke of how he had heard her confession the morning she was killed. 'In that confession,' he said, 'she wasn't preparing herself for death, she was preparing herself for life. Her murder really is the horrible waste of a beautiful life.'[515]

The day after her funeral, a photograph of Barbara in her coffin appeared on the front page of *The Irish News*. A teddy bear is at her shoulder, and three of her dolls lie at her feet. She is wearing a favourite outfit as well as 'her most prized rings and a simple silver necklace'.[516] Kevin and Margaret stand over their daughter's coffin; Kevin strokes her hair. They had invited *The Irish News* to take the picture 'in the hope of sending a stark message to the gunmen'.[517]

In that day's editorial, the newspaper wrote of the debate among republicans regarding a second ceasefire. 'Those who advocate a return to all-out violence must know that they are not talking about some glorious military engagement between rival armies. What they really mean is nine-year-old girls lying in coffins surrounded by their teddy bears.'[518]

✳ ✳ ✳ ✳ ✳

Name: *Darren Murray*

Age: *12*

From: *Portadown, Co Armagh*

Date of Death: *10 / 10 / 1996*

Darren Murray loved taking things apart. 'He could take a telly apart, he would take a stone apart to look into it,' says his mother Marie Therese. The 12-year-old was 'a funny wee lad, adventurous, and above all curious,' she adds. 'I remember him coming in the door from school singing, "Mummyyyyyyy".'

He had just started at Drumcree High School, where his favourite subject was IT, but he was also creative, and had made many pieces of artwork. He loved The Wolfe Tones and Take That and could often be spotted in the street wearing his Celtic or Manchester United jersey.

There was no doubt about his favourite food. 'He couldn't go a week without his beloved pizza and chips.'

Among his friends, Darren was outgoing. 'He was the leader as he always seemed to keep the craic going,' remembers Marie Therese. 'I was blessed to have a son that would go through life with that cheeky wee smile on his face. He loved nothing better than a practical joke.'

But the Troubles deeply affected Darren, she explains. At a car boot sale, she handed him a pound coin; he returned with a body alarm. He was scared 'in case the Protestants attack me', he said.

The family lived just off the Garvaghy Road in Portadown, which was at the centre of the Drumcree stand-off between the Orange Order and nationalist residents which had raised sectarian tensions in the town. Darren had been the victim of sectarian and racist – he was dark-featured – abuse.

'He used to run messages for the police to the shops to get 20p, but when he saw the trouble on the TV he got upset and scared,' says Marie Therese.

His sister Maria, who was 14, said Protestant youths had been taunting Darren; without looking, he ran across the road to get away from them, and was struck by a van. Maria said the group cheered when Darren was hit.

'I blame the siege of Drumcree,' Marie Therese told *The Irish News* at the time. 'It has made Catholic children bitter and Protestant children bitter … It has cost a young life.'[519]

Darren was transferred to the Royal Victoria Hospital in Belfast where he survived on a life-support machine until it was switched off two days later. 'I couldn't bear to hold his hand, because I knew if I did I would never let go,' says Marie Therese.

She credits her faith with helping her survive the loss of her son. 'I have never done the "what if" – it doesn't help,' she says. 'Even though my Darren has passed, I feel him close to me every day looking after our family.'

❋ ❋ ❋ ❋ ❋

Falls Road,
West Belfast, 1996.

Members of the Orange Order make their way down Garvaghy Road in Portadown amidst increased security presence. Opposite: Garvaghy Road residents protest against the Orange Order march.

1997

- Lance Bombardier Stephen Restorick is the last soldier killed by the IRA

- The IRA declares a fresh ceasefire

- LVF leader Billy Wright is killed by the INLA inside the Maze prison

- Victims of loyalist violence include Robert Hamill in Ballymena and 16-year-old James Morgan in County Down

- Labour's Tony Blair becomes British prime minister and appoints Mo Mowlam as Northern Ireland secretary

- In the Republic, Albert Reynolds becomes Taoiseach and Sinn Féin takes up its first Dáil seat

- The RUC decision to force a controversial Orange Order parade down Garvaghy Road in Portadown leads to rioting in nationalist areas

- *Titanic* is the summer blockbuster movie.

GARVAGHY ROAD
RESIDENTS COALITION

Name: *James Morgan*

Age: *16*

From: *Annsborough, Co Down*

Date of Death: *24/07/1997*

James Morgan loved the summer. Every year, the family went on holiday to Killarney, County Kerry, for a week to escape the Twelfth; the 16-year-old had been working with his father on a building site, and had money in his pocket. 'He was like a millionaire that week,' says Philomena. 'He saw The Wolfe Tones, and went to see Brendan Grace twice – he was up at the bar talking to him afterwards.'

It was also the first time his parents had seen him drinking, though they reckoned the pint probably wasn't his first. 'I said, "Do you want an orange or a beer?" explains his father Justin. 'He said, "I'll have a beer," and he had a pint of Harp.'

James and his best friend Nathan were inseparable; they saw each other every day. The journalist Susan McKay described how 'James would arrive and tap on the window of Nathan's bedroom, Nathan would open it, and James would climb in'.

The friends 'climbed mountains, threw stones at targets, lit bonfires. They'd pool their money, hitch to Newcastle and try and win enough money on the seafront slot machines to buy bottles of cider.'

'We used to get chairs and sit out in the field looking out at the stars and talking,' said Nathan.[520]

A favourite hangout was a nearby outdoor pursuits centre – with the added attraction of the girls who arrived on their Duke of Edinburgh expeditions. James was tall – over six foot – and 'kept himself well', according to his mother – 'nice white shirt, always spick and span, and loved the jeans', she says. He also loved music, especially Guns 'n' Roses, which James and Nathan would listen to on the stereo he carried on his shoulder.

James had sat his GCSE's that summer, and was awaiting the results; before that, there was a whole month of holidays left to enjoy.

It was a pouring wet afternoon; as usual, James headed over to Nathan's house. When a car stopped to offer him a lift, his parents said he would have jumped in to get out of the rain.

They had picked him up knowing he was a Catholic. James was beaten to death with a hammer, then his attackers tried to set his body on fire before dumping it in a sinkhole used by farmers to dispose of the bodies of dead animals.

Nathan and James's younger brother, Jerome, 'went out and sat and stared into the night sky until they found a constellation to name after their lost friend'.[521]

At James's funeral, Fr Finbar Glavin said that all those who had contributed to sectarianism in any way must bear some responsibility for his death, and that the brutality of James's murder had shocked the entire community. 'The murderers will remember the death forever,' he said.[522]

One man was later sentenced to life imprisonment for the murder; the court was later told that an accomplice had 'regrettably escaped justice'.[523]

James's parents opened their son's GCSE results after his death; they were excellent, as had been expected. When the envelope came through the door, the project he had made in woodwork class was still sitting in the hall; it sits there still. 'It's in the same place where he left it. We've never moved it.'

✳ ✳ ✳ ✳ ✳

Children pass burnt-out vehicles on way to school, North Belfast. Opposite: Omagh bombing memorial service, August 1998.

1998

- The Good Friday Agreement, signed in April, establishes a new Northern Ireland Assembly and other political structures designed to give parity of esteem and aspiration to both communities

- Despite the opposition of the DUP, in May the Agreement is endorsed in a referendum, by 71% of voters in Northern Ireland and 94% in the Republic

- Brothers Richard, Mark and Jason Quinn die in a loyalist petrol bomb attack on their home in Ballymoney, County Antrim, on 12 July

- In August a Real IRA car bomb in Omagh kills 31 people, including eight children and unborn twins; the Real IRA subsequently declares a ceasefire

- *Godzilla* is the summer blockbuster movie, while Furby is the must-have Christmas toy.

Name: *Richard Quinn*

Age: *10*

From: *Ballymoney, Co Antrim*

Date of Death: *12/07/1998*

'Richard was a devil, but he had a big heart.' He and his three brothers – 12-year-old Lee, Mark, who was 9, and 8-year-old Jason – were well known in the Carnany estate. 'They were just boys,' said their mother Chrissie. 'They were into everything, but everybody liked them.'[524]

The boys liked to have a bit of fun, said their father, John Dillon, and were 'very active and high-spirited'.[525] They loved living on the estate, according to John; that summer, they spent their time playing in the street, or at the local community centre, or with their grandmother, Irene, in nearby Rasharkin.

As the twelfth of July – always a flashpoint in Northern Ireland – drew nearer, sectarian tensions were heightened by the continuing standoff between the Orange Order and nationalist residents at Drumcree, in Portadown.

A Catholic living in a mainly Protestant estate, Chrissie was from a mixed family; her partner was a Protestant, and she had deliberately not brought the boys up as Catholics. They had helped build the Eleventh Night bonfire in the estate and had played around it with their friends before heading home; Chrissie had told them to be home early as she was afraid of trouble.

Chrissie had been threatened; other Catholic families in the estate had received bullets in the post, and that night she was so worried about an attack on their home that she had stayed up until 3.30 am.[526]

An hour later, the petrol bombs came through the window. Chrissie was 'woken up by the children's screams. I ran to their room to try and get them out but I couldn't find them because of the smoke and flames.' She thought her sons had managed to escape. 'The heat got unbearable and I had to jump out of the window.'[527]

An eyewitness told how she couldn't see the house, only smoke. 'One of the wee ones was upstairs – Richard. I tried to get up twice but I couldn't, the heat and smoke was that bad. I shouted and he said, "I am in a corner." Another neighbour told the boy to go to the front of the house to the stairs. That's when he shouted that he couldn't find the stairs, then the whole stairs went up in flames.'[528]

David Hetherington, a neighbour, said he saw Richard at the window. 'He said he was getting hot. He said he was frightened and he said his feet were burning. I asked him to get out and he said he couldn't.'[529]

Chrissie said she had no doubt the Drumcree stand-off was responsible for the deaths of her sons. 'It had everything to do with it.'[530]

The RUC chief constable, Ronnie Flanagan, said it was 'the sectarian murder of three children asleep in their beds. That's not protest – that's murder. The loss of three children as they slept in their beds changes everything.'[531]

Shock at the boys' deaths, and the widespread outrage and condemnation that followed, effectively ended the protests surrounding the Drumcree stand-off. A local man was later jailed for life for their murders; in police interviews he said three others, who were members of the UVF, had been involved.[532]

The boys were buried from their grandmother's home in nearby Rasharkin; the *Coleraine Chronicle* showed an image of their three white coffins being carried through the streets under a banner headline, 'Our Saddest Day'.

❋ ❋ ❋ ❋ ❋

Name: *Mark Quinn*

Age: *9*

From: *Ballymoney, Co Antrim*

Date of Death: *12/07/1998*

The Quinn boys all looked alike. A family photograph showed the four boys – Lee, the eldest, who was 12, 10-year-old Richard, Mark (9) and Jason (8) – all smiling broadly. 'Mark was a good wain,' said their mother Chrissie. 'Jason was a good wain.'[533]

Lee was the only one of the brothers to survive the fire. He had been staying with his grandmother, Irene, so was not there when the petrol bombs smashed through the windows of the house in the Carnany estate, trapping his three younger brothers in the flames.

Images of the funeral show the shell-shocked child clinging tightly to his mother and grandmother as they walked behind his brothers' coffins; he stands over their graves, leaving a black and white floral football as a tribute.

The sectarian attack came at a time of heightened tensions over a stand-off over an Orange Order march in Drumcree. A number of Catholic families on the estate had already moved out; among them, Irene Quinn. 'I left the estate a few days before, because I felt uneasy living there,' said Irene. 'Chrissie never wants to go back. She got no warning or nothing … I'm a Protestant, my daughter's a Catholic, we are a mixed family.'[534]

The boys' great-uncle Harry Patton, a member of an Orange lodge near Ballymoney, said he would never parade again. 'There is no road worth three lives. It's ridiculous. The Orange Order and Garvaghy Road residents should talk to each other face to face. They should have cancelled the stand-off after this.'[535]

Mark, Richard and Jason's deaths were the effective end of the Drumcree protests; though the stand-off continued, the violence that had resulted was largely halted. One man was later sentenced to life imprisonment for their murders.

Among those who sent their condolences to the boys' mother was the US President, Bill Clinton. 'Your family's tragedy redoubles our determination to do all we can to make sure that others need not have to experience what you are so courageously facing,' he wrote.

'May you take comfort in all the love that surrounds you and may God welcome Jason, Mark and Richard into the eternal embrace of his love.'[536]

✳ ✳ ✳ ✳ ✳

Name: *Jason Quinn*

Age: *8*

From: *Ballymoney, Co Antrim*

Date of Death: *12/07/1998*

Jason Quinn had just celebrated his eighth birthday.

He and his brothers were pupils at Leaney Primary School in Ballymoney; their school principal, Joe McConaghie, said, 'The Quinn boys were loved and adored by all their fellow pupils and staff at our school – we are all deeply shocked by this tragedy.'[537]

Jason and his two older brothers, Mark and Richard, died when their house in the predominantly Protestant Carnany estate was petrol bombed; they were targeted because they were Catholic.

Yet their family was a mixed one. 'Religion was not the divisive issue with her [their mother Chrissie] as it is to many others,' the *Coleraine Chronicle* wrote. 'The children were happy at school and that was what mattered most to her. They played with other children in the estate and went to the community centre, where young Jason had recently drawn a dove of peace in a special project.'[538]

Their murders sparked condemnations from around the globe. Among them was a message from the secretary of state, Mo Mowlam: 'Last night a family in Ballymoney went to bed as a family. When they woke up this morning three of them, three young boys, were dead. That was a family that has never done anybody any harm.'[539]

In the aftermath of their deaths, Mowlam was among many who called for a peaceful resolution to the parading dispute at Drumcree, which had stoked sectarian tensions. 'I feel a sense that the terrible images of a fire-bombed home in Ballymoney flashed around the world have strengthened the resolve of responsible people here in Northern Ireland to build a better future,' she said.[540]

The following year, a local man was jailed for life for their murders. A few months previously, the Quinn boys' former home had been knocked down. A playpark now stands in its place as a memorial to Richard, Mark and Jason.

Name: *James Barker*

Age: *12*

From: *Buncrana, Co Donegal*

Date of Death: *15/08/1998*

James Barker's favourite outfit was his Chelsea football strip. He had turned 12 on 2 August; the gear had been his birthday present. 'He'd been wearing it practically every day since,' remembers his mother, Donna-Maria. 'He'd wanted to wear it that day but I said no, put something else on, and I'll wash it.'

The Barker family had moved to Buncrana, County Donegal, from England to give their four children a better quality of life, with James's father Victor commuting back and forth to his legal practice in Surrey.

A pupil at Foyle Preparatory School in Derry, James was the goalkeeper in the school football team and was also a member of the cub scout pack and wanted to be a lawyer like his dad. 'When he steps down, I will step up,' James had written in a school essay. 'I will live in my dad's house and my dad can move over to Ireland to have a rest.'[541]

That summer, the Barkers had a visitor: Lucrecia Blasco Baselga – who was known as Uki – was staying with them as part of a Spanish exchange; her brother Fernando, who was the same age as James, was staying with the family across the road but was always over at the Barkers' house.

James had been due to caddy for Victor, who was playing in a golf tournament that day, but changed his mind at the last minute and decided to go on a trip to Omagh with the Spanish students. 'It was natural for a child,' said Victor. 'He would much prefer to be with his friends than lugging his father's golf bag around.'[542]

Donna-Maria gave the children a lift to the bus. 'James was such a little gentleman, he said "Uki, you sit in the front and I'll sit in the back." I had the funniest feeling,' she says. 'James was so excited, he just jumped out of the car. I didn't call him back, but I remember him waving to me and smiling. When I looked in the mirror I felt such a yearning, I wanted to stop and put him back in the car but because I'd seen him smile I didn't, I just drove off.'

James and Fernando were with two other friends from Buncrana, Oran Doherty and Shaun McLaughlin, in the centre of Omagh when the Real IRA bomb exploded.

A policeman later recalled seeing 'a boy lying injured … gasping for breath' among the rubble. 'A male civilian put the boy's head in his hands to comfort him. Another civilian put a cushion under the boy's head.'[543] James was taken to hospital where he underwent an emergency operation, but doctors were unable to save his life.

Eight children were among the 29 people who died in the bomb, as well as unborn twins. It was the highest death toll of a single incident of the Troubles.

Donna-Maria was taken to the makeshift mortuary in Lisanelly army barracks in Omagh to identify her son. 'His eyes, I remember thinking what beautiful emerald green eyes he had,' she says. 'I knew he had green eyes but I never realised how beautiful they were until that moment.'

When the family returned home from Omagh, 'all I could see was his Chelsea outfit blowing in the wind on the washing line'.

'Four days before he was killed, we were walking on the beach in Buncrana. [His younger brother] Oliver was running ahead and James was in the water. He turned round and said, "Mum, this is the best time of my life."'

✳ ✳ ✳ ✳ ✳

Name: *Fernando Blasco Baselga*

Age: *12*

From: *Madrid, Spain*

Date of Death: *15/08/1998*

In the photographs, they are smiling. A group of Spanish students pose for the camera as a souvenir of their trip to the Ulster American Folk Park outside Omagh; later, they would sign the visitors' book. Fernando Blasco Baselga added his name, an excited, 12-year-old's scrawl. Beside it, he writes 'Viva España'.

'I remember Fernando smiling a lot,' said his mother, Lucrecia. 'He was obedient, full of fun, a good eater and very affectionate. He loved playing with his friends.'[544]

It was Fernando's second summer in Ireland. One of a family of six from Madrid, he and his brother and sister were staying with families in Buncrana, County Donegal, in order to learn English. 'He liked going,' said Lucrecia. 'The families treated our children very well.'[545]

'Fernando was the same age as James and he was staying with the people opposite, but he was always with me because his sister Lucrecia was staying with us,' says James Barker's mother Donna-Maria. 'I always remember Victor [my husband] would sing the Abba song "Fernando" to him and he didn't know what it was.'

The children had just arrived in Omagh when the bomb exploded. Fernando died instantly; James Barker and two other children from Buncrana, Oran Doherty and Shaun McLaughlin, were also killed. Fernando's sister Lucrecia was seriously injured.

Fernando had been desperately unlucky, the coroner later told the inquest into his death. Struck by a piece of flying debris, if it had hit him almost anywhere else his injuries would have been superficial. Instead it sliced his spinal cord, below his left ear. He would have been immediately unconscious; death was inevitable.[546]

The family's Catholic faith was a comfort to them. 'He was such a good boy that the Virgin wanted to take him with her,' his grandmother said.[547]

'We will never know what would have happened if Fernando's life had carried on,' says his mother, 'but I feel calm and in peace because I'm sure he is in Heaven.'

The family keep Fernando's final letter to them – and a packet of Polo mints. 'Besides sending us lots of kisses and telling us that the weather had changed he told us he was sending us a packet of sweets and he did it,' says Lucrecia. 'He put the sweets inside the envelope and sent them. We received the letter with the sweets after he died. He was saying goodbye to us and that he loved us a lot.'[548]

✳ ✳ ✳ ✳ ✳

Name: *Breda Devine*

Age: *20 months*

From: *Donemana, Co Tyrone*

Date of Death: *15/08/1998*

Breda Devine had been born three months prematurely, yet survived her early challenges to grow into a bright and boisterous toddler. 'We are very aware that Breda was a special child who struggled bravely against all the odds,' parish priest Fr George Doherty told mourners at her funeral.[549]

On the afternoon of 15 August 1998, the 20-month-old was in the centre of Omagh with her mother, Tracey, uncle Gary and his fiancée, Donna. 'This was a special shopping trip to get shoes for Breda to go with a little dress she was going to wear to her uncle Gary's wedding,' said Breda's aunt Marina Devine. 'She was his goddaughter and she was going to the chapel to be a flower girl.'[550]

They were making their way across Market Street when the bomb exploded. Her uncle found her still strapped into her buggy, covered in rubble.[551]

Traffic warden Rosemary Ingram later recalled how Breda fought for life. 'I held that child to my heart, I shushed and cooed and told her, "Come on, come on wee pet," and then I screamed that I needed to get this baby to the hospital.

'Her wee face was black with debris, soot and dust, her clothes were covered so much that I couldn't even make out the colour of the outfit. But there it was plain as day, a heartbeat bumping along fast and furious in her chest, thump, thump, thump. I'd never seen anything like it. And I thought there was hope, I believed there was a chance that she'd open her eyes and my heart raced along with hers.'[552]

Critically ill in hospital, Tracey was unable to attend her daughter's funeral. She was not told Breda had died until six weeks later. The last of the injured to be released from hospital, Tracey returned home just in time for Christmas. 'The three other children need me and I miss them. I had to push myself because I knew the kids were at home waiting for me,' she said.

She told *The Guardian* she 'could never forgive the killers, but she hoped the peace process would succeed'.[553]

Name: *Oran Doherty*

Age: *8*

From: *Buncrana, Co Donegal*

Date of Death: *15/08/1998*

Oran Doherty was desperate to go on 'the Spanish trip'. Each year, a group of Spanish students came to Buncrana and stayed with local families; Bernie Doherty was unsure whether her son Oran, at only eight years old, was old enough to go with them to Omagh.

Oran's cousin Emmet was going, as were some of their older friends from Knockalla Drive – among them, 12-year-old Shaun McLaughlin. 'That morning Shaun called and Oran wasn't ready … I remember saying to him, "Now will you watch these boys?" He said yes, Patricia – my sister – had already warned him. "I've to look after Oran."

'Then away they went, and I remember them going down the brae and watching until they went out of sight.'

Oran loved football, particularly Celtic, and had received a Celtic tracksuit for Christmas. He played for the local underage team, Buncrana Hearts, and had already won plaques for his footballing skills. He also enjoyed fishing and had shown an early interest in Irish dancing.

'When Riverdance was on Eurovision I remember him watching it with me,' says Bernie. 'Any time me and him were in the house on our own he would have gone round the house dancing like Michael Flatley. But if anybody came in, no way, he wouldn't have wanted anybody thinking that he liked Irish dancing. He certainly wouldn't have let his brothers see it, or his daddy.'

A 'thoughtful boy' who was full of questions, he asked his mother about the Good Friday Agreement and images he'd seen on television of the Quinn brothers, who had died after loyalists petrol bombed their home in Ballymoney, Co Antrim, the previous month.

Just as he'd promised, Shaun kept an eye on Oran in Omagh. The pair were with their friend James Barker when they heard there was a bomb scare. An eyewitness later told Bernie that she had seen the boys together just before the

Real IRA car bomb exploded. 'She saw them standing and they were all happy, and she said, "I can tell you he didn't look frightened or anything."'

Bernie remembers two gardaí coming to tell her Oran was missing. 'My sisters told me it wasn't like a cry I let out, it was like the wail of a banshee.'

The boys had a joint funeral; Oran's coffin was draped in a Celtic flag, and he was buried in his Celtic jersey.

'I don't know if he would have been a great footballer or not,' says Bernie. 'He was only eight, so we didn't really get a chance to know. But he loved football and he loved Celtic, because his daddy loved Celtic. Even today – and I don't know if it's because of Oran or not – but his brothers, they all like Celtic to win.'

⁕ ⁕ ⁕ ⁕ ⁕

Name: *Shaun McLaughlin*

Age: *12*

From: *Buncrana, Co Donegal*

Date of Death: *15/08/1998*

In June 1998, Shaun McLaughlin met Irish president Mary McAleese in Dublin; two months later she attended his funeral. A pupil at Scoil Íosagáin in Buncrana, 12-year-old Shaun had been among six students chosen for the visit to Áras an Uachtaráin, where he gave the president a poem he had written for peace.

> Orange and Green, it doesn't matter
> United now, don't shatter our dream
> Scatter the seeds of peace over our land
> So we can travel hand in hand
> Across the bridge of hope.[554]

Photographs of the trip showed Shaun laughing and playing on the lawns of the Áras – a typical 12-year-old 'like any other father's son', as his father John would later describe him.[555]

That August was a warm one, and Shaun – a keen footballer who played for a local underage team – was often out playing football with the other boys in Knockalla Drive late into the evening.

On the morning of 15 August, he and eight-year-old Oran Doherty – who lived across the road – and their friend James Barker were among the local children getting ready to leave for a trip to the Ulster American Folk Park near Omagh.

In the afternoon, the group travelled into Omagh; the boys had just come out of some shops in Omagh's Market Street when they heard there was a bomb scare. 'I got scared,' Oran's cousin Emmet McLaughlin told the inquest into their deaths. 'Shaun, Oran and James [Barker] went on down the street. I said no, but because they went, I followed. Suddenly there was a giant bang. When things stopped falling everywhere I could see people all around me were badly injured.'[556]

News of the tragedy filtered back slowly to Knockalla Drive. 'This day last week we were playing football, now they're to come home in boxes,' said a friend of the McLaughlin family, Martin O'Donnell.[557]

Shaun, Oran and James were buried after a joint funeral at St Mary's Church, Cockhill, where Shaun had been an altar boy. Fr Shane Bradley told mourners that Shaun was a 'great little lad' with 'a wicked smile and always in good form'.[558]

Among the many tributes paid to Shaun, it was his smile that was always remembered. 'The one memory I have of him is of his happy, smiling face.'[559]

✳ ✳ ✳ ✳ ✳

Name: *Maura Monaghan*

Age: *20 months*

From: *Augher, Co Tyrone*

Date of Death: *15/08/1998*

Maura Monaghan was 'a beautiful, curly-haired angel who was loved by everyone'.[560] Twenty-month-old Maura died alongside her mother Avril, grandmother Mary Grimes, and unborn twin sisters, five members of the same family wiped out by the Real IRA car bomb which exploded in Omagh in August 1998.

The family had gone into Omagh for a shopping trip to celebrate her granny's birthday. A shop assistant in RD Kells' drapery shop, Sharon Robinson, later told the inquests into their deaths that she had served Maura and her family – 'a little girl with black curly hair and a white dress with navy bib and flower on it'.[561]

They left the shop, Avril carrying Maura over her shoulder. As they walked out, both Maura and her mother waved at Sharon. They were at the door of the shop when the bomb exploded.[562] Sharon said that 'when she got to her feet she saw there were nine people in the shop who were all dead and they included the grandmother, mother and child.'[563]

An army doctor later recalled how a medic collapsed after he turned over Avril Monaghan's body to find toddler Maura underneath. 'The child was lying with her hands crossed on her chest,' he said.[564]

About two thousand mourners attended their joint funeral in Clogher, County Tyrone. Maura's father Michael carried his three-year-old son in his arms as he followed the coffins of his wife and daughter into the church; beside him were his two young daughters, the eldest only five years old, looking lost and bewildered.

'Among the many wreaths at the graveside was a pink teddy-bear for the baby from her older sisters and brother. An accompanying note read: "To a beautiful and cheeky sister, you will be missed always."'[565]

❋ ❋ ❋ ❋ ❋

Name: *Monaghan Twins*
Age: *Unborn*
From: *Augher, Co Tyrone*
Date of Death: *15/08/1998*

Avril Monaghan's twin daughters were due in September 1998; on 15 August they died in Omagh along with their mother, 20-month-old sister Maura and grandmother Mary Grimes.

'Had Omagh not happened and the twins they were expecting been born next month,' wrote Frank McNally in *The Irish Times*, 'the Monaghans would have had six children under the age of seven. Father Lawrence Dawson, the parish priest in Clogher, would probably have baptised the new babies, as he did her [Avril's] other children. Instead he will be assisting at the funeral.'[566]

'She [Avril] was a loving wife and daughter and she goes to God with full hands with Maura and her two unborn children and we cannot forget them,' Fr Dawson told mourners. 'They are very much part of this morning's ceremony.'[567]

At the inquests into the Omagh deaths in September 2000, the Monaghan family solicitor, Barry Fox, applied for the twins to be declared as 'full parties' to the inquest proceedings, which would also raise the official death toll from the Omagh bomb from 29 to 31.

In a statement read by solicitor Edwin Colton after the inquest, the Grimes/ Monaghan family said that there had been 'aspects in the aftermath of the catastrophe which we found unhelpful, and in some cases, quite hurtful. We refer to the weekly, if not daily references in the press and in most news items, of the families of the 29 victims of the bombing, when in fact 31 lives were lost. The unborn twins would at this time be preparing for their second birthday.'[568]

The state pathologist for Northern Ireland, Professor Jack Crane, said the twins had not been physically injured in the explosion, but their mother's uterus had been lacerated, causing their deaths.[569]

The coroner, John Leckey, said that as far as he was concerned 31 people died, but for legal reasons he could only claim jurisdiction over 29. 'They were living, healthy babies, though unborn,' he said.[570]

He said he would write to the Department for Public Prosecutions to inform them that the unborn twins had been killed as a result of the bomb, and to urge it 'to press for child destruction charges against anyone apprehended'.[571]

Ruth Dudley Edwards, in her book on the Omagh bombing, includes the girls' names: Eimear and Evelyn.[572]

On the family headstone in the small, country graveyard in Clogher, County Tyrone, the twins are remembered alongside their mother and sister. 'All separated from us on the 15th August 1998.'

✳ ✳ ✳ ✳ ✳

Name: *Alan Radford*

Age: *16*

From: *Omagh, Co Tyrone*

Date of Death: *15/08/1998*

Alan Radford and his sister Claire couldn't have been closer. With only a year between them – Alan was 16, Claire 15 – 'everything was shared between me and him,' says Claire.

'He had my back and I had his. Every evening we would have had our wee chat at the end of the night, and Mum would be constantly saying, "You two get to bed." We were at the same school and walked to and from school together, and we still filled each other in on how our days had been.'

Alan had just finished at Omagh High School that June, and was awaiting his GCSE results. He was hoping to go to Omagh College of Further Education to do a catering course. 'I had to laugh at that,' says Claire. 'Alan hated the sight of blood. I said to him, "How are you going to cut up meat?"'

Every Saturday Alan went into town with their mother Marion, a single parent, to help her home with the shopping. 'He did that without any grudge,' says Claire. 'He was always helping people.'

He and Marion were close. 'One of the last films he went to see was *Titanic* – we were obsessed with *Titanic* history. They went to the cinema to see it, it was maybe a three- or four-mile walk, and then the two of them walked home on a cold, starry night. He was as proud as anything to be taking his mum to the cinema.'

Alan also loved music, and was a 'massive Celine Dion fan. To have her singing the main song for that film, it was his dream.'

He also had a comical streak, and loved watching Rab C. Nesbitt and *Police Academy*. 'He used to do some laughing at that,' says Claire.

The funniest was when Claire was in trouble. 'That was the best ever. I always knew when I was in trouble, for Alan would come to the front door before I would get it open and he would go, "You're dead," laughing. He knew the antics I'd been up to but he would never drop me in it. There was always good craic between me and him.'

That Saturday afternoon Alan and Marion were in the town centre as usual; Alan wanted to open a bank account before starting his college placement in September. He had just left Marion in the greengrocer's at the bottom of Market Street. 'He was in front of the bomb car when it exploded,' his sister says. 'The chances are, if he'd stayed where he was, he'd still be here.'

The Real IRA car bomb left bodies and debris strewn over a wide area; Alan's brother Paul was among those who went to look for him. 'Thankfully Alan was one of the first to be lifted off the street,' says Claire. 'He had died rapidly.'

The week after he was killed, Alan's family received his GCSE results. He passed.

✳ ✳ ✳ ✳ ✳

Name: *Lorraine Wilson*

Age: *15*

From: *Omagh, Co Tyrone*

Date of Death: *15/08/1998*

Lorraine Wilson and her best friend, Samantha McFarland, dreamt of travelling the world together. Fifteen-year-old Lorraine wanted to become an air hostess – 'for a few years' – then settle down at home in Omagh and become a chef.[573]

The 'maternal figure' at home, Lorraine would often have dinner ready for her parents, and looked after her nine-year-old brother Colin, who had learning difficulties, making him toys out of cereal boxes and other pieces of cardboard. 'When she had any spare time, she would curl up in an armchair reading love stories.'[574]

When she went out with her older brother and sister, Lorraine's mother, Ann, knew her younger daughter would look after the older pair. 'If they went to a dance and couldn't get in, it would be Lorraine who would phone to let us know what they were doing or where they were going.'[575]

Lorraine and Samantha, who was 17, collected for charities such as the RNLI and USPCA, and volunteered in the Oxfam shop in Omagh. 'These were girls who were concerned about the Third World and people less well off than themselves,' said the principal, Bill Harper.[576]

A 'model pupil' at Omagh High School, Lorraine also 'served with distinction' on the school hockey team. 'We have a prize night each year and at the last one, she was on stage line dancing.'[577]

That Saturday Lorraine and Samantha were at work in the Oxfam shop. Told of the bomb warning, they locked the shop and made their way, as directed, down Market Street. 'They refused an invitation from a friend to go to the Kozy Corner pub for a drink, as they had the keys to the shop and wanted to be ready to reopen it. She [Lorraine] was last seen by an acquaintance of Samantha's, sitting on the windowsill of Kells' drapery shop.'[578] The car containing the bomb was parked beside her.

Lorraine was buried wearing her mother's wedding dress; her school friends made a guard of honour at her funeral. 'She would have laughed at the teachers standing here,' said Elaine Ross, whose younger sister Angela was in Lorraine's class at school. 'She was a very bubbly girl.'[579]

Omagh High School lost two pupils, Lorraine and 16-year-old Alan Radford, in the Real IRA atrocity; a significant number of former pupils were also killed.

'The ones who died were the ones about whom I would feel, "Here are people who have been a success,"' said principal Bill Harper. 'They have the personality, the values and the character that you would wish young people to hold.'[580]

'They both wanted to achieve at school and they both wanted to travel,' Samantha's brother Richard told mourners at her funeral. 'She can now travel with Lorraine wherever she wants, because the human soul has no boundaries.'[581]

✳ ✳ ✳ ✳ ✳

Night of horror relived

■ Above — Felix Rooney, who survived a bomb attack on troops, examines the damage [from a] booby-trap which killed two of his friends and seriously injured two soldiers. Right — Kev[in] [is pictured se]cond from right), as he was pictured in the Irish News just over a month ago. He died [from] from hideous injuries he received in Thursday night's bomb blast. Below — From left [two] boys who died as a result of the INLA explosion, 14-year-old Stephen Bennett and 11-yea[r old] [to]day.

The Irish News
AND BELFAST MORNING NEWS

No. 33,576   BELFAST, SATURDAY, MAY 16, 1981   10p

Girl, 9, is killed in gun blitz on house

By Ruth O'Reilly

A NINE-YEAR-OLD girl was shot dead and a man critically injured in an attack on a house in north Belfast last night.

And a caller to the *Irish News* claiming to represent GHQ staff of the INLA using a coded message blamed the "Gino Gallagher" faction of the organisation for the attack.

INLA group accuses rival faction of murder

A number of men pulled up in a car, believed to be a white Peugeot 405, and one got out, opening fire through the

run round and police had surrounded the house. I explained that I was a nurse and I ran into the house.

"The fella was still conscious. The girl was unconscious, lying on her back. I put her in the recovery position and dressed her wounds. There was a faint pulse.

"I did what I could until the ambulance came. They put an airway in. I would say she was dead by the time we got [her into the ambulance]."

BLACK DAY FOR NORTH

Primate grieves on the day of four funerals

P.M. says 'No' to plea

"A black day in the history of the North" — that was how Cardinal Tomas O Fiaich yesterday referred to the four funerals of people "who should not have died," as well as the death of a policeman in a rocket [attack] on an RUC Land-rover.

Funeral of Francis Hughes — with masked escort

Pope, still in intensive care, is making steady progress, says bulletin

POPE JOHN PAUL, still in intensive care after Wednesday's assassination attempt, made steady progress yesterday

and it was too soon to foresee the longterm outlook.

Dr Emilio Trisotti, chief physician at the hospital, said: "There is still the danger of in-

Buses stoned

Balcony bomb mows down children and soldiers

The Irish News
AND BELFAST MORNING NEWS

ESTD. 1855   No. 33,948   FRIDAY, SEPTEMBER 17, 1982   10p (15p in the Republic of Ireland)   127TH YEAR

Little boy fights for life after blast kills friend

By Una Murphy

A 14-year-old boy was killed and his 11-year-old companion critically injured when a bomb exploded at Divis Flats on Belfast's Falls Road last night.

Stephen Bennett (14), from Whitehall Walk in the complex, died when the device went off as he was walking down Callingtree Walk with two friends, shortly after 7.30 p.m.

■ Children look into a military ambulance at Cullingtree Road as a soldier with leg wounds is given treatment.

Pictures by
BRENDAN MURPHY and
ALLAN McCULLOUGH

Poor areas take

---

around 6 p.m. propped against a hedge at Rugby Road.

The RUC said the responsibility for the murder "clearly lies with the terrorists who conceived and constructed this lethal device."

One of the two boys who had been with Patrick Smith at the time of the blast, 16-year-old Brian Molloy was seriously ill in hospital with leg injuries yesterday but 15-year-old Paul Sykes escaped unhurt but shocked.

Yesterday he relived the horror of finding his lifelong friend blown to bits after the blast.

He said that he and his two friends had been riding their

The INLA last night claimed responsibility for the explosion which killed 16-year-old schoolboy Patrick Joseph Smith in Belfast's University area.

The boy, who lived in Rutland Street, died instantly when a bomb attached to a motorcycle exploded as he and two friends were cycling along Rugby Road.

The INLA said the bomb had been intended for members of the security forces.

Earlier the Provisional IRA

INLA moto death

PATRICK SMITH

bicycles along Rugby Road their way to visit a priest Wednesday night.

Heavily armed police escort children on their way to school during the Holy Cross dispute in north Belfast in 2001. Opposite: The IRA's weapons are put beyond use.

2001-5

- Sixteen people die, including at least five in loyalist feuds, and a further five Catholics are killed in loyalists attacks; among the victims is *Sunday World* journalist Martin O'Hagan

- Loyalist protests take place outside the Holy Cross Girls' Primary School in Ardoyne in Belfast from June to November 2001

- The contentious issue of IRA arms decommissioning leads to the resignation of David Trimble as First Minister; decommissioning finally begins in October 2001

- The Police Service of Northern Ireland (PSNI) is established, with the aim of recruiting Protestants and Catholics on an equal basis

- Assembly elections in 2003 leave the DUP and Sinn Féin as the largest parties

- In July 2005, the IRA announces the end of its military campaign. In September, the decommissioning body announces that it has put all of its weapons beyond use

- Apple releases its iPod in 2001, while Kylie tops the charts with 'Can't Get You Out Of My Head'.

Name: *Thomas McDonald*

Age: *16*

From: *White City, North Belfast*

Date of Death: *04/09/2001*

Thomas McDonald was 'a typical teenager'. The 16-year-old was 'happy go lucky and full of life', according to his grandmother Gladys McDonald.[582] 'He always had a pretty girl on his arm,' she said, 'and like the rest of the boys his age, he was no angel. But he was such a loveable character.'

A pupil at Glengormley High School, he had chosen not to return to school after the summer, and was hopeful that he had found a job as an apprentice tiler. A supporter of Linfield FC, he was also a member of Whitewell Defenders Flute Band.

Sectarian tensions were high in north Belfast amid the loyalist protests around the Catholic Holy Cross Girls' Primary School, and there had been clashes between rival Protestant and Catholic groups around the interface area that divides the White City estate, where Thomas lived, from the nationalist Lower Whitewell Road.

Thomas had appeared in court for riotous behaviour; he was 'just a typical Protestant teenager', his aunt said. 'They all think they have to defend their area.'[583]

Thomas threw a brick at the windscreen of a car coming out of a Catholic estate; as he pedalled away on his bike, the driver – a 32-year-old mother of six – drove after him, mounting the footpath and knocking him off his bike.

'The only small comfort was that his mummy was with him at the end,' said Gladys. 'She took him in her arms and repeated over and over again, "Oh my Thomas, my son." He just moved his wee arm a bit, but didn't say anything.'[584] Newspaper photographs showed Thomas's mangled bicycle still lying beneath the fluttering police tape.

Thomas was buried in his flute band uniform. Friends laid flowers at an impromptu shrine at the spot where he was killed; at night, they slept beside it 'to guard it from attack'.[585]

As his funeral was taking place, a bail application by the woman accused of his killing was taking place in Belfast's High Court. She was later convicted of manslaughter.

The judge said he was convinced she had 'deliberately and consciously' driven her car at Thomas in order to cause him 'very serious injury', but he did not believe she intended to kill him. He said she had 'lost control' when the brick hit her car in what he described as 'a calculated and unprovoked assault'.

Thomas's mother, Pauline McDonald, said she hoped her my son's face 'flashes in front of her and I hope she will never sleep another night's sleep in her life'.[586]

The then first and deputy first ministers, Reg Empey and Seamus Mallon, said, 'This sectarian strife which places children in the front line is creating an extraordinary dangerous situation for all of us.'[587]

✳ ✳ ✳ ✳ ✳

Name: *Glen Branagh*

Age: *16*

From: *Tiger's Bay, North Belfast*

Date of Death: *11/11/2001*

Glen Branagh was less than a week away from his seventeenth birthday. A member of the local youth club, one youth worker described him as 'exuberant, full of life, and with a lot of promise'.[588] Nicknamed Spacer, he was 'a bit wild – but not a bad boy, not a bully or a vandal'.[589]

He was also a member of the UDA's youth wing, the Ulster Young Militants. The journalist Susan McKay quotes Glen's friend Billy: 'He was as game as a badger. He would have taken on Goliath.' Others, McKay notes, 'say he was just young and impressionable'.[590]

That Sunday afternoon, they were both out rioting. The ongoing loyalist protests at Holy Cross School in Ardoyne, another part of north Belfast, were continuing to stoke sectarian tensions, and there was 'recreational rioting' at the North Queen Street interface most weekends.

Trouble had broken out following a Remembrance Day service in Tiger's Bay, and a line of police in riot gear separated the two sides. The police saw Glen emerging from a crowd of loyalist rioters with a 'fizzing object' in his hand. As he was preparing to throw it at police lines it exploded, injuring his head, arm and hand.[591]

Claims by loyalists that Glen had been a 'hero' who had picked up a device thrown by the nationalist side were simply not true, the police said.[592]

Assistant Chief Constable Alan McQuillan said Glen's death was 'a disaster waiting to happen', and that those responsible were the loyalist paramilitaries who had given him the bomb. 'The 16-year-old lad killed was sent out … to do this. Somebody gave him that device, and somebody set this up.'[593]

Glen was buried the day before his birthday. 'Men and boys dressed in black trousers, white shirts and black ties bearing a UDA crest followed the coffin,' *The Guardian* wrote. His coffin was covered in a UDA flag, and accompanied by floral tributes bearing the slogans 'T[iger's] Bay Young Gun' and 'UYM'.[594] His image later appeared on a mural in Tiger's Bay celebrating the Ulster Young Militants.

Whereas most of Glen's contemporaries supported Rangers FC, the newspaper reported that Glen had been laid to rest in a Celtic FC shirt. 'He was just a wee lad who supported Celtic,' said a loyalist source, 'and thought that sport should remain separate from everything else.'[595]

✳ ✳ ✳ ✳ ✳

Name: *Thomas Devlin*

Age: *15*

From: *Somerton Road, North Belfast*

Date of Death: *10/08/2005*

Thomas Devlin was always making his friends laugh. 'It seemed to be his gift,' said his friend Hugh.[596] Another friend told his parents she remembered him laughing a lot. 'He had a great sense of humour and he was a very kind person,' according to his parents, Penny and Jim.

A pupil at Belfast Royal Academy, Thomas wanted to study either law or computing when he left school. He loved computers, and when he wasn't out with his friends, Thomas 'could be found at one computer or another, playing games or just tinkering', his friends said.[597]

He was studying music for GCSE and played the tenor horn – 'he didn't much like practising it' – though his favourite music was power and heavy metal. A strong swimmer, he was 'good at practical things' and had built a treehouse at his grandparents' farm in Armoy, County Antrim.

Thomas also loved animals, and among his pets was his Great Dane, Rosie. 'He was lying on the floor in front of the open fire watching the television,' remembers Penny, 'and the dog wanted to lie there as well but Thomas refused to move, so she just lay on top of him until he did so – she did weigh 13 stone.'

He had gone through a Goth period in his early teens, says Penny, and 'insisted on wearing all black, including black jeans'; one summer, he had dyed his black hair bright red. A member of the Boys' Brigade, in his last year he would go 'with his uniform on underneath his Goth clothes, and take them off just before he went in'.

On Saturdays, he would head into the city centre – regarded as 'neutral' – where he had made friends with other Goths, as well as skaters and punks, from all parts of Belfast; though raised a Catholic, he was the son of a mixed marriage, and his parents had deliberately sent him to schools that had pupils from a range of backgrounds.

'Thomas could make fun out of doing nothing,' says Penny. 'On the night he was killed, he was with his friends walking home, believing that he was safe – he had no reason to believe otherwise.'

The teenagers had been to the local shop to buy sweets and fizzy drinks; one of Thomas's friends was to stay over at his house, and the pair planned to play computer games. Thomas was only yards from home when they were attacked; he tried to run away, but was stabbed nine times.

His killer was later sentenced to a minimum of 30 years in jail, and his accomplice received 22 years. The two men were also convicted of the attempted murder of Thomas's friend Jonathan.

The judge said it had been an attack on 'utterly defenceless and harmless boys'. He said that the killing was not motivated by sectarianism, but the pair 'held deeply ingrained sectarian attitudes towards Catholics'.[598]

Thomas's parents say they have no doubt their son's murder was sectarian, and that he should be remembered as one of the child victims of the Troubles.

Days after Thomas's murder, Jim told the BBC that his son 'was the next generation coming up. He was across all the divides and taken away by someone who sought otherwise.'[599]

In their son's memory Penny and Jim set up the Thomas Devlin Memorial Fund – which provides bursaries for young people to pursue studies in music and the arts – in order to raise public awareness about the effect and impact of violence on young people.

'Thomas was, and his friends are, the future for Northern Ireland,' his parents wrote on the Fund's website. 'It is vital that Thomas's generation have hope and confidence for their futures.'

✳ ✳ ✳ ✳ ✳

Martin McGuinness and Ian Paisley
sign the St Andrews Agreement.
Opposite: Operation Banner –
soldiers leave Bessbrook.

2006-7

- The St Andrews Agreement is signed between the DUP and Sinn Féin, paving the way for power-sharing between the two parties in a restored Assembly

- Sinn Féin agrees to support both the PSNI and the justice system

- Operation Banner: the British army's military involvement in Northern Ireland comes to an end after almost four decades, concluding the longest military operation in its history

- Ian Paisley and Martin McGuinness are sworn in as First and Deputy First Ministers of a power-sharing government at Stormont

- At cinemas, Daniel Craig debuts as James Bond in *Casino Royale*, while the Nintendo Wii is the must-have console at Christmas.

Name: *Michael McIlveen*

Age: *15*

From: *Ballymena, County Antrim*

Date of Death: *08/05/2006*

It was an ordinary Saturday night. Fifteen-year-old Michael was out with friends; they had been to the town's cinema complex, and stopped for pizza on the way home.

A student at St Patrick's College in Ballymena, Michael loved combat games, and was a marshal in a cross-community combat group. He also loved football, and supported Celtic and Manchester United.[600]

As a Catholic in the predominantly Protestant town, Michael was no stranger to sectarianism; an assault three months previously had left him needing stitches.[601] But Michael loved Ballymena – it was where his friends were, and though the family had moved to Scotland for a time, he had been glad to come home.

'He was a big flirt and a very likeable wee fella,' said one female school friend. 'He always kept us going in class but he did that to everybody. He was very popular.'[602]

One woman described meeting Michael for the first time at her grandson's eighteenth birthday party. 'A lot of teenagers sit together and don't bother with older ones like me but Michael wasn't like that … he was a bashful wee boy because I went to take a photograph and he was shy.'[603]

It was just after midnight. Michael and his friends were attacked by a Protestant gang. They chased the boys for a mile until he was cornered by a high wall, and beat him with a baseball bat.

His family allowed *The Irish News* to take a photograph of Michael as he lay on a life-support machine in hospital, tubes coming from his mouth, as they said their final farewells. The hands of his loved ones rest on his chest, and his uncle kisses his nephew's forehead.

'He was 15, just 15,' said another uncle. 'He was a quiet wee teenager … he stood for his sister's baby last week. Now he is dead. It is such a waste.'[604]

The journalist Susan McKay described how Michael's seven-year-old brother Sean had been given money to go and buy sweets in the hospital shop. In the shop, all the newspapers had photographs of his brother on them, so he bought them all, and some lollipops. 'When he got back to the ward where Michael was lying, he laid the papers out and set a lolly on top of each of them.'[605]

As Michael's remains were brought home, his friends waited outside the house, dressed in Celtic jerseys with his nickname – Micky Bo – on the back; some held red roses. At his funeral, the priest said that Michael had shared his last meal on earth – a takeaway pizza – with a Protestant friend.[606]

Four men were later convicted of Michael's murder, and a number of others were convicted of lesser offences. A 'lethal cocktail of drugs, drink, youth and sectarianism provided the context in which this murder occurred', the judge said.[607]

Following his death, Michael's family and friends were among many in Ballymena and beyond who called for an end to sectarianism.

'There's maybe a turning point within Ballymena,' said PSNI District Commander Terry Shevlin. 'Not just with young people but adults who at times behind the scenes would orchestrate young people to get involved in sectarianism – I think now's that time … in memory of Michael McIlveen, to put an end to that.'[608]

※ ※ ※ ※ ※

15-year-old James Kennedy was one of five people killed in a Loyalist attack on Sean Graham's bookmakers, February 1992.

6

Legacy of the Troubles

'The bullets that killed James didn't just travel in distance,
they travelled in time. Some of those bullets never stop travelling.'

Belfast is a city of memorials. Plaques, monuments, even shrivelled bunches of flowers mark the spot where its people died, its landscape forever marked by the blood that seeped onto its streets.

On a gable wall in south Belfast is one such memorial; in the lexicography of the Troubles, the phrase 'Sean Graham's bookie's' is the only explanation needed. Anyone who lived through it can picture it: the shopfront they saw on the news, the loyalist gunmen who sprayed the premises with bullets, and the five people they killed.

Around the corner is a stone laid on the twentieth anniversary of the killings in 2012. It bears pictures of the five victims – the youngest, James Kennedy, was only 15. Below is the inscription: 'This memorial serves as a reminder of the suffering that was caused, the collusion that lay behind it, and our determination that truth and justice will ultimately prevail.'

As a testament to the Troubles, it could stand for many such atrocities. Yet beyond the five who are commemorated on the memorial are other victims.

James's mother Kathleen died almost two years to the day after her son. 'The whole time after she only crossed the door once,' says James's brother David. 'She wouldn't leave the house, she wouldn't eat, she just gave up. Our mother was dying in front of us and we were still too young to understand what was going on.'

Her husband Jack had no doubt his wife died of a broken heart. 'The bullets that killed James didn't just travel in distance, they travelled in time,' he said in a newspaper interview. 'Some of those bullets never stop travelling.'[1]

A version of that statement is also inscribed on the memorial at the bookie's; it is also on James's headstone. 'It's true what he said, isn't it?' reflects David. 'Those bullets never stop travelling.'

It is February 2019. Ann Maguire sits in the conference room in the offices of Relatives for Justice on the Glen Road in west Belfast.

On the table in front of her is a thin manila folder. It contains a newspaper cutting, a photocopy of a page from *Lost Lives*, and a photograph of her nine-year-old brother Hugh. She was 11 when he was killed in west Belfast in 1980; she is now 51.

'This is all the information I have in relation to my brother,' Ann explains. 'It consists of about three pages.' Hugh was found lying injured in the road; he had either been hit by an iron bar which had bounced off a British army vehicle, or struck by the vehicle itself.

She opens the folder and sets each document on the table in front of her, explaining how the now defunct Historical Enquiries Team (HET) contacted her 'out of the blue' in 2012, but when the HET was suspended in 2013 she 'let it go'.

'I thought, *Well, he's gone, my mum's gone, my dad's gone, what can I do?* Something at the back of my head wouldn't let me rest. I thought, *I want to see these reports.* I'm of an age now where I'm thinking, *I want to know what happened to my brother. I want to know was it a complete accident or was someone actually responsible.* I don't want to wait until I'm 70 or 80 and think, *I wish I'd found out.* I've made up my mind. I want to know.'

She lifts up Hugh's photograph. 'He's only about seven there. He's handsome, isn't he?'

It took Ann until the end of 2018 to make contact with Relatives for Justice. 'It's emotional,' she says, 'but I want to do it. This is my file, and there's nothing there.'

Some relatives, like Ann, have just begun to ask questions. All too often, Troubles deaths were simply not investigated, or the investigation that did take place was limited. Of the 186 children included in this book, the majority – approximately 42.5% - were killed by republicans; loyalists were responsible for 27% of deaths, and security forces for 26%.

This final figure, comprised of the children killed by either the British army or the RUC, is significantly higher than the percentage of deaths caused by the security forces over the course of the Troubles. Lost Lives attributes 361 deaths out of 3,720 to the security forces, or approximately 10%.

Conversely, the percentage of deaths attributed to republicans is lower among the child casualties, at approximately 42.5%, as compared to 54% of all Troubles-related deaths. The IRA was responsible for the majority of these. The percentage of loyalist killings among children is also slightly lower, at approximately 27% rather than 30%.[2]

In six cases, it is simply not known who was responsible. 13-year-old Martha Campbell was killed as she walked round to her friend Geraldine's house in west Belfast in 1972. The HET report into the her death states, with some incredulity, that 'it is difficult to imagine that a child could have been shot dead in the street, and no investigation of the killing took place'[3] yet this is exactly what it concludes: 'A child was shot to death in a public street and the matter was never effectively investigated.'[4]

The HET was set up in 2005 by Northern Ireland's then Chief Constable, Sir Hugh Orde, in order to re-examine all Troubles-related killings. In some cases, it represented the first substantive investigation into a loved one's death; for some families it provided answers, and for others, additional evidence. For others, its links to the police raised questions over impartiality when investigating killings by the security forces, and in 2013 the HET was criticised by police watchdog HM Inspectorate of Constabulary, which found it had investigated cases where security forces were involved with "less rigour" than others.[5]

It was wound up the following year – with the PSNI citing financial pressures – and was replaced by the Legacy Investigations Branch (LIB), part of the Police Service of Northern Ireland. In practice it is limited in funding and scope; the House of Commons Defence Select Committee was told in 2017 that out of more than 900 deaths remaining to be investigated, the LIB's "active caseload" was 14.[6]

In Northern Ireland, the failure to deal with the past continues to haunt the present and future. At the time of writing, the North has been without a government for more than two years; 'legacy' is one of the sticking points.

The 2014 Stormont House Agreement suggested four new institutions – among them, a Historical Investigations Unit (HIU) to take forward outstanding investigations into Troubles-related deaths, an Independent Commission on Information Retrieval (ICIR) to enable family members to seek and privately receive information about the deaths of their relatives, and an independent Oral History Archive (OHA) to enable people from all backgrounds to share experiences and narratives related to the Troubles. These plans were put out to consultation in 2018, with more than 17,000 people responding. In July 2019, the Northern Ireland Office published an analysis of their responses. While it was 'inevitable' that there would be 'different priorities and contrary views', its report said, 'the overarching message from the vast majority of those who have responded to the consultation is clear: the current system needs to be reformed and we have an obligation to seek to address the legacy of the past in a way that builds for the future.'

Many families continue to campaign for fresh inquests, which would allow them to find out how their loved one died.

Prior to 1980 the modern verdict of 'unlawful killing' did not exist, and coroners' powers were extremely limited – for example, they lacked the power to compel witnesses. The vast majority of Troubles-era inquests returned open verdicts.

Of the 186 children killed as a result of the Troubles, there have been convictions for murder or manslaughter in less than 15% of cases. All those convicted have been either loyalist or republican paramilitaries, or their associates.

A soldier was found guilty of the unlawful killing of 12-year-old Kevin Heatley in Newry in 1973; his conviction was quashed on appeal. At the time of writing, he is the only member of the security forces to have been convicted in connection with the death of a child.

Annette McGavigan was also shot by the British army; her brother and sister, Martin and May, began campaigning on their sibling's behalf almost twenty years ago.

'Annette was one of the forgotten,' says her sister May. 'She was so innocent, and good, but her name was never mentioned. I thought to myself, *No, we need to try and find out as much as we can about what happened to her.*'

The 14-year-old had been let out of school early and had gone to watch a riot near her home in Derry's Bogside in September 1971; really, Martin says, the girls had gone to check out 'the talent'.

A soldier fired into the crowd, killing Annette, who was still wearing her green school uniform. The British army claimed they had shot an IRA gunman – a claim which has always been denied by local eyewitnesses.

The McGavigans – and others whose loved ones were killed by the security forces – maintain that the lack of a proper inquiry into their deaths means there is a legal obligation for them to be investigated now.

From 1970 until September 1973 the existence of an informal agreement between the Chief Constable of the RUC and the G.O.C. of the British army meant that army killings were not investigated by the RUC, but by military police.

This meant that, according to Dr Patricia Lundy of Ulster University, 'the interviews appear to have been conducted informally with no assessment of criminal responsibility.

'The role of the RMP officer seems to have been simply to record the facts as described by the soldier, rather than to probe or question with a view to ascertaining whether or not the action had been justified or whether the soldiers' actions were lawful.'

She cites evidence given by a military witness to the Saville Inquiry into Bloody Sunday: 'It was not a formal procedure. I always wore civilian clothing and the soldier was usually relaxed. We usually discussed the incident over sandwiches and tea.'[7]

In 2003, a judicial review into the death of Kathleen Thompson - a mother of six shot dead by the British army in her garden in the Creggan area of Derry in 1971 – found that the investigation into her death was not effective, thus setting a precedent for the re-examination of other cases.

In Annette's case, 'there has never been a proper, rigorous investigation,' says Paul O'Connor, the director of the Pat Finucane Centre (PFC), which supports the McGavigan family.

'The inquest was deeply inadequate – it returned an open verdict and the family were not legally represented, only one witness was interviewed, there was no proper forensic or ballistic examination, and the bullet was not recovered.

'There was never a subsequent police investigation. The soldiers involved were never interviewed under caution, and therefore were never challenged about their accounts.

'The soldier who fired the shot was alive when the HET were involved, and he refused to talk to them, and that investigation was never completed.'

The McGavigans want their sister's death properly investigated, and the British army's claim that they shot a gunman publicly overturned; the PSNI is currently reviewing her case and considering if there is there is enough evidence for a full investigation.

In February 2019 Northern Ireland's Department of Justice released £55 million which would allow 52 legacy inquests – covering 93 deaths – to proceed.

Among them will be an inquest into the death of Margaret Gargan, a 13-year-old girl who was one of five people (including three children) shot dead by the British army in west Belfast on the evening of 9 July 1972.

'Most of the families want another inquest because there was no challenge,' says Margaret's brother Harry. 'Nobody said to the soldier, "Well, you said this," like is happening with the Ballymurphy [massacre] inquests now. I just want to hear them being challenged over what they said originally.'

For many families, 'dealing with the past' is also about pursuing not just truth, but justice.

For the family of 15-year-old Daniel Hegarty – who was shot dead by a soldier in Derry in 1972 – a fresh inquest paved the way for a decision by Northern Ireland's Public Prosecution Service (PPS) in April 2019 that a soldier was to be charged with his murder.

After the inquest decision was announced, Daniel's sister Margaret Brady went up to the cemetery to tell him. 'We said, "You can rest in peace now, son," and then we went and we told my [deceased] ma and da, "You can rest now in peace, and may God forgive that soldier."'

The prosecution of former British soldiers for Troubles-related killings is a deeply controversial issue. There have been accusations of a 'witch-hunt' against former soldiers and claims that they are being disproportionately pursued.

There have been protests, most notably in regard to the so-called Soldier F, who faces charges of murdering two people and wounding four others on Bloody Sunday in Derry in January 1972.

In 2018, the then British prime minister, Theresa May, told the House of Commons that it was 'unfair' that only members of the security forces were being investigated in connection with the Troubles; the then Secretary of State, Karen Bradley, was among those who claimed there was a disproportionate emphasis on the actions of the police and former soldiers.

'There is very little emphasis on the actions of paramilitary terrorists,' she said.[8]

In 2017, the DUP MP Jeffrey Donaldson said that "the reality" was that "90% of the resources of the Legacy Investigation Branch … are devoted to investigating 10% of the deaths during the Troubles, and 10% of its resources are devoted to investigating 90% of the deaths."[9]

PSNI figures obtained by the BBC disputed these claims: they stated that the LIB was to re-investigate 1,188 deaths not previously considered or completed

Memorial quilt by the South East Fermanagh Foundation, commemorating victims of the Troubles.

by the HET. 530 of these related to republicans, 271 to loyalists, and 354 to the security forces.

The HET, the BBC stated, had previously reviewed 1,626 cases, of which more than 1,000 were attributed to republicans; 32 were related to the security forces.[10]

'Just because you wear a uniform, you shouldn't get off with murder,' says Daniel's sister Margaret Brady. 'Should you be the pope or the queen of England, if you commit murder you should stand trial. Nobody should be above the law.

'We always forgave the soldier,' she adds. 'This was never a witch-hunt. It's not about hatred, it's not about anger. Regardless of who or what did the killing, the law has to be upheld.'

For the Hegarty family, there was relief, but also sadness. 'We're glad now that the PPS has taken on board that he was murdered, and we were telling the truth all the time and that Daniel posed a threat to nobody. We're just totally sad that our younger sister, who passed away, wasn't here to see this.'

Her sentiments are shared by many. A couple of months before Daniel was killed, another Derry teenager, 15-year-old Manus Deery, was shot in the head by a soldier. He had been eating chips with his friends; the British army had maintained that the soldier had fired at a gunman.

His sister Helen campaigned for years for a fresh inquest into his death, and in 2017 the coroner ruled that he had been 'totally innocent'. Yet in Manus's case there can be no prosecutions. The soldier who fired the fatal shot is dead.

'I would have liked to have seen him in court, of course I would,' said Helen. 'I think the delays in all these cases are despicable, because people are dying, relatives are dying. This place can't move forward until these legacy cases are dealt with.'[11]

David McCafferty agrees. His 15-year-old son – also called David – was killed on the same night as Margaret Gargan. 'I want to see them paying in some way, because they murdered them kids.'

Would he like to see somebody in court? 'I'd love to see it.'

'It'll be up to them'uns to decide whether to prosecute or not,' Margaret's brother Harry tells David McCafferty.. 'What you say won't make any difference.'

Harry is ambivalent about a prosecution. 'It's just important for me to see the facts,' he says.

'Justice is different things to different people,' points out Julie Livingstone's sister Elizabeth. Julie was shot and killed by a plastic bullet in west Belfast in 1981. 'The soldier, we know he was a Welsh Guard and I'm sure he would be easy enough to identify, but there's too much water under the bridge for me,' says Elizabeth.

'I just hope he's had sleepless nights, I hope he has a conscience and I hope he's suffered guilt because he shot an innocent child. It wouldn't help me for him to be prosecuted, but I know that some of my family would like to see that.'

Yet the reality is that, for many, prosecutions are unlikely. 'James was a little English boy in Northern Ireland, he didn't know anything, and I really do feel he deserves justice,' says James Barker's mother Donna-Maria.

He was one of eight children and unborn twins killed in the Real IRA bombing of Omagh. No-one has ever been prosecuted in a criminal court for the explosion.

'I went to court some of the times, and the police, they know who was responsible, but I don't think I will see it [a prosecution] in my lifetime.'

Some have sought apologies; Mark Eakin, whose 8-year-old sister Kathryn was among those killed in the IRA's bombing of the village of Claudy, County Derry, in 1972, spoke to the North's then deputy first minister Martin McGuinness 'several times' after making a direct appeal to him on BBC radio. For Mark, a private apology to him from the former IRA leader went some way to acknowledging those Mark describes as 'the forgotten victims' of Claudy.

In 2010 a report by the Police Ombudsman revealed that in 1972 the RUC believed a priest, Fr James Chesney, was the IRA's director of operations in south Derry and had been directly involved in the Claudy bombings; the police never called him in for questioning, and he was instead transferred to another parish.[12]

'It was covered up, and still to this day it's been covered up," says Mark. "Even when it came out about Father Chesney, everyone knew about Father Chesney. I don't remember the names, but my mother could have told you a list of names of people as long as your arm of those who were involved in Claudy.

'Not one person was responsible, a lot of people were mixed up in it, and a lot of people have become mixed up in it since trying to cover it up. More money's been spent trying to keep it quiet than trying to sort it out.'

In regard to Northern Ireland's past, much remains to be 'dealt with'. Recent revelations as to the nature and extent of security force collusion in loyalist killings – not least in regard to the five people killed in Sean Graham bookie's – has left many questioning how much more is yet to be revealed, and how much ever will be.

Films like *Unquiet Graves*, about the Glenanne Gang, and *No Stone Unturned*, which investigates the Loughinisland massacre, have brought questions of legacy and collusion to a wider audience than ever before. In the absence of prosecutions, they have at least brought families a measure of consolation that what happened to their loved ones – and, in some cases, exactly who was responsible – is now in the public domain.

Amid the continued absence of an official position on legacy, much of the campaigning – and much of the progress – has been carried out by victims' and survivors' groups, individual family members, film-makers, journalists and arts practitioners.

Denis Bradley was the co-chair of the Consultative Group on the Past, which in 2009 reported its recommendations as to how Northern Ireland should respond to the Troubles. Though overtaken by controversy following a leak to the media over a proposed payment to victims of £12,000, ten years on Denis Bradley remains convinced that their proposals represented the best chance Northern Ireland has had of making some headway.

'Acknowledgement would be the underlying ground to it, but other families will say, "I want justice," or "I want truth." So acknowledgement is running under all of that – it's a very undefined word but it's an important word – and what we were suggesting was a way of packing that with a legacy commission and also an investigation branch.

'It doesn't give the victim all the power, but what it does give is acknowledgement. It gives you options, but you are not in total control of this.

'It will be victim-centred but it will not be victim-led because society has a right in this too and society is going to do this because it's the right thing to do and then it's going to shut it down.

'You either do this in the next five years or forget it, so we're challenging you too, but the problem is at the moment nobody's challenging anybody, we're going ad hoc from one situation to the next situation.'

'I went into past fairly cynical as to whether anything should be done,' says Bradley. 'What changed me was I began to think we will not get through the politics of this situation unless we have some mechanism with dealing with it.

'I keep using the image of a mucky field. It's a swamp we won't be able to get through, and that's kind of where we are at the moment.'[13]

Claire Radford is doubtful. Her 16-year-old brother Alan was among the victims of the 1998 bombing of Omagh; she points out that the Omagh victims 'fall outside the legacy issues'.

'Everybody signed the Good Friday Agreement on the 10th April and thought that was the end of it. Alan was killed in so-called peace times.

'We are still appeasing terrorists. What happened is whitewashed, because we're OK with dealing with what happened before the Good Friday Agreement because that suits us, but anything afterwards, we're completely lost.

'Terrorists are being appeased and nothing is being done for the victims. I want Alan's murder accounted for. The Troubles were supposed to be over, so let's address it properly.'

She is doubtful that a measure such as a truth commission would be effective. 'I can see the reason why people want to pursue it, but the outcome will never be what you actually desire. You will never get full transparency, never get full truth.'

She is adamant she will continue to campaign on her brother's behalf; so too will David Kennedy. Once his father Jack campaigned on behalf of his brother James and the other victims of the attack on Sean Graham's bookmakers; now his father is dead, it has fallen to David to continue to speak up on his brother's behalf.

'It's a faceless thing isn't it,' says David. 'Who do you blame for it, is it the state, the British, does it go back to the prime minister? How do I feel about it? I don't really know. But someone could've stopped it. How can you justify it? I know loads of people have been killed, but my brother was only 15.'

David now has two sons of his own; the eldest is 11-year-old James. 'James is into computers and he typed his name into Google and it brought up everything that happened to [his uncle] James. He said, "Daddy, I typed in James Kennedy and look what it brought up," and I said, "No, you shouldn't be looking at that."

'At my father's funeral a couple of years ago the priest said about James getting murdered and when we came out of church James said to me, "See, I told you my Uncle James was murdered."'

When he's ready, David will tell his sons how and why their uncle was killed, and why he continues to campaign on his behalf. Until then, he tells his eldest son: 'You've been named after your Uncle James and he's proud of you.'

First day of 1994 IRA ceasefire.

Endnotes

Children's Biographies

1. McKittrick, David, Kelters, Seamus, et al., *Lost Lives: The Stories of the Men, Women and Children Who Died as a Result of the Northern Ireland Troubles*, Mainstream Publishing, 2008, p34.
2. Father tells of his son's 1969 killing by British army for the first time, *The Irish Times* 4/8/98.
3. National Graves Association, *Belfast Graves*, AP/RN Print, 1985, pp85–6.
4. Army Deny Gas Caused Death, *The Times*, 21/4/70.
5. Callaghan: No CS gas ban, *Irish Press*, 15/5/70.
6. CS gas 'did not kill baby', *Irish Press*, 4/6/70.
7. Child Shot in Cowboys and Indians Game, *Irish News*, 11/12/70.
8. Game of Cowboys Ends in Tragic Death of Child, *Evening Herald*, 11/12/70.
9. Ibid.
10. Death notices, *Irish News*, 11/5/70.
11. Creggan Blaze: 5 Die Through Misadventure, *Irish News*, 11/12/70.
12. 'Three Die After Explosion in House', *The Irish Times*, 27/6/70.
13. 'Violent Bogside Reaction to Derry Fatality', *Derry Journal*, 27/7/71, p5.
14. Kevin Myers Witnessed the Horror and Chaos Following Internment on August 9th, 1971, *The Irish Times*, 10/8/96.
15. De Baroid, Ciaran, *Ballymurphy and the Irish War* (Revised Edition), Pluto Press, 2000, p72.
16. *Lost Lives*, *op. cit.*, pp79–90.
17. *Lost Lives*, *op. cit.*, p90.
18. *Lost Lives*, *op. cit.*, p92.
19. Shot Derry Youth Found Dying, *Irish Independent*, 20/8/71.
20. White, Robert W., *Out of the Ashes: An Oral History of the Provisional Irish Republican Movement*, Merrion Press, 2017, p402.
21. O'Doherty, Shane Paul, *The Volunteer: A Former IRA Man's True Story*, Strategic Book Group, 2011, p75.
22. Shock death of boy at 16, *Evening Herald*, 20/8/71.
23. Horror as Sniper Kills Baby, *Irish Independent*, 4/9/71.
24. Shot Girl's Mother Collapses Near Graveside, *Derry Journal*, 7/9/71.
25. Angry Scenes After Derry Child Is Killed by Army Vehicle, *Derry Journal*, 10/9/71.
26. Soldier Fainted as Child Died – Inquest, *Belfast Telegraph*, 11/12/71.
27. Ibid.
28. *Irish Press*, 11/9/71.
29. Angry Scenes After Derry Child Is Killed by Army Vehicle, *Derry Journal*, 10/9/71.
30. MacAirt, Ciarán, *The McGurk's Bar Bombing: Collusion, Cover-up and a Campaign for Truth*, Frontline Noir, 2012.
31. McGurk's Bar Massacre: The Day my Life was Shattered, *Belfast Telegraph*, 1/3/11.
32. Blast that killed 15 may have been IRA error, *The Times*, 6/12/71.
33. Press release by the Police Ombudsman for Northern Ireland, 21/2/11, https://cain.ulster.ac.uk/issues/police/ombudsman/po210211press.htm.
34. McGurk's Bar Massacre: The Day my Life was Shattered, *Belfast Telegraph*, 1/3/11.
35. Two Babies Among Victims of Belfast Explosion, *The Irish Times*, 13/12/71.
36. Let Bombers See Victims, says Coroner, *The Irish Times*, 28/7/72.
37. Coalisland Youth was Unarmed when Shot – Inquiry, *The Irish Times*, 23/12/71.
38. Four Die in NI Explosions, *The Irish Times*, 20/12/71.
39. *Lost Lives*, *op. cit.*, p133.
40. Body of Youth Found with Gun in Pocket, *Evening Herald*, 12/1/72.
41. Man Shot Dead in Belfast, *The Irish Times*, 13/1/72.
42. Youth Found Shot Dead in Belfast House, *Irish News*, 12/1/72.

43. Appendix II: Provisional Republican Roll of Honour, in White, Robert W., *Out of the Ashes: An Oral History of the Provisional Irish Republican Movement*, Merrion Press, 2017.
44. 200 Teenagers at Belfast Boy's Funeral, *The Irish Times*, 15/1/72.
45. Youngest Ever Mayor is Elected by Town Council, *Meath Chronicle*, 27/6/12.
46. Women in Struggle interview, Ógra Shinn Féin, 15/9/09, http://sinnfeinrepyouth.blogspot.com/2009/09/women-in-struggle-interview-with.html.
47. Ardoyne Commemoration Project, *Ardoyne: The Untold Truth*, Beyond the Pale Publications Ltd, 2002, p110.
48. Ibid., p111.
49. Ibid., p111.
50. Ibid., p111.
51. Ibid., p113.
52. Ibid., p113.
53. Soldiers Charge Funeral Mourners, *Irish Independent*, 23/2/72.
54. IRA Honours at Derry Boy's Funeral, *Derry Journal*, 29/2/72.
55. Inquest on shooting of Derry youth, *Irish Press*, 12/7/72.
56. IRA Honours at Derry Boy's Funeral, *Derry Journal*, 29/2/72.
57. *Lost Lives, op. cit.*, pp157–8.
58. Shot Boys Inquiry Demand, *Evening Herald*, 2/1/72.
59. Two Boys Die in Van Horror, *Irish News*, 2/3/72.
60. Ibid.
61. *Lost Lives, op. cit.*, p159.
62. *Tyrone Democrat*, 9/3/72.
63. Fr Faul, Denis & Fr Murray, Raymond, *The RUC: The Black and Blue Book*, 1976, reproduced in http://cain.ulst.ac.uk/issues/police/docs/faul.htm
64. http://jeeves701.tripod.com/greaterclonardexprisonersassociation/index.html.
65. National Graves Association, *Belfast Graves*, AP/RN Print, 1985, p89.
66. Ibid.
67. Three Provisionals Die in Explosion, *The Irish Times*, 10/3/72.
68. Relatives for Justice, *In Your Own Words: Understanding the Troubles: Interview with Flo O'Riordan by Mark Thompson*, 28/7/10.
69. *Interview, Wave Trauma Centre*: http://storiesfromsilence.com/margaret-delaney/.
70. National Graves Association, *Belfast Graves*, AP/RN Print, 1985, p90.
71. *Lost Lives, op. cit.*, p169.
72. *Interview, Wave Trauma Centre*: http://storiesfromsilence.com/margaret-delaney/.
73. Funeral of shot Belfast boy, *Irish News*, 25/3/72.
74. Death notice, *Irish News*, 25/3/72.
75. *Interview, Wave Trauma Centre*: http://storiesfromsilence.com/margaret-delaney/.
76. National Graves Association, *Belfast Graves*, AP/RN Print, 1985, p90.
77. Ibid.
78. Ibid.
79. De Baroid, Ciaran, *Ballymurphy and the Irish War*, Pluto Press, p100.
80. Shot Youth was in IRA, *Irish Independent*, 28/3/72.
81. *Lost Lives, op. cit.*, p170.
82. Two Men Hurt by Gunfire in Belfast, *Irish Independent*, 27/3/72.
83. Francis Rowntree killing 'not justified' – coroner', *BBC News*, 17/11/17.
84. IRA bullet kills child in Army post attack, *News Letter*, 1/5/72.
85. Provos Blame Child's Gunshot Death on Orange Elements, *Irish Independent*, 1/5/72.
86. *Lost Lives, op. cit.*, p180.
87. Inquest Verdicts on Six Violence Victims, *The Irish Times*, 7/7/72.
88. Father in Jail when Child Died, *Irish Press*, 1/5/72.
89. Volley at IRA Man's Funeral, *Irish Independent*, 17/7/72.
90. Historical Enquiries Team: *Review Summary Report concerning the death of Martha Ann Campbell*, undated, p18.
91. *Lost Lives, op. cit.*, p188.

92. Boy Dies, 2 Others Hurt in City Shootings, *Irish News*, 19/5/72.
93. Teenager Shot Dead, 2 Others Wounded, *The Irish Times*, 19/5/72.
94. Ibid.
95. Boy Dies, 2 Others Hurt in City Shootings, *Irish News*, 19/5/72.
96. Teenage Boy Shot Dead, *Irish Press*, 19/5/72.
97. Manus Deery: Witness Describes Night 15-year-old was Killed in Bogside, *BBC News*, 26/10/16.
98. Derry teenager 'totally innocent', says coroner, *BBC News*, 10/4/17.
99. *Irish News*, 30/5/72.
100. Shot Girl Loses Fight for Life, *Irish News*, 31/5/72.
101. *Lost Lives, op. cit.*, p194.
102. https://api.parliament.uk/historic-hansard/written-answers/1972/jun/21/joan-scott.
103. *Lost Lives, op. cit.*, p194.
104. Ardoyne Commemoration Project, *Ardoyne: The Untold Truth*, Beyond the Pale Publications Ltd, 2002, p120.
105. Ibid., pp120–1.
106. *Lost Lives, op. cit.*, p199.
107. Ardoyne Commemoration Project, *Ardoyne: The Untold Truth*, Beyond the Pale Publications Ltd, 2002, pp120–1.
108. Ibid., pp124.
109. Leaflet, *Springhill Westrock Massacre July 1972*, The Springhill Westrock Massacre Committee, 2019.
110. Booklet, *The Springhill Massacre, early 1990s*, quoted O Bradaigh, Seosamh, https://seachranaidhe1.blog/tag/irish-republican-army/page/5/
111. Unnamed friend of Margaret Gargan, quoted in Leaflet, *Springhill Westrock Massacre July 1972*, The Springhill Westrock Massacre Committee, 2019.
112. Leaflet, *Springhill Westrock Massacre July 1972*, The Springhill Westrock Massacre Committee, 2019.
113. Ibid.
114. Ibid.
115. Correspondence between the HET and Madden and Finucane Solicitors, quoted in *Relatives for Justice, Gerard Gibson: Murdered by the British Army, 11th July 1972*, undated, p13.
116. McKay, Susan, *Bear in Mind These Dead*, Faber & Faber, 2008, p34.
117. Ibid., p33.
118. Mother of Shot Boy Savagely Assaulted, *Irish News*, 13/7/72.
119. McKay, Susan, *Bear in Mind These Dead*, Faber & Faber, 2008, p35.
120. 'Life' for Rapists and Child Murderers, *Irish Independent*, 23/5/73.
121. Ibid.
122. Troubles Victim So Young his Family Never Had Chance to Take Photograph, *News Letter*, 28/9/17.
123. Bloody Friday, *BBC NI*, broadcast July 2012.
124. Ibid.
125. Ibid.
126. Taylor, Peter, *Provos: The IRA and Sinn Féin*, Bloomsbury, 1998, p150.
127. Seven killed in the carnage at Oxford St. Bus Station, *Belfast Telegraph*, 22/7/72.
128. Starmaker's Tears for a Life Cut Short, *Belfast Telegraph*, 22/7/72.
129. Ibid.
130. Bloody Friday, *BBC NI*, July 2012.
131. Messenger Boy who Predicted his own Fate, *Belfast Telegraph*, 22/7/72.
132. Bloody Friday, *BBC NI*, July 2012.
133. Tribute to boy hero of Bloody Friday, *Belfast Telegraph*, 15/3/73.
134. Bloody Friday, *BBC NI*, July 2012.
135. *Lost Lives, op. cit.*, p240.
136. Daniel Hegarty's Family 'Overwhelmed' by Inquest Findings, *BBC News*, 10/12/11.
137. My Little Sister will Always be Eight, the Age she was when I saw her Murdered in Claudy, *Belfast Telegraph*, 30/8/10.
138. Ibid.
139. Public Statement by the Police Ombudsman Relating to the RUC investigation of the alleged involvement of the late Father James Chesney in the bombing of Claudy on 31 July 1972, 24/8/10.

140. My Little Sister will Always be Eight, the Age she was when I saw her Murdered in Claudy, *Belfast Telegraph*, 30/8/10.
141. Two Shot Dead in Belfast City Street, *Irish Press*, 28/9/72.
142. Man on Parole Shot Dead in Belfast, *The Irish Times*, 29/9/72.
143. *Lost Lives*, *op. cit.*, p269.
144. Ibid.
145. Unarmed N'Stewart Youth Shot Dead by UDR Patrol, *Ulster Herald*, 14/10/72.
146. Ibid.
147. Ibid.
148. Ibid.
149. Relatives for Justice, *In Your Own Words: Understanding the Troubles: Interview with Mark Thompson*, 5/7/2010.
150. Ibid.
151. Ibid.
152. Ibid.
153. *Lost Lives*, *op. cit.*, p281.
154. Shots at Youth's Funeral, *Belfast Telegraph*, 19/10/72.
155. *Lost Lives*, *op. cit.*, p288.
156. Tribute to Angels Blown Up 30 Years Ago, *The Mirror*, 31/10/02.
157. *Lost Lives*, *op. cit.*, p289.
158. Tribute to Angels Blown Up 30 Years Ago, *The Mirror*, 31/10/02.
159. Ibid.
160. Bomb Deaths Recalled, *Irish Independent*, 28/3/81.
161. Horror on Halloween, *Evening Herald*, 1/11/72.
162. UDA Men Jailed for Life, *The Irish Times*, 17/12/81.
163. Tribute to Angels Blown Up 30 Years Ago, *The Mirror*, 31/10/02.
164. Ibid.
165. Dockland Tears for 2 Little Girls, *Irish News*.
166. Boy (14) Shot Dead in Belfast, *Irish Press*, 28/11/72.
167. Ardoyne Commemoration Project, *Ardoyne: The Untold Truth*, Beyond the Pale Publications Ltd, 2002, p158.
168. Ibid., pp158–60.
169. Ibid., p161.
170. Ibid., pp159–60.
171. Ibid., pp160–61.
172. *Lost Lives*, *op. cit.*, p305.
173. http://stellamarissecondary.com/pupilsdeceased.html.
174. O'Malley, Padraig, *Biting at the Grave: The Irish Hunger Strikes and the Politics of Despair*, The Blackstaff Press, 1990.
175. TD Calls for Investigation into 1972 Belturbet Car Bombing, *The Irish Times*, 30/12/17.
176. *Lost Lives op. cit.*, p311.
177. Hooded Body Found in Beauty Spot Outside City, *Irish News*, 31/1/73.
178. *Lost Lives*, *op. cit.*, pp321–2.
179. Newry 1916 Easter Commemoration Association, Facebook post, 17/7/15.
180. Schoolboy Shot Dead – MP Accuses Army of Murder, *Newry Reporter*, 1/3/73.
181. Ibid.
182. Ibid.
183. Funeral of 12-year-old Kevin Heatley, *Newry Reporter*, 8/3/73.
184. *Lost Lives*, *op. cit.*, p335.
185. Corporal Jailed Over Shooting of Boy, *The Irish Times*, 16/3/74.
186. British Soldier is Cleared of Killing, *The Irish Times*, 22/6/74.
187. Northern Ireland Families Challenge May's Defence of Army, *The Irish Times*, 15/11/16.
188. Families Challenge MoD and Prime Minister in London, Pat Finucane Centre, 26/10/17 available at http://www.patfinucanecentre.org/state-violence/families-challenge-mod-and-prime-minister-london.

189. Note on sources used: unpublished research, Andy Tyrie Centre, east Belfast, & pamphlet, UDA Roll of Honour.

190. Condition of Boy Shot on Grosvenor Road Still Critical, *Irish News*, 22/3/73.

191. Coogan, Tim Pat, *On The Blanket: The Inside Story of the IRA Prisoners 'Dirty' Protest*, St Martin's Griffin, 2002, p97]

192. Coogan, Tim Pat, *The Troubles: Ireland's Ordeal 1966–1996 and the Search for Peace*, Arrow Books, 1996.

193. *Lost Lives*, *op. cit.*, p343.

194. Catholic Youth is Shot Dead, *Irish News*, 21/3/73.

195. Ibid.

196. Note on sources – all references from Ardoyne Commemoration Project, *Ardoyne: The Untold Truth*, Beyond the Pale Publications Ltd, 2002, pp179–85.

197. Kicked to Death by British Troops; article Tommy Corr, undated.

198. Ardoyne Commemoration Project, *Ardoyne: The Untold Truth*, Beyond the Pale Publications Ltd, 2002, p188.

199. Ibid., p186.

200. Ibid., p189.

201. *Lost Lives*, *op. cit.*, p351.

202. HET report, quoted in Smith, Micheál, *The Impact of the Parachute Regiment in Belfast 1970–1973*, The Pat Finucane Centre, 2018, p82.

203. *Lost Lives*, *op. cit.*, p358.

204. Two More Fatal Shootings, *Irish News*, 18/5/73.

205. National Graves Association, *Belfast Graves*, AP/RN Print, 1985, p112.

206. *Lost Lives*, *op. cit.*, p358.

207. Ibid.

208. The Terror of the Troubles: When the Macabre was Mundane, *The Irish Times*, 7/4/18.

209. Paul, 4, Died in Crossfire, *Irish Independent*, 29/5/73.

210. Myers, Kevin, *Watching the Door: A Memoir 1971–1978*, The Lilliput Press, 2006, p153.

211. *Lost Lives*, *op. cit.*, p371.

212. Ibid., pp371–2.

213. Who Killed Henry Cunningham?, *The Irish Times*, 14/5/05.

214. Egan, Jo, *The Crack in Everything*, script – performed Playhouse, Derry, November 2018.

215. Interview with Robert Cunningham, *Wave Trauma*, www.storiesfromsilence.com/robert-cunningham.

216. Who Killed Henry Cunningham?, *The Irish Times*, 14/5/05.

217. Egan, Jo, *The Crack in Everything*, script – performed Playhouse, Derry, November 2018.

218. HET report.

219. Murdered teen remembered in bursary, *Inishowen News*, 22/10/10.

220. *Tírghrá: Ireland's Patriot Dead*, National Commemoration Book, Dublin, 2002, p121.

221. Provos Killed in Attack on Army Base, *Irish Independent*, 18/8/73.

222. *Tírghrá: Ireland's Patriot Dead*, National Commemoration Book, Dublin, 2002, p121.

223. Victimisation Link in Killings, *Irish Press*, 28/8/73.

224. 'Why Did the IRA Kill my Brother?', *The Irish Times*, 30/1/04.

225. Report of the Historical Institutional Abuse Inquiry, findings Volume 1 p190.

226. Egan, Jo, *The Crack in Everything*, script – performed Playhouse, Derry, November 2018.

227. Derry Shocked by Shooting of 14-year-old Girl, *Derry Journal*, 16/11/73.

228. IRA issues apology for killing Derry girl in 1973, *The Irish Times*, 24/6/05.

229. M62 IRA Coach Bombing, *News Letter*, 5/2/19.

230. Murder on the M62, *Yorkshire Evening Post*, 4/2/04.

231. Motorway Terror and a 40-Year Fight for Justice, *Yorkshire Post*, 1/12/14.

232. *Lost Lives*, *op. cit.*, p435.

233. M62 IRA Coach Bombing, *News Letter*, 5/2/19.

234. Motorway Terror and a 40-Year Fight for Justice, *Yorkshire Post*, 1/12/14.

235. Ibid.

236. *Lost Lives*, *op. cit.*, p421.

237. Van Bomb Blame Put on British Unit, *Evening Herald*, 11/3/74.

238. Ibid.

239. Ibid.

240. Bomb Tragedy Deplored by Priest, *Irish Press*, 13/3/74.

241. Dublin 1974 Bombings Survivor: It Needs to be Talked About, *The Irish Times*, 12/11/18.

242. Worst Moment for Heavy Casualties, *The Irish Times*, 18/5/74.

243. Grimmest place in Dublin was morgue, *The Irish Times*, 20/5/74.

244. Mullan, Don, *The Dublin and Monaghan Bombings*, Wolfhound Press, 2001, p95.

245. Report of the Independent Commission of Inquiry into the Dublin and Monaghan Bombings (Barron Report), 29/10/03, as reproduced at https://cain.ulster.ac.uk/events/dublin/barron03.pdf, pp286–7.

246. Teenage Girl Dies in Belfast Car Bomb Blast, *Irish Examiner*, 10/9/74.

247. *Lost Lives, op. cit.*, p458.

248. Slanted Against War, *Irish Press*, 4/1/75.

249. UFF Admit Killing of Schoolgirl, *Irish Independent*, 11/6/74.

250. Dark Art from the Killing Fields, *Irish Independent*, 16/1/05.

251. Two Jailed for Life in North, *Irish Examiner*, 3/12/74.

252. Boy Tells how his Chum 13 was Murdered, *Irish News*, 16/8/74.

253. Ibid.

254. *Lost Lives, op. cit.*, p472.

255. One Dead, 3 Wounded as Murder Gangs Strike, *Irish Independent*, 20/9/74.

256. Youth (15) Shot Dead in Belfast, *Irish Independent*, 19/9/74.

257. Death notice, *Irish News*, 20/9/74.

258. Commemoration to Mark 40th Anniversary of Teenager Volunteer's Murder, *Cross Examiner*, 13/10/14.

259. Ibid.

260. *Tírghrá: Ireland's Patriot Dead*, National Commemoration Book, Dublin, 2002, p149.

261. Council Want Inquiry into Shooting, *Newry Reporter*, 24/10/74.

262. Army and Residents Differ Over Shooting of Newry Youth, *Newry Reporter*, 24/10/74.

263. Newry Youth's Death, *Newry Reporter*, 24/10/74.

264. Volunteer Michael Meenan Remembered In Derry, thepensivequill blog, 13/11/14.

265. Youth Dies in Car Bomb Blast, *Derry Journal*, 1/11/74.

266. Death notices, *Derry Journal*, 1/11/74.

267. All quotes in this section from *Remembering Ethel and John*, DVD, 2014, supplied by McDaid family.

268. Priest Refers to Lame Excuses, *The Irish Times*, 22/1/75.

269. *Lost Lives, op. cit.*, p512.

270. Thousands Take Part in Peace Marches, *The Irish Times*, 27/1/75.

271. National Graves Association, *Belfast Graves*, AP/RN Print, 1985, p130.

272. *Tírghrá: Ireland's Patriot Dead*, National Commemoration Book, Dublin, 2002, p166.

273. Lost Lives, *op. cit.*, p528.

274. Belfast Inquests on Three Victims of Bullets, *Irish News*, 31/10/75.

275. National Graves Association, *Belfast Graves*, AP/RN Print, 1985, p130.

276. Cadwallader, Anne, *Lethal Allies*, Mercier Press, 2013.

277. Slaughter on Way to Play School, *Irish News*, 14/6/75.

278. Ibid.

279. Ibid.

280. Death notices, *Irish News*, 14/6/75.

281. Protestant Tears for a RC Victim, *Irish Independent*, 17/6/75.

282. Murdered Day After He Left School, *Irish News*.

283. Elliott, Marianne, *Hearthlands: A Memoir of the White City Housing Estate in Belfast*, The Blackstaff Press, 2017, pp175–6.

284. Murdered Day After He Left School, *Irish News*.

285. Lost Lives, *op. cit.*, p551.

286. http://stellamarissecondary.com/pupilsdeceased.html.

287. *Lost Lives, op. cit.*, pp552–3.

288. Army Maintain Shot Youth was Armed, *Irish News*, 16/7/75.

289. *Lost Lives, op. cit.*, p1346.

290. Death notices, *Irish News*, 14/7/75.

291. *Lost Lives, op. cit.*, p559.

292. Teenager 'May have been Shot Dead by Soldier in 1975', *Belfast Telegraph*, 20/1/16.

293. Girl (4) Died in Crossfire Yards from her Own Home, *Belfast Telegraph*, 5/2/76.

294. *Lost Lives, op. cit.*, p560.

295. Memories of a Friend and Comrade, *An Phoblacht*, 26/11/98.

296. Ibid.

297. *Tírghrá: Ireland's Patriot Dead*, National Commemoration Book, Dublin, 2002, p171.

298. Memories of a Friend and Comrade, *An Phoblacht*, 26/11/98.

299. *Lost Lives, op. cit.*, p566.

300. Ibid., p567.

301. Ibid., p566.

302. Watertown Public Opinion, 18/7/75, as quoted in Fr Faul, Denis & Fr Murray, Raymond, *Rubber & Plastic Bullets Kill and Maim*, p15.

303. Ibid.

304. *Sunday Times*, 5/10/75, quoted in Fr Faul, Denis & Fr Murray, Raymond, *Rubber & Plastic Bullets Kill and Maim*, p15.

305. Ibid.

306. Boy Dies from Bullet Injuries, *The Irish Times*, 9/1/76.

307. Inquest into Plastic Bullet Killing of Child Reopened, *Irish News*, 7/7/14.

308. Watertown Public Opinion, 18/7/75, as quoted in Fr Faul, Denis & Fr Murray, Raymond, *Rubber & Plastic Bullets Kill and Maim*, p15.

309. Girl of 6 Killed Instead of Father, *Irish News*, 31/10/75.

310. Ibid.

311. *Lost Lives, op. cit.*, p591.

312. Ibid.

313. Two Belfast Funerals – with a Difference, *Irish Independent*, 4/11/75.

314. Cadwallader, Anne, *Lethal Allies*, Mercier Press, 2013, p136.

315. Six are Killed in Another Week-End of Violence, *Belfast Telegraph*, 9/2/76.

316. 8 Victims Die of Violence in Two Days, *Irish News*, 9/2/76.

317. Schoolboy Dies in Bomb Blast, *Craigavon Times*, 11/2/76.

318. *Lost Lives, op. cit.*, p623.

319. Brother and Sister Die in Booby-Trap Blast, *The Mid-Ulster Mail*, 13/2/76.

320. 8 Victims Die of Violence in Two Days, *Irish News*, 9/2/76.

321. Six are Killed in Another Week-End of Violence, *Belfast Telegraph*, 9/2/76.

322. 8 Victims Die of Violence in Two Days, *Irish News*, 9/2/76.

323. Rev. McCrea's tribute to victims, *The Mid-Ulster Mail*, 13/2/76.

324. Cardinal Warns the Men of Violence, *Irish News*, 9/2/76.

325. Double Grave for Bomb Victims, *The Irish Times*, 12/2/76.

326. Boys Going Home to Safety Met Death in Blast, *Irish News*, 16/3/77.

327. Ibid.

328. Open Verdict on Fuel Tank Blast Boy, *The Irish Times*, 17/3/77.

329. Murdered by the Glenanne Gang: 'Patrick Lived Till the Ripe Old Age of 13', *The Irish Times*, 2/5/15.

330. Eleven in Hospital after Bomb Blast, *Evening Herald*, 18/3/76.

331. Cadwallader, Anne, *Lethal Allies*, Mercier Press, 2013, p169.

332. Justice Denied as Crusading Dad of Boy Killed in 1976 UVF Bomb Dies, *Belfast Telegraph*, 4/4/17.

333. Murdered by the Glenanne Gang: 'Patrick Lived Till the Ripe Old Age of 13', *The Irish Times*, 2/5/15.

334. Ibid.

335. Baby and Sister Die in 'Gun Car' Crash, *Irish News*, 11/8/76.

336. Ibid.

337. Ibid.

338. Ibid.

339. Peace Groups Springing Up All Over the City, *Irish News*, 16/8/76.

340. 'Get Out', Women Tell IRA', *Irish News*, 12/8/76.

341. Legacy of NI Peace Movement, *BBC News*, 11/8/06.

342. Fr Faul, Denis & Fr Murray, Raymond, *Majella O'Hare: Shot Dead by the British Army 14 August 1976*, pamphlet, 1976, p21.

343. Ibid., p22.

344. No Closure for O'Hare Family, *The Irish Times*, 28/3/11.

345. Fr Faul, Denis & Fr Murray, Raymond, *Majella O'Hare: Shot Dead by the British Army 14 August 1976*, pamphlet, 1976, p23.

346. Brady, Brian, Fr Faul, Denis & Fr Murray, Raymond, *British Army Terror: West Belfast September October 1976*, pamphlet, undated, p24.

347. Youth Admits Murdering Shop Girl, *The Irish Times*, 27/9/77.

348. Girl (14) Among NI's 3 Weekend Victims, *The Irish Times*, 8/11/76.

349. *Lost Lives, op. cit.*, p687.

350. Schoolgirl Murdered by Sniper, *Irish Independent*, 8/11/76.

351. *Irish News*, 29/11/76.

352. Ibid.

353. Ardoyne Commemoration Project, *Ardoyne: The Untold Truth*, Beyond the Pale Publications Ltd, 2002, p278.

354. Ibid., p280.

355. Ibid., p278.

356. Ibid., p279.

357. Ibid., p279.

358. Mourning for Fourth Dead Pupil, *Irish Independent*, 10/12/76.

359. Ardoyne Commemoration Project, *Ardoyne: The Untold Truth*, Beyond the Pale Publications Ltd, 2002, p278.

360. Child Among This Year's First Bomb Victims, *The Irish Times*, 1/1/77.

361. On his First and Last Holiday – the Young Victim of Terror, *Evening Herald*, 5/1/77.

362. Judge Recommends 30-year Jail Terms, *The Irish Times*, 27/5/78.

363. On his First and Last Holiday – the Young Victim of Terror, *Evening Herald*, 5/1/77.

364. Still Burdened with Pain of her Little Boy's Murder by the UVF, *Irish News*, 7/4/07.

365. Boy, Uncle Murdered, *Irish Press*, 11/4/77.

366. *Lost Lives, op. cit.*, p715.

367. The Guilty, *Irish Press*, 21/2/79.

368. Too Scared to Make Safety Jump – Friend, *Belfast Telegraph*.

369. *Lost Lives, op. cit.*, p740.

370. We Loved Lesley … You Wonder What she Would be Like Now?, *News Letter*, 29/9/17.

371. Booby Trap Bomb Kills Girl and Father, *Belfast Telegraph*, 8/2/78.

372. Troops and Police Search Wide Area after NI Killings, *The Irish Times*, 10/2/78.

373. 'These Murderous Acts' Condemned, *Irish News*, 9/2/78.

374. https://www.liverpool.ac.uk/media/livacuk/irish-studies/research/A,Patchwork,of,Innocents.pdf

375. Fire Deaths were Murder – Police, *Irish News*, 13/2/78.

376. Ibid.

377. Ibid.

378. *Lost Lives, op. cit.*, p745.

379. Ibid., p769.

380. Ibid., p769.

381. Found Guilty of Killing RUC Man, *Irish Press*, 29/7/80.

382. *Lost Lives, op. cit.*, p777.

383. Found Guilty of Killing RUC Man, *Irish Press*, 29/7/80.

384. Plea for End to 'Terrible Slaughter', *The Irish Times*, 27/2/79.

385. http://storiesfromsilence.com/countess-mountbatten-2/.

386. Hon Timothy Knatchbull: 'Wrong' twin finds peace, *Sunday Times*, 23/9/09.

387. Knatchbull, Timothy, *From a Clear Blue Sky: Surviving the Mountbatten bomb*, Arrow books, 2009, p11.

388. Ibid., p130.

389. Prince Charles Visits Lord Mountbatten 1979 IRA Murder Site, *BBC News*, 20/5/15.

390. Hon Timothy Knatchbull: 'Wrong' twin finds peace, *Sunday Times*, 23/9/09.

391. After Mountbatten: the Many Victims of the Mullaghmore Bombing, *The Irish Times*, 17/5/15.
392. Hon Timothy Knatchbull: 'Wrong' twin finds peace, *Sunday Times*, 23/9/09.
393. Charles can Expect Bittersweet Emotions on Arrival in Mullaghmore, *The Irish Times*, 20/5/15.
394. Four Shot Dead at Start of New Decade, *Irish News*, 2/1/80.
395. Girl Shot Dead at a Belfast Roadblock, *The Irish Times*, 1/1/80.
396. Call to Try Soldiers for Killing of Girl, *Irish Press*, 3/1/80.
397. United Drive Against Death Risk Joyriders, *Irish News*, 6/2/80.
398. Ibid.
399. Joyrider, 16, Shot Dead, and Second 'very low', *Irish News*, 1/4/80.
400. Priest Says Young Joyriders Face 'Instant Death', *Irish Press*, 2/4/80.
401. Killing of boy joyrider 'callous, cold-blooded', *Irish Independent*, 2/4/80.
402. Priest Says Young Joyriders Face 'Instant Death', *Irish Press*, 2/4/80.
403. Ibid.
404. *Lost Lives, op. cit.*, p833.
405. Police Ombudsman's report, 2007.
406. Desmond Guiney Laid to Rest as 5,000 Watch, *Irish News*, 13/5/81.
407. Dead Boy's Mother's Appeal to Parents, *Belfast Telegraph*, 9/5/81.
408. Milkman Hurt in Stoning 'Dangerously Ill', *Belfast Telegraph*, 6/5/81.
409. Innocents Killed as Riots Swept Across City, *Irish News*, 6/5/81.
410. Boy Who Died in Riots Buried, *The Irish Times*, 13/5/81.
411. Second Child Hit by Plastic Bullet, *Irish News*, 20/5/81.
412. Fr Faul, Denis & Fr Murray, Raymond, *Rubber & Plastic Bullets Kill and Maim*, undated, p30.
413. Relatives for Justice, *In Your Own Words: Understanding the Troubles: Interview with Mollie Barrett by Mark Thompson*, 7/7/10.
414. Ardoyne Commemoration Project, *Ardoyne: The Untold Truth*, Beyond the Pale Publications Ltd, 2002, pp361–2.
415. Ibid., p362.
416. Relatives for Justice, *In Your Own Words: Understanding the Troubles: Interview with Mollie Barrett by Mark Thompson*, 7/7/10.
417. Relatives for Justice, *In Your Own Words: Understanding the Troubles: Interview with Mollie Barrett by Mark Thompson*, 7/7/10.
418. Ardoyne Commemoration Project, *Ardoyne: The Untold Truth*, Beyond the Pale Publications Ltd, 2002, p363.
419. Relatives for Justice, *In Your Own Words: Understanding the Troubles: Interview with Mollie Barrett by Mark Thompson*, 7/7/10.
420. *Lost Lives, op. cit.*, p871.
421. Relatives for Justice, *In Your Own Words: Understanding the Troubles: Interview with Mollie Barrett by Mark Thompson*, 7/7/10.
422. Victim's Last Minutes – By Shop Owner, *Belfast Telegraph*, 16/3/82.
423. We Feel No Hatred, Say Boy's Parents, *Belfast Telegraph*, 16/3/82.
424. School Closes as Pals Grieve at Alan's Burial, *Belfast Telegraph*, 18/3/82.
425. Ibid.
426. Fr Faul, Denis & Fr Murray, Raymond, *Plastic Bullets – Plastic Government: Deaths and Injuries by Plastic Bullets, August 1981–October 1982*, undated, p11.
427. Ibid., p11.
428. Ibid., p12.
429. *Lost Lives, op. cit.*, p904.
430. INLA Claim Motorcycle Death Blast, *Irish News*, 4/6/82.
431. Ibid.
432. Pope's Message for Family of Blast Victim, *Irish News*, 5/6/82.
433. Ibid.
434. Boy Survivor Lives Terror Again, *Irish News*, 18/9/82.
435. Former INLA Member Dies in Hospital Following Milltown Shooting at Republican Plot, *Irish News*, 18/5/19.
436. Belfast Bomb Kills Boy of 14, *Irish Independent*, 17/9/82.

437. Mothers' plea to Divis Flats bombers, *Irish Press*, 18/9/82.
438. Ibid.
439. Divis Blast Deaths: INLA Members 'Flee to Republic', *Irish Independent*, 21/9/82.
440. INLA Prisoner Set for Freedom, *Belfast Telegraph*, 5/3/99.
441. Mothers' plea to Divis Flats bombers, *Irish Press*, 18/9/82.
442. Catholic Anger as Second Child Dies from INLA Bomb, *Irish Independent*, 18/9/82.
443. Bitter Controversy Surrounds Shootings, *Derry Journal*, 26/2/85.
444. Massive Security at Strabane Funerals, *Derry Journal*, 26/2/85.
445. Families Awarded Money over SAS Shootings, UTV, 7/5/02.
446. Village Mourns Three 'Lovely' People, *The Irish Times*, 25/7/88.
447. *Irish Press*, 25/7/88.
448. Families of Victims Killed Near Border Call for Garda-PSNI Inquiry, *The Irish Times*, 9/12/13.
449. Bishops Unite in Peace Call at Hanna Funeral, *Irish Examiner*, 29/7/88.
450. Dream Holiday Ended in Horror, *Irish Independent*, 25/7/88.
451. Boy was not Rioting when Killed, Inquest Jury Finds, *The Irish Times*, 29/6/90.
452. Family wants Inquiry into Plastic Bullet Killing, *The Irish Times*, 30/3/90.
453. English Ghettos Offer Little Safety, *The Irish Times*, 28/10/89.
454. Serviceman and Baby Murdered in Germany, *Belfast Telegraph*, 27/10/89.
455. 'Apology' for Slaying Baby Met with Scorn, *Belfast Telegraph*, 28/10/89.
456. Ibid.
457. IRA Admit Killings – 'Regret' Over Baby, *Belfast Telegraph*, 27/10/89.
458. Taylor, Peter, *Provos: The IRA and Sinn Féin*, Bloomsbury, 1998, p279.
459. English Ghettos Offer Little Safety, *The Irish Times*, 28/10/89.
460. 'Craigavon mourns three beautiful lives', *The Irish Times*, 1/4/1991.
461. 'I don't want any other mother to suffer like this', *The Irish Times*, 29/3/91.
462. Ibid.
463. *Lost Lives, op. cit.*, p1232.
464. Two on Murder Charge, *Irish Examiner*, 11/11/91.
465. Anguished Scenes at Belfast Funerals, *Irish Press*, 13/11/91.
466. Two on Murder Charge, *Irish Examiner*, 11/11/91.
467. Death notices, *Irish News*, 11/11/91.
468. NI Men Get 15 Years for Killings, *The Irish Times*, 12/2/93.
469. Ibid.
470. Pitch Battle, *The Guardian*, 22/8/02.
471. St Enda's Glengormley – a club that never took a backward step, *Irish News*, 1/12/18.
472. 'Some of the bullets never stop travelling', *The Irish Times* 5/2/94, p9.
473. *Lost Lives, op. cit.*, p1284.
474. Provo-led Teen Gang Blamed as Boy Dies After Brutal Beating, *Irish News*, 26/3/92.
475. Ibid.
476. Ibid.
477. IRA Denies Role in Youth's Death, *Irish News*, 26/3/92.
478. Action Urged as Teenage Gangs Clash on Streets, *Irish News*, 20/3/92.
479. *Lost Lives, op. cit.*, p1284.
480. In Memory of a Daughter Killed by the IRA: Father Relives Bomb Blast in City, *The Herald*, 10/4/93.
481. Stress Led Bomb Hero to Kill his Girlfriend, *The Independent*, 23/6/93.
482. Warrington Bomb Dad's Anguish, *Manchester Evening News*, 10/8/04.
483. Ibid.
484. I was Holding Warrington Bomb Boy Johnathan Ball's Hand as he was Killed, *Belfast Telegraph*, 4/4/18.
485. Bomb Victim's Mum Had 'Broken Heart', *News Letter*, 14/12/09.
486. Warrington Bomb Dad's Anguish, *Manchester Evening News*, 10/8/04.
487. Parry, Wendy, *Wave Trauma Centre: Stories from Silence*, available at http://storiesfromsilence.com/wendy-parry-2/.
488. Interview with Wendy Parry, *Today with Miriam*, RTÉ, 30/8/18.
489. Parry, Wendy, *Wave Trauma Centre: Stories from Silence*, available at http://storiesfromsilence.com/wendy-parry-2/.

490. Tribute to Tim Parry, https://cain.ulster.ac.uk/victims/docs/group/parry_ball/news/parry_ball_tribute_0308.pdf.

491. Colin and Wendy Parry, parents of Warrington Bomb Victim, *The Guardian*, 31/8/18.

492. Shankill Road Bombing: Pain that is Still Raw 20 Years On, *Daily Telegraph*, 4/5/14.

493. Ibid.

494. Shankill Bomb: The Nine Innocent Victims Who Perished in IRA Attack, *Belfast Telegraph*, 23/10/13.

495. Shankill Bomb: We Still Need Answers Over that Day, says Relative, *Belfast Telegraph*, 22/10/18.

496. Shankill Bomb: The Nine Innocent Victims Who Perished in IRA Attack, *Belfast Telegraph*, 23/10/13.

497. Ibid.

498. Shankill Bomb Bereaved in 'Painful but Necessary' Remembrance 25 Years On, *Belfast Telegraph*, 22/10/18.

499. Interview on *Morning Ireland, RTE*, 23/10/18.

500. Day I Lost Leanne Will Stay with me for the Rest of My Life, Says Shankill Bomb Victim's Mum, *Belfast Telegraph*, 20/10/18.

501. *Shankill bombing*, BBC documentary, October 18.

502. Day I Lost Leanne Will Stay with me for the Rest of My Life, Says Shankill Bomb Victim's Mum, *Belfast Telegraph*, 20/10/18.

503. *Shankill bombing*, BBC documentary, October 18.

504. Ibid.

505. Shankill bomb: Paramedics Recall Horror of Finding Victims, *BBC News*, 21/10/18.

506. Day I Lost Leanne Will Stay with me for the Rest of My Life, Says Shankill Bomb Victim's Mum, *Belfast Telegraph*, 20/10/18.

507. Peace Process is too Late for Victims, *The Irish Times*, 7/12/93.

508. *Lost Lives, op. cit.*, p1339

509. Politicians Warned that Words Can Kill, *The Irish Times*, 9/12/93.

510. Good Samaritan Brian Mourned at School, *Irish Press*, 7/12/93.

511. Barbara was 'Ears' for her Deaf Mum, *Irish News*, 18/3/96.

512. Girl, 9, is Killed in Gun Blitz on House, *Irish News*, 16/3/96.

513. *Lost Lives, op. cit.*, p1392.

514. Murder in Belfast may have links to INLA feud, *The Irish Times*, 5/6/04.

515. 'Waste of a Beautiful Life', *Irish News*, 19/3/96.

516. Tragic Scene Parents Wanted the World to See, *Irish News*, 19/3/96.

517. Ibid.

518. 'Pain Behind the Struggle', Editorial, *Irish News*, 19/3/96.

519. Sectarian Hatred Cited in Death of Portadown Boy, *The Irish Times*, 12/10/96.

520. McKay, Susan, *Bear in Mind These Dead*, Faber and Faber, 2008, p151.

521. Ibid., p156.

522. Villages United in Grief Over Murder, *Irish Examiner*, 31/7/97.

523. *Lost Lives, op. cit.*, p1415.

524. Drumcree is responsible for the death of my boys, *Irish News*, 17/8/98.

525. Innocent victims of arson attack to be buried today, *Irish News*, 14/7/98.

526. Tragic Boys' Final Journey, *Irish News*, 14/7/98.

527. 'Mother Asks: Who Could be So Cruel to do this to my Children?', *Coleraine Chronicle*, 18/7/98.

528. Mother had feared for safety of her murdered children, *Irish News*, 13/7/98.

529. Distraught Mother Flees Petrol Bomb Trial, *The Guardian*, 8/9/99.

530. Drumcree is responsible for the death of my boys, *Irish News*, 17/8/98.

531. World is Horrified by murder of the innocents, *Coleraine Chronicle*, 18/7/98.

532. *Lost Lives, op. cit.*, p1436.

533. Drumcree is responsible for the death of my boys, *Irish News*, 17/8/98.

534. Mother Thought Boys Escaped Fire, *The Irish Times*, 14/7/98.

535. Innocent victims of arson attack to be buried today, *Irish News*, 14/7/98.

536. Clinton's Pledge to Lee, *Irish News*, 16/7/98.

537. 'Why?...', *Coleraine Chronicle*, 18/7/98.

538. 'Mother Asks: Who Could be So Cruel to do this to my Children?', *Coleraine Chronicle*, 18/7/98.

539. Rest in Peace, *Irish News*, 13/7/98.

540. There is hope for the future despite deaths, *Irish News*, 14/7/98.
541. A 12-Year Old Boy's Dreams of the Future, *Belfast Telegraph*, 19/8/98.
542. Omagh Father Condemns Government, *Telegraph*, 6/10/00.
543. Ibid.
544. *Omagh: The Legacy – Ten Years On*, BBC documentary, 2008.
545. Ibid.
546. How Spanish boy, 12, died at Omagh, *The Guardian*, 15/9/00.
547. Omagh Aftermath: Madrid sheds tears for Spanish teacher and pupil, *The Independent*, 19/8/98.
548. *Omagh: The Legacy – Ten Years On*, BBC documentary, 2008.
549. Baby Breda 'a special child', *Belfast Telegraph*, 19/8/98.
550. 'Mother not yet told her baby girl is dead', *Belfast Telegraph*, 17/8/98.
551. *The Irish Times*, 23/9/00.
552. 'Omagh: Ten Years of Hurt', *The Mirror*, 11/8/08.
553. 'Last Omagh Victim is Home for Christmas', *The Guardian*, 23/12/98.
554. 'Sean's Poem for Peace', *Ulster Herald*, 20/8/98.
555. 'Victim's Poetic Plea for Peace', *Donegal Democrat*, 20/8/98.
556. Irish Police Refuse Inquest Evidence, *BBC News*, 25/9/00.
557. 'Buncrana Weeps for Three Local Children and Two Spanish', *The Irish Times*, 18/8/98.
558. 'Sean's Poem for Peace', *Ulster Herald*, 20/8/98.
559. Father Charles Keaney, *The Irish Times*, 18/8/98.
560. A Terrible Beauty as the Bodies are Buried and Ulster Prays for Peace, *The Independent*, 19/8/98.
561. Three Generations of the One Family Killed in an Instant, *Ulster Herald*, 21/9/00.
562. Workers Tell of Unimaginable Horror, *Belfast Telegraph*, 20/8/98.
563. Three Generations of the One Family Killed in an Instant, *Ulster Herald*, 21/9/00.
564. Harrowing Details Entrenched in Medic's Memory, *Ulster Herald*, 21/9/00.
565. 2,000 Mourners Attend Mother and Daughter's Funeral in South Tyrone, *The Irish Times*, 19/8/98.
566. Relatives of Family which Lost Three Generations Prepare for Funerals, *The Irish Times*, 18/8/98.
567. Heartrending Scenes as First Bomb Victims are Laid to Rest, *Ulster Herald*, 20/8/98.
568. Families Appeal to Bombers, *Ulster Herald*, 21/9/00.
569. Three Generations of the One Family Killed in an Instant, *Ulster Herald*, 21/9/00.
570. Omagh Coroner Rules on Unborn Twins, *BBC News*, 28/9/00.
571. Bombers Should Also be Charged with Killing Unborn Twins – Coroner, *Ulster Herald*, 5/10/00.
572. Dudley Edwards, Ruth, *Aftermath: The Omagh Bombing and the Families' Pursuit of Justice*, Vintage, 2010.
573. Ibid., pp15–17.
574. Ibid., pp15–17.
575. Ibid., pp15–17.
576. 'Children have to play; work, smile, cry, just as ordinary children. That's what I want to get back to', *Belfast Telegraph*, 22/8/98.
577. Headmaster Pays a Tribute to Pupils who Perished, *Ulster Herald*, 20/8/98.
578. Dudley Edwards, Ruth, *Aftermath: The Omagh Bombing and the Families' Pursuit of Justice*, Vintage, 2010, pp15–17.
579. 'When they took her, they took an angel', says Lorraine's sister, *The Irish Times*, 20/8/98.
580. 'Children have to play; work, smile, cry, just as ordinary children. That's what I want to get back to', *Belfast Telegraph*, 22/8/98.
581. Community United in Grief as Bomb Victims are Laid to Rest, *Ulster Herald*, 20/8/98.
582. Families United in Grief over Killings, *Belfast Telegraph*, 9/9/01.
583. A ray of hope amid the drizzle and gloom as Thomas is laid to rest in a sea of tears, *Irish Independent*, 8/9/01.
584. Families United in Grief over Killings, *Belfast Telegraph*, 9/9/01.
585. A ray of hope amid the drizzle and gloom as Thomas is laid to rest in a sea of tears, *Irish Independent*, 8/9/01.
586. Woman Guilty of Bicycle Boy's Killing, *BBC News*, 10/1/03.
587. Calls Mount to End Demo as the Violence Spreads, *Irish News*, 5/9/01.
588. McKay, Susan, *Bear in Mind These Dead*, Faber & Faber, 2008, p186.
589. Ibid., p187.

590. The Crying Game, *New Statesman*, 5/6/08.

591. Horror as Youth (16) Dies in Fierce Rioting, *Belfast Telegraph*, 12/11/01.

592. Ibid.

593. Police Hunt Loyalists After Bomb Death, *BBC News*, 12/11/01.

594. Thousands at Funeral of Ulster bomb boy, *The Guardian*, 16/11/01.

595. Ibid.

596. Tribute from Thomas's Friends, https://www.thomasdevlin.com/tributesandtears/friendstribute.php

597. Ibid.

598. Thomas Devlin's Killer Jailed for Minimum of 30 Years, *BBC News*, 11/5/10.

599. Murdered Boy was a Shining Beacon, *BBC News*, 12/8/19.

600. McKay, Susan, *Bear in Mind These Dead*, Faber & Faber, 2008, p197.

601. Michael's Grieving Family Prepare for Final Farewell, *Irish News*, 11/5/06.

602. Shocked Friends and Relatives Grieve for Popular Schoolboy, *Irish News*, 10/5/06.

603. Ibid.

604. Don't Let this Happen Again Plead Murdered Boy's Family, *Irish News*, 9/5/06.

605. McKay, Susan, *Bear in Mind These Dead*, Faber & Faber, 2008, p194.

606. Ibid., p199.

607. Four Jailed for Life for Beating Catholic Teenager to Death, *The Guardian*, 1/5/09.

608. Young People's Plea in Bitterly Divided Town, *Irish News*, 10/5/06

Childhood of the Troubles

1. Hon Timothy Knatchbull: 'wrong' twin finds peace, *The Times*, 23/8/09.

2. Moore, Richard, *Can I Give Him My Eyes?*, Hachette Books Ireland, 2009, p50.

3. Ibid., p52.

4. The Games Children Play, *Belfast Telegraph*, 21/3/73.

5. McCann, Eamonn, *War and an Irish Town*, Haymarket Books, 2018, p105.

6. The Crying Game, *New Statesman*, 5/6/08.

7. Campbell, Julieann (ed.), *Beyond the Silence: Women's Unheard Voices from the Troubles*, Guildhall Press, 2016, p54.

8. Ibid., p61.

9. Ibid., p85.

10. Ardoyne Commemoration Project, *Ardoyne: The Untold Truth*, Beyond the Pale Publications Ltd, 2002, p278.

11. Thousands at Funeral of Ulster Bomb Boy, *The Guardian*, 16/11/01.

12. Starmaker's Tears for a Life Cut Short, *Belfast Telegraph*, 22/7/72.

13. 'I don't want any other mother to suffer like this', *The Irish Times*, 29/3/91.

War on the Streets

1. Father Tells of His Son's 1969 Killing by British Army for the First Time, *The Irish Times*, 4/8/98.

2. Doherty, Tony, *This Man's Wee Boy: A Childhood Memoir of Peace and Trouble in Derry*, Mercier Press, 2016, p110.

3. Mallon, Seamus with Pollak, Andy, *A Shared Home Place*, The Lilliput Press, 2019, p50.

4. O'Callaghan, Eimear, *Belfast Days: A 1972 Teenage Diary*, Merrion Press, 2014, p167.

5. Rolston, Bill, *Children of the Revolution*, Guildhall Press, 2011, p30.

6. Elliott, Marianne, *Heartlands: A Memoir of the White City Housing Estate in Belfast*, The Blackstaff Press, 2017, p166.

7. O'Callaghan, Eimear, *Belfast Days: A 1972 Teenage Diary*, Merrion Press, 2014, p169.

8. Ibid., p296.

9. Ibid., pp50–1.

10. Paramilitary threats forced 52 PSNI officers to move home, *The Irish Times*, 12/9/17.
11. Advertisement, Northern Ireland Office, *Irish News*, May 1981.
12. Dead Boy's Mother's Appeal to Parents, *Belfast Telegraph*, 9/5/81.
13. Department of Education website, https://www.education-ni.gov.uk/articles/integrated-schools.
14. Morrow, Prof. Duncan, *Sectarianism in Northern Ireland: A Review*, Ulster University, 2019, p4.

Families

1. Egan, Jo, *The Crack in Everything*, unpublished script, p9.
2. Interviews with Mollie Barrett & Tina Erskine, *In Your Own Words: Understanding the Troubles:* DVD by Relatives for Justice, 2010.
3. 'Transgenerational Trauma and Dealing With the Past in Northern Ireland', Damien McNally, *Wave Trauma Centre*, March 2014.
4. Troubles 'Linked to Half Mental Health Cases in Northern Ireland', *BBC News*, 5/3/15.
5. Briefing Report: Mental Health Crisis in Northern Ireland, Together for You, 20/2/18, available at https://www.amh.org.uk/wp-content/uploads/2018/02/Briefing-Mental-Health-Crisis-in-Northern-Ireland.pdf.
6. Troubles Created 500,000 Victims Says Official Body, *Irish News*, 27/9/11.

Rubber and Plastic Bullets

1. Curtis, Liz, *They Shoot Children: The Use of Rubber and Plastic Bullets in the North of Ireland*, Information on Ireland, 2nd edition, 1987, p9.
2. Ibid., p9.
3. Army Units to Get Rubber Bullets, *The Irish Times*, 6/8/70.
4. Curtis, Liz, *They Shoot Children: The Use of Rubber and Plastic Bullets in the North of Ireland*, Information on Ireland, 2nd edition, 1987, pp14–15.
5. Ibid., p11.
6. Ibid., p15.
7. Ibid., p29.
8. The Committee on the Administration of Justice, *Plastic Bullets and the Law*, 1985, p3
9. Ibid., p3.
10. Committee on the Administration of Justice, *Plastic Bullets and the Law*, CAJ Pamphlet No. 15, 1990, p3.
11. The Trouble with Plastic Bullets, *BBC News*, 2/8/01.
12. Committee on the Administration of Justice, *Plastic Bullets and the Law*, CAJ Pamphlet No. 15, 1990, pp9–11.
13. Plastic Bullets are Too Dangerous, Says Lecturer, *The Irish Times*, 22/12/76.
14. Curtis, Liz, *They Shoot Children: The Use of Rubber and Plastic Bullets in the North of Ireland*, Information on Ireland, 2nd edition, 1987, p11.
15. Committee on the Administration of Justice, *Plastic Bullets and the Law*, CAJ Pamphlet No. 15, 1990, pp9–11.
16. Plastic Bullets Save Lives, Ulster Police Chief Says, *The Times*, 27/5/81.
17. Inside Belfast: Bad Time to Drop the Low Profile, *The Irish Times*, 7/10/76.
18. Committee on the Administration of Justice, *Plastic Bullets and the Law*, CAJ Pamphlet No. 15, 1990.
19. Curtis, Liz, *They Shoot Children: The Use of Rubber and Plastic Bullets in the North of Ireland*, Information on Ireland, 2nd edition, 1987, p35.
20. Fr Faul, Denis & Fr Murray, Raymond, *Plastic Bullets – Plastic Government: Deaths and Injuries by Plastic Bullets, August 1981–October 1982*, undated, p34.
21. Ibid., p37.
22. Ibid., p34.
23. Ibid., p36.
24. Shallice, Dr Tim, 'The Harmless Bullet that Kills', in Fr Faul, Denis & Fr Murray, Raymond, *Plastic*

Bullets – Plastic Government: Deaths and Injuries by Plastic Bullets, August 1981–October 1982, undated, p20.

25. Curtis, Liz, *They Shoot Children: The Use of Rubber and Plastic Bullets in the North of Ireland*, Information on Ireland, 2nd edition, 1987, p25.

26. The Committee on the Administration of Justice, *Plastic Bullets and the Law*, 1985, p13.

27. Fr Faul, Denis & Fr Murray, Raymond, *Plastic Bullets – Plastic Government: Deaths and Injuries by Plastic Bullets, August 1981–October 1982*, undated, pp41–2.

28. Committee on the Administration of Justice, *Plastic Bullets and the Law*, CAJ Pamphlet No. 15, 1990, p13.

29. Declassified documents from the National Archives on the dangers posed by rubber bullets, Ministry of Defence, available at http://www.patfinucanecentre.org/declassified-documents/declassified-documents-national-archives-dangers-posed-rubber-bullets, pp10-12.

30. *Plastic bullets — plastic death.* Decoding the Declassified documents (Part 1), available at http://www.patfinucanecentre.org/declassified-documents/plastic-bullets-plastic-death-decoding-declassified-documents-part-1]

31. Committee on the Administration of Justice, *Plastic Bullets and the Law*, CAJ Pamphlet No. 15, 1990, p23.

32. Curtis, Liz, *They Shoot Children: The Use of Rubber and Plastic Bullets in the North of Ireland*, Information on Ireland, 2nd edition, 1987, p29.

33. Exhibition, Holywell Trust, Derry, 2018 – get full details Eamonn Baker.

34. The Trouble with Plastic Bullets, *BBC News*, 2/8/01.

35. PSNI Use of Force Statistics, December 2018, pp3–5.

36. Poignant Site Set to Be Named After Clara and Emma, *Andersonstown News*, 17/1/19.

Young Combatants

1. Ardoyne Commemoration Project, *Ardoyne: The Untold Truth*, Beyond the Pale Publications Ltd, 2002, p121.

2. Ibid., p161.

3. Cadwallader, Anne, *Holy Cross: The Untold Story*, Brehon Press, 2004, pp13–4.

4. *Lost Lives, op. cit.*, p1555.

5. Ardoyne Commemoration Project, *Ardoyne: The Untold Truth*, Beyond the Pale Publications Ltd, 2002, p111.

6. Ibid., p121.

7. Ibid., p161.

8. Rolston, Bill, *Children of the Revolution*, Guildhall Press, 2011, p146.

9. Longer, unpublished interview for article published as 'Bloody Sunday: I Think it's Likely There Will Be Prosecutions', *The Irish Times*, 13/3/19.

10. Doherty, Tony, *The Dead Beside Us: A Memoir of Growing Up in Derry*, Mercier Press, 2017, pp248–9.

11. Ardoyne Commemoration Project, *Ardoyne: The Untold Truth*, Beyond the Pale Publications Ltd, 2002, p124.

12. *Tírghrá: Ireland's Patriot Dead*, National Commemoration Book, Dublin, 2002, p121.

13. Ardoyne Commemoration Project, *Ardoyne: The Untold Truth*, Beyond the Pale Publications Ltd, 2002, p161.

14. Crawford, Colin, *Inside the UDA: Volunteers and Violence*, Pluto Press, 2003, p80.

15. Taylor, Peter, *Loyalists*, Bloomsbury, 2000, p90.

16. Ibid.

17. Ibid.

18. Crawford, Colin, *Inside the UDA: Volunteers and Violence*, Pluto Press, 2003, p22.

19. Rolston, Bill, *Children of the Revolution*, Guildhall Press, 2011, p187.

20. Boy (16) Among Two Shot in Belfast Within 24 Hours, *The Irish Times*, 17/2/17.

21. untitled article, *Irish Independent*, 9/12/74.

22. IRA Honours at Derry Boy's Funeral, *Derry Journal*, 29/2/72.

23. First Anniversary Tribute to Young Derry Republican, *Derry Journal*, 27/2/73.
24. *Lost Lives, op. cit.*, p158.

Legacy of the Troubles

1. 'Some of the bullets never stop travelling', *The Irish Times*, 5/2/94.
2. *Lost Lives, op. cit.*, p1553.
3. Historical Enquiries Team, *Review Summary Report concerning the death of Martha Ann Campbell*, undated, p9.
4. Ibid., p18.
5. Historical Enquiries Team treats state cases with 'less rigour', *BBC News*, 3/7/13.
6. House of Commons Defence Select Committee, Investigations into fatalities in Northern Ireland involving British military personnel, part 14, available at https://publications.parliament.uk/pa/cm201617/cmselect/cmdfence/1064/106404.htm.
7. Lundy, Dr Patricia, *Assessment of HET Review Processes and Procedures in Royal Military Police Investigation Cases*, Ulster University, April 2012, available at https://cain.ulster.ac.uk/lundy/2012-04-02_Lundy_HET-Briefing-Paper.pdf.
8. PM: Northern Ireland system investigating past 'unfair', *BBC News*, 9/5/18.
9. Donaldson, Jeffrey, cited in House of Commons Defence Select Committee, Investigations into fatalities in Northern Ireland involving British military personnel, part 17, available at https://publications.parliament.uk/pa/cm201617/cmselect/cmdfence/1064/106404.htm .
10. Troubles legacy cases bias disputed by figures, *BBC News*, 2/2/17.
11. Unpublished article, Freya McClements for *The Irish Times*, 10/4/17.
12. Public Statement by the Police Ombudsman Relating to the RUC investigation of the alleged involvement of the late Father James Chesney in the bombing of Claudy on 31 July 1972, 24/8/10.
13. Freya McClements interview Denis Bradley, unpublished.

Select Bibliography

A Note on Sources

Children of the Troubles is primarily based on original interviews, the majority of which were with relatives of the children killed during the conflict. Unless otherwise specified in the endnotes, the source is an original interview conducted with the named individual by either Joe Duffy or Freya McClements between June 2017 and July 2019.

Books

Ardoyne Commemoration Project, *Ardoyne: The Untold Truth*, Beyond the Pale Publications Ltd, 2002

Cadwallader, Anne, *Holy Cross: The Untold Story*, Brehon Press, 2004

Cadwallader, Anne, *Lethal Allies*, Mercier Press, 2013

Cairns, Ed, *Caught in Crossfire: Children and the Northern Ireland Conflict*, Appletree Press, 1987

Campbell, Julieann (ed.), *Beyond the Silence: Women's Unheard Voices from the Troubles*, Guildhall Press, 2016

Coogan, Tim Pat, *The Troubles: Ireland's Ordeal 1966–1996 and the Search for Peace*, Arrow Books, 1996

Coogan, Tim Pat, *On The Blanket: The Inside Story of the IRA Prisoners' 'Dirty' Protest*, St Martin's Griffin, 2002

Crawford, Colin, *Inside the UDA: Volunteers and Violence*, Pluto Press, 2003

De Baroid, Ciaran, *Ballymurphy and the Irish War* (Revised Edition), Pluto Press, 2000

Doherty, Tony, *This Man's Wee Boy: A Childhood Memoir of Peace and Trouble in Derry*, Mercier Press, 2016

Doherty, Tony, *The Dead Beside Us: A Memoir of Growing Up in Derry*, Mercier Press, 2017

Dudley Edwards, Ruth, *Aftermath: The Omagh Bombing and the Families' Pursuit of Justice*, Vintage, 2010

Elliott, Marianne, *Hearthlands: A Memoir of the White City Housing Estate in Belfast*, The Blackstaff Press, 2017

English, Richard, *Armed Struggle: The History of the IRA*, Macmillan, 2003

Feeney, Harry, *The 14th November: The Day Time Stood Still*, self-published, 2015

Hanley, Brian & Millar, Scott, *The Lost Revolution: The Story of the Official IRA and the Workers' Party*, Penguin, 2009

Knatchbull, Timothy, *From a Clear Blue Sky: Surviving the Mountbatten Bomb*, Arrow Books, 2009

McCann, Eamonn, *War and an Irish Town*, Haymarket Books, 2018

McCann, Michael, *Burnt Out: How 'The Troubles' Began*, Mercier Press, 2009

McGuinness, Michael & Downey, Garbhán, *Creggan: More than a History*, Guildhall Press, 2000

McKay, Susan, *Bear in Mind These Dead*, Faber & Faber, 2008

McKittrick David, Kelters, Seamus, Feeney, Brian, Thornton, Chris & McVea, David, *Lost*

Lives: The Stories of the Men, Women and Children who Died as a Result of the Northern Ireland Troubles, Mainstream Publishing Company, 2008

McKittrick, David & McVea, David, *Making Sense of the Troubles*, Viking, 2012

Moore, Richard, *Can I give Him My Eyes?*, Hachette Books Ireland, 2009

Myers, Kevin, *Watching the Door: A Memoir 1971–1978*, The Lilliput Press, 2006

National Graves Association, *Belfast Graves*, AP/RN Print, 1985

O'Callaghan, Eimear, *Belfast Days: A 1972 Teenage Diary*, Merrion Press, 2014

O'Malley, Padraig, *Biting at the Grave: The Irish Hunger Strikes and the Politics of Despair*, The Blackstaff Press, 1990

Parry, Colin & Wendy, *Tim: An Ordinary Boy*, Hodder & Stoughton, 1994

Rolston, Bill, *Children of the Revolution*, Guildhall Press, 2011

Smith, Micheál, *The Impact of the Parachute Regiment in Belfast 1970–1973*, The Pat Finucane Centre, 2018

Taylor, Peter, *Provos: The IRA and Sinn Féin*, Bloomsbury, 1998

Taylor, Peter, *Loyalists*, Bloomsbury, 2000

Tírghrá Commemoration Committee, *Tírghrá: Ireland's Patriot Dead,* Republican Publications, 2002

Unwin, Margaret, *A State in Denial: The British Government and Loyalist Paramilitaries*, Mercier Press, 2016

White, Robert W., *Out of the Ashes: An Oral History of the Provisional Irish Republican Movement*, Merrion Press, 2017

Newspapers
Andersonstown News
News Letter
Belfast Telegraph
Craigavon Times
Coleraine Chronicle
Derry Journal
Donegal Democrat
Evening Herald
Irish Examiner
Irish Independent
Irish Press
The Irish Times
Mid-Ulster Mail
Newry Reporter
Republican News/An Phoblacht
Ulster Herald

Pamphlets & Reports
The Committee on the Administration of Justice, *Plastic Bullets and the Law*, 1985 & updated, 1990
Close, John, *In Memory of John Dempsey*, undated

Curtis, Liz, *They Shoot Children: The Use of Rubber and Plastic Bullets in the North of Ireland*, Information on Ireland, 2nd edition, 1987

East Belfast Brigade, *UDA Roll of Honour*, undated

Fr Brady, Brian, Fr Faul, Denis & Fr Murray, Raymond, *British Army Terror: West Belfast September/October 1976*, pamphlet, undated

Fr Faul, Denis & Fr Murray, Raymond, *Majella O'Hare: Shot Dead by the British Army, 14 August 1976*, pamphlet, 1976

Fr Faul, Denis & Fr Murray, Raymond, *Rubber & Plastic Bullets Kill and Maim*

Fr Faul, Denis & Fr Murray, Raymond, *Plastic Bullets – Plastic Government: Deaths and Injuries by Plastic Bullets*, August 1981-October 1982, undated

Morrow, Prof. Duncan, *Sectarianism in Northern Ireland: A Review*, Ulster University, 2019

Relatives for Justice, *Gerard Gibson: Murdered by the British Army*, 11th July 1972, undated

Report of the Independent Commission of Inquiry into the Dublin and Monaghan Bombings, 29/10/03, https://cain.ulster.ac.uk/events/dublin/barron03.pdf

Key Websites

CAIN Web Service: Conflict and Politics in Northern Ireland: https://cain.ulster.ac.uk/

http://www.dublinmonaghanbombings.org

Wave Trauma Centre: http://storiesfromsilence.com/

Stella Maris Secondary School: http://stellamarissecondary.com/pupilsdeceased.html

Declassified documents from the National Archives uncovered by the Pat Finucane Centre, available at http://www.patfinucanecentre.org/declassified-documents/

Unpublished Material

Egan, Jo, *The Crack in Everything*, script – performed Playhouse, Derry, November 2018

In Your Own Words: Understanding the Troubles: Interview with Mollie Barrett by Mark Thompson, Relatives for Justice, 7/7/10

In Your Own Words: Understanding the Troubles: Interview with Flo O'Riordan by Mark Thompson, Relatives for Justice, 28/7/10

Picture Credits

Andriy Yankovskyy: x

Alamy: v, xxiii, 43, 116, 120/Alain Le Garsmeur 'The Troubles' Archive; 16, 56, 57, 86–87, 144–45, 165, 261, 301, 315/Trinity Mirror/Mirrorpix; 45, 46, 270, 281, 339/ Homer Sykes Archive; 129, 154/ Keystone Press; 235/Tony Smith; 255/Chris Brennan; 320, 328, 333/Stephen Barnes/Northern Ireland News; 325, 338/Radharc Images; 335/World History Archive.

Belfast Telegraph: 352.

Derry Journal: xxiv, 1, 2, 22–23, 58, 70-71, 114, 119, 135, 181, 231, 304–305.

Getty: vi-vii/Jean-Louis Atlan; 7/Malcolm Stroud; 14, 40/Keystone; 79/Bentley Archive/ Popperfoto; 117, 291/David Turnley; 123/Mirrorpix; 124/Christine Spengler; 186/Independent News and Media; 187, 206/Bettmann; 219/Alex Bowie; 239, 347, 408-409/Mathiew Polak; 253/ Three Lions; 262, 292/Hilton Deutsch; 280/Henri Bureau; 308/Peter McDiarmid; 315/Boris Spremo; 323/Oliver Morris; 346/Richard Baker; 365/Kaveh Kazemi; 384/BWP Media; 387/ Getty images; 391/Robert Wallis; 392, 393/Bloomberg; 410/Peter Turnley.

Pacemaker Press: 208, 244, 263, 302, 306, 307, 309, 316, 334, 339, 351, 385, 396.

Press Association: 207, 245, 271, 278-9, 293, 300, 347, 359/Brian Little, 360, 361/Brian Little, 364/ Paul Faith.

Shutterstock: 15, 282/Peter Kemp/AP.

Victor Patterson: 6, 41, 176.

Sincere thanks to all of the families who provided us with images.

Thanks to CAIN, Relatives for Justice and the Pat Finucane Centre for their assistance in sourcing and supplying images.

The authors and publisher have endeavoured to contact all copyright holders. If any images used in this book have been reproduced without permission, we would like to rectify this in future editions and encourage owners of copyright not acknowledged to contact us at info@hbgi.ie

Glossary

Cumann na gCailíní – often referred to simply as the Cailíní, this was the female equivalent of the Fianna.

Eleventh Night – the evening of 11 July, the night before the Orange Order marks the Battle of the Boyne on 'the Twelfth'. Bonfires are traditionally lit in many Protestant areas.

Fianna – Na Fianna Éireann, the youth wing of the IRA, typically referred to simply as the Fianna. Both the Provisional and Official IRA had their own Fianna organisations. Members were known as Fians, and they were organised into units known as 'slua'.

Historical Enquiries Team (HET) – a special investigative unit of the Police Service of Northern Ireland (PSNI), it was set up in 2005 to re-examine more than 3,000 Troubles-era killings. It was wound up in 2014 and replaced by the Legacy Investigations Branch (LIB).

Interface – an area, often separated by a peace wall or similar structure, where Catholic/nationalist and Protestant/loyalist areas meet

Internment – arrest and imprisonment without trial. Introduced in Northern Ireland on 9 August 1971, it was used overwhelmingly against the civilian Catholic population and, instead of allowing the Stormont government to regain control, greatly increased support for the Provisional IRA in nationalist areas and led to an upsurge in violence by both republican and loyalist paramilitaries. By the time internment was abolished in December 1975 almost 2,000 people had been interned.

Irish National Liberation Army (INLA) – a republican paramilitary group, which was established in 1974 as a breakaway group from the OIRA.

Irish Republican Army (IRA) – a republican paramilitary group, it had been dormant since the ending of its so-called 'border campaign' in 1962, but re-emerged at the beginning of the Troubles. In 1969 it split into two factions, the Official IRA and the Provisional IRA.

Irish Republican Socialist Party (IRSP) – the political wing of the INLA.

Official IRA (OIRA) – one of two factions of the IRA which emerged from a split in December 1969. Dublin-based and influenced by Marxist principles, in the North it was quickly eclipsed by the Provisional IRA. Following the controversial killing of Ranger Best – a Catholic soldier who was home on leave – in Derry in 1972, the 'Officials' declared a ceasefire, though its members continued to be involved in sporadic violence and feuding with the PIRA.

'On the beak' – to skive/mitch school.

Peace line/peace wall – a barrier or a physical wall, sometimes with gates to allow access, which separates Catholic/nationalist and Protestant/loyalist areas.

Provisional IRA (PIRA) – the largest and most active republican paramilitary group during the Troubles, its declared aim was the protection of nationalist communities in the North and the establishment of a 32-county Irish Republic through military means. In December 1969, the organisation known as the IRA split into two factions: the PIRA and the OIRA. The Provisional IRA was responsible for more than 1,700 deaths during the Troubles – the greatest number of any single organisation. It declared its first ceasefire in 1994; its last weapons were decommissioned in 2005.
★ *Please note that we have used the term 'IRA' to refer to the Provisional IRA throughout this book.*

Real IRA – a dissident republican paramilitary organisation. It was responsible for the 1998 Omagh bomb, which killed 29 people and unborn twins. It declared a ceasefire shortly afterwards.

Republican Clubs – the name used by Sinn Féin in Northern Ireland to avoid a ban on the party which had been introduced in the North in 1964. Following the IRA split the name was later used by Official Sinn Féin in the North. It later became known as the Workers Party.

St Patrick's Training School – a residential institution on the Glen Road in west Belfast, it was run by the De La Salle brothers and housed Catholic boys who had been placed there for a number of reasons, including truancy – often as a result of what would now be described as special educational needs – and involvement in civil disorder.

'The Twelfth' – 12 July, the date the Orange Order takes part in parades to mark the anniversary of the Battle of the Boyne.

Ulster Defence Association (UDA) – the largest loyalist paramilitary organisation, it emerged from local community associations in loyalist areas which amalgamated to form the UDA in 1971. Despite its evident involvement in paramilitarism and sectarian killings – primarily through its cover organisation, the UFF – it was not banned until 1992. In 2010 the UDA said it had put its weapons beyond use.

Ulster Freedom Fighters (UFF) – a cover name for the UDA, often used to claim responsibility for UDA killings.

Wain – child

Acknowledgements

Firstly, and most importantly, we wish to thank the families and friends of the children whose lives are remembered in this book. This project simply would not have been possible without you, and we are deeply grateful to you for trusting us with your memories. We hope we have done them justice.

We would also like to thank the victims' and survivors' groups who facilitated many of the interviews upon which this book is based, and which were an invaluable source of support and advice throughout the writing process. Time and time again, you went above and beyond the call of duty in order to ensure that the stories of the people you represent could be heard, and you bear the credit for much of what is contained in these pages.

We wish to acknowledge, in particular, the contributions of the Pat Finucane Centre, especially Paul O'Connor, Sara Duddy, Alan Brecknell and Anne Cadwallader; Relatives for Justice, including Mary Kate Quinn, Paul Butler, Mark Thompson and Andree Murphy; Margaret Unwin of Justice for the Forgotten, Kenny Donaldson of the South East Fermanagh Foundation/Innocent Victims United, Ciaran MacAirt of the McGurk's families, Michael Gallagher of the Omagh Support and Self-Help Group, and Don MacKay of Ulster Human Rights Watch, as well as Julieann Campbell, Jean Hegarty, John Kelly, Adrian Kerr and Rossa Ó Dochartaigh of the Museum of Free Derry.

We are also grateful for the support of many journalistic colleagues throughout Ireland, North and South, including the RTÉ *Liveline* team – Richie Beirne, Tara Loughrey Grant, Laura Leigh Davies, Aonghus McAnally, Hugh Ormond and Fergus Sweeney; *The Irish Times* – especially Martin Doyle, Mark Hennessy and Gerry Moriarty; Eve Blair, Louise Cullen, Ann-Marie Foster, Kevin Sharkey, Peter Stewart, Stephen Walker and many other former colleagues and friends at BBC Radio Foyle/Ulster, and Sean McLaughlin and all at the *Derry Journal*.

Particular thanks are due to Martin Cowley (formerly *The Irish Times* and Reuters), Brian Kernohan (BBC Radio Foyle) and Seamus McKinney (*Irish News*), who willingly gave their time and expertise to proof-read the manuscript and who kept us right throughout.

We would also like to thank our publisher Ciara Considine, copy-editor Aonghus Meaney, designers Karen Carty and Terry Foley and the team at

Hachette Ireland, our agents Niamh Tyndall and Noel Kelly, Niamh McCormack & Caitriona Kelly of Noel Kelly Management, the staff of the Tyrone Guthrie Centre, Annaghmakerrig, Dublin City Libraries and Belfast and Derry Central Libraries, and Professor Mary McAleese, who generously contributed the foreword to the book.

Our thanks, always, to Drew Banerjee, who has been a key part of *Children of the Troubles* from its earliest days, and to our families, who have lived with the children for more than three years – June Meehan, Sean, Ellen and Ronan Duffy, Roberta and John McClements, Irene Bloomfield, Tom Quinsey, and Vincent and Rebecca Doherty.

We would also like to thank the many others who generously offered their time, assistance and friendship and who helped in innumerable ways in the research and writing of this book, including Karina Carlin, Thomas Conway, Amanda Doherty, Tony Doherty, Jo Egan, Harry Feeney, Dr Brian Harvey, Eamonn MacDermott, JJ Magee, Archbishop Eamon Martin, Fr Sean McArdle, Brian McDermott, Martin McGavigan, Jim McGilloway, Caolán McGinley, Philip McGuigan, Susan McKay, David McKittrick, Maeve McLaughlin, Roisin McLaughlin, Brian McMahon, Patrick Mulroe, Frank Murtagh, Pádraig Ó Muirigh, John Peto, Damon Quinn, Ellen Quirke, Billy Rowan, Gary & Patricia Roberts, David Stitt, Minty Thompson, Iain Webster, Paul Welsh & Jude Whyte.

Index of Names